DISCARDED

MAURY MAVERICK: A POLITICAL BIOGRAPHY

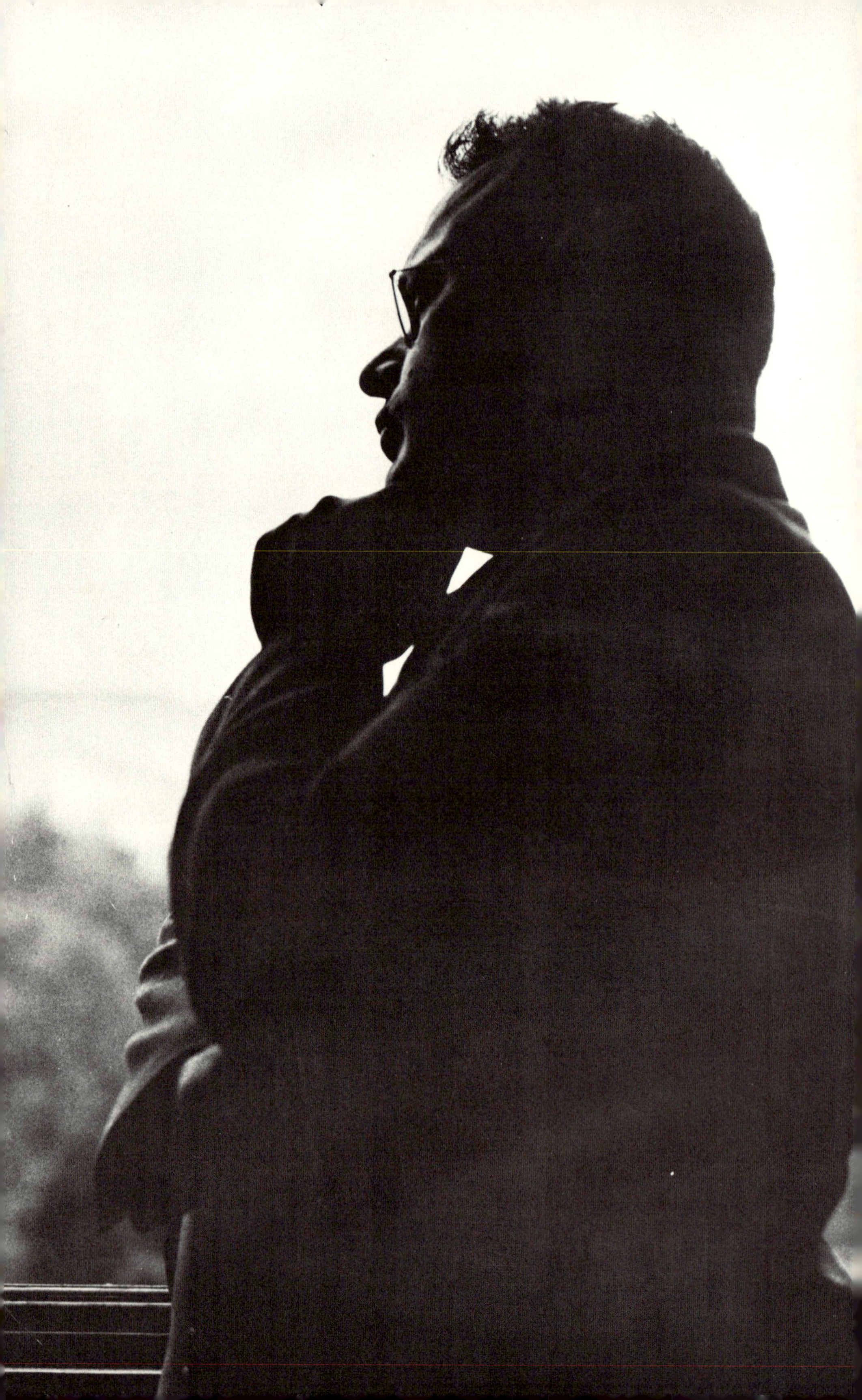

Maury Maverick

A POLITICAL BIOGRAPHY

by Richard B. Henderson

FOREWORD BY JOE B. FRANTZ

UNIVERSITY OF TEXAS PRESS, AUSTIN & LONDON

International Standard Book Number 0-292-70090-3
Library of Congress Catalog Card Number 75-134494
© 1970 by Richard B. Henderson
All rights reserved
Type set by G&S Typesetters, Austin
Printed by The University of Texas Printing Division, Austin
Bound by Universal Bookbindery, Inc., San Antonio

To Dorothy

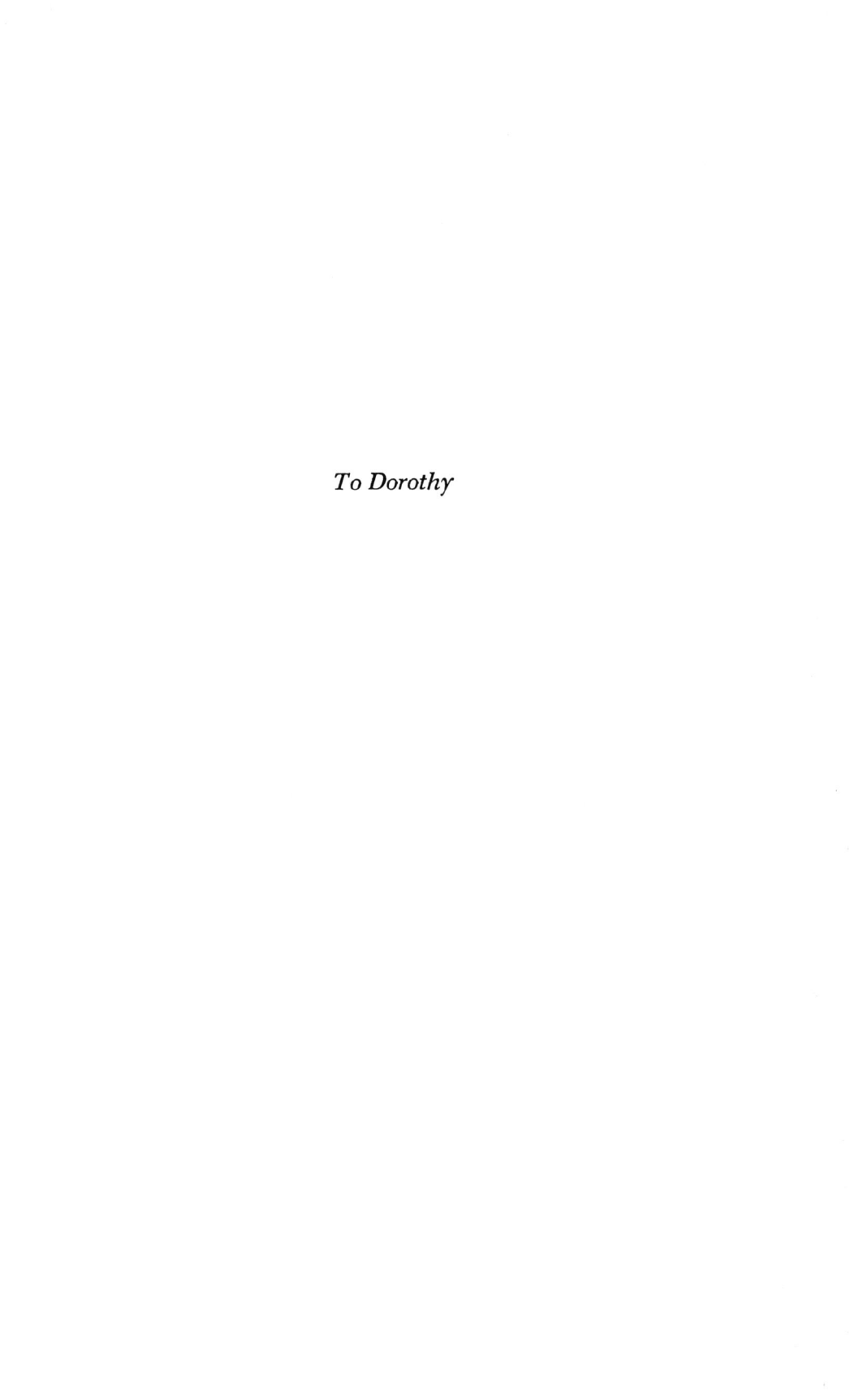

CONTENTS

Foreword xiii
Preface xxi
1. A Maverick American 3
2. The Bootleg Decade 30
3. Maury and His Mavericks 63
4. Two Cowboys Are Better Than One 98
5. Ever Insurgent Let Me Be 131
6. Sultan of the Young Turks 163
7. A Texas La Guardia 188
8. He Stirreth Up the People 213
9. An Isolationist's Change of Heart 232
10. Asia—"Our Biggest Problem" 251
11. Like Ripples on a Pond 271
12. I Am That Gadfly 297
Notes 311
Bibliography 355
Index 371

ILLUSTRATIONS

Frontispiece
Maury Maverick in 1938

Following page 200
1. Maury Maverick, age five months
2. Maverick's birthplace
3. Maverick, age three
4. Maverick, about age thirteen
5. Lieutenant Maverick, 1917
6. Maverick and his fellow Sigma Chi's, 1914
7. Maverick and Terrell Dobbs at Port Aransas, Texas
8. Maverick and Terrell Dobbs at Sunshine Ranch
9. Pat Jefferson, Maury Maverick, and Harry Futrell
10. Maverick with his two pet javelinas
11. Three generations of Mavericks
12. Caricature of Maverick by Walter Karig
13. Maverick is bombarded with "gobbledygook"
14. Freshman Congressman Maverick
15. Mrs. Maverick samples an apple
16. Maverick queries a House colleague
17. Maverick notes an engagement on his office blackboard
18. Maverick heads for his House office, 1936
19. Maverick and five other congressmen with FDR, 1938
20. Maverick returns to San Antonio, 1938
21. Mayor Maverick discusses the restoration of La Villita
22. Maverick and H. G. Wells

23. Rioters protest the Communist meeting in the San Antonio Municipal Auditorium, 1939
24. A mob presses in to prevent the Communist meeting
25. Mayor Maverick speaks at La Villita
26. Maverick speaks at a slum clearance project
27. A busy Mayor Maverick at City Hall
28. Mayor Maverick speaks at La Villita, 1940
29. Maverick prepares to make a network radio address
30. The Texas delegation to the 1940 Democratic National Convention
31. Maverick in the Office of Production Management, 1941
32. Maverick inspects wartime prison industry
33. Maverick and Eleanor Roosevelt inspect the Maryland Penitentiary, 1943
34. Maverick is sworn in as chairman of the Smaller War Plants Corporation, 1944
35. Maverick shows FDR around San Antonio in 1936
36. Maverick arrives at Atsugi Airfield, Tokyo, 1945
37. Maverick and Paul V. McNutt
38. Maverick chats with Dr. Syngman Rhee, 1945
39. Maverick and aides at Guam, 1945
40. Maverick welcomes the Truman family to San Antonio

FOREWORD

Although Maury Maverick has been in his grave for sixteen years as of this writing, he refuses to stay dead and buried. Mention of him occurs frequently in the journals of the nation, and increasing numbers of busy graduate students comb the Maverick papers at the University of Texas Archives to learn more of this unusual man.

For Maury Maverick was unique. I know the clichés ("there'll never be another like him"; "he's one of a kind") said by nearly everyone about anybody the minute after he dies. But a case can be made for Maury Maverick that will lift such statements above the bromidic level.

With their almost three and a half centuries on these North American shores, plus their remarkable skill for breeding tough-fibered men of great courage and personal carelessness, the Mavericks are one of the few families whose name has become a common noun. In the vernacular of the cow camp, a maverick is a calf "who has lost his mother and who don't know who his father was," which is the hyperbolic Western way of saying that a maverick is a stray. Throughout the English-speaking world, a maverick is an independent who goes his own way, swims upstream, runs against the crowd, or refuses to stand hitched. Maury Maverick was all of these things, not an independent for the sake of independence, but simply a man who arrived at his own decisions without considering party, popularity, conformity, or consistency. He went the way his heart and head dictated, in a rare but always honest combination of those two abstractions.

Maury Maverick would have loved the 1960's. He would have

applauded every decision of Earl Warren's Supreme Court, which broadened and further guaranteed individual liberties and group civil rights. From a legal standpoint this past decade has been a confirmation of all that Maury Maverick stood for, of what he fought for, and of those principles that defeated him as congressman and as mayor. He would have been proud that his hometown, San Antonio, sent Texas' first Mexican-American, Henry B. Gonzalez, to Congress. Once San Antonians and Texans got used to the idea of being represented by one of their natives, the people have gone on reelecting Gonzalez, apparently for life. In the Rio Grande Valley, where the *old* families were of Mexican ancestry and the *first* families were from that catch-all group called Anglos, Gonzalez' victory gave the citizens enough courage to send to Washington a second Mexican-American, Eligio de la Garza, as their congressman. Crystal City, whose huge statue of Popeye confirms its claim as the spinach capital of the world, provided an example for other communities when its Mexican-American majority elected a predominantly Mexican-American city council. Now a chicano revolution is sweeping from Texas to California, which should cause Maverick to burst his coffin with a loud *olé*.

Despite a heritage that goes back to the Texas Revolution, Maury Maverick would have hailed the efforts of the Mexican-American to get another tradition off his back—that proud group known as Texas Rangers, whose anti-Mexican sentiments are notorious, albeit for sometimes sound historical reasons. Undoubtedly he would have hailed John F. Kennedy, and he would have lauded Lyndon Johnson for that cloudburst of social legislation his fellow Texan put through Congress in 1964–1965. Maverick would have stood for all the voting, educational, housing, and other rights that brought all Americans under the same set of laws. On the other hand, he probably would have scored Kennedy for the Bay of Pigs and perhaps even for the missile confrontation, and he would have been on Johnson's back for Viet Nam. His sentiments toward President Nixon would have been unprintable, even in these scatological times.

But the developments of the 1960's that would have given Maverick the most pleasure were those guaranteeing the accused the same rights as other citizens and giving all people of this country

Foreword

the right to speak up and out. When, as mayor, he permitted the Communists to use San Antonio's municipal auditorium, he was denounced as a Communist himself. In fact, his accusers charged that he was worse than a Communist, that he was, to use the ultimate epithet, a traitor to his class. It was a night for lynching as the "good people" rioted in downtown San Antonio, and the only difference between SDS rioting on today's campuses and American Legion rioting in San Antonio in 1939 is the age of the people involved. The intemperance and the disregard for reason and justice are identical.

The attempted denial of free speech to American Communists in San Antonio led Maury into one of his few retaliations by pedigree. He took to the air waves to read practically the whole Maverick genealogy from the time they hit Boston Harbor in early colonial days right down to himself, from the heroic Matthew Fontaine Maury on the one side through three and a half centuries of American Mavericks on the other. He called off every patriotic organization to which he belonged by right of heritage or his own participation, and he was by right a Son of practically every one of them. At the conclusion he challenged anyone in San Antonio to equal his credentials as an American. Then he reasserted that, since he believed in America, the Communists could speak. San Antonians of lesser American heritage wanted to burn him at the stake.

Too bad he couldn't have hung around for the censure of Joe McCarthy! Too bad he couldn't have debated Vice-President Spiro Agnew, matching rhetoric for rhetoric. Although sweet reasonableness in their interchange might have been missing, the quotability would have been endless. Agnew would have had in Maverick an adversary who could fight him phrase for phrase, someone the vice-president lacks at this moment. Maverick believed in all the first Ten Amendments, and he would have said so in words that were pungent, earthy, and memorable.

Sometimes Maverick walked a thin line between crude honesty and complete courage. Some of us have long felt that one of his greatest achievements was choosing a wife who could smooth over the cross patches he had scuffed up. Sometimes he seemed to irritate just for the sake of keeping people stirred up. He did not function in an atmosphere of serenity.

For instance, to get street sanitation under control and to insure clean food, the city fathers of San Antonio once banned all outdoor eating places except under the most stringent conditions, an action that resulted in the banishment from the streets of the city's famed and colorful "chili queens." So Maury Maverick was elected mayor, and as mayor had to be accepted as the town's first citizen by people who, though they had known him and his family in perpetuity, nevertheless abhorred Maury's free-wheeling politics. Eventually the mayor attended one of the fancier garden parties, breathed graciousness itself through the receiving line, and then turned to his host and bellowed (there is no other word nearly so precise). "You-all know that it's against the law to have outdoor eating places. You bastards passed the law yourself. I'm giving this party fifteen minutes to get these tents down and all this food indoors, or the police will be called!" For the remainder of the party he was hardly the most popular guest present.

I first saw Maury Maverick at a meeting of the Texas State Historical Association in Austin while I was still a student. I knew him by fearful reputation, which came from reading such disapproving newspapers as the *Dallas News* and the *Fort Worth Star Telegram*. At the annual luncheon of the association, listed in the program for noon, the two or three hundred people attending the luncheon insisted on visiting in the corridor while the association director did his best to move them into the hotel dining room. Being in that cooperative student phase, which dates me, I went into the dining room where the tables were set, with the salad and shrimp cocktail already by each plate. There, near the center of this sizable banquet room, sat Maury Maverick, alone, hunched over his plate, eating away at his shrimp cocktail. Someone behind me said, "Why Maury Maverick, what are you doing in here alone!"

"The program said this lunch was at noon, and by God I follow the program!"

Stories like this are legend. Walter Prescott Webb, the historian, went to a stuffy black-tie dinner at which the speechmaking was interminable. James P. Hart, then chancellor of the University of Texas, did what any decent American would—he dozed. Here came a note from Maverick to Webb: "Your damned chancellor is asleep!" Webb, no mean man with a quip himself, scribbled in reply, "Maury, you're jealous!"

Maury Maverick, Jr., who naturally inherited some of his father's characteristics, tells how his father sent for the family after suffering the heart attack that finally killed him. Maury, Jr., arrived at the hospital, was told to go right into the room, and tentatively knocked on the door. In that high-pitched voice that Maury alternated with his foghorn, the father said:

"That you, son?"

"Yes, papa."

"Come over by the bed, son. You know, this is it."

The Mavericks are honest to the end, and Maury, Jr., did not give false words of comfort.

"Yes, papa, I know."

"Son, you and I have never been very close."

"I know, papa."

"I think it may have been my fault." His son didn't argue.

"But I want you to know that I'm proud of you, son."

"Well, thank you, papa," said Junior, somewhat flustered by this show of unusual parental sentimentality.

"Yes, son, I'm real proud of you—I'm proud that you didn't turn out to be a horse's ass like Elliott Roosevelt!"

The younger Maverick says, "Those were my father's last words to his son, and I cherish them. I know of no other son who received such a benediction from his father."

They tell the story, possibly apocryphal, that in those last moments Maverick sent for an Episcopal priest. Whoever was with him was shocked and remonstrated that Maverick was showing a sign of weakness, that he had never needed a priest before. According to the story, Maverick then said, in language that for a university press must be expurgated somewhat: "I don't need no damned priest; but who knows, there may be something after all to that crap, and at this stage I'm too weak to take any chances!"

Maury Maverick's widow later married Walter Prescott Webb after an intervening eight years. When she first began to go out again, her first more or less date was with an old bachelor friend named Sam Zisman, an urbanologist of considerable renown. Undoubtedly there is something portentous about a widow's first appearance on the arm of a new man, particularly when he is a bachelor not known for squiring unattached women. Although Zisman had been a close friend of the Mavericks for years, and under ordinary circumstances neither he nor Mrs. Maverick would have felt anything unusual about being together, on this occasion they felt, in the words of Steve Allen, "this could be the start of something big." They were dining when who should walk in but Maury, Jr. He spotted them, and in a style reminiscent of his father, walked over to Zisman, stuck out his hand, and said impishly, "Hello, Daddy." According to Mrs. Maverick, this took the bloom off any promise of flowering romance. She and Sam Zisman continued to see each other only as lifelong friends until he died in the spring of 1970.

Being a congressman, writing articles for national magazines, leading a national liberal group, and receiving widespread approbation and condemnation are all stimulating activities, as Maury Maverick found out. But probably the greatest thing that happened to Congressman Maverick was to discover that he was basically not a Texan, not a Southerner, but an American and a citizen of the world. When he was in Congress, that great body worried about such bills as the one branding lynching a federal offense and another seeking to eliminate the poll tax. When these two bills came up in the 1930's, Maverick found himself isolated from his Southern compadres as he assailed the theses that a man must pay to exercise his right to vote, and that a man with dark skin has no right to his day in court. Despite all the blood of the Mavericks, the Maurys, and the Fontaines of Virginia in his background, and with all the Southwestern tradition stemming from old Sam Maverick forward, this scion of first families from Massachusetts to Texas was not only cut off politically from his neighbors but almost ostracized for voting what he believed was right and just.

However, the pain of ostracism hurt even worse when the good people of San Antonio, many of them friends from boyhood, turned their backs on him. Surprisingly, Maverick never became bitter. He formed no permanent alliances with anyone, but entangled himself only with principle. I once heard him say in a conversation that "any man who holds public office and expects gratitude is a damn fool. No one remembers you for what you did yesterday. A politician does what he thinks is right, and if he is satisfied that he

Foreword

has done just that, then he has enjoyed a sufficient political career. But gratitude—hell, there ain't no gratitude!"

His schooling, as Richard Henderson points out, never reached tidy conclusions, but his education never stopped. Outfitting himself with a board made to his specifications, he read and wrote in bed through the night. He could not tolerate a library of clean, well-ordered books. He wrote all over the pages and blackened the margins, arguing, cross-referencing, and amplifying. His is one library that must be investigated if the researcher is to know Maury Maverick. The books themselves are not remarkable, but the marginalia overwhelms. Thus another man, racked with pain and never able to sleep well, enriched himself more than a man with a healthier body likely could have or would have. Sweet are the uses. . . .

In the daylight hours Maverick was likely to be seen anywhere —in the workroom of an expensive Philadelphia jeweler designing a handsome silver bowl, in Mexico choosing cloth and conferring on techniques of weaving, or in Tokyo talking lacquers with a Japanese artisan. His curiosity was boundless, equaled only by his energy, his imagination, his creativity, and his courage. A squirrel by nature, he collected almost everything and saved accordingly. He had the autograph of every president (as well as those of the flag-raisers at Iwo Jima), coins, and medallions by the bucketful. I doubt that he ever saw a commemorative china plate he did not purchase. Sixteen years after his death his widow is still searching for places to put the stuff, even after having placed a considerable portion in the University of Texas Archives and distributing still more to relatives and friends. I remember one party at Walter Webb's Friday Mountain Ranch, with about thirty men present, when Maury showed up late. He brought commemorative plates of San Antonio for everyone.

Of course, when San Antonio staged its delightful world's fair in miniature, a jewel known as HemisFair, San Antonio's current crop of city fathers rightly bowed low for the worldwide applause they received for their taste in underplaying the world's fair theme. A part of the delight in HemisFair came from the city of San Antonio itself, a collection of blithe spirits with the same lilt of life that distinguishes Rio anytime or Munich at the height of its May wine festival. Visitors loved the people of San Antonio, and they loved the San Antonio River, which could have been any other major city's sewer, but was instead a picturesque, even romantic walk. Although Maury Maverick, long gone, was never acknowledged as the father of San Antonio's downtown river beauty, it all started with his utilization of federal grants that changed an eyesore into a pathway of civic pride. The same can be said about La Villita, that bit of native quarter and craft that Maverick exhumed from the past, which San Antonio continues and reveres.

While Maverick was alive, Texas' conservative newspapers thought that he was directly descended from the devil, and they fought him with their best editorial weapons. When he died, however, they discovered that a fresh quality had been withdrawn from the sometimes sterile Texas scene. And if newspapermen miss anyone, it is a man who provides good, colorful copy. In noticing his death, they lauded his historic antecedents and his influence. They applauded his having coined the word *gobbledygook* for officialese; they repeated his often quoted remark (Mr. Vice-President, please note) that "newspapermen are the most underpaid and overprivileged guys in the world"; and they also smiled at his definition of a Latin American as "a Mexican who has paid his poll tax." *Time* called him a "dumpy, dynamic, Texas Democrat," while the *Dallas News*, never in his corner, proclaimed that he was "an honest demagogue" who "had faith in what he did." The *News*, which, like most Texas newspapers and a majority of Texas Democrats, had supported Eisenhower in the 1952 election, repeated Maverick's charge that Governor Allan Shivers' repudiation of the Democratic national ticket that year was tantamount to "having a big wedding and taking the wedding vows to honor and obey, then dishonoring your wife and killing her."

Two days after his death on June 7, 1954, the *News* opined that Maverick was not just another politician, but was truly "as maverick as his name."

That he was.

JOE B. FRANTZ

PREFACE

One day in April 1952 I walked into the lobby of San Antonio's old Plaza Hotel to register as a participant in a five-day seminar on international relations, sponsored by the Brookings Institution. A bit of good fortune had put me, a greenhorn instructor of government, in the company of distinguished professors, college and university presidents, admirals, generals, colonels, and assorted dignitaries from San Antonio's political and business community.

I registered early, and as I turned to cross the almost empty lobby, a short, fat, graying man with powerful shoulders and an impressive mien thrust out his hand and rumbled, "Ah'm Maury Maverick." I had never seen him before, but my mind raced back to a graduate course in public administration and a lesson on "gobbledygook," and some vague recollection that this was a man of importance. We got acquainted, and he seemed not to mind that I knew very little about him, but I have gathered that he would have minded had I been nearer his age.

The next day fortune again threw me in with him as we were assigned to the same panel for the entire session of mock planning on foreign policy—much as it might be done in the State Department. In those four days I saw a number of facets of the character of this remarkable man. I was impressed—and fascinated.

Perhaps he was even less inhibited than usual in view of the fact that the director had said that all remarks would be off the record, but I saw Maverick display the fearless candor that endeared him to some and made bitter enemies of others. He grumbled and muttered through the meals, eating rapidly and impatiently and bullyragging several members of the State Department

Policy Planning Staff for their timidity in the face of threats from Senator Joe McCarthy, who was riding high at the time. Maverick tossed them such rhetorical questions as how did they define the "free world"—did it include "that great democrat, Fulgencio Batista" and that "little sonofabitch playboy, Bao Dai?" His glare swept the table as he dared anyone to deny that Bao Dai was a little sonofabitch playboy.

When Maverick accepted the director's invitation to address the entire assembly, I saw the sledgehammer wit that provoked gales of laughter as he told the conferees that he had had researchers to comb through all the archives back to ancient Babylon, and they were unable to turn up a speech worse than the one delivered that week by Secretary of State Dean Acheson. During this speech the audience applauded often and vigorously, but when the time came to vote on a policy proposal, Maverick lost. His reaction was a wry grin and an undismayed, "Once more I am happy to be a part of the intelligent minority."

I saw some of Maverick's high jinks when he dashed from the building to get a key to the city of San Antonio to present as a "decoration" to a young colonel who had the temerity to suggest that he did not see anything wrong in trade with Communist nations. I saw Maverick, too, as a generous, thoughtful man as he hosted a dinner for delegates at his beloved La Villita and when he offered to take my wife and me on a tour of the historic sites in the Alamo City in "the old Buick." There were, on the other hand, many things I did not see, but this was true of many men who thought they knew him well, and that is what makes the story.

Two years later Maverick was gone, and the opportunity to tell his story fell to me. In the course of my research, I interviewed his old friend President Harry S. Truman. I naively stated to Mr. Truman that it was my firm intention to be objective in my study of Maury Maverick. I was met with a burst of laughter and a confident, "Nobody can be objective about Maury Maverick." He is probably right.

We are all obliged to pay, even if it is only "in ink," as Maverick once put it, those who have made our work possible or who have helped to smooth out the rough road. My greatest debt is to Mrs. Walter Prescott Webb (formerly Mrs. Maury Maverick) and her

Preface xxiii

children, Mrs. Terrelita Maverick Clinton and Maury Maverick, Jr. They not only extended to me the privilege of complete and, for a time, exclusive access to Maury Maverick's papers and library, but they also answered an untold number of questions with admirable candor and yet freed me from the possible bane of a family-approved biography. On the contrary, they urged objectivity.

The late Walter P. Webb earned a large payment "in ink" for the kind extension of his good offices in introducing me to the Maverick family and for his advice and encouragement.

There are few genuinely self-made men. Credit must be given to those people who have helped us to develop whatever talents we have. My greatest debts in this area are to Senator Walter Richter; the late James Taylor, professor of history and chairman of the Social Sciences Division at Southwest Texas State University; Joe Bill Vogel, formerly a professor of journalism at the same institution; and Professors Thornton Anderson and Franklin L. Burdette of the University of Maryland.

An important part of the research and writing of this book would have been impossible without the time provided by a research grant from the Danforth Foundation and a research grant and faculty development leave from Southwest Texas State University. Too numerous to mention are those omnipresent and too often unsung collaborators of all researchers: the personnel of the Southwest Texas State University Library, the University of Texas Library, the University of Texas Archives, and the San Antonio Public Library. I owe special notes of thanks to Charles T. Morrissey for examining the Franklin D. Roosevelt papers for me, and to Dr. Chester V. Kielman, archivist of the University of Texas at Austin, for his assistance in the use of the Maury Maverick papers.

R. B. H.

MAURY MAVERICK: A POLITICAL BIOGRAPHY

A Maverick American

WHEN NEWSPAPER REPORTERS turned to their typewriters on June 7, 1954, to report the death of Maury Maverick, they summoned a wide variety of expressions to illuminate the many facets of his character and career: "New Deal evangelist," "political warhorse," "honest demagogue," "fiery little Texan," "political patriarch," "brilliant student," "able-organizer and administrator," "champion of small business," and "clean-up mayor of San Antonio."[1]

The *New York Times* praised his "bulldog courage and disarming sincerity,"[2] and later members of Congress described him in such terms as "brilliant," "highly intelligent and intensely patriotic," "courageous and forthright," "shockingly frank, but refreshingly candid," and "a man of great vision and understanding."[3]

Maury Maverick was all of these things and many more; he was one of the most colorful and vital figures of recent American political history. The story of his career and its impact upon our political life has been told only in fragments from time to time.[4] The former New Deal congressman, mayor of San Antonio, and chairman of the World War II Smaller War Plants Corporation preempted the best of all possible titles for a study of his career when he chose *A Maverick American* as the title for his semi-autobiographical book published in 1937. He was a maverick American, not just a maverick Texan. He was truly "unbranded," the dictionary meaning of the term that his grandfather contributed to the American lexicon.[5] He was, as well, a maverick legislator, mayor, and thinker.

The Mavericks were dissenters and independents before the political connotation was given to their name. Samuel Maverick of Pendleton, South Carolina (Maury's great-grandfather), and his son, Samuel Augustus Maverick, were sharply critical of the exaggerations of their fellow South Carolinians with respect to the allegedly oppressive Tariffs of 1824 and 1828. Samuel A. Maverick, a young lawyer and recent graduate of Yale, presented a closely reasoned argument *against* nullification, secession, and extreme states' rights postures in general. When his father delivered a speech to counter the arguments of his neighbor, John C. Calhoun, the younger Maverick challenged a heckler in the audience to a duel and slightly wounded the fellow in the contest.[6]

The younger Samuel's unpopular position forced him to give up his aspirations for a political career in South Carolina, and, at his father's suggestion, he went to manage a plantation in Alabama. When stories of the great adventure in Texas began to reach him, he determined to go there. He arrived in the small village of San Antonio de Bexar in the fall of 1835, within weeks of the inception of the Texas Revolution.[7]

After he had played one of the leading roles in the Texas Revolution,[8] Samuel A. Maverick was a delegate to the convention that prepared the Texas Declaration of Independence in 1836, but he had no hand in it. High waters delayed his arrival until March 3, the day after the document was completed. He was permitted to sign it, however, and he later participated in the drafting of the Constitution of the Republic of Texas.[9]

The first Texas Maverick was a land speculator—with perhaps the largest single set of holdings in the state. His biographers depict him as a man of almost unbelievable integrity and modesty. Though twice elected mayor of San Antonio, many times to the

Texas Congress and State Legislature, and finally Chief Justice of Bexar County, he is said never to have sought or campaigned for an office.[10] He also showed the extraordinary tenacity and unbending will when doing what he thought right that was later exhibited by his grandson.

An example of the Maverick character is to be found in the Perote Prison story. In September 1842 the Mexican government sent a major expedition, headed by General Adrian Woll, to regain Texas. The forces invaded San Antonio, and, in the course of their victorious battle, Sam Maverick was taken prisoner. He and his fellow prisoners were forced-marched eighteen hundred miles to Perote Prison in Mexico. During almost unspeakable hardships—chained and in ill health—Maverick had an opportunity to win freedom from President Antonio Santa Anna if the Texan would promise to support a token reannexation of Texas by Mexico.[11]

The United States minister, General Waddy Thompson, reported that Maverick replied, "I cannot persuade myself that such an annexation on any terms, would be advantageous to Texas, and I therefore cannot say so, for I regard a lie as a crime, and one which I cannot commit even to secure my release; I must, therefore, continue to wear my chains, galling as they are." Thompson offered the comment, "Such an act recorded by Plutarch would have added another page as bright as that which perpetuates the noble constance and heroic virtue of Regulus." Thompson reported further that he was soon able, as a "personal favor" to him, to secure the release of Maverick and two other prisoners.[12]

Six children survived from the ten born to Samuel A. and Mary Maverick. The youngest son, Albert, was the father of Maury Maverick. There is no colorful career to report for Albert Maverick, but there was nothing tame about his youth. As a boy he hunted, fished, and learned the ways of the Texas wilderness with a famed Indian fighter and scout, Polycarpio Rodriguez. The account of his school years is filled with recitals of youthful pranks and assorted mischief. A fellow student at the University of Virginia described Albert as having too much "animal spirit" for serious scholarship. It was alleged that he once stole the great iron gates at the entrance to the university, and Maury Maverick took great delight in chiding his father about an escapade in which the elder Maverick drank too much wine and performed the never-to-be-duplicated feat of climbing one of the university's stately columns.[13]

After one year at the University of Virginia, Albert was advised that his professors had given him passing marks on the condition that he not return. The final phase of his education took the unusual form of a walking trip across England from Liverpool to Dover with some days spent in the British Museum, followed by a seven-month stay in Paris. The trip, and particularly the stay in Paris, seemed to be a sobering one. He found Paris to be a shocking "den of immorality" with some women showing their legs "as high as the knee," but he said he managed to find lodging with "a good honest family." He spent seven months studying independently and learning to speak French. On his return to the United States in March 1877, he went straight to Piedmont, Virginia, to claim his promised bride, Jane Lewis Maury, a direct descendent of the Reverend James Maury, Thomas Jefferson's first teacher.[14]

Maury Maverick frequently referred proudly to his namesake, Matthew Fontaine Maury, the famous nineteenth-century pioneer in the field of oceanography. His biographer's description of his characteristic attitudes toward matters academic bears an uncanny resemblance to the characteristics of Maury Maverick. Matthew Maury did poorly on examinations at the United States Naval Academy. His apparent mediocrity was attributed to the fact that his fellows made high grades by answering "mainly in terms of the books" without understanding what it was all about. "Maury's mind had original habits. He was by nature a trail-blazer. He could not so well follow other men in speech and thought—he thought and spoke for himself."[15] Elsewhere he is described as "stout," "largely self-educated," and an opponent of "humbuggery"—a no less accurate portrait of Maury Maverick.[16]

Almost immediately after his marriage to Jane Maury, Albert took her to the Maverick homestead in San Antonio. After a short stint in a low-paying clerical job, he tried ranching near Bandera, Texas, for a few years, but a severe drought drove the growing family back to San Antonio. There Albert Maverick managed the Maverick Land Office and made general investments in San Antonio real estate and business operations, activities for which he had little ability or interest. Though the tall, handsome Albert faithfully went "down to the office" on every working day until he was eighty-seven years of age, he didn't belong there. He became, by all accounts, a quiet, retiring, scholarly type, with a strong attachment to family and home. Unlike his father and son, he did not hold public office. This "beautiful man," as Mrs. Walter P. Webb describes him, was almost Thoreauvian in his love for nature and his joy in working with his hands, qualities that, despite vast differences in their personalities, were as evident in the life of Maury Maverick as in that of his father. Some of Albert Maverick's most absorbing activities were such things as keeping records of the chilling Texas northers as they swept in over the hills into San Antonio and carefully noting the arrival and departure of the purple martins that came to the large house he had erected for them near his veranda. He made saddles for all of his children and melted down Mexican pesos to fashion heavy buckles for the belts that he made for all of his sons. The family referred to them as Maverick belts, and Maury Maverick kept his until the day he died.[17]

A biographer who had no difficulty finding noteworthy achievements and honors of other members of the Maverick family, said only that Albert was a "progressive citizen of San Antonio" and "a pioneer for the conservation of the natural beauty of our city, having publicly objected to the destruction of the cypress trees as early as 1882."[18] Albert Maverick was generous "to the point of eccentricity," and he let the major part of an inherited fortune simply slip through his hands. He sustained serious losses in periods of financial panic and depression, but one reason for this was that he would not collect rent from distressed tenants.[19]

Jane Maverick was a short, bustling woman with a strong, commanding personality. Albert was head of the house, but she was the manager. As Maury Maverick explained, "My mother has executive ability, running the place and doing the ordering and the talking for both. My father is a quiet man."[20] Jane was no mere housewife. A houseful of children and a lack of formal education did not prevent her from becoming a literate woman, knowledgeable about public affairs. She traveled occasionally, and in later years when the children were grown she made carefully prepared speeches to local clubs concerning her experiences.

Albert and Jane had eleven children; the eleventh was Fontaine Maury Maverick. Though he steadfastly maintained that he was brought by a wise and loquacious old stork,[21] he was born on October 23, 1895, at the grand old Maverick home at 218 Avenue E, just off San Antonio's Alamo Plaza. His father put him down as a "cheerful" small boy,[22] and Maury himself described his boyhood as "free and easy"—listening to the band on the square, buying tamales and Mexican sweets at the chili stands.[23] He demonstrated quite early that he had inherited some of Papa's youthful mischief-making. Palmer Giles, a rancher who lives near Comfort, Texas, was a boyhood playmate and school chum of Maury Maverick. Giles tells a tale of one of the more extravagant stunts engineered by Maury at the age of seven or eight. The Giles and Maverick parents were chatting in the parlor while the boys went off to play. Maury and his brother George asked Giles if he would like to take a bath. Giles responded that he had had one that week, but Maury repeated the question with a wink. He and George then led the perplexed Giles down a long porch to a large, completely tiled bathroom. The boys then took off their clothes, placed thick towels under and around the edges of the door, closed the door tightly on the towels, and proceeded to fill the entire bathroom with water about three feet deep. After frolicking about for a time, the boys drained and cleaned up the "swimming pool," and the parents were apparently none the wiser.

In 1905, when Maury Maverick was nine years old, the family moved to what they came to call Sunshine Ranch, in what is now suburban San Antonio but which was then in the countryside overlooking the city. There Albert built a large, plain two-story house with a long porch and an upstairs gallery designed to catch the prevailing breeze. The view from this spot is still impressive, but the visitor in those days could see "a wide-spreading valley, the wastes of green mesquite and yellow stubble, and the distant town half drowned in purple mist, the few high buildings very white and stately, suggesting Venice."[24]

The Albert Mavericks were "getting along," but they were far from wealthy. Nonetheless, the big, plainly furnished house was a Sunday afternoon Mecca for the many members of the Maverick clan and their friends. Everyone knew that the children were invited, and the atmosphere was one of warm family ties, great fun, and a vigorous exchange of ideas. Albert carved the roast with great aplomb and presided over the dinner with quiet dignity, but later the children gathered on the veranda to eat watermelon, cavort, and perform tricks, while the adults gathered inside for stimulating discussions. The Mavericks were a lively and opinionated bunch, and the discussions would often become arguments, but Jane Maverick would not permit the participants to engage in personalities.[25]

It was a good life—virtually ideal as well as idyllic—that young Maury Maverick had at Sunshine Ranch. He sometimes milked the cows, became fascinated with the life of bees as he gathered their honey, and, as he candidly told a reporter in later years, "pitched hay, but not much." He had no great liking for farm and ranch chores and at times could be counted upon to get into some sort of scrape when they were assigned to him. At the age of fourteen he was driving a small herd of horses across the country for his uncle. The trip was hot and dusty, and Maury decided to stop for a soft drink in the German community of Fredericksburg. An old German innocently suggested that a strapping boy doing a man's work might well consider a bottle of beer rather than soda water. After four bottles, Maury had more than a little difficulty rounding up the horses and barely managed to mount his own. He failed to say how he managed the rest of the trip.[26]

It was about this time that Fontaine Maury Maverick, according to his own account, became just plain Maury Maverick, but his amusing tale of how it happened is probably spurious. The story goes that he was riding in a wagon heavily loaded with the honey that he had helped gather, and the old driver couldn't get the horses to pull a steep grade. He turned and asked Maverick for his full name, and when he heard, "Fontaine Maury Maverick," he angrily said, "You'll have to drop part of that name or these horses will never make it up this hill. Make up your mind, son, which you are willing to drop." Maury said, "I'll drop the Fontaine," and the horses made it up the hill.[27] A more likely explanation is that he dropped the name later on because some of his college friends used to poke fun at him for it, addressing him with such verbal caricatures as "Fontice."[28]

Maury Maverick once wrote that his mother gave him "many spankings to no avail," but that he deserved one thousand from his father who gave him only two,[29] but he enjoyed the sort of relationship with both of his parents that most boys would order if they could. The occasional firmness and parental advice was tempered by understanding, deep affection, and often a dash of wit. Maury was no more than ten or eleven years of age when he announced (inspired perhaps by his father's youthful adventures) that he was going to California. He saddled up his pony and gathered a few provisions as his mother and father tried to dissuade him. When they saw that he was determined, they exacted the promise from him that he would stop for a week at the Giles' Ranch near Comfort. After Maury had left, Mrs. Maverick called Mrs. Giles and said, "My little boy is leaving for California on his pony. Please delay him as long as possible when he gets to the ranch." Maury and his weary pony survived the hot seventy-mile trip through rugged country, and the strategy worked. He and his playmate, Palmer Giles, spent half the summer doing all the things that boys of ten and eleven do in that wild hill country, and then Maury saddled up and headed for home.[30]

Much of the correspondence between Maverick and his parents reveals affectionate joshing and the indulgence of doting Mama and Papa. When Maury was attending the University of Texas he wrote to Papa to request some money to attend a football game in Houston. He explained that the trip would involve night travel, requiring enough money for a "birth" both ways. Albert responded, "I'm glad I can send you the money; I had no idea you were in such a delicate condition."[31] (This was often the style in which Albert chided various of his children into better spelling and writing habits.) When his son was a young lieutenant in France, Albert wrote (after occasionally sending him a hundred dollars), "Call on Gen. Persh., & see your pay is doubled. Say it is imperative because your father insists on your employing a guardian & I want him to be a responsible person."[32]

In one of his books Maury Maverick jocularly characterized his mother as having "slightly Fascist tendencies" and at another point referred to her as a "Mussolini."[33] Thus the first pass to the gallery of the United States House of Representatives that freshman Representative Maury Maverick sent to his mother was filled out in the name of "Signora Mussolini." Another card, however,

A Maverick American

asking that courtesies be extended at the White House, was made out to a "Little Jane Maury." The cards were attached to a pseudo-formal letter that read:

Dear Mrs. Maverick:

I hope you will visit Washington sometime and hear me speak. . . . Try to remember this: it is harder to be a congressman than a mother. You only have eleven children and 65 grandchildren. I have a quarter of a million.

Respectfully,

Maury Maverick

(Your Congressman)

Mama responded archly with a note addressed to the "Most hon. Congressman," giving him a "special invitation to Sunshine Ranch," but, she concluded, "Please don't bring your quarter of a million children." The note was signed, "Signora Mussolini."[34]

There was nothing typical about the education of Maury Maverick. He volunteered the information, not proudly, but candidly, that he "never graduated from anything."[35] He began a program of desultory (at first) self-education at the age of twelve or thirteen that was to continue to his death. There were many serious books in the Maverick home, and the family read and discussed them. Maverick said that he was reading Greek philosophy at the age of twelve,[36] and at another point explained, "At home I read books in a wide range, from the causes of the Crimean War to books by dead philosophers—and dead books by living ones. I had subscribed to the Appeal to Reason, a socialist publication from Girard, Kansas, and read every issue of it. I had met old Gene Debs. I thought then he was a great man, and I think so now."[37]

In addition to reading "every issue" of *Appeal to Reason* in his early teens,[38] Maverick read Robert Hunter's *Poverty* at the age of thirteen.[39] Hunter's book examined the extent, evils, and necessary remedies of poverty in the United States and mentioned suggestions and criticisms from such leading economists as Richard T. Ely and John R. Commons.[40] In this book Maverick read of the downtrodden "struggling up the face of a barren precipice," because of the "brutal power of the economic forces which dominate their lives."[41] The impact of books of this type and readings of this sort was obvious in Maverick's lifetime of evangelistic efforts in behalf of all sorts of programs to alleviate the condition of the poor.

The Southwestern intellectual equivalent of derring-do pulp magazines and other schoolboy contraband when Maverick was a boy was the *Iconoclast*, a paper written in Waco, Texas, by William Cowper Brann, a character as fabulous as Maverick.[42] Brann was a self-taught philosopher-journalist who left home for a newspaper career at the age of thirteen. Another maverick, he spent his spare time reading "science, philosophy, history, biography and general literature." He wrote some of the most colorful prose that was ever applied to paper in the United States. Defense of intellectual freedom was his forte, but he was likely to direct a withering blast at anything that happened to strike his fancy. "He was a hater of shams and defied every form of fraud, hypocrisy and deceit. . . ."[43] Roy Bedichek refers to Brann as a "provincial Voltaire" who opposed injustice, cruelty, senseless repression and "hocus pocus," but "in the heat of controversy he was, like the great Voltaire himself, guilty of each of these abominations, as who is not?"[44] The paper is said to have reached a circulation of ninety thousand at the time of Brann's death—extraordinary even today for a publication of its type.[45] Editorial comment on his death came from every part of the United States.[46]

Maverick was too young to have subscribed to the paper, but he said that he read the two-volume collection[47] at the age of eleven.[48] He never stated that Brann influenced him, but there is a considerable parallel between some of the best of Brann and the character and attitudes of Maverick. This is particularly true of the readiness of both men to leap to the defense when any attempt at suppression of freedom of expression was made.[49] Another strong parallel was to be found in the opposition to sham and hypocrisy evidenced by both men. While reading one of Brann's speeches, Maverick marked with approval: "One may . . . have Plato at his fingers' ends and ever remain a fool."[50]

But drawing too much of a parallel would be an injustice to Maverick. Brann's bottle of vitriol poured forth racist outbursts—even to advocating the killing of the "buck Negro"[51]—and his motives were often questionable.[52] Also, Maverick expressed disagreement with Brann's essentially negative approach. For ex-

A Maverick American

ample, Brann said of his role as iconoclast, pessimist, and skeptic, "I am no perfectionist. I do not build the spasmodic sob nor spill the scalding tear because all men are not Sir Galahads in quest of the Holy Grail, and all women with two pair of reversible wings and the aurora borealis for a hat-band." This statement must have piqued Maverick the reformer at some later reading, for he wrote opposite it in the margin, "I am not envisioning a perfect society —but at least a *moving* one."[53]

Maverick's claims concerning his early reading were apparently not idle boasts. At least as early as the age of seventeen, he was keeping an annotated notebook with the title, "Books I Have Read." Most of the works listed were political and social histories, with some novels of the same genre. Maverick did not merely read such books, he studied them. An appreciation of how effectively he used books can be gathered from the following entry, written when he was nineteen:

Civil History of the Confederate States—J. L. M. Curry, 1901—B. F. Johnson-Richmond, Read June 1915.
 The author should take into consideration the fact that the Civil War was over in '65, and that Confederate money is now no good. He is too extreme—rather narrow-minded. He is almost as bad as some old narrow-minded northerners who write about how they saved the North or rather the "union" against the rebels, etc. and talk about the "noble blacks" and the war as one of "civilization vs. barbarism."[54]

In another entry, Maverick described *The Citadel* by Samuel Merwin as the story of a young member of Congress sent there "by the interests." Maverick then suggested that the political novel form "could be used by professors who write on Political and Social Economy. It would be sure to create public interest and educate the public, who otherwise would read trash."[55] Thus young Maverick anticipated the current use of novels as vehicles to learning in political science courses in the colleges and universities.

Despite Maverick's references to the dominant role of his mother, his father was the primary influence on Maury's early ideas. Albert Maverick and his son read and discussed together the works of Thomas Paine and Thomas Jefferson,[56] and the elder Maverick taught his son the lessons of free inquiry and freedom of expression.[57] The atmosphere in the home was conducive to the development of liberal views on most subjects. As to religion, for example, Maverick's parents were devout in their own way, but they were not regular churchgoers. As Maverick explained, his father did not try to dictate his children's thoughts; rather, he hoped that they would develop their own. "He merely offers information, so that they will not go into the world as a set of nitwits. As for our economic or religious opinions, he cares nothing."[58] Something of the father's views are reflected in this representative excerpt from his fragmentary diary, written during the depression years:

May 7, 1932—The money interests who own our Government got our baby President Hoover, several weeks ago, to make a special appeal to the people not to hoard money. What a mockery, & how transparent! The golden stream of interest (usury) flows east and north . . . to the overfilled coffers of the usurers, who own & act through the banks concerned only in increasing their capital—not in the increasing misery of the people. The government should own all the banks, & interest by degrees, abated, and made illegal. Employment should be furnished to the people, in road building & public works—to make them self-respecting & not paupers, & more, a limit must be set to a man's possessions & *service* become the badge of honor, service for all, for the common good.[59]

The range of Albert Maverick's knowledge and interests is revealed in this passage from a letter to Lieutenant Maury Maverick in 1917: "Let us hope help can get to Italy in time to ward off a surrender, & mingle our tears over Kerensky, discredited. Every man is doomed to failure in the case of Russia—hordes of semi-civilized wild people suddenly given power, & German intrigue & strategy will profit by it. Peace is a long way off."[60]

Maverick's early self-education was not confined to books and father-son discussions. Family gatherings were often the occasion for discussions and, more likely, heated debates on public affairs. His home and relatives' homes were fairly frequent stopping-off places for important public figures—it was in this way that he met William Jennings Bryan, for example. Maury's watchful eye also caught the political ferment that was going on about him during his grammar school and high school years. He told of his earliest recollection of being induced to do some serious thinking for himself by the sight of a man being mobbed and driven from San Antonio's Alamo Plaza as he tried to make a speech.[61] As a

A Maverick American 15

grammar school student in 1909, he watched and heard Francisco I. Madero and his supporters plan the revolution by which Madero was soon to become president of Mexico.[62] Two years later, at San Antonio's Maine Avenue High School, Maverick and his friends organized a discussion club called the Atheneum Association. Shortly after its organization, General Bernardo Reyes came to San Antonio to attempt to establish a revolutionary force to overthrow Madero.[63] Reyes was living with his family and some assistants on San Pedro Avenue, near the high school. Students generally favored Madero, and they subjected Reyes' home to rock throwing and other harassment. The Atheneum group sought to make amends by inviting Reyes to speak to the student body, and Maury Maverick was the spokesman for the group. His friend Hobart Huson said, "Maury made a brave, but excruciating, effort as interpreter," but nonetheless he was able to convey the message to Reyes.

The school authorities had not been consulted, and they strongly opposed the invitation. Other school clubs adopted resolutions against having Reyes speak. Association members were attempting to find another location for the speech, but before they could do so, Reyes returned to Mexico. Huson concluded that "Maury Maverick got his first lesson and experience in creating publicity, which served him well in future years."[64]

In 1912, without having completed high school, Maverick boarded a steamer at Galveston for Virginia Military Institute by way of New York and Washington. He rode most of the trip in the steerage, though he had first-class passage. He discussed socialism, Henry George and the single tax, Karl Marx, and the "Wall Street exploitation" of Cuba with the steerage passengers. He ate the steerage fare and typically began to discuss ways and means of getting something done about it. The first mate labeled him an agitator and ordered him to eat in the first-class accommodations.[65]

In Washington, sixteen-year-old Maverick stayed for a time with his uncle, Congressman James L. Slayden, an outstanding pacifist,[66] and insisted on being introduced to Congressman Victor Berger and Senator Robert M. LaFollette. Maury's recollections of his year at Virginia Military Institute consisted of two parades celebrating the election of President Woodrow Wilson and an "average" scholastic record.[67] He kept a "Maury Maverick Memory Book" in which he recorded the expected pranks, "gripes" at cadet officers, demerits, and such entries as "Penalty drill today in overcoats. Cold." A letter of July 10, 1917, in the "Memory Book" certified that Maverick had "a good record [at VMI]" and "successfully completed the topics of instruction in the fourth class." The book also revealed the youthful Maverick to be harboring the typical homesickness and sentimental attachment to Sunshine Ranch and his native Texas. Snapshots depict a stocky, tanned youth with a shock of unruly hair and an air of mischief—indeed, beneath one photograph Maverick wrote, "a creation of the devils: devilishly short, and devilishly ugly."[68]

On his return to Texas in 1913, Maverick enrolled at the University of Texas "in journalism," according to his account.[69] It appears, however, that he enrolled in a basic prelaw curriculum and elected a course in journalism during his sophomore year. He did work on the *Daily Texan* (the student newspaper) as a reporter and later as an issue editor from time to time during the 1914–1915 academic year.[70] The scanty records available show that he took two years of English, German, and public speaking and one year each of mathematics, English history, geology, American history, journalism, and government. His grades were poor.[71]

By his own admission and the testimony of professors, Maury Maverick had little patience for the formal aspects of his schooling. He not only found his courses to be dull and turned to his own reading list, but he also spent considerable time in frivolity and roistering about the campus. Professor Brooks thought that Maverick had merely fallen victim to the middle-aged man's common obsession of imagining himself as a "regular heller" in his undergraduate days,[72] but it is just as likely that Maverick did not exaggerate his student high jinks. After one drinking spree at a football game, he scrawled some outrageous obscenities on a postcard and mailed it to a friend, and it was only by the intervention of some influential friends of the family that he was saved from indictment by a federal grand jury.[73] In his first book Maverick gave a lengthy recital of expulsions and near expulsions for hazing students, "rotten-egging professors," painting the water tank and "being a very poor student."[74] The late Walter Prescott Webb, a distinguished American historian and close friend of the Mavericks, delighted in telling the story of Maverick's lament to the dean,

"Why do you always call *me* in when something goes wrong around here?"[75] Dr. Lewis H. Haney, one of Maverick's instructors and now professor emeritus of economics and lecturer at New York University, testifies, "My recollections of Maury as a student are that he took little interest in scholarly attainments, and did not apply himself diligently to his studies. He had more interest in outside activities on the fun-making and social side of college life."[76]

Maury admitted to participation in the publication of an underground newspaper, the *Blunderbuss*, which appeared on the University of Texas campus each April Fool's Day. It had the primary objective of lampooning and even slandering members of the faculty. The issue printed April 1, 1915, bears the unmistakable stamp of Maury Maverick, though the identity of editors and writers was carefully concealed. A front-page story concerning "egg-throwing" has the flavor of Maverick-via-Rabelais—whose works he reread dozens of times. Also, the paper has several fictitious items about Maury Maverick, such as "Mr. Maury Maverick has established a select matrimonial bureau at his apartment on Nineteenth Street. The Blunderbuss desires to wish him success in his undertaking as we know no one knows 'em better than he does."[77]

But there were items on the plus side of the ledger. Dr. Haney said that Maverick had an "alert and active mind. He was an independent thinker to the extent of being a non-conformist."[78] He banded with some fellow recalcitrants in the organization of a group known as the Campus Buzzards. "We proclaimed ourselves," he said, "as carrion philosophers and permitted no reading except that which was prohibited."[79] He learned about the things that interested him by attending bull sessions with some of the younger professors, going to labor meetings, and listening eagerly to such speakers as Scott Nearing, "who had the impudence to suggest that lynching of Negroes should stop."[80] One of the young professors who joined these bull sessions, poet and author Stark Young, wrote of Maverick, "I remember him as one of the vivid figures in my Texas acquaintance. He had a vigorous, independent and original way of thinking and speaking."[81]

Maury's unsuccessful second year at the University of Texas exhausted Papa's patience; it was time for the young man to get to work. Maury received an offer of a job as a reporter on the

Amarillo Daily News on August 18, 1915, and he accepted immediately.[82] The job paid sixty dollars per month for, as Maury put it, "Title: city editor. Real position: local reporter."[83] Maverick seemingly did well at the *News*. One of his journalism instructors (addressing him as "Execrable Copy Reader, Pathetic Reporter and Sad City Editor") told Maverick that he would soon "be able to write as good a story as any of them."[84] His aunt and mentor, Ellen Maury Slayden, who wrote *Washington Wife*,[85] said, "This is good newspaper work. I had no idea Maury could do so well."[86] She later wrote to him:

My dear old Boy,
   You made a terrible hole in the family circle when you went away....
   I feel kind of proud of you myself, because, you see, I had quite a hand in raising you.
   I am really surprised at your good lines, but I am afraid you are elaborating your news with a little too much imagination, and overworking your superlatives.

Ellen Slayden suggested to him that a year out of college would help him: he could go back "as a man and not just a boy who has to work off his foolishness."[87] But encouragement and admonitions were not enough to keep Maverick on the job in Amarillo. Letters from his mother indicated that he was suffering from a combination of discouragement over his low pay and position and homesickness. Mrs. Maverick told him to stick to the job—that his father had started to work in his youth at thirty-five dollars a month and that the family was essentially broke at the moment.[88] Aunt Ellen gave similar advice and held out the promise of better things. She implied that she would help him to go to Columbia University the next year to study under Talcott Williams, the outstanding journalist and critic, and she enclosed a piece entitled "The Creed of a Great Newspaper."[89]

Despite the influence that Mrs. Slayden exerted upon Maury in other matters, it was to no avail on this occasion. In a few days he had presumably persuaded his parents to permit him to return to the University of Texas—this time to the Law School.[90] Maverick later boasted that he had "jammed all my three years of law into one."[91] Though this statement may sound extravagant, it is not far from the absolute facts. His record card in the University of Texas Law School shows that he took thirteen courses with an average grade of 79. The record indicates that he received a grade of 80 in "International Law A" by taking the examination without having attended classes. Dr. A. Leon Green, distinguished professor of law and one of Maverick's instructors, says that these scores are only respectable and would not represent the high level of achievement as the same scores would today.[92] Nonetheless, Maverick's feat was rather remarkable. He took and passed the Texas bar examination in Austin in May 1916. It is impossible to determine the level of his performance on the examination because the Clerk's Office of the Texas Supreme Court has no records of such matters prior to 1919.

Dr. Green says that Maverick continued some of the pranks and frivolity in law school, but he adds: "I never doubted Maury's ability, and his salty way of putting things even then was extremely refreshing. He gave no quarter to any one and asked none. Were he in law school today he would be tops in any company. Law teaching has finally caught up with his spirit. This is confirmed by the fact that in his later years he was a favorite with law students and faculties all over the country. It is a pity he died when he was needed most. . . . His is a rare spirit and should be an inspiration to all youngsters who aspire to public life or who have an interest in public men and affairs."[93]

Professor Brooks, who was president of the American Political Science Association in 1940, said of Maury's outlandish study habits: "Evidently his intellectual curiosity was insatiable. Given a really understanding tutor he would have forged ahead at a tremendous intellectual pace."[94] Maverick did not have a tutor, but he was able to profit in his youth and early manhood from the sage advice of another self-educated Maury of rather remarkable attainments—his Aunt Ellen. She never attended a "real school," but she read widely and traveled to international peace meetings with her husband, James L. Slayden, a congressman from San Antonio. Her abilities were such that she contributed articles to *Century* magazine and various newspapers on such topics as political problems in Mexico.[95] The caliber of her advice to young Maverick as he began practicing law in San Antonio at the age of twenty can be seen in the following letter:

To Maury Maverick, In Re plumb nonsense.

Your first fee has given much pleasure, amusement & interest not only to your present correspondent, but to the Representative from your Congressional district and a number of our friends. I am torn by conflicting emotions over it, and if your legal advice isn't too expensive, an opinion from you would be welcome. I wish to keep the draft (for 15 cts. only) as a thing of interest to you, say, 20 years from now, and yet with the world's finances in their present state am I justified in letting all this money be idle? Tell me, how am I to eat my cake and have it, if you can. Before discussing the bargain we made about the books you were to have for your first fee, I want to say a few words "in re" *the* importance of a lawyer's cultivation of the judicial rather than the prejudicial order of mind and speech. "The falsehood of extremes," the fact that there are "two sides to every question," and that "the truth lies between two extremes" are axioms that every lawyer should keep in mind, or else—he is never likely to make a Judge of the Supreme Court. Now you know that I am not a thick & thin admirer of Woodrow Wilson, but I consider your strictures upon him much too severe. Many wise & good men agree with his views, *even* on the Mexican question in which he seems to you & me so woefully mistaken, so it behooves us to withhold severe judgment lest we should be proved in the wrong. Besides, he was elected to the Presidency by the votes of the party of which you claim to be a member, and until the majority of the party decides that he no longer represents them satisfactorily, it is more loyal and much more dignified to speak of him with respect and restraint or not at all. This does not mean approval of him, or that you will not vote for another Democrat when you get the chance, but merely that you think violent opinions violently expressed are a poor form of party loyalty, bad taste & bad politics. It is a grave reflection upon the collective wisdom of your party in electing him which the enemy is sure to seize upon as proof that the Democratic party is unfit to be trusted with the government. As to your saying that because of your dislike of Wilson your 'first vote may be lost or else cast for Hughes,' your Uncle Slayden tells me to remind you that unless you have thought over the party principles for which the two men stand very thoroughly and decided you agree with the Republicans rather than the Democrats, you are making a grave political mistake to declare yourself as considering the possibility of voting against your party. The action, of course, would ruin you, but the mere declaration would be sure to embarrass you in the future if you wished to be active or influential in politics. 'No one wants a wobbler.' So much for him, and I want to add that a vote is a very sol-

A Maverick American

emn privilege, and remind you of the French proverb, ' 'Tis the first step that counts.' So I hope your vote will be cast 'soberly, discreetly and in the fear of God.'

Now, about the books or book. I am really sorry that you refuse the History of the U.S. tho I must admit that its standing as history is not very high. Still, it is worth reading . . . but if you won't have it, I have in mind another book, "America and Her Problems" by d'Estournelles de Constant, which I am finding most interesting, and which is of sufficient importance for *two* copies of it to have been sent to us from different sources. I presume that you do not propose to confine your study and interest to the courts of S.A. or even the problems of the state of Texas, so it may be good for you to look at our national problems for a while thro' the eyes of the wisest of living French writers and historians. I have met the Baron several times in this country & in Europe, and found him as simple-mannered and quizzically wise & observant as only the wise Frenchman can be. . . .

With Best Love,
Aunt Ellen[96]

As early as the spring of 1916, while still a law student, Maury Maverick was attempting to get into some military service. He sought the help of his uncle, Congressman James L. Slayden, and that of Senator Morris Sheppard in an effort to secure a commission in the U.S. cavalry. Maverick hoped to get into the fighting in Mexico. Sheppard wrote that he remembered him "quite well" from a meeting in Amarillo and that it would be a pleasure to recommend him for a commission if war with Mexico should break out.[97]

With characteristic audacity Maverick seized what he thought was the ultimate opportunity to realize his ambition for a commission. General John J. Pershing was stopping over in San Antonio at a time when Maverick was attending a dance at a local hotel. Pershing and a fellow officer were looking in on the dance when Maverick spotted the general and dashed over to introduce himself. Then he asked his dancing partner to dance with the startled Pershing and asked another girl to dance with Pershing's friend. The officers stayed for awhile and seemed to enjoy themselves immensely. The next day Maverick called General Pershing and asked if he would like to see the historic sites of San Antonio "in my car." After some hesitation, Pershing agreed, and Maverick begged enough money from his father to rent a car for the excursion. He then picked up the same girls and proudly drove his captive general and his aide around the city. At the end of the sightseeing tour, Maverick thought the time was ripe to put the bite on the grateful general. But when he asked Pershing to help him get a commission, the crestfallen Maverick heard the general say, "Son, I'll tell you what to do. You go out to Fort Sam Houston and enlist, and you can tell them you have my recommendation."[98]

When the United States did become involved in World War I, Maverick was one of the first men in San Antonio to enlist in the Army.[99] In the spring of 1917 he was sent to the Federal Reserve Student Training Camp at Camp Funston, Leon Springs, Texas, where he was commissioned a second lieutenant in the Army Reserve on June 11, 1917. He kept up a constant barrage of letters, mainly to Representative Slayden, in an attempt to get an overseas assignment. He tried to get transferred to the air corps and even threatened to resign his commission and join the Canadian forces in order to get overseas.[100] Slayden told him to "keep his shirt on," that policies could not be changed for an individual: "Even [Theodore] Roosevelt who has influence with hundreds of thousands of people almost as crazy as he is could not alter the predetermined course of events."[101]

Maury was sent to join the First Colorado Infantry at Trinidad, Colorado, in September, 1917, and it was soon ordered to the Fortieth Division training base at Camp Kearney, Linda Vista, California. He was put in charge of a machine-gun company and was promoted to first lieutenant in the National Guard on December 21, 1917.

Maverick's first baptism of fire was in a different sort of war, which he was to fight in for the rest of his life—the struggle for human rights and human dignity. Many of the men under his command were of Mexican descent. Despite Maverick's repeated speeches emphasizing our great heritage of liberty and the necessity for "making the world safe for democracy," when questioned as to why they were fighting, these men could answer only, "De draft board, he send me here."[102] Maverick persuaded the division commander that these men were being misunderstood and abused simply because they did not understand English. He organized language classes for the men and was doing reasonably well with

A Maverick American

them when a graver problem arose—two of the men deserted and were picked up in Mexico. Maverick was appointed to defend them. He reported, "I studied all about a soldier's constitutional rights—and also got some books on the subject of natural rights. At the trial, I quoted the statements of James Otis and Sam Adams on Natural Rights, made preceding the American Revolution." He went on to argue that these men did not understand what the war was about, that they knew nothing of American customs or the English language, and that it was therefore improper for them to have been drafted. He said he could not tell them why we were fighting, because he really didn't know either. Maverick was threatened with court-martial himself, but the commander relented and issued a memorandum (which Maverick did not mention in his own account of this affair) commending the Texas lieutenant for "his interest in conducting classes for soldiers of Mexican extraction." On the basis of Maverick's contention that the two men had acted out of ignorance rather than cowardice and that they needed help, the commander said that he desired that "this officer [Maverick] take personal charge of the instruction of the two men."[103]

In the summer of 1918 Maverick was shipped overseas. After several days of "drunken brawling" in England,[104] he landed in Cherbourg on September 4, 1918, as the band on the dock played the *Marseillaise*. In two days he was in the serious and gory business of fighting a war. He joined the First Division at Sarcy, France, as it was moving up to Saint-Mihiel and the front. During the battle of Saint-Mihiel, Maury was working with the regimental headquarters, directing the bringing up of ammunition. While reconnoitering a route for his ammunition wagons, he happened upon twenty-six German soldiers who, as Maury explains with unmatched candor, demanded to be captured and conducted to the rear.[105] Before and after this battle, Maverick had written to his parents that the German soldiers were cowardly, "immoral to obscenity," and that they would not die "like men."[106] He was soon to make a radical change in his views.

After the battle of Saint-Mihiel, Maverick sought and obtained a transfer back to his company and was made executive officer under Lieutenant Frank Felbel, a more experienced officer. There is none of the usual Maverick humor in his grim account of his part in the Argonne offensive, for which he received the Silver Star for gallantry in action. In powerful writing that compares favorably with that of Erich Maria Remarque,[107] he tells a story of stumbling, almost blind, into the Argonne forest at two o'clock on the morning of October 1, 1918, of a loss of communications, of the sudden loss of his company commander, of companions blasted to pieces before his eyes, of heroics by inadvertency or instinct, and then of shell fragments biting into his shoulders and back as he stumbled through shell holes. In the unpublished account he dictated shortly after his experiences, he said: "How did you get back? The way it was with me, I could walk a little bit you see; I was staggering around. I tried to walk and then I got wounded again. I got lost and went back to the German lines. I went in the opposite direction to where I wanted to go and then I had to crawl back.... I crawled back all the way."[108]

After this experience Maverick said that the "Germans were good fighters—I did not find any 'Kamerad' stuff that is talked about."[109] He later said he did not deserve his medals and offered two pithy asides on the subject of heroism and medals. "The line between coward and hero is sometimes very indistinct. Men are suddenly brave or suddenly cowardly. In one moment of emotion they are likely to be branded for life, one way or the other—and wrongly.... Medals are not to reward brave men, but to keep men brave, and make them fight. The ruling classes have always attempted to build up the hero idea. It stops men from thinking."[110]

In a moment when he was "half-drunk and bored," shortly after arriving in France, Maverick sat on the side of the road to Saint-Mihiel and wrote a half-serious, half-facetious will in which he specified that all young male heirs must never shirk military service. On June 8, 1931, perusing his notes and records as he often did, he wrote that he was ashamed of the document and attached the following commentary:

> This document is kept in order that possibly some young man may run across this—and possibly I will save him from being a damned fool. If you go to war—but DON'T DO IT—don't get dramatic—NOBODY GIVES A DAMN ABOUT YOU, except your parents, and they can't help.

A Maverick American

This will is a fine example of VALOR (bunk), Unselfishness (childish egotism), and the rest of the traits the BIG BOYS work on us to go and murder somebody as their collectors. This letter is a true example of human vanity and false family values.

Remember—it takes MORE GUTS to refuse to fight, than it does to prance around in a uniform, and get shot at.[111]

The almost fatally wounded Maverick finally made his way back through French-American lines to a field hospital, where he collapsed from loss of blood. When the field hospital was brought under enemy shell fire, he was moved to Base Hospital 115 at Vichy. After extensive surgery, it took him more than a month to get back on his feet, and he never fully recovered from the effects of his wounds.[112] He apparently recovered enough, however, for a bit of revelry in Paris before the return voyage to New York in December of 1918.[113] After a two-week sojourn in New York, he was sent to the Base Hospital at Fort Sam Houston, San Antonio, where he was discharged on February 16, 1919.[114] On January 1, 1920, Maverick received a copy of general orders citing him for "gallantry in action and especially meritorious service," for which he was later awarded the Silver Star.[115]

Almost immediately after Maverick had returned to his law practice in San Antonio, he was on his way abroad again, mainly to do some legal research in Dublin, Ireland, concerning a legacy left to the Right Reverend J. W. Shaw, archbishop of New Orleans.[116] This trip lasted from early March to August of 1919. It is not treated in Maverick's semiautobiographical *A Maverick American*, and it is worth noting here only for whatever insight it offers into the development of the future politician. On the first leg of his trip he stopped off to see his devoted mentor, Aunt Ellen, who reported that "seeing Maury was just one more delight that I hadn't counted on. He . . . fussed with & abused his Uncle Sully & me as if he had been 3 yrs. old. His Uncle Sully was so overcome when he saw his wounds that he had to turn away & couldn't speak."[117]

Scraps of records that Maverick kept indicate that much of his time was spent in traveling about the British Isles with major stops in Dublin, Edinburgh, and London. Though he apparently made a nice vacation out of the trip, he maintained the serious interests that were a part of his continuing self-education. He developed the habit at this time of jotting notes concerning people he had met and places he had visited and the habit of reading and studying as he traveled. In Dublin he bought a book of instructions on how to learn the Irish language and a series of public-affairs pamphlets such as *The Nature and Rights of Property* and *Origin and Nature of Civil Authority* by Reverend M. M. O'Kane, both published in Belfast in 1917, as well as *Ulster's Opportunity: A United Ireland* (Dublin, 1917) by "an Irish K.C."[118]

It seemed that during this trip Maury's indulgent and devoted mother and aunt were engaged in a contest to determine which of them could present the most extravagant evidence of his prowess as a lady killer. Mama wrote that she had told a girl who complained that Maury's love letters were of no more than four lines that she "thought that was doing beautifully when one considered how many love letters you had to write."[119] Less than two weeks later she made the following report: "The entire town is consumed with curiosity about your trip to Europe. Some girls insisted on knowing where you were & Ellen S. told them 'the Crown Prince of G. was suing for a divorce & that you were correspondent.' To Mac Houston she told 'that you had been hastily called to the Peace Convention to take Clemenceau's place.' "[120]

But Maverick's days as a peripatetic bachelor were numbered. Shortly after he returned to San Antonio in the summer of 1919, he was attending a party at what is now the Texas Military Institute. A pretty, vivacious young woman was there named Terrell Louise Dobbs, who was living with her aunt and uncle, Dr. and Mrs. Thomas Terrell Jackson, in San Antonio. A friend, George Clifton, said to Miss Dobbs, "I want to introduce you to Maury Maverick; he's going to give a party at Sunshine Ranch, and he'll invite you." The two met, and Maverick invited her to the party. Maury Maverick was anything but handsome, indeed his nickname was "Ug," but women were attracted to him, and he was cocksure and persistent. Miss Dobbs sensed his design at first meeting and wrote to her sister, "This man thinks he's going to marry me, but he's not." She later received the formal invitation and a dance program that had been hand painted by Mrs. Albert

A Maverick American

Maverick, but she did not go to the party. Instead she went on a trip to Port Aransas with her aunt and uncle. The day after his party, Maverick called Miss Dobbs and announced that he was coming to Port Aransas. She met him at the ferry, and he asked her to marry him on the spot. She refused, and explains today with a coquettish air, "I was only nineteen, and besides, I had a few other things going at the time."

Thereafter, Maverick moved in steadily. He came to the house ostensibly to see her uncle and went to political meetings with him. But all the while Maverick was bombarding her with flowers, and he gradually ran off his less persistent rivals until Miss Dobbs agreed in December that she would marry him. They were married May 22, 1920, in San Antonio.[121]

Terrell Maverick had wanted to be a June bride, but had she been there would have been no time for a honeymoon trip, because Maury Maverick had committed himself to be on hand in San Antonio to campaign for his uncle, Representative James L. Slayden, who faced a tough contest that he was to lose. This was Mrs. Maverick's initiation into politics, and, as she explained in 1962, "From that summer political activities in general and the Democratic primary elections in particular have dominated and enriched my life."[122] It was an exciting life that she led as the wife of Maury Maverick—"I was never bored," she said. It is doubtful that she ever bored her husband or anybody else for that matter. She is to this day a pretty, petite woman of great charm, enthusiasm, and verve. She had little formal education, but, like Ellen Slayden, she learned rapidly and outstripped many people with formal educations.

Maury Maverick was the dominant figure in his family, but Mrs. Maverick said, "Though I learned a lot from him, he didn't smother me." Her role was not limited to that of the attractive wife and mother who stands in the background of the spotlighted public figure. She had her own views, and Maverick respected and sought them. She not only accompanied him at political conventions and the like, but she was an active participant in her own right on many occasions. She gave him good-humored but unflattering criticisms of his speeches and decisions, and she helped to assuage his wounds, both real and political. Her talents can be readily perceived in the preface she wrote for Ellen Slayden's *Washington Wife*.[123]

Two children were born to Maury and Terrell Maverick—a son, Maury, Jr., on January 3, 1921, and a daughter, Terrelita, on January 10, 1926. Maverick was, like his father, a devoted family man. He had a good relationship with his children, not unlike that with his own father. He spent as much time with his children as he could, taking them on trips and swimming excursions. He also passed on to his children his father's love of nature and animals. Maverick once returned from a trip to Mexico with a pair of javelinas (peccaries), which he named Anthony and Cleopatra. Kept in the yard as pets, one eventually died and the other had to be shipped off to the zoo when it playfully sank its teeth into a visitor's hand. On another occasion he brought back a black bear and a mountain lion, which he gave to the San Antonio Zoo.[124]

Maury, Jr.'s first recollection of his father was the sight of a "tremendous series of scars" that covered his body, and the agony that he suffered. Young Maury recalled that when he was about the age of seven his father would get up in the middle of the night and sit in a bathtub of hot water to ease the recurring pains from his wounds. Maury, Jr., would wander into the bathroom and stand there while his father talked to him about such subjects as world peace. "Papa always talked to me like an equal of sorts—always took me with him," said Maury, Jr., as he explained how his father showed him around Washington and introduced him to "great old-time newspaper people" and political leaders. He particularly remembered meeting Senator George Norris, regarded by his father as "the greatest living American."[125]

The correspondence between Maury Maverick and his son and daughter in their youth reveals the same sort of affectionate jibes and good-humored criticism that was used by Albert Maverick—though Albert would not have been as earthy as this father and son. After one of several complaints from teen-aged Maury, Jr., concerning his assignment to latrine duty at Texas Military Institute, the parental advice was:

As for being corporal of the crapping can, there was once a great General in Athens who came back, and purposely to insult him, they

A Maverick American

put him in charge of the garbage and trash of the city and the emptying of the crappers. In order to humiliate his enemies, he made Athens the cleanest and most beautiful city in the world.

Therefore, if you wish to be famous, keep the toilets clean and you will go down in history as the greatest corporal who ever lived.[126]

On another occasion, Maverick's teen-aged scion wrote to complain bitterly that he had not received a football letter to which he was sure he was entitled. He said that since his father had taught him that "you can't cuss" in letters, he would have to say that he had been "sexual intercoursed."[127]

The Bootleg Decade

MAURY MAVERICK'S RETURN to civilian life had taken place at the beginning of what he called the Bootleg Decade. He was elected president of the San Antonio Bar Association at the age of twenty-four in 1919, married in 1920, and by the middle 1920's was raising a family and seemed to be on the road to stodgy and stultifying respectability. He joined the Kiwanis Club and the Lions Club and "made speeches about Progress (of the wrong kind) and Thrift (which also turns out to have been of the wrong kind) and attended church once in a while." But the maverick inclinations were never clearly suppressed. He fought the Ku Klux Klan, headed off a movement to prevent violinist Fritz Kreisler from playing in San Antonio, and tried to liberalize his Bar Association. As its president he created and edited a little paper, *The Whereas*, for which he wrote a piece entitled "Koo Klucks Kondemned." Maverick, as the self-appointed "Imperious Gizzard," had held a "called meeting" attended only by himself at which the "Koo Klucks" had been judged as wearers of nightgowns who were "fully as mentally developed as an ape."[1]

It was not long before the practice of law began to pall for

Maverick's restless mind. He also explained that his effectiveness as a lawyer was often damaged by his tendency to sympathize with the opposite party in his law cases.[2] In 1922 he became manager of the Hillyer-Deutsch-Jarett Lumber Company, and about two years later, with some assistance from his father, Maverick joined a friend in the organization of the Kelley-Maverick Lumber Company. He moved into the construction business and started to get "middlin' rich" ($50,000 to $60,000),[3] but he later said that "Hoover got it all."[4] In one of his displays of remarkable candor and self-criticism, he wrote. "The houses that I and others built were a disgrace to this country. This is no confession, but a fact. That is the reason that the government should subsidize housing. Human beings should not have to live in the rotten habitations handed to them by speculators."[5]

Maverick was also moved to criticism of himself and his society by his experiences on a grand jury in February and March of 1924. He kept a notebook of "strictly private papers" on the entire course of events and included various musings on the nature of justice. He began his notes with the observation that laws on statutory rape and seduction were "barbaric." He wrote, "I must read more, and think more, of this subject."[6] He later followed through on this implicit promise by studying some works in sociology. In one of them he wrote that his experience with the grand jury had presented him "with all of the malformations of society," and had caused him to begin a study of sociology and, more specifically, criminology.[7]

In his "grand jury notebook" he told of the near-indictment of a Mexican-American for robbery before Maverick's insistence upon a more careful examination of witnesses revealed that no robbery had been committed! He commented:

Human beings seem to take human life very lightly, but they must remember that the lowest person on earth, whether he be Mexican or Negro, or anyone else, is entitled to full justice before the law; *in fact, such people are entitled to it more than any other because they have less knowledge and money to work themselves out after they have been charged with a crime.*

It seems that if some dumb, ignorant person commits some bungling crime, he is jerked in before the Grand Jury, charged with it and indicted because they have the dope on him, but that the real criminals are never caught. Take a man who has committed his first crime, which is really not criminal in its nature. He is guilty, there is no doubt about it. According to the law, he should go to the penitentiary and does, serves two years and returns to society. He finds it hard to get a job and has no character or courage left . . . he does not think he has committed such a great sin so he resentfully sets about to make himself an efficient criminal. This he does, and when he perfects himself, he commits robberies just heretofore mentioned, makes no mistakes, gets what he wants and stays out of jail. This is a sociological problem of course, of which the Grand Jury has no cognizance.[8]

After a recital of various other cases that appeared before the grand jury, Maverick expressed the opinion that punishment was always "personal"and "vindictive." He felt that men must determine the real nature of crime—that they should study the heredity, physical make-up, emotional stability, environment as a youth and the present home conditions of an alleged criminal before determining his fate. It was Maverick's judgment that criminals should be examined by a board of "say six men—2 doctors, 2 lawyers, and 2 laymen" before disposition of their cases. But he came to the bitter conclusion that such a proposal was impossible because lawyers and doctors were afraid of public opinion where rape and the like were involved. He wrote, "Our theories of government and of religion are all against it"; all we apparently want is the type of government that "prohibits absolute anarchy."[9]

This grand jury experience was not the only impetus to reading, study, and research for Maverick. He seemed to have an almost insatiable curiosity about all sorts of subjects, and he had the drive to pursue each of them until he felt that he was reasonably knowledgeable in that area. The 1920's marked the real flowering of Maverick's intellectual and scholarly interests. He was largely responsible for the establishment of a Carnegie Library in San Antonio, and he joined with friends in the establishment of the San Antonio Open Forum discussion group, which met at the old Main Avenue High School. In his brassy fashion he fought for a more salubrious scholarly climate at the University of Texas, and he embarked upon a renewed, major regimen of reading and study that made him a scholar of considerable attainment.

Perhaps the least-known qualities of this extraordinary Texas politician were his serious scholarship and his capacity for original

The Bootleg Decade

thought. Why should his erudition have been relatively obscured? The reasons are several, but all are interrelated. For one thing, Maverick never tried to hide his poor academic record in college; in fact he called attention to it.[10] Also, as a part of his studied irreverence, he developed a fondness for joshing, needling, or even baiting the professors. The classic example was his treatment of his friend Dr. Rexford Guy Tugwell, who tried out one of his speeches on Maverick while the two were visiting Laredo, Texas. When the New Deal braintruster reached a point at which he spoke of workers and farmers "combining their genius" and forming a "nodule," Maverick exploded, "Rex, I am sore and insulted, and do not want to hear any more."

"Why?" asked Tugwell.

"What in God's name is a nodule?" said Maverick.

"A nodule is—" began the professor.

"Stop! Stop!" Maverick shouted. "Don't tell me. Whenever you use a word that I don't understand, it makes me mad. I am an American! The word nodule is not understood by the American people, nor is it understood by me, which makes it worse—and I do not want to know what it means. Nobody wants to listen to your academic phrases. Nodule my eye! Put your speech in simple language. I never heard of a 'nodule' before, so I don't like it. Besides," Maverick continued, "it sounds like sex perversion."[11]

Maverick was given to the use of such deliberate exaggerations in order to make a point; his vocabulary was as extensive as that of most educated people, but he was very impatient with attempts to communicate with ordinary people in such language. Also, subsequent passages dealing with the above episode indicate both a genuine desire on the part of Maverick to bring about more effective communication and a desire to lash back at Tugwellian remarks about "demagoguery," from which Maverick seemed to be smarting:

Out there in these open spaces we enacted a scene which dramatized one of the fundamental failures of the Administration. Professors with wonderful ideas—but professors who can afford to have Olympian contempt for the politician, since they do not have to be elected.

No man could be elected, or if elected by accident, no man could stay in office if he used this Tugwellian jargon of abstruse and incomprehensible polysyllables. . . .

The professorial jargon is an answer to an inferiority complex. The professor is at a loss in crowds, and to vindicate himself he uses big words which no one can understand. Since he cannot be elected himself, he builds up a distrust for the politician who can. For myself, I find it hard enough to be a progressive, thinking official, and at the same time get elected; but that is the only way we can accomplish anything: by being elected.[12]

Maverick also avoided what he considered the curse of identification with the scholar by eschewing some of the stereotyped symbols. In 1932 he made a Washington Day address on San Antonio radio station WOAI. Requests for copies of the speech poured in from ten states as well as from many points in Texas, many of these people asking for copies of the "lecture" by Mr. Maverick![13] Two years later, while campaigning for Congress, "Professor" Maverick indicated that there would be no more of this political luxury. He said, "My friends came to me and told me that I was delivering good lectures to a college class-room, but that they were poor political speeches."[14]

Various drafts of a number of his later speeches show clearly how he excised words he thought might be troublesome to his audiences or brand him with the mark of the intellectual. For example, a first draft of a radio address in 1936 started out with a reference to "anomalous situations," and wound up with a reference to "peculiar situations" in the final draft. When Maverick wrote a review of Wertenbaker's *Torchbearer of the Revolution*, he devoted an entire paragraph in his first draft to the consideration of the possibility of this book leading to more study of the "Virginia mind" and the influence of delusions of aristocracy. He omitted this passage completely in his second draft, and it did not appear in the published version.[15]

His interest in promoting the cause of clear writing and speaking gave rise to the contribution for which Maverick is probably best known, the coinage of the word *gobbledygook* and the elaboration of his argument for terse, lucid prose.[16] After taking such a positive stand, he could scarcely run the risk of being caught in the use of anything vaguely resembling professorial jargon.

Finally, the scholarly side of Maury Maverick was obviously obscured by his personal characteristics and appearance—a greater contrast to the stereotype of the scholar would be difficult to find. He was a bullish, lusty, brash type, given to the earthiest sort of language, and he could slug it out with the best of them in the political arena. He just did not fit the part of the intellectual; it would be like expecting a giant football tackle to play Mozart on a spinet. Also, most newspaper reporters were much more interested in telling their readers about the Maverick who was "knocking them dead" or "rolling them in the aisles" of the House of Representatives. Scholarship generally makes poor copy.

But there were more than a few indications that Maverick had not only a great respect for scholarship and the scholars, but even that he aspired to the groves of Academe himself. He was drawn to academic men, and they in turn were drawn to him. In the same book in which he lambasted Tugwell and other professors, Maverick could write, "The march of the professor is the greatest advance in the history of our government. We are just beginning to slough off the philosophy of 'Old Rough and Ready.' It's high time."[17]

Even in his student days, when much of his time was spent in sniping at professors, Maverick could leap to their defense if a serious charge were made. When he was a sophomore student at the University of Texas, he saw a letter in the *Daily Texan* by Harrison F. Lane (an admitted pseudonym) attacking a professor for baiting students and "pouncing on some luckless freshman." Replying the next day, young Maverick said that the professor's action was "fully warranted" on the basis of the students' "utter lack of preparing their lessons and being boneheads." He said he had been one of the victims, and that he had deserved it. His conclusion was that the professors were entitled to more respect, and he characterized the student's failure to sign his name as a cowardly act.[18]

In the 1920's, despite his poor academic record and his own reputation as a campus playboy and ne'er-do-well, Maverick was greatly disturbed by what he conceived to be happening to his University of Texas. Big-time football was then coming into its own in the Southwest and other parts of the country, and, moreover, university administrators and faculties were not only plagued with the problems of financing the growing institutions but were also beset with the poking and probing of legislatures and boards of regents bent upon preserving religious and political orthodoxies.

In a statement prepared sometime in the summer of 1923, Maverick charged that the University of Texas was becoming demoralized through the reprehensible actions of the Board of Regents and its chairman, H. J. Lutcher Stark. One of Maverick's specific indictments was:

> Recently they wasted their time passing unnecessary resolutions on the religious views of the professors. Then they did something smaller and meaner than any Spanish Court of Inquisition ever did—they called in Dean H. Y. Benedict and tried to give him the third degree on his religious views, asking him, among other things, none of which were any of their business, of what church he was a member, and if he had baptized his baby. Church affiliations, and baptism of professors' babies hardly constitutes the regents' business. Yet the ex-students stood by and I heard not one word of condemnation from any ex-student over the State. I have talked to numbers of ex-students who seem to think it amounts to nothing, but it is as vital a question as can be imagined.[19]

Old-timers at the University of Texas remember this incident, but it apparently took place behind closed doors and the newspapers avoided it. On July 11, 1923, the *Daily Texan* and the *Austin American* simply reported that the Board of Regents had, without explanation, passed a resolution prohibiting any "infidel, agnostic or atheist" from holding any position with the university. Such a person could not be hired, nor could anyone "continue in office" unless he believed "in God as the supreme being and the ruler of the universe." The *American* made no comment on the resolution, and the *Texan* simply stated that the resolution was probably designed to do no more than "reassure the people of the state as to the university's position on religion" and to "quiet" criticism of religious views at the university. An editorial the next day, however, complained of lengthy closed meetings of the Board of Regents and suggested that "some progressive college" might try holding board meetings that would be open to the public.

As Robert H. Montgomery, professor emeritus of economics at the university, remembers this incident, which most of his colleagues knew about at that time, Dean Benedict held his own in

The Bootleg Decade

the encounter. When a member of the Board of Regents asked him if his beliefs would comport with their newly adopted resolution, Benedict is said to have asked if his belief in an "anthropomorphic God" would be satisfactory. The puzzled regent looked around at his equally bewildered colleagues and asked them if they thought that would be all right, and they, with some uncertainty, voiced approval.

Further charges by Maverick in the 1923 statement involved the machinations by which Stark attempted to make the governor of Texas, Pat M. Neff, the next president of the university. Maverick said that Stark was a "willing tool" who was "trying to work something out for himself." The presidency was vacant at this time, and it was reported in February of 1923 that Neff and Stark had conferred at length and that the governor would soon be offered the presidency, to be assumed at the end of his term as governor. What proved to be an abortive "Stark for Governor" movement was also reportedly underway in Austin.[20] In May, Raymond Brooks of the *Austin American* said that the regents would probably offer the presidency to Neff, and if that were to happen, he would accept.[21] A few days later the executive council of the ex-students association went on record as opposing the selection of Neff.[22] Later in the month the regents named W. S. Sutton as acting president, and though the presidency was eventually offered to Neff, he declined, and the post went to Dr. W. M. W. Splawn, a member of the Texas Railroad Commission and former chairman of the economics department at the university.[23]

The development of athletics, particularly football, as a consuming mania of university students, ex-students, and regents began in the early 1920's. At the University of Texas the turning point seemed to be about 1921. At that time the week's athletic events were taking up the lead story space in the *Daily Texan*, and, though there were some editorial murmurs against overemphasis on athletics in the early part of 1922, by May of that year the editor wrote apologetically that he could do no more than provide the students with what they clearly wanted.[24] By the mid-twenties the entire front page of the *Texan* was frequently devoted to athletic contests.

Maverick deplored this trend. In his statement he charged that the regents and many of the ex-students were guilty of fostering athletics at the cost of other aspects of education. He admonished, "A stadium is not of itself a healthy sign. At the peak of the wealth of Rome, there was a fine coliseum, a fine place for the rabble to go to watch the gladiatorial sports, but it was the beginning of degeneracy, which finally ruined the empire. A stadium might be a healthy sign, if education flourished commensurately, but it does not."

Football, said Maverick, was a particular mania of Lutcher Stark, chairman of the Board of Regents. Stark had announced in November of 1922 plans for a concrete stadium designed to seat "between fifty and sixty thousand people," and he became chairman of the drive to raise funds for it.[25] When such matters were brought before an ex-students meeting in San Antonio in 1924, Maverick rose and told President Splawn and his fellow ex-students that "athletics, booze and society" were ruining the university. He wanted to know who could justify the construction of a unit of a million dollar stadium—"a temple of athletics"—while students were freezing and experiencing various other discomforts in "flimsy shacks [on] the campus." He was ready to raise funds, he said, but not for athletics.[26]

Maverick's reward was condemnation in the *Daily Texan* for a "vicious attack" that was not worthy of comment. But two years earlier another editor of the *Texan* had called attention to the conditions Maverick described. In February of 1922, regents were urged to have a look at the dilapidated shacks in which many students lived. These quarters were described as having large cracks in the floors, walls through which dust and dirt sifted, and inadequate heat. A year later another *Texan* editor complained that half of the work of the university was still being done in more than twenty wooden shacks that "clutter the campus." He pointed not only to heating problems, but also to the problem of maintaining an atmosphere favorable to learning in shacks nearly wide-open to the outdoors.[27] Maverick could have used other ammunition to demonstrate that threats to the development and maintenance of a first-rate scholarly community at the University of Texas existed in this period. A considerable number of faculty members left the university in August of 1921 when a faction of the Texas House of Representatives known as the "salary slashers" pushed through a cut in faculty salaries by a two-to-one vote as part of a

The Bootleg Decade

general retrenchment program. The measure was defeated in the Texas Senate by one vote, but only after severe criticism was leveled at the Legislature by an aroused press.[28]

It seems likely that Maverick's concern for the scholarly community could be attributed in part to his own incipient aspirations to the professorial. In later years such a suggestion was made by a distinguished professor, the late Robert C. Brooks, Joseph Wharton Professor of Political Science at Swarthmore College and president of the American Political Science Association. Brooks wrote in 1938, "No doubt it will grieve the Congressman sadly, but it must be said that, much as he affects to deride professors, he possesses many traits of that species." The Swarthmore professor backed up his contention with a recital of Maverick's reading habits, his writing of book reviews, and, finally, a "typical academic lecture" that Maverick gave at Swarthmore with the "characteristic fault of such discourses, the effort to cover too much ground."[29] The clinching evidence of Maverick's yen for the halls of ivy is to be found in a letter in which he applied for a position in political science at the University of Chicago after his defeat in the race for a third term in Congress. His application was rejected pending the appearance of his second book, *In Blood and Ink*, a study of constitutional development in the United States with particular emphasis on economic justice and civil liberties, and he did not subsequently pursue the matter.[30]

But Maverick pursued diligently his renewed program of self-education in the 1920's as he began to build an impressive personal library of serious works in the areas of ethics, philosophy, sociology, and political science. A great many of these books were conveniently marked with the dates on which he read them. Others, even more conveniently, contained liberal annotations by Maverick, reaching on occasion such researcher's riches as a half dozen tipped in sheets of Maverick's commentaries. At one point he even indulged himself in the minor conceit of writing a note to his biographer to explain, "I didn't mark the above passage, Aunt Ellen did."

An anonymous newspaper reporter wrote in 1937: "Anyone who assumes that Maverick is just a clown will be surprised to learn that he became a member of the bar at the age of 20 and that he was president of the San Antonio Bar Association at 24. He knows his Shakespeare, his Milton and his Greek mythology. His brother, Dr. George Maverick, tells me that Maury is one of the leading authorities on Erasmus in this country, but George is an industrial research chemist and you know what unreliable fellows scientists are."[31]

It is often anybody's guess what an authority is, but it is not open to question that Maverick was a careful student of Erasmus. His library contained eight different works on Erasmus, most of them with liberal annotations by their owner. His wife said that there were a number of others that have since disappeared (perhaps given away—if Maverick liked a person, he would sometimes impulsively give him a book.) Maverick's copy of Preserved Smith's *Erasmus* contained a letter, pasted inside the front cover, from the Cornell University Erasmus scholar in which he thanked Maury for his criticisms of the book and concluded, "I shall learn something from your dissent." Still another volume is inscribed, "For Maury Maverick, whose ideas helped create this edition of Erasmus, Sincerely, Pascal Covici" (publisher).[32]

As he read Erasmus, Maverick marked with approval such passages as those in which Erasmus was cited in favor of freedom of expression and in opposition to the likes of unwarranted search and seizure. He particularly emphasized this passage: "[Sir Thomas] More would die for his faith, and would have you punished for yours; Erasmus would be companionable and chatty and courteous and tolerant even to an infidel . . . he let his mind play freely on the sacred arcana of the traditional faith; that he recognized reason as the final arbiter in these matters as well as in social and political affairs—all this is the noble genius of Erasmus."[33]

There is a strong indication that Maverick got some of his penchant for pricking bubbles of conceit and letting "very dry sawdust out of stuffed shirts"[34] from sources other than William C. Brann. He was an inveterate reader of Voltaire's *Candide* and the works of François Rabelais. He was so delighted with *Candide* and the great Dr. Pangloss, who taught "metaphysico-theologo-cosmolonigology," that he often mentioned it in letters to friends and acquaintances throughout his life. A copy of this book was his most characteristic gift to persons who took his fancy. A former assistant and friend tells the story of Maverick, then chairman of the

The Bootleg Decade

Smaller War Plants Corporation, stopping on a New York street and turning to him to say, "Have you read *Candide*?" When the response was no, the bustling Maverick pulled his friend into a bookstall and bought him the book.[35]

Maury had several unexpurgated editions of Rabelais that he read and reread throughout his life. He chuckled and chortled over the doings of Panurge, Pantagruel, and Gargantua and even kept a copy handy in the "library with plumbing."[36]

Most of Maverick's reading was nonfiction, but there were other works of fiction that particularly interested him. He read James Joyce's *Ulysses*, probably because he found out that he wasn't supposed to, and then became so interested in Joyce's style and technique that he attempted a Maverick novel in that mold, though he said that he did not "consciously plagiarize" Joyce. He made this statement when he sent a partial rough draft to his friend H. L. Mencken, who commented: "I confess that this stuff seems rather obvious to me. But it certainly falls in with the fashion and so I believe that if you complete the book there may be some chance to publish it. Probably no American publisher would tackle it, but in Paris there are several firms that specialize in such extremes. One of them during the past three or four years has printed five or six books of genuine importance, including Ludwig Lewisohn's last novel and the first book of Ernest Hemingway."[37] Maverick was disgruntled by Mencken's lack of enthusiasm, and the book was never finished.[38]

Another of Maverick's favorites was Anatole France. He apparently read everything the French satirist wrote. In his copy of France's *The Latin Genius*,[39] he noted that he had read the book in September 1924, and his interest in France is demonstrated by the fact that Maverick inserted in the book no less than eight articles on the French novelist, beginning with a newspaper clipping reporting his death in 1924.[40] Maverick's views indicated that he was probably attracted to and influenced by what Robert Dell referred to as France's "benevolent cynicism" and his exposure of the "follies of patriotism," that is, in its excesses.[41]

Other fiction that interested and impressed Maverick was Hugo's *Les Misérables*; *The Four Horsemen of the Apocalypse*, by Vincente Blasco Ibáñez; the works of Henry Fielding (particularly *The History of Tom Jones*); Cervantes' *Don Quixote*, and Proust's

Swann's Way. Maverick kept several editions of *Alice in Wonderland* and used quotations from it frequently in his speeches and writings.[42] Though he read very widely, he seems not to have paid much attention to lighter fiction.[43]

Maverick's study of nonfiction works was remarkable for a lawyer-businessman who had made a poor academic record in college. It is, of course, impossible to know all of the books he read, but a more-than-representative sample can be found in those that he either noted as having read or marked with varying amounts of annotation. Most of this reading was in the areas of religion and moral philosophy, political theory, history, and, more specifically, civil liberties and pacifism.[44] The list provides an outline of the causes that Maverick was to champion in his public career (see Bibliography).

It appears that he read nearly everything that was available by or about Thomas Jefferson, but he did most of his marking and annotations in Albert J. Nock's *Jefferson* and in *The Writings of Thomas Jefferson*, edited by Andrew A. Lipscomb, the twenty-volume memorial edition. In the Nock book Maverick marked several passages dealing with the right of revolution and gave particular emphasis to, "The spirit of resistance to government is so valuable on certain occasions that I wish it always to be kept alive. It will often be exercised when wrong, but better so than not to be exercised at all."[45] Maverick's extensive markings in the memorial edition of Jefferson were almost entirely confined to moral philosophy and religion, particularly liberal Christianity. For example, he gave heavy marking to this passage: "And the day will come, when the mystical generation of Jesus, by the Supreme Being as His Father, in the womb of a virgin, will be classed with the fable of the generation of Minerva in the brain of Jupiter. But we may hope that the dawn of reason, and freedom of thought in these United States, will do away all this artificial scaffolding, and restore to us the primitive and genuine doctrines of this the most venerated Reformer of human errors."[46]

At the age of 29, Maverick indicated that he was impressed by religious passages in other works, one of which was particularly related to politics and public morality. He marked these passages heavily with red pencil, whereas he usually marked or noted with ordinary pencil or pen. He noted the argument of Dr. L. P. Jacks,

The Bootleg Decade

professor of philosophy at Oxford and a leading Unitarian, to the effect that there was little hope of educating and freeing the minds of the people through politics because the politician seeks nothing but power, and then he underlined heavily, "The quest of the human spirit is Goethe's dying cry, Light—more Light. And it is from these men [those outside of politics] that I look to get a nobler system of education. They will compel the politicians to act, perhaps get rid of the present race of politicians altogether."[47]

In George Bernard Shaw's preface to *Androcles and the Lion*, Maverick marked passages indicating the trend in his thinking that linked liberal Christianity to social justice. He underlined one passage in which Shaw wrote that Christ "advocates communism, the widening of the private family," and "the organic conception of society in which you are not an independent individual but a member of society."[48] Maverick then placed a large *X* beside a passage beginning, "He was to take away the sins of the world by good government, by justice and mercy, by setting the welfare of little children above the pride of princes."[49]

In addition to reading Ruskin, Proudhon, and others, Maverick seems to have hung on every word of Sinclair's *The Cry for Justice: An Anthology of the Literature of Social Protest*. In addition to marking dozens of passages, he prepared an index inside the front cover to those items he considered most important. For example, he cites "The Wrongfulness of Riches," by Grant Allen, and the passage, "If you are on the side of the spoilers, then you are a bad man. If your are on the side of social justice you are a good one. There is no effective test of high morality at the present day save this."[50] Maverick also marked and carefully indexed related remarks by William Lloyd Garrison, James Oppenheim, Martin Luther, Vergil, Henry David Thoreau, Ruskin, Abraham Lincoln, and O-Shi-O (an eighteenth-century Japanese scholar).[51]

Maverick's ego and determination to do his own thinking could be seen in his markings in Emerson's writings. He was particularly interested in the essay "History" and in Emerson's contention that history is "in the soul" of men who make it—"all must be explained from individual history."[52] In "Self-Reliance," Maverick underlined, "Familiar as the voice of the mind is to each, the highest merit we ascribe to Moses, Plato and Milton is that they set at naught books and traditions, and spoke not what men, but what they thought."[53]

When Maverick read plays in these early years, he turned to Molière, Shakespeare, Ben Johnson, Shaw, and particularly the social-problem plays of Henrik Ibsen. His favorite poet was Rabindranath Tagore, and he indicated that he read Tagore's philosophical works as well, though none appeared in his library.[54]

While still in his regimen of reading, roughly about 1928, Maverick began to make some tentative expressions of his ideas. First it was in the attempted war novel, next it was in some lines of verse and finally in speeches and memoranda as he decided to make the move into politics in 1930.

A year before the 1929 crash, he began to express his concern with what he felt to be the inequities and injustices of our economic and social system; he had already been active in defense of the rights of individuals and in support of the American Civil Liberties Union. He dashed off some verses that, though they may not bring him posthumous fame as a poet, revealed his attempts to pin down some of the ideas that were chasing around in his head. One untitled fragment reads in part:

> I hate but one thing: intolerance
> And I am intolerant myself.
> Give us, let us have, force upon us, tolerance. . . .
> Damn these pious grafters, these hoarders, these smiling, sniveling,
>   grapplers of what really belongs to the people.
> Damn the machines, the roaring, flaming furnaces,
> The thunder of industry and noon-day luncheon clubs;
> Can't you hear babies crying and dying—
> Old men, old women moaning and lonesome and sick—
> Oh, God damn your rotten soul in hell,—your system.

The effect of these reflections on his conscience may be seen in:

> DEFEAT
> There are two human stinks
> The stink of over-eating, over-smoking; the stink of success, of supercilious smiles, and
> The stink of hunger, malnutrition, the stink of failure, of smiles forced through the smoldering fires of disease.
> All this EATS on me
> Well, who cares? Not even me—

The Bootleg Decade 45

In another untitled fragment he questioned his own motives and sincerity: "Who is this Maury Maverick?/ Bum, villain, leader or hick?/ Are these true, honest and loyal aspirations/ These big, noisy and egocentric gyrations?"[55]

Maverick was vaguely seeking some sort of New Deal before the depression created the urgency. After having analyzed the factors contributing to a great disparity between the lot of the wealthy and that of the poor, he considered the solutions offered by doctrinaire philosophies. In his unfinished war novel (1928), he has Lieutenant Harrick (obviously Lieutenant Maverick) express the opinion that the Bolsheviks "bore us all," for they are "tiresome, they often smell bad, and they know nothing of American psychology."[56] But Maverick *did* know something of American psychology. His Harrick rejected the socialists as providing an intellectual diet of "milk and water" and as having "no leadership." Said Harrick, "Radicalism in this country must be American. We have no proletariat, no working class—only people who expect to get rich."[57] This assertion anticipated the thesis so ably presented by Arthur N. Holcombe twelve years later.[58] A key point in Holcombe's thesis concerning the middle class as the foundation of our political system is that regardless of statistics of income levels, most Americans think of themselves as middle class—there is no proletariat.

With his office as tax collector as a springboard, Maverick began to make speeches and to engage in actions that reflected the results of his extensive reading and thinking. His first speeches were appraisals of what had created the depression; these were followed by another set suggesting what was to be done. In what appears to have been his first radio address, he charged the American people with having been blind or delinquent in their failure to meet the problems arising from the end of the frontier and the mounting complexities and interdependence that came with industrialization. He blasted the political leadership (and himself, by implication) of the 1920's in this tirade: "During this time that we were so carefree, men who roared about religion and who had small souls, men who prated about their knowledge but who had no brains, men who spoke of vision but who had no vision, all the puppets of the special interests, political buffoons, rode into office and wealth and bureaucratic jobs in our government. They are out of touch with the heart and soul of America—indeed, they have never been in touch with the people, their needs, their aspirations, their objectives."[59]

Maverick, then, anticipated not only the New Deal, but the type of leadership that would make it. With remarkable prescience, he said that Lincoln had been a great man because "he sensed the sweep of a powerful feeling among the people and became its spokesman," and he gave this description of the "next great man": "He isn't going to be an expert who sits down and draws up a plan that he believes ought to work according to the old rules. He's going to be a man who can sense the trend of the times. He'll be more of a spokesman for the muddled ideas in the public mind than he will be a prophet. So many of our political prophets have led us astray that we wouldn't believe them now even if they told the truth."[60] Maverick could have been referring to Franklin D. Roosevelt. He had met FDR, and had said in 1929 that he was the only man who could be elected on the Democratic ticket.[61] But he may have been expressing Maverick aspirations as well.

What the men of the New Deal arrived at, essentially, was a loose plan for popping timbers in here and there to try to shore up a tottering economic and social system. Though some absolutists served to prod, few of these men were doctrinaire or felt that they had *the* plan, for this is the "genius of American politics," as Professor Boorstin has so aptly and provocatively explained.[62] When asked for his impressions of Maverick's philosophy, Arthur M. Schlesinger, Jr., wrote in part, "One felt about him that he revived and expressed the sound, native American instinct for freedom as the way in which democracy makes its progress—the same instinct one found in different ways in men like Lincoln, Mark Twain, the La Follettes, Frederick Jackson Turner."[63] Boorstin had used the names and ideas of two of these men, Lincoln and Turner, to illustrate his thesis.[64] The pattern of eclecticism, however, is not cut to an exact fit for Maury Maverick. It fitted at times, but he was more radical and more inclined to some philosophical absolutes than many of his contemporaries.

As a part of his regimen of serious reading in the 1920's Maverick had read some of the works of Mohandas K. Gandhi, and he wrote the following commentary to an Indian author with whom he had discussed Gandhi: "You say to hell with politics. Well, I just can't help it, but politicians irk me so that I must hurl bricks and must get very angry. Deep down in my heart I think Gandhi is one of the world's greatest men and possibly the greatest man of all time, and that his principles are right, but I can't stand for them personally. Action I must have."[65]

Maverick found his opportunity for action in a political upheaval beginning to take shape in San Antonio at the end of the decade. In 1929 growing resentment against the machine-ridden politics of Bexar County and San Antonio began to boil up in the Alamo city. On November 23, 1929, a weekly tabloid newspaper, *The Bexar Facts*, appeared on the streets of San Antonio with the avowed purpose of printing the "truth" that other newspapers would not touch and of exposing the city-county "ring,"[66] which has been referred to as one of the most "durable, solidly entrenched political machines in the United States."[67] Earle B. Mayfield, a former U.S. senator and member of the Texas Railroad Commission, charged in a gubernatorial campaign speech in San Antonio in 1930: "The Bexar County machine can give Tammany Hall of New York lessons when it comes to holding crooked elections and counting candidates out who have been honestly elected. This machine not only pays the poll taxes for several thousand fictitious persons and distributes these poll taxes to its henchmen who vote five to fifteen times in each election, but goes so far as to have the tally sheets made up the night before the election."[68]

On another occasion, William Aubrey, styled as the dean of the San Antonio Bar, said in a radio address in San Antonio: "Bexar County has become a byword for the impurity of its elections. This notoriety is not based on idle rumor but is the inevitable result of exhaustive and published investigations by an unprejudiced congressional committee, the reports and indictments by your grand jury, by the action of your own District Attorney's office and by official prosecutions instituted by your Attorney General based upon independent examination of the facts involved and supported by the affidavits of some of your best fellow citizens."[69]

The Bexar Facts kept up a barrage of criticism of the "ring" and all its works throughout late 1929 and early 1930. There were attacks upon the city-county machine for condoning the existence of a state-wide liquor-combine headquarters in San Antonio,[70] and exposures of poll-tax frauds, favors to pet contractors and either blandishments or threats to still the voices of opponents. In February 1930 Donovan Weldon, editor of *The Bexar Facts*, openly charged what he had been hinting at for some months—that Frank Huntress (publisher of the *San Antonio Evening News* and the morning *Express*) had "played false to those who had confidence in him and his newspapers." Weldon said that while he was city editor of the *News* he was "under strict orders to allow nothing to be printed which might injure Mayor C. M. Chambers, the City-County political ring, or any of its members."[71] Aubrey later charged that the *Express* was the "organ of the Ring," and Frank C. Davis, a leader of the Citizens League, told a meeting that the "Morning Excuse" and the "Evening Nuisance" had "deliberately lied" and had engaged in "unwarranted partisanship" and "unwarranted attacks . . . upon a majority of the people" of San Antonio.[72] Weldon on occasion urged his readers to get their daily news from the *San Antonio Light*, a Hearst paper.[73]

Maury Maverick had no official connection with this new publishing venture, but his close association with the tabloid paper and its causes was obvious from the outset. In one of the early issues, the story of Maury's successful fight against a traffic ticket became a vehicle for praising him as a "free-thinker, businessman and traditional foe of machine government." It also proved to be the occasion to anticipate that machine forces would try to bring up past misdeeds of Maverick such as the time when he "whipped a city policeman on Houston Street" in 1925 for calling him "vile names what would force any red-blooded Texan to use his fists."[74] In the next issue of the paper, following a recital of machine activities, there was a report that "people" were urging Maverick to run for sheriff. Again Maverick was characterized as a "fighting free-thinker" not aligned with any faction—the kind of "honest and fearless" man needed.[75]

The first report of organizational efforts against the "ring" came in the January 3, 1930, issue of *The Bexar Facts*. Opposition to machine government had been growing steadily for years, and now seemed to be "crystallizing . . . into a concrete foundation for an organization to oppose ring candidates at the polls."[76] Two weeks later an unsigned letter to the editor expressed the opinion that there were not ten men who would have "guts enough to oppose the ring openly," but in the same issue there was an account of a meeting of "fifty leading business and professional men" for planning purposes and for discussion of the issue that was to prove to be the opening gun of the campaign against the machine. In connection with this report, Maverick was quoted in opposition to a major city bond issue proposal. He said that the bond issue was unnecessary and designed only to satisfy the machine's "own political purposes."[77] A week later, amidst reports of defections and dissension in the machine, there was a story of a meeting of businessmen at the home of Walter W. McAllister (now mayor of San Antonio). J. Roy Murray, an automobile dealer, was quoted as saying that the group planned to support a complete ticket against the "present administration."[78] These meetings laid the groundwork for the emergence of the San Antonio Citizens League a few months later.

Before the Citizens League emerged, there was another organization with a similar name, the San Antonio Civic League. This group of businessmen had secured a nonprofit corporation charter from the state of Texas. Maury Maverick was chairman of the board of directors and presided at the first meeting in the Menger Hotel on February 21, 1930. This group apparently faded out as the later San Antonio Citizens League was organized.[79]

In late February Maverick began to write a series of articles in *The Bexar Facts* in which he charged that the bond issue was unnecessary and demanded that there be an independent audit of city expenditures. As the series went on he added an attack upon recent city attempts to annex farm and ranch land adjoining San Antonio. Maverick had a personal interest in this matter; his father, Albert Maverick, had filed suit to prevent the annexations.[80] The bond issue provided the basis for the reform movement's first test against the machine, and Maverick's carefully drawn arguments played a major role in that fight. In private notes, however, he credited the *San Antonio Light* with "getting the ball rolling" in the bond issue fight.[81]

In March the machine struck back at the relentless hammering of *The Bexar Facts*. Editor Weldon and fourteen news vendors were arrested and charged with violation of an archaic city "advertising" ordinance. After an impassioned defense argument by attorney Walter Groce (assisted by Maury Maverick and others), the defendants were acquitted.[82]

During April *The Bexar Facts* began the exposure of poll-tax frauds by printing affidavits of aliens and minors who had had poll taxes bought for them and delivered to them by representatives of the machine.

At a mass meeting on April 7, 1930, more than two thousand citizens gathered to oppose the bond issue. A resolution was adopted to establish a permanent organization to fight the city-county machine. This was the nonpartisan (for a short time) Citizens League of San Antonio. A. B. Weakley was elected chairman of the meeting and the organization. Maury Maverick made one of the major speeches to the gathering. In his address he chided the city administration for providing a dance hall for Negroes instead of the library for which funds had been originally allocated and then, adding insult to injury, requiring them to pay rent for the facility. Mayor Chambers made the mistake of labeling the participants in this meeting "a few clowns and soreheads." The meeting was not even mentioned by the Huntress papers.[83]

The Bexar Facts continued to expose poll-tax frauds and was able to report the arrest of deputy poll-tax collectors for racketeering as the election drew near. On May 5 the bond issue was defeated by a narrow margin of 17,575 to 17,483. The paper charged that more than one thousand illegal votes had been cast in the bond election.[84] This contention proved to be correct; almost two months later city attorneys reported that 1,166 illegal votes were cast in the election.[85]

With the bond election victory behind them, the Citizens League moved on to the next phase of their struggle with the now foundering machine. On May 16 Maury Maverick presided at a meeting of the league at which *The Bexar Facts* reported that there were "riotous cheers" for the leaders and a determination to do battle. The same issue of the paper carried an advertisement in which the league announced: ". . . the Citizens League was organized for the purpose of striking off the shackles of the political ring which has dominated the City and County for many years, and restoring free government in San Antonio and Bexar County."[86]

The organization met at Beethoven Hall on May 19 to select a

The Bootleg Decade

nominating committee to name a complete slate of candidates for all local offices in the approaching Democratic primary.[87] On June 4 "thousands" met and accepted the slate provided by the committee, which had named candidates from legislative seats down to local precinct chairmen. The nominee for county tax collector was Maury Maverick. In a major spread in *The Bexar Facts*, he was characterized as "an active defender, frequently against organized odds, of the civil liberties and public rights," and praised as the man primarily responsible for the establishment of a Carnegie Library in San Antonio.[88] Maverick said privately that his reason for accepting the nomination was that he felt that he could perform the public service of eliminating bogus poll taxes, of which there were seven thousand according to his estimate.[89] In political advertisements, which he wrote himself, he urged his supporters to elect the entire ticket—the important thing was a Citizens League victory, not his personal victory.[90]

The league slate for the Democratic primary was endorsed by the respected Republican (!) Congressman Harry M. Wurzbach in a speech at Alamo Plaza July 3. He said, in part, that "honest service cannot be reconciled with the acts proved against the ring candidates. Honest public service and stealing elections won't mix." He said that he held most county officials responsible for participation in election irregularities, and said of the Citizens League, "There is not a man on the ticket who is a spoilsman."[91]

On July 31 the Citizens League and Maury Maverick won a sweeping victory over the now discredited and disintegrating machine.[92] In typical Maverick fashion, no sooner had he won the office of tax collector than he began to urge that it be abolished. In December of 1930 the "militant leader of the Citizens League" was quoted as advocating that the offices of tax collector, tax assessor, and county treasurer be combined into one office. He said that in this connection he had been conferring with legislative leaders of a movement to provide meaningful home rule for Texas counties in order that they might effect savings of thousands of dollars.[93] The movement, of course, has not yet succeeded.

The position of tax collector is more important than it may sound, for Bexar County was and is one of the largest (290,000 population then) metropolitan areas in Texas, and the office had the all-important responsibility for issuance of poll-tax receipts.

Maverick was credited with carrying out his campaign promises and with doing a good job of reorganizing the office, sharply reducing costs of operation, facilitating the payment of poll taxes and generally conducting an efficient operation.[94] When he was attacked by the almost always hostile *San Antonio News* for ignorance and inefficiency,[95] he addressed this memorandum to his employees:

> Here's what we'll do: BE STILL MORE EFFICIENT. Treat everybody fairly. If you know of some man who calls himself my enemy, FORGET IT. Treat him with the utmost courtesy, and let him realize this is a PUBLIC OFFICE where everybody gets a SQUARE DEAL. In the Courthouse, DON'T TALK POLITICS, but what is much better, HIT THE BALL. Let us always DO OUR DUTY and treat people of this County just as they are treated by any intelligent business concern.
>
> Let there be no waste of time, money or equipment. Let us conduct an office which will be a credit to the whole STATE OF TEXAS. And if by any chance you wish to play politics for me—then play it by giving QUICK, HONEST, AND COURTEOUS SERVICE.[96]

In his first term as tax collector Maverick saw the depression "hit like a cyclone," and by the middle of 1932 he viewed its effects on San Antonio as terrifying.[97] Before that date he had already been engaged in a number of relief activities. For example, he organized and directed a "Babies Ball" to raise milk money for indigent children, and, as commander of the Veterans of Foreign Wars, he spent his own money to aid fellow veterans.[98] But by 1932 circumstances had worsened and many citizens of San Antonio and Bexar County were in a desperate plight—it was reported that as many as eleven thousand applications for relief had been made.[99]

Maverick rolled up his sleeves and began to practice what he had read and preached. He urged Governor Ross Sterling to provide relief assistance, and he joined in the establishment of a Central Veterans Committee for aid to veterans and their families. When the Central Relief Committee for San Antonio was established, Maverick asked the governor to appoint him to the chairmanship of the Finance Committee, which was to disburse the funds received by the state from the Reconstruction Finance Corporation. In addition to managing the funds, Maverick wrote many letters soliciting contributions to supplement the limited

The Bootleg Decade

amount provided through state assistance, and he had considerable success.[100] The substantial nature of his contribution may be judged from the following letter from W. M. Cadmus, secretary of the C. Spangler Lodge of the Brotherhood of Railroad Trainmen in San Antonio:

> Your activities are well known to the membership of this organization in which you have shown the unselfish spirit so necessary at this time. It is known that you have personally furnished supplies, and personally supervised distribution, as well as giving time and energy to the point of personal hardship in having shelter made available to the destitute.
> The thanks of this lodge is hereby extended to you, Mr. Maverick. Your activities in relief work will go down in history as an outstanding example of sacrifice for starving humanity.[101]

Maverick's major venture as a member of the Central Veterans Committee was the establishment of what began as a camp for transient veterans and then became an experiment in communal living. The War Veterans Relief Camp was organized on October 18, 1932, at Exposition Park in San Antonio, where remnants of the Bonus Army were camping. Maverick was designated director and R. R. Rogers was the camp commander. At first the camp was only a place where transients might get a meal and a place to sleep in nondescript shelters. Food was provided partly through relief funds and partly through contributions of local merchants and farmers. The first camp census (October 19, 1932) listed forty-three adults and thirty-two children. Maverick kept up constant correspondence and leg work securing salvage cooking equipment, surplus army clothing, and other necessities for the increasing number of camp dwellers.

On November 21, 1932, a terse "Colony Order No. 2" appeared, informing residents that, "Effective this date this camp will be known as the Diga Colony, Frio City Road and Mr. Maverick will be known as the Colony Director. It is desired that the word 'camp' be dropped from the record and conversation entirely."[102] The order signaled the move of the camp to a thirty-five-acre site that Maverick had secured from the Humble Company and announced the launching of an original self-help community, the Diga Colony.[103]

Maverick conceived of a utopian scheme by which the unemployed transients might completely rehabilitate themselves. He said that the basic aims were to provide "Housing, regular and proper diet, education, character building and a normal life." It was his view that widespread unemployment and indigence made it necessary to "start the recolonization and repatriation of the people and somehow have a change in the economic order and in this way people will be finally adjusted."[104]

The tireless and idealistic tax collector secured a number of boxcars from the Missouri Pacific Railroad[105] and had the cars moved to the site. Somehow, somewhere he was able to "chisel," as he put it,[106] enough materials to permit colonists to convert the cars into decent habitations. Maverick was also the inspiration for programs of training in various crafts. Some food was grown in the colony area, and labor was bartered for farm products in the surrounding area. A clinic and an employment agency were also established. Maverick, with the zeal of a make-the-world-over-today reformer, even had Dr. Robert H. Montgomery, an economics professor at the University of Texas, give lectures in economics to the youths in order that they might understand the problems they faced and the significance of such experiments as Diga.[107]

A fairly rigorous discipline was maintained for all colony residents. Breaches in discipline would result in expulsion from the colony, and the records reveal several such actions. Children were required to attend school and parents had to give a strict accounting of any tardiness. Parents who were not working were expected to perform kitchen duty or supervisory work in the common dining hall. Maverick was responsible for the rule that men who earned money outside the colony were required to donate one-third to one-half of their earnings, depending upon whether they were single or married, to the Diga Colony Fund. Curt notices appeared from time to time with such messages as: "Effective this date and until further orders all men in the Colony, not on special duty, will answer roll call in front of the office at 7:45 A.M. . . . for work instructions," and "Effective this date there will be no men leaving the colony, at any time, without permission from Mr. Rogers, Colony Commander."[108] Though Maverick reported a population of "250 to 300" for Diga Colony,[109] the official records showed a peak census of 171 on January 14, 1933.[110]

The colony was apparently well managed, and it reached a near self-sustaining basis midway in its life span of about one year. Robert Kelso, field director for the Reconstruction Finance Corporation, called it "one of the most effective demonstrations of self-help for the unemployed" he had seen in his travels across the country.[111] The *Houston Chronicle* published a major feature article on the colony and expressed the opinion that it was "unquestioned that Camp Diga is performing a valuable public service. Besides sustaining individuals and families who might be on charity . . . it is strengthening or restoring the morale of persons who, although they might have been 'down' were not yet 'out.' "[112] By February 1933 the experiment had attracted the attention of the *Christian Science Monitor*, and it was said to be the subject of study by people from all over the United States.[113]

The idea for Diga was entirely Maury Maverick's. He was termed the "guiding spirit" of a "vision of an idealist come true."[114] The colony was not, of course, a completely original idea, but it was an original venture in its time and place so far as Maverick was concerned. A few experiments were going on in other parts of the country at this time, and reports of some of them were getting into the radical publications.[115] The *Monthly Labor Review* (to which Maverick subscribed) did not report such experiments until March 1933.[116]

The people in the colony had no ideological objections to the venture, because, as Maverick explained: "None had ever heard of socialism—except as some vague thing that was 'bad.' As for Communism, all they knew was that it was Russian, unpatriotic, and sinful. As for the word 'collectivism,' it was just a word that had gotten misplaced. In many contacts, I found that their idea of 'capitalism' was a state of society in which you can be hungry for a while, but you will finally get a good job, and possibly have others that can go hungry or work for you."[117]

Maverick's communistic experiment went the way of most such experiments, because people did not "understand cooperation for the common good." He later declared, "Two economies cannot exist side by side within a given area, especially a money and a non-money one. Such things as 'Epics' and the like are bound to be failures because they represent a patchwork economy."[118] As was often the case, Maverick's pungent humor masked his disappointment with the results when he commented, "Our men began to get work on Army projects. One worked thirty hours in a week and got a dollar an hour. He had been the meekest, most respectable and hard-working man in the colony. He drew his thirty dollars. He arrived on the scene tight as a drum, swaggering down the street. He beat his wife, turned capitalist, and left."[119]

Maverick concluded that the experiment had been valuable as a phase in the "story of the development of the American mind," and that it had helped his own thinking to develop. He reasoned that such experiments were likely to succeed only if they were isolated from the rest of society and if they had the "binding power" of some religion. He said that Diga was a laboratory in which he learned the "utter futility of makeshift economics," and that "the condition of a laborer in Northhampton, Massachusetts, has a direct effect on a worker in Tucumcari, New Mexico." The economy of the nation cannot be, he said, "a hodgepodge of conflicting systems and plans."[120]

It was after Diga was underway that Maverick undertook another venture that he said would probably bring charges of publicity seeking. Before he had engaged in his efforts in behalf of the transient unemployed, Maverick had done some field research to discover the true proportions and gravity of their problems. He did this by dressing as a hobo and mingling with the people as they alighted from the freights in San Antonio. Now he conceived of doing this on a broader scale. In December 1932 the governor appointed Maverick, at his own behest, to make a "survey of destitute people in the state, particularly in reference to destitute transient population."

Accompanied by two friends, Pat Jefferson and Harry Futrell, Maverick dressed as a hobo and made a swing through part of Texas to study at first hand the plight of the transient unemployed. He admitted that at first he was not too effective as an "amateur bum"—some of the authentic tramps wanted to know where he had gotten a shave and how he managed to get fat. He also failed the test when he attempted to eat some of the hobo fare; he had to rush to a secluded spot with his two companions and vomit. As he described the scene, "Pat jumped up and down and nearly laughed himself to death. Harry, however, a sympathetic soul, looked on

The Bootleg Decade

and suddenly he joined in. It was a fine duet. I feel sure that Harry must have done this as a gesture of true brotherhood."

Though they actually "rode the rods" to some extent, the three "hobos" cheated by keeping a car planted in the towns they visited, and they would slip off to get a decent meal from time to time. But despite Maverick's lighthearted treatment of some events on the trip, the three did sleep in the hobo jungles in Houston and Waco and saw the incredible degradation of people who were not ordinary tramps. Many were youths, male and female, and sometimes entire families were aimlessly drifting about the country on the freight trains. In his message to Governor Sterling after the trip, Maverick made an impassioned plea for some action to alleviate a situation in which such youths were "spending their formative years in flophouses, jails, jungles, or any available shelter, begging, panhandling, and, incidentally, starving part of the time, living miserably on a wholly improper diet, with no sanitation, no medical attention." Maverick told the governor that there were some fifty to seventy-five thousand "destitute, shelterless, homeless people" who were willing to work but could find no jobs. He urged that these conditions be recognized as a national problem and that the information be given to the federal government with a view to the development of national policies to meet such problems. To the extent that he was able to do so, Maverick took direct action in San Antonio. He organized transient relief stations where these people could get a simple but decent meal, and he even provided them with information as to the best travel routes and "the best places to board trains without getting into trouble."[121]

Maverick moved to action on still another front in the late 1920's. He had joined the American Civil Liberties Union shortly after his return from World War I, and he gave as his reason for joining: "In the World War, I was so impressed with human injustice, . . . that I have a hatred of all kinds of these things."[122] As one writer put it, foremost among the things for which Maury Maverick would "fight, bleed and die"[123] was the protection of civil liberties. The development of his thought should be of particular interest to students of civil liberties, because Maverick's intellectual convictions were constantly meeting the acid tests of having to stand beside some "enemy of the people," or suffer the abuse and ingratitude of those he defended or even listen to the cries of an angry mob that wanted to "Hang Maury Maverick to a sour apple tree."[124]

That Maverick should have been concerned with civil rights and civil liberties requires little analysis or explanation; that he should have been one of the most resolute champions in modern American history does. He probably would have agreed that his penchant for defending the rights of the individual, and the underdog in particular, stemmed in part from the fact that he was the youngest child in his family—battling for status and recognition.[125] Secondly, the principle of the free, inquiring mind—making its own findings and its own choices—was preached and practiced in his home. Finally, a man who made intellectual insurgency a fetish would naturally stand for as complete freedom of expression as he could get.

Maverick also indicated that he was inspired to the defense of civil liberties by the example of his grandfather, Sam Maverick. Maury wrote a cousin in 1930 that the elder Maverick came to Texas with a "solemn understanding of the Bill of Rights," and with the principles of the Declaration of Independence "in his heart and soul." He continued, "You will remember, he was not a member of any church, and yet, when the Know Nothing movement hit Texas, just as the Ku Klux movement hit a few years ago, he helped to wipe them out and Texas' name was not blotted by the disgraceful tactics of that organization in other parts of America."[126]

Maverick told an audience in Boston in 1937 about another Sam Maverick whom he claimed as an ancestor ("sixth great-grandfather"). This Sam was "in continuous hot water with your authorities because he believed in civil and religious liberties."[127] In his first book, Maverick spoke proudly of this ancient Maverick being fined 150 pounds for raising a row over violations of civil liberties.[128]

As Maury defended Communists during the period from 1928 to 1930, he began to have some misgivings about extending protection to them. He defended some friends of Communist leader Benjamin Gitlow in 1930 and then listened to them boast that they would "defy the police" and not abide by the law.[129] (When one of them

The Bootleg Decade 59

came to his tax collector's office and insisted upon taking Maverick as his "comrade," the furious Texan said, "Get out, you son-of-a-bitch!")[130] After several earlier notes of complaint, Maury addressed a lengthy letter to Forrest Bailey of the American Civil Liberties Union, complaining that the Communists whom he had defended had charged that he was no better than the persons who would not defend them, because he would not welcome them with open arms. He asked Bailey:

Why should I go out of my way to help a bunch of people, who do not recognize the ordinary process of law, who do not themselves recognize the Bill of Rights under which they claim freedom of speech and who by their freedom of speech would take away my liberties. There is a point for you, and I want your committee to pass upon it and I do not want any set of theorists to pass on it, but I want you, Baldwin, Hays and other old trusties to pass on it. . . . Like Rabelais, I do not mind doing heroic deeds, but give me a definite principle and a definite thing to establish for a definite person.
Lastly, listen to this: Don't you "members of the Board" sit up there on your golden thrones . . . and in your theoretical somnolence chide me for my narrow-mindedness.[131]

There is little doubt that Maverick's questions were no more than rhetorical—a bit of grumbling. He resented both the ingratitude and abuse of the Communists and what he felt to be the sometimes gratuitous advice and proddings of the ACLU and some of the defendants in the cases. In fact, he had provided the answer to his own question in the following passage from the same letter, "If principles of liberty are involved, which may become law by virtue of appellate decisions, then of course, irrespective of all questions, we should enter and make a fight."[132] Bailey's answer to Maverick was a generally routine response to such questions and differed little from his own statement just quoted.[133]

There was no slackening of Maverick's civil liberties efforts. In the same month, he wrote to the district attorney in Dallas, urging prosecution of persons who had kidnapped and beaten two Communist party organizers. Maverick said that the country should know that "Texas protects the Bill of Rights and freely and gladly allows freedom of any form of speech."[134] In April 1931 he was fighting attempts to pass criminal syndicalist laws in the Texas

Legislature[135] and applauding the Governor's decision to permit Communists to come to the Capital and "talk themselves out."[136]

Maverick was often wrestling with himself—fighting the indigenous prejudices that surrounded him as well as expressing his resentment toward those people who advised him but who were not in the sweaty arena. His strong and nearly always consistent defense of civil liberties and civil rights was made all the more remarkable by the fact that he did not win this struggle within himself until his later years. He often raised such questions in private until the last five years of his life. His support for the ultimate in freedom of expression and procedural guarantees for the Communists (as well as his support for equal rights for racial minorities) derived from intellectual convictions. He heartily disliked the Communists and their tactics, perhaps even "despised" was often the more correct word, and he was quite sensitive to Northern liberals' complaints about conditions in the South; he opposed social equality for the Negro until about 1950, and even then he had some misgivings about it.[137] In his usual pungent style, Maverick once wrote to his son: "Lord God, I have spent my life fighting for minorities. But what have they done for me? They have shit on me; but I hasten to say, having washed, I am ready to go on defending them. But every now and then I get tired of that stuff. . . . Prejudice is inherent in every religion, race, creed or nationality. We Protestants have it, as others do. The thing to do is to try to level it down as much as we can."[138]

Maury, Jr., told me that his father had said at a later date, after a particularly trying bout over civil liberties, "Don't do anything for minorities with the expectation of getting something in return, even if it's just gratitude; if you do, they will break your heart. Do for them because its the right thing to do and for no other reason."[139]

Maverick was not defending civil liberties with an eye to the ballot box. His worst enemies would not make that charge against him. A San Antonio newspaper that rather consistently treated him with indifference or condemnation said, "There have been those who questioned the sincerity of Maverick's liberalism, thinking that he was trimming his sails to the contemporary national political wind—but the questioning was infrequent and the questioners mostly obscure. This newspaper was not one of them."[140]

The Bootleg Decade 61

Against the advice of friends, Maverick decided to make the race for a congressional seat in 1934. An opening that he had anticipated presented itself in the form of the creation of the new Twentieth District of Texas, taken from the Fourteenth District represented by Richard M. Kleberg. The Twentieth District is confined to Bexar County. Maverick had supported Kleberg in his race for the Fourteenth District seat in a special election in 1931 with the understanding that Kleberg would support Maverick in his bid when the new district was established, and he had that support.[141]

In this first congressional campaign, Maverick's back injuries caused him to stagger and provided his delighted opponents with the whispered charge of drunkenness. He reported that he ignored the charge because he much preferred it to the truth.[142] The truth was that a tumor had developed on his upper spine as a result of his war wounds, and the pressure on his spinal cord had not only produced his unsteady gait but had caused his eyes to bulge and gave him excruciating pain.[143] Albert Maverick wrote in his "Private Notes," April 11, 1933, that his son was "intensely nervous and restless—too heavy & lacks exercise—systematic exercise—slips down in a big chair, brings his right hand back around his head & presses the left side—talking the while by fits and starts. He is suffering all the time & gets next to no sleep. . . . All comes, no doubt, from the wound on his spinal column, rec'd. in the Argonne some 15 years ago. It makes me cry—quietly & to myself." Albert wrote again in August 29, 1934, "Physical infirmities result from his wounds. He suffers constantly. Activity—mental and physical—is necessary."[144] As his father indicated, the pains goaded Maverick into almost frenzied activity—a set of habits he was never to relinquish even after the reasonably successful operation he had after the election.

The ailing Maverick led a field of five candidates in the first Democratic primary, but he lacked the necessary majority for the nomination, which was tantamount to winning the seat in Congress. He had ahead of him a bitter campaign against the runner-up, Mayor C. K. Quin, who was to remain his arch foe in later political battles. The doughty Maverick was charged by his opponent with "morals unworthy of a congressman," "affiliations with Communists," and the desire to "supplant the American Flag with the red flag of Russia." Frank C. Davis, speaking for

Quin, pointed out that Maverick was a member of the American Civil Liberties Union, "that organization which stands for communism and anarchy."[145] A campaign broadside headed, "American Citizens Beware," warned of the dangers of electing the radical Maverick. This sheet, issued by the "Klu [sic] Klux Klan Committee," featured a picture of Quin in KKK garb with the caption, "Our Congressman," and the injunction: "All 100% Americans will vote for a Real Patriot!"[146]

At this early date, however, such charges were not as likely to be effective as they were to be in Maverick's later contests. The real struggle was between Maverick's Citizens League supporters and a revived city-county machine backing Quin. Maverick won an impressive runoff primary victory of 20,411 to 17,210, and one of America's most spectacular congressional careers had been launched.[147]

Before he could go to Congress, however, Maverick had to go to the Mayo Clinic for the critical surgery that he had needed for years. His condition was precarious, and his wife was warned that the worst might be expected. The operation involved removal of the tumor and sawing off the back part or lamina of each of the vertebra from his skull to his shoulders. Maverick said that the operation had saved his life and that all of the "bad features" were gone, but thereafter he was not able to turn his head in the normal fashion. People often thought he was being impolite when he turned his back to respond to someone standing or seated at his side, but it was the only way he could turn his head.[148]

Maverick almost had to be carried about during his first weeks in Congress, but with the help of two canes he recovered in about five or six months.[149] He retained something of his rolling gait, but it was not so pronounced as before the operation. Whatever his physical condition, Maverick did not permit it to interfere with his activist role in the House of Representatives, which he assumed from the outset.

Maury and His Mavericks

IT WAS ONLY a matter of days after his arrival in Washington in January 1935 that delighted newsmen were filing lively stories about one of the most colorful men who had ever entered the United States House of Representatives.

What manner of man was this Maverick?

The spectator who looked down from the House gallery saw a squat, broad-framed, bench-legged man about forty years old with the general appearance of a bulldog or a big bullfrog. His widow still chuckles about an incident that occurred when the late Senator Harry F. Byrd of Virginia was showing a group of constituents through the nation's Capitol. As Byrd brought his brood into the House gallery, he noticed Maverick coming down the aisle below and remarked, "There comes Maury Maverick, looking like a big toad." Mrs. Maverick, who was sitting nearby in the gallery, turned and said, "Excuse me, Mr. Byrd, but that's my husband." The courtly Byrd turned several hues and without a word moved quickly on with his party.[1]

Maverick's weight ranged from 175 to 230 pounds, and he was closer to the higher side of that range most of the time. He usually lost the sporadic battles he waged against the extra pounds. He often made weight charts from the cardboard inserts found inside folded shirts and posted these charts on the wall over the bathroom scale. His wife and daughter "helped" by attaching to the sides and bottom of the charts such gentle reminders as a picture of a prize hog from a recent fat-stock show.

Maverick could not even find victory in his most successful bout with his weight problem. A couple of years out of Congress, as mayor of San Antonio, he had trimmed his bulging paunch down to near the vanishing point. Accompanied by his wife, he went into a San Antonio clothing store to buy a suit to fit his new figure. As he boasted of his achievement to a salesman he knew quite well, Maverick stepped back, said, "See," and sucked in his belly. Though his trunk was large, his hips were relatively small, and to the horror of the salesman and in full view of the first-floor customers, Maverick's pants fell to the floor. A matronly woman looked over and said, "There's our disgusting mayor; now I *know* I'll never vote for him." Maverick struggled manfully but unsuccessfully to get his belted trousers up as the salesman helped him to hobble off to a dressing room.[2]

Maverick was fat, but his deep chest, heavily-muscled shoulders and thickset legs gave an impression of power rather than pudginess. His hands were blunt, square, and capable looking, and his large head was topped by a thatch of dark brown hair that curled up in rebellious fashion above his broad brow.[3] In later years, however, his hair was a more closely cropped gray. From his early thirties he wore somewhat old-fashioned metal-rimmed spectacles through which his gray-green eyes stared piercingly. The nose was large and blunt; the mouth generous with full lips, the lower sometimes a bit pouted. His jowls were heavy, but his chin and jaw were strong and determined in their cant. Altogether he was a man people did not soon forget.

In private conversation Maverick spoke in a modulated rumble that could rise to a crackling higher pitch in moments of excitement. In public speaking he exhibited most of the arts of volume, tone, pitch, and timing with seeming effortlessness. The speech drafts from which he spoke, however, show a very careful preparation by heavily penciled notations of "slow here," "rising inflection," "up tempo," or "softly."

A contemporary observer, who said that Maverick had "taken a running broad jump onto the nation's front pages," described him in action on the floor of the House: "His five feet and a little over are not impressive. But his resounding voice rolls out from his barrel chest and his words ring up into the House galleries. His round face grows red with conviction as he unloosens a stinging accusation and then his blue eyes pop with mischief as he swings to raillery."[4]

His private speech was extremely earthy and nearly always generously interlarded with profanity. The world of his philosophical and political enemies was pretty generally populated with "bastards" and "son-of-a-bitches." But Maverick often used this language to give an appearance of a roughness he did not feel; that is, it was a mask for his sentimentality. Indeed, he was a user of what might he called affectionate profanity. I deemed it the final touch of approbation to be introduced by him to Mrs. Maverick as a "God damned professor." Maverick admitted to as much in the preface to his first book, where he related his cussing at a reference librarian in the Library of Congress and said, "For indeed, it is a happy friendship that I have with this fellow; he knows that my bellowing, like his pretense of ignorance, are kindly shams and frauds that bind us together."[5]

He could be seen at times and by some people as the exhibitionist, the clown or buffoon.[6] His very appearance and name caused some persons to see "bull" or "belligerence."[7] Some conservative opponents (and even some nervous supporters) saw him as a grown-up adolescent, ready to wreck things in order to strike a fanciful pose.[8] Though Maverick was not conceited in the sense of boasting of his achievements, he did want to be noticed—he demanded attention for his ideas and opinions. But his challenges were not for ego appeasement alone, and he knew what he was doing. As he said to a reporter in 1937: "I found by being pleasant the party leaders did not remember me. Then I began to question their actions, make suggestions that irritated them. They remembered me. Having placed me in the category of a crackpot, they began to show me some consideration. They consulted me about legislation they thought I might be for or against."[9]

Maverick *was* often tough and blunt. He said that facts themselves were "tough, hard, mean" things,[10] and he had a passionate hatred of "all pretenses, hypocrisies, and superficialities," which made many people uncomfortable targets of his barbs, or, more often, thunderbolts.[11]

One of Maverick's worst failings, and at the same time one of his great assets, was his studied irreverence. He had a tendency to make provocative "digs" at various groups or institutions or personalities. He did not do this out of pure cussedness, but rather as a gambit designed to draw peoples' attention, stir them up, and bring on some lively conversation. Former President Harry S. Truman interpreted this trait another way. When queried about Maverick's irreverence, Truman said, "He wasn't irreverent; he was like me, he said what he thought." Truman said that the query reminded him of an incident in which he had been treated to some of Maury's irreverence. On one of his visits to San Antonio, the president decided to pull Maverick's leg a bit by asking him, "Maury, what's this Alamo thing you have here?" Truman reported that Maury bristled and growled, "If you want to see it, say so, but I don't want to hear anybody calling it the 'Alamo thing.'" "And," Truman concluded with obvious delight, "I was the President of the United States!"[12]

When Maverick offered himself as a candidate for Congress in 1934, he presented his philosophy of representation to Bexar County voters in terms not unlike Edmund Burke's famed speech to his constituents.[13] He declared: "I intend to be independent and courageous and I will not indulge in indecent personalities. I expect to be faithful and loyal to my district, but not to be a cheap pork-barrel congressman; I expect to be true to my principles, and not to be deflected by unfair criticism by some irresponsible source, or by pressure from those who are powerful and selfish."[14] In a 1935 address to the House of Representatives, Maverick omitted a passage that had appeared in his original draft: "Now we came to Congress, not to follow the mob, nor to follow ill-advised opinions, but to lead the people, possibly, in the right path."[15] But in a later speech he was not afraid to say with sheer audacity, "As for me I am throwing in with the Yankees and the liberals, the agriculture boys of the West—and the big-city Democrats too. That is the only way the Democratic Party can do a good job and serve America." He rubbed in a bit of salt with a final remark to the effect that the South was not entitled to any special favors and that labor was entitled to protection as much as "cotton plantation owners and ranchmen and rice growers."[16]

This attitude was widely recognized as contributing to his eventual defeat. As the *Philadelphia Record* said, "He preferred to follow his principles and did not make the least effort to conceal them even in the cases where they offended the prejudices of his constituency."[17] *Fortune* magazine summed up Maverick's concept of the role of a representative in this way, "He had a rather cavalier attitude about voters, preferring, oddly in a politician, to allow ideas he actually had to become known and to think that voters should make up their minds on the basis of the record."[18]

Maury Maverick would not use demagoguery, at least not with respect to any important matters, as he once put it.[19] It is remarkable that he even discussed his demagoguery publicly and vowed that he would do it no more.[20] Maverick did, for the most part, refrain from such tactics. If he had been looking for a vote-getter, he could very well have endorsed or at least side-stepped the Townsend Plan, which had considerable support in Texas. Far from doing this, he branded the proposal as "fantastic" and "brazen, unconscionable, and hopeless." When asked why he was so positive when he could have at least straddled the issue, Maverick said, "Having died twice in France, it isn't worthwhile to avoid one political death by being a demagogue."[21]

Ten years away from the legislative scene, Maverick clearly indicated what he thought a representative should and should not be in this advice to young congressmen:

For a quarter-century, I have seen young handsome men, full of ideals, spring into Washington. I have seen many slink away, heavy of soul, fat of head, lazy, stupid, traitors to the people who sent them there. I have seen others stay to lobby for the special interests whom they originally fought against in Congress and which they now serve like dull, political eunuchs in the harem of a pasha.

The pressure on you to follow in their footsteps will be great.

Everything you do that is new or that inconveniences anybody will bring self-righteous criticism, pious warnings. Often when you act as a true statesman you will be ridiculed and thought a fool. Many times they will try to work through your wife and kids, holding out the bribe of better clothes, a better home, better schools, protection against the unending insecurity for your family that will haunt you. But don't give in. Do what *you* think is right.

You face what Joseph Conrad tried to write about, that is, being alone. But if you can feel and see beyond the fake forest built around you by newspapers, selfish people and special interests, the world is with you.[22]

Friends, enemies, and neutrals testified that Maury Maverick was one of the most radical members ever sent to the United States House of Representatives. He was not just radical "for a Southern member," he was as radical as United States representatives get. He consorted with the left wing of the American labor movement, tried to pass general civil-rights legislation, and fought loud and long against the House Committee on Un-American Activities. His office became a sort of informal headquarters and sometime clearing house for various liberal causes.

Maverick's physical disability at the time of his arrival in Congress had won him an office, number 101 in the old House Office Building, on the street level close to the subway to the Capitol. The office was cluttered and jammed with too many filing cabinets. The walls were covered with his personal picture gallery, and various bits of Texana were scattered about in other places. A row of Texas cactuses in a long window box was silhouetted in the window of the reception room. Behind Maverick's desk was a special, high-backed chair designed to support his weakened neck, and to the side there was a large blackboard on which he posted his various commitments. The office was also frequently cluttered with promoters of liberal causes and other Maverick well-wishers, and it was for this reason that he and a few of his fellows cornered some small rooms on the fifth floor for use as hideouts. There Maverick might be found by a favored few, hunched over his well-thumbed copies of Montesquieu, Montaigne, Hume, Bryce, and others—one hand supporting his head. Stanley High, one of the favored few, said that Maverick was "obviously one of the heavy-thinking contingent," but that he was too politic to "parade his knowledge on the floor of the House where an erudite man may be suspect." High also testified to Maverick's radicalism, saying that he was one of the foremost spokesmen for the "radico-liberals"

Maury and His Mavericks

throughout the country. The orthodox leaders were wary of Maverick, said High, and "his enemies called him a wild man."[23]

High was clearly an admirer of Maverick, but an amiable Maverick critic in South Carolina, after voicing "avowed Tory sympathies," gave a similar appraisal. He said that Maverick was clearly a "radical" or "leftist," but not a "blackguard." He praised Maverick's erudition and talent as a writer for radical publications and defended him against the "average nice fellow in Congress from the South" who would set Maverick, or any man of cultivation and talent, down as a "crank." The South Carolina editor concluded, "Maverick seems to be an original sinner, and we have come to the stage that we wink at political sin if only a little of it be original."[24]

Though High said that Maverick was too politic to do so, he *did* show some of his erudition on the floor of the House, but consistent with High's claim, Maverick often did it in such a manner as to lampoon the erudition.[25] For example, he prepared his own report on a resolution designed to permit United States officers to accept foreign medals, with the primary aim of chiding his colleagues for devoting their attention to minor matters instead of considering the welfare of the nation—"a mere local matter." With tongue far into cheek, he said:

> Since this matter of medals touches all the heights and depths of civilization . . . it is not to be treated lightly. It must be treated philosophically. Now the heaviest philosophy for the occasion is that of Hegel who handled everything dialectically. This method calls for the division of every . . . argument into these parts: thesis, antithesis and synthesis. It may not be generally known, but thesis, antithesis and synthesis form the basis of all argumentation. . . . This was proved beyond any doubt by Dr. Hegel, a distinguished philosopher.

Hegelian Truth

Applying the reasoning of Hegel to the problem before us, the burning issue of medals, we are compelled to take the case philosophically in the following manner:

Thesis
1. If a citizen is not worthy, he should not have a medal; and if he is worthy, he does not need it.

Antithesis
2. To insist on his having it is . . . the antithesis.
Synthesis
3. Don't let him have the medal.[26]

The uncongressman-like activities of Maverick in the world of books and ideas included writing book reviews for the *Congressional Record*. When he encountered what he thought to be an important book, he considered it his duty to apprise his less-enlightened colleagues of its value and to encourage them to read it. In February 1937 he had included in the *Record* a column by Gail Borden of the *Chicago Times*, February 28, 1937, which twitted Maverick for his presumptuousness, but then styled part of the review as a "masterpiece of review like one of the old masters in that craft." Maverick promptly announced that he was entering another book review for the benefit of his colleagues.[27]

Maverick was also asked to review books for various other publications. One of the better ones was done for the *Baltimore Sun* on Walter Lippmann's *An Inquiry into the Principles of the Good Society*. After reading the book, Maverick had the Library of Congress send him Lippmann's columns for the past year and he read them. He then had his estimate of Lippmann as a thinker and a personality corroborated in an exchange of letters with Charles A. Beard, General Hugh S. Johnson, and Stuart Chase. Armed with such impressive backing, Maverick sailed into Lippmann with the usual gusto. He said, "The non-reading elite who live in big houses will buy it, read a few chapters, gain solace and recommend it as sound," but he marked out of his original draft the more pungent observation, "I am sure his former comrades will say, 'Lippmann is the opium of the Rich.'"[28] Maverick apparently thought this line was hitting a bit below the belt. His analysis (which was done before nearly all others) anticipated the criticisms to be found in the liberal journals. His main quarrel with the work was that the "good society" would somehow be based upon collectivist principles and techniques without being collectivist.[29]

Maverick had the faculty, often missing in politicians, of being able to laugh at himself. Indeed, this was a part of the clown myth; but he was more than a clown, he was a genuine humorist. He

Maury and His Mavericks

could be extremely serious when he felt it necessary, but he had a puckish humor which at least one book reviewer compared with that of Mark Twain.[30] His private correspondence and conversation were enlivened by hilarious anecdotes and remarks—some of them unprintable. Walter Webb said that Maverick originated the expression when he told some ostentatiously liberal friends, "I'm so liberal I say 'chigro' instead of 'chigger.'" When a witness reported that he had heard the "clink of silver dollars" as Maverick allegedly distributed money for illegal poll-tax payments, the irrepressible defendent is said to have turned to his lawyer and whispered, "It's a damn lie! It was paper money."[31]

In the course of one of his campaigns Maverick was talking to a group of the Mexican-Americans, who made up such a large part of his constituency. When he referred to them several times as "Mexicans," a nervous aide whispered to him that these sensitive people preferred to be called "Latin Americans." Maverick quickly turned to the assembled group and said, "If you paid your poll tax, stand up." When a goodly number complied, Maverick declared with a grin, "You are Latin Americans; the rest of you are Mexicans." All but a few "Mexicans" laughed then at this imaginative distinction and many of them like to tell the story today.[32]

No writer (or reader) of scholarly works could fail to appreciate Maverick's response to the paraphernalia of scholarly writing:

> For his documentation smacks of vindictiveness rather than professoriality. We feel he is thinking: "Yes, they doubt me—curse them, here is *Ibid.*, I, 344; ² *Adams, Diary*; *King's Corr.*, V., *31*; all this my dear sir, at the bottom of each page—that proves it. And moreover (Bowers still speaking) here upon page 513, you see this (*Aside*— damn your Federalist and Tory hides and such as may disbelieve me), my bibliography, which is headed: "BOOKS, MANUSCRIPTS, PUBLIC DOCUMENTS, CONTEMPORARY PAMPHLETS AND NEWSPAPERS CITED AND CONSULTED," and it is thorough—and cursed be he who says it is not accurate, nor enough.[33]

Maverick seems to have originated the perfect squelch type of letter to answer insulting notes from correspondents. The much-quoted classic was his response to a two-thousand-word letter lambasting Maverick and the New Deal. He replied:

Honorable Robert E. Price
2045 East Wood Street
Decatur, Illinois
Dear Sir:
>Ph-t-t!!
>
>Very truly yours,
>
>Maury Maverick[34]

An equally good and only slightly more wordy example, previously unpublished, was the result of a letter from a radio listener who had heard one of Maverick's network speeches in defense of the New Deal. The writer called Maverick a "rabble rouser" who was out for some political reward. Maverick responded:

Honorable A. B. Smith
The Oaks
4238 Broadside Ave.
Minneapolis, Minnesota
Dear Friend Smith:
>Go jump in the lake, you old bull frog. I mean any one of the beautiful ten thousand lakes in Minnesota.
>
>Very truly yours,
>
>Maury Maverick
>
>P.S. Don't do it—you will ruin the lake.[35]

Maverick also had a propensity for pulling off elaborate gags done up in some sort of pseudo-official trappings. Three months after his arrival in Congress he concocted a ceremony in the Republican cloakroom in which he knighted left-wing Republican Representative Vito Marcantonio with the Order of the Pink Elephant and designated him as the Pink Pachyderm of Congress. In the presence of Marcantonio's more conservative colleagues, Maverick pinned a tiny pink elephant with a blue ribbon on the New York representative and presented him with an elaborately decorated scroll that congratulated him for being an "off-color Republican."[36]

As a member of the Texas Philosophical Society, which was apparently a bit shy of philosophers, Maverick once had the task of sounding out members for suggestions for future meetings. After gathering the responses, he addressed this combination of whimsey and irony to his fellows:

MEMBER SAYS WE SHOULD CONSIDER PHILOSOPHY
(An Eccentric Suggestion)
Now it becomes my painful duty to relate a multilateral insult. It is that our organization should devote itself, at least to some extent, to our purposes—this person must be an eccentric. Anyhow, this wicked character suggested that we give some attention to philosophy. I move he be thrown out, without trial or due process of law, of course.

He went even further and made the gross suggestion that teachers of philosophy in our various institutions of learning might be taken in as *auxiliary members.*

OUR PURPOSELESSNESS MUST BE PRESERVED

The foregoing we could hardly bear, permitting Ph.D.'s to be almost our intellectual or social equals—and to mingle with us as secondary members of the Texas Philosophical Society. If this passes, I shall demand that these Ph.D.'s be segregated and make affidavits that they will not overthrow our Society and its purposelessness.[37]

Maverick's high order of intellectual integrity was testified to by friends and enemies. Webb said his integrity was "unflinching,"[38] and Herbert Corey wrote in the *Nation's Business*, "One of the most acid critics said of him: 'He is fundamentally honest. He could not be induced or bullied into surrendering his principles. He makes up his own mind.' "[39] A businessman wrote of Maverick, "I have known Maury for twenty years and doubt that any man in America is better qualified to advise new congressmen. Stentorian of voice, subtle as a brass band, courageous, sincere and frank, he has haunted phonies and fence-straddlers throughout his public career. Those who don't like him respect his patriotism, guts and brilliance."[40]

Despite his attention-getting antics and truculence, the rough-tough Maverick had great compassion for his fellow man. It was this quality that Mrs. Eleanor Roosevelt singled out when asked to give her estimate of Maverick. She said, "I would say that Maury Maverick was fearless and warm as a man. He had compassion for all men, even those in prison."[41] President Truman said, "He was always on the right side—the side of the little fellow."[42] Maverick once said that he considered "human compassion" to be the fundamental difference between a "progressive" and a "conservative."[43] Maverick was a man of great sentimentality and sensitivity. He wept openly as he watched newsreel pictures of young men marching off to war,[44] and he once wrote that the reason he had always thought Anatole France's *The Crime of Sylvester Bonnard* to be a "beautiful book" was because "the main idea is that there is only one thing worth while, and that is sentiment."[45] The late Arnold Ben Wacker, assistant professor of business administration and economics at Our Lady of the Lake College in San Antonio and a speech-writing assistant and admirer of Maverick, gave the candid appraisal that Maverick loved the poor and the downtrodden in the abstract, but that at times had the human failing of many liberals of not being able to "enthuse" about it in person-to-person relations with such people.[46]

It is difficult to find superlatives adequate to describe the phenomenal impact of this Texas whirlwind on Congress and the national consciousness when he took his place in the House of Representatives in January 1935. Few freshman members of Congress have equaled his performance. Rather than awaiting a nod from the thrones of the wise and mighty, Maverick was engaging in vigorous debate before his chair was warm. At the beginning of his second year, he paid his respects to the tradition of quiescent first-timers, and then said bluntly, "I represent my people, so I will speak."[47]

His unmatched candor and audacity, even when dealing with the president, became the talk of Washington. One reporter gave an account of Maverick's unsuccessful attempts to secure an appointment with Stephen Early, secretary to President Roosevelt, which culminated in this tart letter to FDR: "I am having difficulty in reaching Mr. Early. Will you be so kind as to help me in making an appointment with him?" The next day Early called Maverick.[48]

One of Maverick's best friends, the late newsman and novelist Walter Karig, gave him some of his own medicine after failing several times to find the congressman in his office. Karig penciled on a sheet of typing paper an excellent caricature of Maverick, picturing him as a horned, snorting bull rushing somewhere headlong, and above the drawing he jotted the note, "Dear Voroshilov: You're getting as hard to reach as Steve Early. Karig." Maverick preserved the caricature and wrote on it the comment, "This is really great, aggressive art. He told me off.—M."[49] Karig also did a pretty neat job of capturing the image of Maury Maverick in words. Karig said that when he went to heaven, he fully expected to find "at the Golden Gate St. Peter, baffled by my unscheduled arrival, will say he'll have to see the Boss' brain truster about me; and up will ride you, in a chariot towed by all the beasts in Revelations. You will say: 'What goddam gate crashing son of a bitch is this?' And at that time, Maury, please remember that the applicant is your awed and devoted admirer."[50]

In a matter of months the name and appearance of Maury Maverick was known throughout the United States. A careful student of Texans in the New Deal has said, "Unquestionably, the most meteoric rise in Congress during the New Deal was that of Maury Maverick of San Antonio . . . one of the best known congressmen in the nation."[51] In his first year, Maverick was the primary subject of sixteen items in the *New York Times* as compared with nine items concerning the majority leader, William B. Bankhead.[52] Articles and editorials about the ebullient Texan appeared in dozens of newspapers from the *Seattle Times* to the *Miami Daily News* when he fought the military disaffection bill in July of 1935.[53]

The Maverick fame was more than a matter of being a showman or good copy. He was being taken seriously by a great many people, including a considerable segment of the House of Representatives. He had not been in Congress two months when he organized his liberal friends into a Maverick bloc with which both legislative and executive leadership was compelled to reckon—indeed, it might well be said that it was at times the leadership. The regular leadership of the House, Speaker Byrns and Majority Leader Bankhead, was essentially conservative and had no great enthusiasm for more New Deal programs.

Texas and the nation were strongly supporting Franklin D. Roosevelt and his New Deal when Maverick entered Congress. Economic conditions were improving, and the off-year Democratic gains in House and Senate seats were almost unprecedented. Arthur M. Schlesinger, Jr., viewed the 1934 election as having also strengthened presidential influence on the Hill by bringing in a new breed of Democrats—among them "the more responsible members of the Maury Maverick group in the House"—who were both dedicated liberals and party regulars.[54] This analysis was frequently valid (perhaps then depending upon one's interpretation of "responsible"), but it did not apply to some of the key issues that came to the fore in the House in 1935, and there were indications that men like Maverick looked upon the election results as a mandate to move the New Deal further and faster than Roosevelt had planned.

Maverick and his cohorts were also determined to oppose FDR's position on what was characterized as the number one issue as this session of Congress opened, the proposal for funding the World War I veterans bonus. Moreover, the Maverick group was to lock horns with Roosevelt on neutrality policy. The threat of an aggressive totalitarianism in Europe was just beginning to emerge at this time. On the day Congress met, beleaguered Abyssinia was asking the League of Nations to take measures to ensure peace between that small African nation and Mussolini's Italy, while reports from Berlin told of an unusual meeting of Nazi leaders to demonstrate the German nation's unity under Adolf Hitler. The mood of the United States was becoming increasingly isolationist, and Maury and his Mavericks reflected that mood.

Maverick wrote next to nothing about his group of fellow liberals, and the size, nature, and degree of influence of the group have been treated variously. When queried about the paucity of information concerning the Maverick bloc, his widow said that much of its maneuvering was hush-hush, and that her husband had followed some advice from Jesse Jones to the effect that the best investment a politician can make is in a telephone bill: "You get quick connections and there is no record."[55] There is no evidence that Maverick ever claimed to be *the* leader of the group, but he was given the honor by virtually all of the sources that treated the movement. The *Washington Herald* reported that the name of the group was taken from Maury Maverick, "a leading spirit in the movement."[56]

Indeed, one person who attended the meetings of the Mavericks said: "During the early period of Maury's tenure in Congress (I think he was almost single-handedly responsible) he called together a group of young liberal Congressmen at a fish restaurant named Hall's Restaurant. We used to go there once a week. Some 15 or 20 young Congressmen would meet with 10 or 12 executives from various agencies downtown, such as Ickes' Public Works Administration, Isador Lubin from the Department of Labor, Isadore Strauss, from the Public Housing Administration. . . . Henry Wallace often came to the meetings. Harry Hopkins came."[57]

The first public mention of the Mavericks appeared on March 10, 1935, when the *Washington Herald* reported that the Texas freshman had joined with thirty-four House colleagues to form the group and that the members had adopted a twelve-point liberal program of action. Paul J. Kvale, Minnesota Farmer-Laborite, called the meeting and presided. Six days later the *Herald* reported that the group was made up of seven Wisconsin Progressives, three Farmer-Laborites, sixteen Democrats, and eight Republicans.[58]

Speaker Byrns was reported to have indicated that possible disciplinary action against the Democrats in the group would be taken by the Democratic leadership.[59] Representative Claude A. Fuller (D.-Ark.) made a full-dress attack upon the insurgents on the floor of the House on March 14. He ridiculed "these Moseses who are going to lead us to the promised land" and charged that they had "formed a bloc for the purpose of controlling legislation hereafter." Kvale was singled out as the "dictator" of the group, and Fuller said that the group was intent upon breaking down the two major parties. He also insisted upon reading all of the names of those members attending the meeting, told the Democrats that they got in on Franklin D. Roosevelt's coat-tails and warned that they might not be back next time.[60]

Maverick hurried to the floor when he heard of Fuller's attack, but he arrived just as the Arkansas congressman was leaving the chamber. Maverick stopped him and growled, "I don't care if you've been around here twenty years, you can't shove that sort of stuff down my throat."[61] He told a reporter, "They are trying to bluff Democratic members and keep them from joining. They can't bluff me. I didn't ride into office on the coat-tails of the President; I rode in on my own."[62] Maverick then obtained five minutes for a reply to Fuller's remarks. The irate Texan termed Fuller's attack upon "certain new members of the House" a cowardly one. In a defiant tone he told his colleagues and the Democratic leaders: "I have never made a personal attack on any Democrat or on the Democratic Party since I have been a member of the House. Of course, I have not been here very long. I will never attack a Democrat unless he attacks me or some group of persons with whom I associate, and I think that I have the right to associate with whom

I please. I have a right to study, to attend open forums, discussion groups, lectures—and to improve my mind if I want to. . . . I did not come here to be loud-mouthed, I did not come here to talk all the time, but I think it is necessary on this occasion to say something." Maverick went on to say that he had never heard Fuller say anything progressive since he had been in the House. As far as insurgency was concerned, Maverick protested that he was not trying to start a third-party movement, but that he was being just as independent as President Roosevelt had been when he was in the New York Legislature.[63]

Representative Gerald J. Boileau (Prog.-Wis.) launched another counterattack against Fuller the next day, charging that the "chairman of the Democratic patronage committee" was trying to intimidate Democrats. He intimated that the leadership had chosen Fuller to act as hatchet man.[64] Though there is no definite evidence to support this charge, the *New York Times* reported that Speaker Byrnes had "made no secret of his opposition" to the group.[65]

It was the *Times* which gave the first definitive report on the Mavericks. Thirty-four members were reported to have answered a "roll call" in a meeting of the group on March 16, 1935. Maverick said that there were thirty more who would identify themselves with the program, but other members differed with him. The March 16 meeting adopted a sixteen-point program containing these policies: federal regulation of credit and currency; abolishment of the issuance of tax-exempt securities; increased inheritance, income, and gift taxes on a graduated basis; refinancing of farm debts on long-term, 1.5 percent interest; lower interest rates on home loans; guarantee to farmers their average cost of production plus a reasonable profit; limitation of hours of labor in industry; insurance to labor of "its inherent right to bargain collectively"; public works appropriations to provide employment; federal aid to education; "government ownership of all natural resources and monopolies vested with public interest"; "deprofitizing" of war; avoidance of "foreign entanglements"; adequate provisions for the payment of sickness, old-age, and unemployment benefits; protection of freedom of speech and the press; and liberalization of House rules.[66] The policy committee of the group consisted of Maverick, Kvale, George J. Schneider (Prog.-Wis.), Kent E. Keller (D.-

Maury and His Mavericks

Ill.), William Lemke (R.-N.D.), Melvin J. Maas (R.-Minn.), and Fred C. Gilchrist (R.-Iowa).[67]

Less than one month from the day its program was offered, the organization, formally known as the Progressive Open Forum Discussion Group, was referred to as "a decisive factor in House strategy," and its solid vote was credited with swinging the House from the Vinson Bonus Bill to the Patman Bonus Bill. The Vinson bill provided that certificates held by World War I veterans would be funded by whatever method might be devised by the Treasury Department; the Patman bill called for outright payment by currency expansion.[68] FDR wanted no bonus bill, and the House leadership had tried to block consideration of such a measure. In an unexpected move by Representative Wright Patman of Texas and his Maverick supporters, the Vinson measure, "with all the prestige of the American Legion endorsement behind it," was rejected.[69] The key vote in this heated and much-publicized struggle was on a motion to recommit the Patman bill. The attempt failed by a narrow margin of 207 to 204.[70] The House and Senate then passed the Patman bill, but it was vetoed by President Roosevelt. The following year, however, a measure akin to Patman's proposal was passed over Roosevelt's veto.[71]

Another major area to which Maury and his Mavericks turned their attention in the spring of 1935 was neutrality and related legislation, and their first big victory was said to have been the rewriting of the administration's war-profits bill.[72] Maverick had returned from World War I with a passionate hatred for warfare and was determined to do all that he could to prevent the involvement of the United States in any future war. He made what was apparently his first antiwar speech in San Antonio in November of 1933. It was a slashing attack on those men who "enjoy the fabulous profits from this death and destruction of their fellow men." He said that war results in an "international loss of respect for human values, and of ordinary rational conclusions," and argued that war might be prevented if "by federal enactment we should eliminate in advance any chance of profits."[73]

In a campaign speech the next year, with more accurate foresight than he perhaps realized, he said, "The next war will be fought by air bombardment of great cities, and against such bombardments there is no means of defense. Enough planes will be able to tear up dozens of great cities, kill and spread murderous gases and hideous death-dealing diseases. Millions of innocent persons, who didn't want to be in the war, who hate no one, and who wear no uniforms and carry no guns, will lose their lives." He concluded that we must remove the economic causes of war— that refusals to trade, artificial restrictions, and "economic nationalism in general" would bring on war.[74]

Maverick was not clearly an isolationist. He once said, "I have been called an isolationist and praised because I am an isolationist, but I am not."[75] The distinction may be a matter of hair-splitting, but he was a pacifist of sorts who favored an adequate national defense, U.S. participation in the World Court, and the general principle of international cooperation. Maverick had been in Congress no more than a few days when he delivered one of his most widely quoted pithy remarks—his capsule commentary on the absurdity of war. Former representative Jeannette Rankin (R.-Mon.) was asked in hearings before the House Military Affairs Committee if she would not do everything she could to help her country win a war if it should become involved in one. Representative Rankin answered with the question, "Will someone please tell me who won the last war?"—at which point Maverick interjected, "Who won the San Francisco earthquake?"[76]

In a few months Maverick had an opportunity to bring his views to bear on some specific legislation. Representative John J. Mc-Swain (D.-S.C.), chairman of the Military Affairs Committee, had been attempting for years to develop an acceptable measure that would prevent profiteering in time of war. On February 12, 1935, he reported from his committee a measure that was said to have been authored primarily by General Hugh S. Johnson and Bernard Baruch.[77] The bill was designed to "prevent profiteering in time of war and to equalize the burden of war and thus provide for the national defense and promote peace."[78] When the bill came up for a special order from the Rules Committee on April 3, Maverick attempted to have it returned to the Military Affairs Committee. He argued that the measure had no chance in the Senate unless it contained an effective tax provision, which had to originate in the House.[79] He was unsuccessful in this attempt, but in the ensuing proceedings he and his Mavericks brought the measure around to what they wanted. Maverick charged that the bill not only would fail to take the profit out of war, but that its loosely drawn provision on conscription could involve the drafting of labor or almost anyone. He was supported in these arguments by Representative Everett M. Dirksen (R.-Ill.), who called for a "real bill" to prevent profiteering and one that would not "regiment our entire nation in time of peace."[80]

Chairman McSwain and his supporters said that the 100 percent war-profits tax that had been recommended by the committee report could not be included in the measure because such a provision would have to come from the Ways and Means Committee. When one member said that a "sister bill" would be forthcoming from Ways and Means, Maverick said, "I'm afraid 'sister' is never coming. That is the trouble."[81] The Mavericks were determined to include the 100 percent war-profits tax in the bill without sending it to the Ways and Means Committee. On April 6 the *Congressional Record* simply reported that McSwain offered an amendment to impose the tax, with the explanation that Senator Arthur H. Vandenberg had told him that this would give the Senate something to work with.[82] *Newsweek* reported, however, that McSwain had "dug his heels in" against the war-profits tax, but that he "walked over to *Maverick's* desk and gave in." The magazine credited the Mavericks, and Maury in particular, with forcing the change and also bringing about the deletion of the objectionable conscription provision.[83] Though the Mavericks were successful in putting this war-profits measure of their own design through the House, it was to bog down in the Senate during the rest of Maverick's tenure in Congress.

There was greater success on the next project, however, and it was to make Maury Maverick one of the leading spokesmen for neutrality legislation in the Congress. In his second month in the House of Representatives he made a full-dress speech for neutrality legislation. He said that he started with the premise that a nation that will not fight will not survive, but that a nation must not fall under the influence of profit makers or it will "fight itself to death." He asserted, "Candor compels me to say that every war that has been fought has been fought for trade, money, avarice, and gain." Ten years later (September 9, 1945) he penned a marginal note in his own copy of the *Congressional Record*: "I think this is crap. 10 years later. M." On November 7, 1951, he added: "Still think it is crap; but it is far deeper than I ever thought—but now, for sure, I don't know what to think—M."[84] But he believed it then, and he went on to present a program for avoiding involvement in war: public ownership of munitions manufacturing, an embargo on shipments of munitions to other countries, reasonable military preparation to meet technological changes in warfare for purposes of defense, a more friendly attitude toward foreign nations, greater world trade and an end to "economic nationalism," and a government-owned "central bank of issue" that would permit "the government of the United States —which belongs to the people—to finance itself."[85]

The revelations of the Nye Committee (chaired by Senator Gerald P. Nye) concerning the activities of the munitions industry in World War I and the attendant publicity stimulated a popular demand for neutrality legislation in the spring of 1935. In response to this demand, President Roosevelt sought proposals for neutrality measures from the State Department, but none was forthcoming because the department was beset with controversies as to the type of legislation needed. Roosevelt literally turned the matter over to Congress, specifically to the Nye Committee.

Even before Nye and his associate, Senator Bennett C. Clark, could introduce neutrality resolutions in the Senate, Maverick introduced his own resolution with the key provisions calling for an embargo on arms and contraband materials to *all belligerents* and a ban on travel on belligerent ships. The key point on which Maverick, Nye, and Clark locked horns with the president was this "impartial embargo"—the president could exercise no discretion as to the nations to which the embargo could be applied.

Some indication of the importance attached to Maverick in this struggle may be seen in the fact that when he asked Secretary of State Cordell Hull to support his proposal, Hull called Maverick into a conference to explain to him the complexity of the neutrality problem and to urge upon him the need for continued study of the problem.[86] Various peace groups rallied to the support of Maverick's position and began to pressure congressmen on the Maverick resolution. Professor Robert A. Divine called him the "most vocal advocate of rigid neutrality" in the Congress and said that pressure by the first termer forced hearings on neutrality resolutions in June of 1935. The legislation was not reported at this time, but the hearings served to spark further national demands for action on a neutrality policy.[87]

After some complex legislative maneuvers in the Senate and fruitless negotiations with the administration, the Pittman resolution, which embodied essentially the Nye-Clark-Maverick position, was passed by the Senate on August 21, 1935. Maverick led nine congressmen to the White House the next morning to urge President Roosevelt to support the Pittman resolution. Roosevelt refused at the time and said that he wanted more discretionary power. One source reported that Maverick told him, in effect, "You ain't a-going to get it."[88] Another source recorded that Maverick told the president he was going to get mandatory neutrality legislation whether he wanted it or not.[89]

No doubt for a complex of reasons, including the fear that neutrality forces would block other major legislation, Roosevelt changed his mind that afternoon and the measure was passed the next day. The only concession he was able to exact was that the embargo would be limited to a six-month period. The Mavericks grumbled over this concession but accepted it with the announcement that they would return to the fight in the next session.

On the domestic front Maury Maverick was a devoted champion of the Tennessee Valley Authority. He characterized it as "the greatest social program of this administration or any other administration in the history of the United States."[90] He argued that TVA was an attempt to substitute care and forethought in the development of a region for the wasteful, hit-or-miss methods of rugged individualism—"make more profits and let the country wash away."[91] In May 1935 Maverick saw his chance to strike a blow for TVA. A bill designed to clarify and extend its powers was before the House Military Affairs Committee, of which he was a member. The measure was primarily directed at circumventing a recent Federal district court ruling that had left in doubt the legality of the TVA's distribution of electric power in the territory surrounding its plants on the Tennessee River. Maverick was first credited with "exposure of the utility company intrigues" against TVA as a result of an incident that took place at the hearings.[92]

Representative Andrew J. May (D.-Ky.), also a member of the

Military Affairs Committee and an arch foe of TVA, had made the mistake of distributing to his colleagues a mimeographed abstract of the comptroller general's audit of TVA operations that had been prepared by a Colonel James E. Cassidy. Maverick demanded to know who Cassidy was. Cassidy said that he had done "a great deal of gratuitous work for this committee. . . . I am not employed by anyone." He gave his occupation as engineer, but refused to give the names of clients. He said he had written the abstract as a personal favor to Representative May, and had had it mimeographed "for nothing" by a utility company attorney. May himself volunteered that he was going to have the mimeographing done by "a friend in the National Coal Association," but C. A. Beasley, counsel of the Alabama Power Company (a major opponent of TVA) was in his office at the time and offered to do the mimeographing. The following exchange then took place:

"I don't have utility and coal officials sitting around my office," growled Maverick.

May peered over his glasses. "Is that intended as a personal remark?"

"You can figure it out anyway you please," bristled Maverick.

"I'll figure it out outside if you want!" the sixty-year-old Kentuckian said, taking off his glasses.

"I'm afraid," mocked the stocky Texan, a World War veteran and twenty years May's junior.

After the hearing resumed, Maverick remarked heatedly that Cassidy should be thrown out of the hearing, and Cassidy apparently invited him to try. Arthur E. Morgan, TVA chairman, who was then testifying, said that Cassidy had asked to be named supervisor of the construction of Norris Dam, telling TVA that he "had influence in Washington." Morgan also said that Cassidy had later sought an appointment as an "expert chemist," but TVA did not make an appointment after investigation of his qualifications. "I think we should throw this colonel out," Maverick roared. But no action was taken, and May told reporters he would have the incident expunged from the record of the hearings. After adjournment of the hearings, Maverick promptly issued a statement that "an immense, crooked lobby is trying to defeat the TVA. It is rotten and disgraceful."[93]

A few days later it was reported that the TVA bill had been

tabled by the committee by a vote of thirteen to twelve. Maverick was said to be "determined" to get the bill out of the committee and on its way to passage, and he was described as conducting a "one-man drive" to do so.[94] Though Maverick denied it, the irrepressible Texan had had an interview with FDR concerning the key amendments to the TVA Act and had been "commissioned to father the measure," in view of the fact that McSwain (chairman of the Military Affairs Committee) was "off" the bill.[95] Whatever the case, on July 8, 1935, Maverick had another victory over his committee chairman. On that date McSwain announced that the committee had reported the bill by a vote of thirteen to twelve. He explained that the bill was a modification of his own measure and indicated he was not too happy about it, but he would not discuss any of the speculations as to the authorship of the changes.[96]

The next day Maverick gave a lengthy opening address on the measure, consuming much of the attention of the House for three days.[97] On July 10, after a plea by Maverick, the House removed all of the restrictive provisions that President Roosevelt had found objectionable and in addition eliminated a provision that would have placed the financial affairs of TVA under the control of the comptroller general. The *Washington News* hailed the action as a "smashing comeback" that would extend "the scope of the administration's 'electric rate yardstick' project."[98] The bill was passed by the House and Senate July 11, but a conference committee was necessary.[99] Maverick continued to maintain a watchful eye over the legislation. When it went to the conference committee, he closely questioned Representative McSwain on the choice of what Maverick thought were unfriendly conferees. He withdrew a formal protest on the matter, but indicated that he wanted his misgivings to be a matter of record and for them to serve as a warning to his opponents.[100] The conference committee's report was accepted by the House on August 21, but not without a considerable debate in which Maverick took a leading part.[101] The Senate added its approval the same day without further debate.[102]

Further evidence of Maverick's influence in maneuvering for passage of the TVA amendments was given in an account by Rodney Dutcher, who reported that because coal region congressmen opposed TVA, Maverick went to Senator Joe Guffey of Pennsylvania and said, in effect, "No TVA bill, no Guffey coal bill."

Guffey then got busy in support of the TVA measure. Later, with the aid of the Mavericks, the Guffey coal bill passed the House by a narrow margin.[103]

Another example of the extraordinary influence that this freshman Texas congressman had won was his leadership in the fight for legislation to control the public utilities holding companies. The *Washington Daily News* reported in July 1935 that the Democratic leadership had admitted it was "peeved" because Maverick and John E. Rankin (D.-Miss.) had been consulted by Roosevelt on the "death sentence" provisions of the public utilities holding company bill,[104] and Ruth Finney reported in the same paper in August that Maverick was "largely responsible for getting the president's TVA bill through the House in the form he wanted it. He took the lead in organizing members of the holding company fight, and has been active on half a dozen other matters."[105] Albert Warner also reported in the *New York Herald Tribune* that President Roosevelt had personally encouraged Maverick and Rankin to lead the fight for the "more drastic" versions of the TVA and holding company legislation.[106]

The Wheeler-Rayburn public utilities holding company bill contained a drastic provision that would have empowered the Securities Exchange Commission to compel dissolution of holding companies that could not appropriately justify their existence—this was the "death sentence" clause. Utility companies exerted desperate efforts to head off this drastic provision. Representative Rankin reported that his telephone was tapped. A Western Union official testified to a special Senate investigating committee that utility interests sent hundreds of telegrams to congressmen opposing the legislation and signed the names of persons who had no idea that their names were being used. Less than three weeks later the originals of such wires were burned in the basement of the Western Union Office, though originals were normally kept for at least one year.[107]

Maverick made several carefully researched and documented speeches on the holding company legislation on the floor of the House and over national radio networks. TVA director David E. Lilienthal wrote to him, "I was lucky enough to be near a radio the other night when you were speaking on holding companies. Your speech was a crackerjack, and you have an unusually smooth radio voice. I wish you would send me a copy of the text of your remarks."[108] Later FDR adviser Felix Frankfurter favored Maverick with this note: "It was a very great pleasure to meet you. You really invigorated my belief in the possibilities of wise and democratic government. I have no doubt that persistent efforts like yours to mobilize the progressive forces in Congress to secure agreement on essentials and fight together for them, will greatly promote the achievement of legislation in the country's interest and ward off attempts to divert such wholesome legislation as the Senate Holding Company bill."[109]

Finally, Maverick was responsible for bringing about a major strategy meeting to aid the passage of the death sentence clause, and he came very near to success. A meeting was held at the Reconstruction Finance Corporation, which included Thomas Corcoran ("Tommy the Cork," an FDR aide), Representative Rankin, Benjamin Cohen, Representative R. Owen Brewster (R.-Me.), Maverick, and several other administration advisers. Maverick reported that at the meeting Brewster had said that he favored the death sentence clause, that he would make a speech for it in the House and that he could probably swing twenty-five Republican votes for it. Brewster not only failed to follow through, but he voted against the bill. He subsequently claimed that Corcoran had threatened to cut off the Passamaquoddy Dam project in Maine unless Brewster voted the right way. Corcoran said that actually what had happened was that he had told Brewster in an encounter immediately before the vote was taken that he could not be trusted to help the administration on the Maine project in view of his "sudden change of attitude on the death sentence."[110] Brewster's remarks in a final brief encounter had indicated to Corcoran that the Maine congressman was not going to be able to resist pressures of the power interests. A Rules Committee hearing subsequently revealed that Corcoran's account was correct.[111] Though the death sentence clause was defeated, a modified version that was scarcely more pleasing to the power industry was passed and signed into law on August 26, 1935.[112]

Maverick's preoccupation with other important legislative matters in his first year in Congress did not divert him from his lifelong interest in the cause of civil liberties. Roger N. Baldwin, director of the American Civil Liberties Union for thirty-three years, had this to say about Maverick's defense of civil liberties:

Maury's unique role as a battler for civil liberties in Congress was due to the unusual combination of conviction, wit, a sense of strategy and a canny estimate of the weak spots in the opposition. He knew how to disarm opponents by appearing more patriotic than they. He joined the unimpeachable organizations like the Sons of the American Revolution, and he never tied up with any other revolution. He was as homespun as the Bill of Rights. I, who also had no other platform, flirted with movements I thought headed for strengthening it, to my later disillusion; but not Maury. It was a position not based on good politics, but good sense.

During his terms in Congress his office was the center of all efforts for civil liberties legislation; he headed the liberal bloc; he ignored the false saviors of civil liberties like Marcantonio. He fought Dies. If he and I ever differed, I would think how in the light of hind-sight that he was right and I wrong. Among the handful of civil rights champions in Congress over the years, Maury stands out as the most devoted and the most skillful in achieving what he went after.[113]

Maverick was always a devoted, if at first a somewhat uncritical, supporter of the natural rights doctrine. His earliest ideas were derived from the writings of Paine and Jefferson,[114] but he also read Hugo Grotius, and in later years, Samuel von Pufendorf.[115] Maverick told the story in his first book of making a study of natural rights when he was appointed to defend two deserters in World War I. He said that he particularly used natural rights arguments of James Otis and Sam Adams in the summation to the court.[116]

According to Maverick's statement (and there is nothing comparable to it in all the vast collection of his papers), the greatest influence on the further shaping and reinforcement of his ideas in the Congressional years came from the late Charles W. Ervin, American socialist, journalist, and labor leader.[117] This "influential, if little-known, figure in American politics,"[118] a Norman Thomas type of socialist, used to come to Congressman Maverick's office in the 1930's and talk for hours with the Texan on political philosophy and public affairs.[119] Maverick called Ervin "the greatest scholar of humanity" he had ever met,[120] and told him in 1951, "You were the first great and solid inspiration in my life. . . . You taught me the excellent purposes of a free country in an affirmative manner. In other words, you gave me my start in having what understanding I have. I am glad to report also that I have not gotten worse, and a little better, and I understand race problems much better than when I used to know you."[121] Ervin's philosophical position is best divined from his comments (in one of the later notes to Maverick) on the Soviet Union: "The idiotic Secret Service from Russia once reported me to their employers as a 'Jeffersonian Socialist and a fanatic on free press and free speech!' " On the Declaration of Independence he said, "Red-headed Thomas took Burlamaqui, a Swiss on Liberty, read Grotius, a Dutchman, Pufendorf, a German, Beccaria, an Italian, and Locke, an Englishman, and fused their ideas in the 112 words."[122]

But Maverick was an outspoken champion of freedom of expression before he met Ervin. The Texas congressman's arrival in Washington marked the approximate beginning of the modern era of legislative investigations into the political orthodoxy of various segments of American life and of proofs of one's loyalty and patriotism. In a 1934 campaign speech Maverick told Bexar County voters: "It has always been the practice of those fearful of democracy to suppress the free expression of new ideas, to thwart new purposes and practices, to undermine all new experiments and to cling to the past with a death grip.... All reactionary power comes through force of some kind, not through intelligent leadership. Against their opponents, these political bigots and reactionaries have no weapons except treachery.... The truth will not sustain them, so they must fly to untruths." There was a time, he said, when we burned witches, but "in a hundred years American civilization had progressed so the people didn't keep a stake and fagots in the public *square*, but they wrote the stake and fagots *into the law.*"[123]

Maverick was one of the early advocates of a literal interpretation of the guarantees of freedom of expression in the First Amendment of the Bill of Rights. In his first important address in Congress on civil liberties he said of the First Amendment, "It did not designate the character of speech, and does not say Republican papers or Communist papers or any other kind of papers. It says, 'freedom of speech and press,' and that is what it means, and for a good reason. If you suppress one philosophy or idea, you can suppress others; therefore, the only guaranty we have of free government is free speech."[124] The notion of a near-absolute freedom of expression is more recent than is often realized. As Professor John P. Roche has explained, the position in defense of the ultimate in free expression is "a modern development" resulting, at least in large part, from the "great legal migration" to Washington in the 1930's.[125] Maury Maverick was an outstanding member of this migration that laid the groundwork for the view now prevailing on the United States Supreme Court.

Maverick first applied and polished his ideas in 1935 and 1936 against the military disaffection bills. The so-called "Tydings-McCormack Bill," as it was to be termed after it reached the House, was designed "to make better provision for the government of the military and naval forces of the United States by the suppression of attempts to incite the members thereof to disobedience." The proposed statute would make it a crime if a person "with intent to incite disaffection advises, counsels, urges or solicits any member," or "publishes or distributes any book, paper, print, article, letter or other writing" counseling the same.[126]

The bill passed the Senate by unanimous consent June 24, 1935, after a brief explanation by Senator Millard E. Tydings (D.-Md.), its author, who said that the measure was requested by the War and Navy Departments.[127] Representative John W. McCormack (D.-Mass.), chairman of the Special Committee on Un-American Activities, had introduced the same text in the House.[128] Maverick launched an intensive campaign against these measures months before either of them received any favorable action. The first week in March 1935 he began a softening-up process by delivering a major speech on freedom of expression. He pointed to the extraordinary provisions of the bill, which would permit search warrants to be issued to take "from any house or other place where it may be found, or from any person . . . any book, pamphlet, paper, print, article, letter, or other writing" of the character described in the law, and that this section would "put a dangerous power in the hands of the military, which they might use indirectly to persecute whom they pleased among the civilians."[129]

Maverick then began a letter-writing campaign to round up members of the House and Senate to oppose the measure. He wrote to dozens of key members and received favorable responses from most of them. His correspondence folder indicates that he was virtually in charge of the successful efforts to organize opposition to the measure on the part of prominent civil liberties spokesmen, such as Dr. Charles A. Beard, Professor Karl N. Llewellyn, Frederick A. Ballard (ACLU lawyer), and Professor Zechariah Chaffee, Jr.[130]

The unrelenting Texas congressman then directed a lengthy statement to Secretary of the Navy Claude A. Swanson, lecturing him on the lack of need for such a measure. He particularly singled out Swanson's complaint that literature handed out to sailors was "carefully worded to avoid the insurrection and sedition statutes," and said that if such was the case, it should not cause a sailor "to commit insurrection and sedition." He then gave Swanson a lengthy lecture on the history of loyalty and sedition statutes, which were likely to have "the opposite effect desired." If sailors were prohibited from reading certain literature, their natural response would be, "Well, there must be something to that." Suppression, said Maverick, would strengthen Communist appeals. He also upbraided Swanson at some length for permitting admirals to speak and write in behalf of such legislation.[131] Swanson's stiff reply simply reiterated his previous "views and recommendations."[132]

When hearings were held by the House Committee on Military Affairs, Maverick, Beard, Llewellyn, Representative Vito Marcantonio (R.-N.Y.), Ballard, and Allan S. Olmstead, another ACLU attorney, appeared against the bill. When the two-day hearings were concluded, the bill was reported with an amendment requiring that publication or advice to promote disaffection must be accompanied by "the intent to incite."[133] Maverick and Congressman Paul J. Kvale (Prog.-Wisc.) prepared a fourteen-page, documented indictment of the measure. They cited statutes and cases giving adequate protection against any conspiracies against the armed forces. They quoted testimony of Assistant Secretary of the Navy Henry L. Roosevelt that Communist influence on the Navy was "absolutely infinitesimal." They cited various cases of abuse of sedition statutes in the World War I period, presented a résumé of the history of civil liberties, and concluded: "This measure, put forward apparently casually and in as inconspicuous a manner as possible, is a direct, unnecessary, and wanton assault on freedom of the press and of speech, and on our traditional rights of immunity against unreasonable search and seizure. At the very least, it is a sop designed to cater to the prejudices of these so-called patriotic groups who think that the most becoming garb for the Statue of Liberty is a strait jacket and that American freedom consists of allowing the liberties of the people to be anesthetized into a complete coma."[134]

Before the report had been made to the House, Maverick charged that the decision to report the bill had been made without a quorum present in the committee and that most of the members had not read the bill. He said, "Strangely enough, the newspapers did not at first pay any attention to it, although it primarily violates the right of freedom of the press."[135] He then introduced into the *Congressional Record* a column by Walter Karig attacking the bill and commending Maverick as the only congressman who had voiced public objection to it.[136] The column was dated July 15, 1935, and the official report was not made to the House until July 22.[137] Apparently Maverick had given the report to Karig and other newsmen in advance.[138]

Maverick attacked the bill again August 1 in a radio address over WOL, Washington, D.C., and WMCA, New York, in which he referred to the measure as a "Stalin-Hitler bill" that some people sought to be "grafted on a free people."[139] Press releases on the talk were sent to 350 daily newspapers throughout the United States.[140] In two weeks Maverick was able to introduce into the *Record* editorial protests against the measure from all of the New York newspapers, most of the news magazines, the Scripps-Howard newspapers, and fourteen other representative newspapers—he said there were "hundreds" of others.[141]

Maverick and Representative Kvale were commended by Maverick's friend H. L. Mencken for carrying on the fight against the McCormack bill. The Baltimore journalist concluded, "It is a sad commentary upon the present estate and the Bill of Rights that, in a Congress of 531 members, these hobgoblins are left to wage their uphill combat alone. . . . As for Dr. Tydings, he abandons fair play and common sense to aid and abet a passel of silly Red-baiters."[142]

While he was carrying on the fight against the military disaffection bill, Maverick was also challenging with equal vigor and

Maury and His Mavericks

articulateness the Kramer Bill, offered by Representative Charles Kramer, a fellow Democrat from California. The gist of this measure was that it would be a federal crime for anyone knowingly to make any statement advocating or urging the overthrow of any government in the United States, or to print, publish, issue, edit, circulate, sell, distribute, or display any written matter containing any such statement. The bill provided for a fine of up to $5,000 and imprisonment of not more than five years, or both, for persons convicted of these offenses.[143]

A few days before the bill was reported by the Judiciary Committee, the chairman, Representative Emanuel Celler (D.-N.Y.), introduced into the *Record* a set of lengthy minority views that followed very closely the argument Maverick had presented to the committee.[144] Celler, as a matter of fact, cited the views "forcefully and ably" presented by Maverick.[145] Three days later Maverick indicated that he was astonished that the bill had been reported by the committee and referred to it as a "killer of American liberty." In a brief speech, he told his colleagues:

Force begets force. Hatred begets hatred. And if we start jailing people for talking and writing, however irresponsible or wild these utterances may be, we are leading ourselves into trouble, and we already have dozens of laws to protect this Government against criminal and overt acts; this Kramer bill is absolutely unnecessary. The worst thing about these anti-sedition bills is that they will be misused against innocent people for the suppression of opinions, the prevention of freedom of press; will be an instrument of widest oppression, will cause fanatical actions throughout the country.[146]

In the hearings on the Kramer bill, Maverick pointed out that Jeffersonian Republicans had been convicted under the Sedition Act of 1798 for statements no worse than, "Mr. Adams has only completed the scene of ignominy which Mr. Washington began," and wondered how many Democrats would be convicted of saying, "Mr. Hoover has only completed the scene of ignominy which Mr. Coolidge began."[147]

Neither the Kramer bill nor the Tydings-McCormack military disaffection bill came up before the House in this session (largely because of the blasts of Maverick and others), but they were not dead and Maverick was to move in for the kill in the next session.

Unlikely as it may seem, Maury Maverick busied himself with many other projects during his first year in Congress. He, with audacity uncommon to freshman members, urged various reforms of Congress and Congressional procedure. After a little more than a month in the House of Representatives he was calling for more clerical assistance. He argued that Congress was at a great disadvantage—all the people "at the other end of the Avenue" had to do was "press a button" to get statistical data and the like.[148] On another occasion he chided his party leaders for their failure to follow regular procedures. He wanted to know whether Calendar Wednesday "was going to be passed forever."[149]

One of his projects that reflected a lifetime interest concerned the promotion of national parks and the preservation of historic sites in the United States. He introduced a number of bills and resolutions directed toward this end and was rewarded by the passage of a measure to establish a National Parks Trust Fund Board authorized to accept and administer funds and properties donated for national parks.[150] Later in the year he secured passage of a measure to provide for restoration of historic sites. The measure established an Advisory Board on National Parks, Historic Sites, Buildings and Monuments whose members were to be selected from among "the professions of history, archaeology, architecture and human geography." In his own bound copy of the parts of the *Congressional Record* in which he had figured, Maverick expressed pride in this achievement and attached a clipping concerning the award of $45,000 from the National Parks Service for reconstruction of an outdoor theater at San Jose Mission State Park, the site used for San Antonio's famed *Drama of the Alamo* production.[151]

In 1935 Maverick began his attack on the Supreme Court that was to culminate eventually in his introduction in the House of Representatives of FDR's court-packing plan. In June he gave a lecture to his colleagues on the need for a flexible constitution and criticized the Court for incorrect reasoning in striking down New Deal legislation.[152] In a national radio address the same month he attacked the Court again and called for a national constitutional convention to consider the "unique" siuation in which elected representatives could not legislate for the "betterment of the people."[153]

Finally, when the House of Representatives was considering

the appropriation of funds for a Texas Centennial commemorating the Battle of the Alamo, Maverick made a speech in which he anticipated the concept of the War on Poverty of the 1960's. Maverick said:

> The example of the Alamo should not be lost to us. If a man will willingly lose his life for the liberty of his people and for posterity, certainly now a man should be willing to lose his political life in standing up for the things that are right and just. The thing that faced the Texans was political tyranny; what we face now is a tyranny of the special interests against the Government of the United States. . . .
> "Patriotism," according to Dr. Samuel Johnson, is sometimes "the last resort of the scoundrel"—and it is likewise the most precious thing to a decent human being. But I think it fair to say that there is a changing concept of patriotism . . . *the war to make the world a decent place to live in,* the pioneering of science, government, progress, has just begun. *Those who are willing to be the new soldiers and pioneers* will have a harder enemy to meet—the special interests, the exploiters, the gods of Greed and Hate—and they will use persecution, ridicule, hate.[154]

After the adjournment of the first session of the Seventy-Fourth Congress, Maverick busied himself with the continuing promotion of legislation that interested him, but he also found time to poke into a few affairs in his home district and around the country.

On the return trip from Washington, he made a swing down through the TVA country, inspecting dams and telling the people of the South that their future was tied to FDR and the Democratic party.[155] Maverick was riding the crest. At home he issued statements on everything, attended groundbreaking ceremonies for a new post office in San Antonio, listened to statements of praise from his old political enemies, and was invited to address the Texas Senate. In his speech he rapped Democrats who were apologetic about their party and told the Senators that President Roosevelt was "the best President the South has had since the administration of Andrew Jackson." "Our duty is to take a militant stand for the party," he said.[156]

In October he tore into the San Antonio Chamber of Commerce in a Kiwanis Club speech for its failure to make public a four-month-old report of a health survey of San Antonio made by the surgeon general of the United States Health Service. The Chamber of Commerce had asked the study to be made, but had, in what Maverick called a "silly, foolish and cowardly" attitude, suppressed the report for fear that it would "hurt San Antonio." Maverick felt that this was shortsighted and that it was time for the people of San Antonio to face the facts of the health situation in their city.[157]

From San Antonio Maverick made another swing up into several adjoining states. Attending a reunion of the 157th Infantry of Colorado, with which he had served in World War I, Maverick was depicted as "breathing fire and brimstone" as he held forth on conservation, freedom of speech, and neutrality. His opinion of the United States Chamber of Commerce was reported to have been "blistering and edifying, but scarcely printable."[158] A few days later Maverick was in New Mexico and Arizona looking over conservation projects and "furthering two of his favorite measures, providing for preservation of historical sites and Spanish colonial missions."[159]

Reporters in El Paso were able to find some quotable Chamber of Commerce remarks by Maverick when he returned to Texas. The congressman sat in the Hotel Paso del Norte and sipped coffee while he flayed the national secretary of the Chamber of Commerce for remarks to the effect that FDR's advisers sounded like "on to Moscow." He said that local chambers should not be flattered by the visits of the likes of the secretary and that the national Chamber of Commerce was the "most dangerous enemy of America." He said that rather than representing the ordinary businessman, the Chamber of Commerce represented the "big industrialists and war munitions manufacturers."[160]

A week later Maverick was off to Saint Louis for a speech to the Saint Louis Civil Liberties Committee at Sheldon Memorial. He made "characteristic attacks on the military disaffection bill, the American Liberty League and Jouett Shouse, the Chicago Tribune and Hearst newspapers, and on Comptroller General McCarl, whom he described as a 'noisy little nuisance with a flowing tie and a Napoleonic complex.' " He was "of course" for the First Amendment freedoms with no exceptions and the right of free expression, especially for those persons who were "weak, unpopular, or in the minority, and those who we, or others, may classify as simple-minded, subversive or crazy."[161]

Maury and His Mavericks

Back in Texas again in December, Maverick treated Galveston and Houston audiences to blistering attacks on the big-business-oriented American Liberty League as "tin-horn fakers of liberty," "degenerate fascists," and "concession Communists" who seek a concession for monopoly from the government and then "enjoy their license from a subservient government which they own." Maverick said that he could match them in name-calling, and there seems to be little doubt that Liberty Leaguers would agree.[162] At Houston Maverick said that he was supporting the New Deal Agricultural Adjustment Act and he did not care whether "Mr. Clayton [W. L. "Will" Clayton, a wealthy Houston cotton exporter] liked it or not."[163]

It was just before his return to Washington for the opening of the second session of the Seventy-Fourth Congress that Maverick chose to issue a statement to the press strongly condemning the Townsend Plan. He said it was a "brazen, unconscionable and hopeless demand on the poor people" that would "financially wreck the country."[164] The *New York Herald Tribune* editorialized, "All honor to Maverick," for opposing the Townsend Plan and for not trying to make political hay of it.[165]

After one year in Congress, the fame of Maury Maverick had spread far and wide. He was where he wanted to be, and he was making the most of it.

Two Cowboys Are Better Than One

MAURY MAVERICK opened his second year in Congress with some more of his attention-getting antics and further demonstrations that he was a man to be reckoned with.

Franklin Roosevelt gave his State of the Union address on January 3, 1936, to an unprecedented night joint session of Congress. His inflammatory message contained a reference to his having "earned the hatred of entrenched greed." Though this may have been more of a "radicalism of rhetoric" rather than deeds,[1] Republican leaders were incensed. They accused FDR of using the performance of his constitutional duty for unfair political advantage. When the Republicans asked for radio time to answer the president, in jumped Maverick. He had had some time scheduled for the following Saturday on the NBC network, and in a "generous and sarcastic" mood he wired NBC: "I see by the papers that the Republicans want radio time. Inasmuch as I believe that they will do more good for the Democratic party than if I speak, I will be pleased to give up my time Saturday, which ought to partially cover their demands. I do this for your convenience and for the benefit of the Democratic party."[2]

Two Cowboys Are Better Than One

Roosevelt was no doubt amused and pleased by Maverick's impulsive impudence, and the president also implicitly recognized the Texas congressman's leadership role in a friendly note three days later. Maverick had sent him a silver spur—one of the Texas mementos he typically sent to friends. Roosevelt responded, "That is a grand spur. I shall dig it in. Wear its mate yourself. Two cowboys can ride herd a whole lot better than one!"[3] This flattering metaphor did not prevent Maverick, of course, from sometimes spurring his mount in to cut off part of the herd and head it off in a divergent direction. Also, some people probably thought Maverick's credentials as a cowboy were somewhat suspect when, a few weeks later, he ran the risk of alienating quite a few of his constituents by grumbling to a reporter that he was getting a little sick of cowboy tunes. "Everytime I turn on the radio or go to a show I hear some guy hollering something about the lone prairie," he said. "Cowpunchers don't sing much either, let alone hang around a fire and yell in one another's faces over a guitar."[4]

Early in 1936 Maverick was admitted to practice before the United States Supreme Court, and by that time he had become quite well acquainted with several of the justices, among them Associate Justice Benjamin Cardozo. His relationship with Cardozo was the basis for one of the most painful yet hilarious encounters ever recorded.

Maverick went to one of Carl Sandburg's lectures at a Washington high school. He had not seen Sandburg since a meeting with him and folklorist J. Frank Dobie in the 1920's, but Sandburg spotted him in the audience, called out to him and "passed a few compliments." After the meeting Sandburg asked Maverick if he would introduce him to Justice Cardozo. Maverick made the arrangements, and the two went to visit the justice in his apartment. Sandburg and Cardozo complimented one another extravagantly, and then, suddenly, Sandburg asked if he might recite a poem for Cardozo. When Cardozo expressed his enthusiastic agreement, Sandburg, "oblivious to his audience," began to recite in blank verse. "Roaring at the top of his voice," he delivered a blistering and very long diatribe against all judges "who sell their souls" and the like. Maverick said that Cardozo's hair was no whiter than his face.

When Sandburg finished, he said, "Judge, what do you think of that?"

The shattered Cardozo could barely choke out, "Mr. Sandburg, I would not condemn the whole judiciary," and Maverick was amazed to hear Sandburg respond, "Why not? They are destroying the country," and more in a similar vein. He assured Cardozo that none of the judges was "worth a damn." At a break in this fantastic harangue, Maverick was finally able to steer Sandburg out of the apartment after a quick exchange of perfunctory words of leave-taking.[5]

Maverick was also giving plenty of attention to serious business. Immediately upon his return to Washington in December 1935 he was conferring with Senator Nye on the establishment of a special steering committee to guide the Nye-Clark-Maverick neutrality measure, which was designed to replace the temporary neutrality law passed in the last session. Maverick was convinced that the Congress wanted a rigid, unqualified bill that would compel the president to place an embargo on shipments of all munitions and materials of war to any belligerent nation.[6] At this time he received a clipping from historian Charles A. Beard that contained a report of the 1935 convention of the American Political Science Association. In the news story, Beard had been quoted as saying, "representatives in Congress, such as Maverick of Texas, know their history, and they intend to keep the power of making war in the legislature where it belongs under the Constitution."[7]

There were new problems to reckon with in this session, however. Since the passage of the temporary neutrality act of 1935 (destined to expire on February 29, 1936), Italy had launched its attack upon Ethiopia on October 3, 1935. The president and others interested in neutrality legislation quickly learned that the restriction of raw materials and other goods could be as important as embargoes on armaments. Though the 1935 law limited embargoes to actual arms, attempts were made to apply a "moral embargo" on shipments of goods that could aid in war. The lack of success of this attempt by the Roosevelt administration helped to stimulate a drive for such restrictions in a new neutrality act.

The measure offered by the administration on January 3 was remarkably close to what the neutrality bloc wanted. It provided for continuation of the impartial arms embargo, a mandatory ban

Two Cowboys Are Better Than One 101

on loans to belligerents, and a quota system under which the president could limit the export of raw materials that he judged to be critical to average amounts exported before a war. The president was given some discretion in this measure. The ban on loans did not prevent him from exempting short-term commercial credits, and a provision left it up to his discretion to declare that trade with belligerents would be at the trader's own risk.

Nye, Clark, and Maverick indicated that they were surprised at the strict provisions of the administration measure, but they still pressed for the more rigid approach embodied in their bill, which they introduced the same day. It called for automatic declaration of trade quotas by the president upon outbreak of war, automatic imposition of an arms embargo, a requirement that the president prohibit absolutely travel by American passengers on belligerent vessels, no presidential discretion with respect to short-term commercial credits, and restrictions on the method by which the president would determine trade quotas.[8]

There seemed to be considerable ground for a compromise between the administration position and that of the neutrality bloc, but, as Beard had indicated, Maverick and his associates wanted the Congress to control the power of making war, and President Roosevelt, having already made many concessions to them, was not in a mood to yield much more. The waters were soon to be muddied even more, however, by the opposition of business groups and Italian-Americans to any trade restrictions on materials other than arms. Maverick was one of the most adamant advocates of the trade restrictions. He did not care if it hurt business, and he even went so far as to say that he would just as soon close the ports of Houston and Galveston if it would save lives. He was also concerned about the wording that permitted the president to invoke an arms embargo "upon the outbreak of or during the progress of any war," which might permit the president to wait indefinitely before invoking the embargo. Maverick sought and obtained wording that required the president to act as soon as he found a state of war to exist.[9]

Neither the administration bill nor the Nye-Clark-Maverick bill was destined to pass. The strong pressure from the business groups and Italian-Americans and the adamant position of Maverick's element ultimately forced the administration and its supporters to accept a compromise bill that dropped the trade quotas and essentially extended the 1935 act to May 1, 1937, with the additional feature of a ban on loans to belligerents. Though the compromise measure incorporated the more definite language that Maverick had sought concerning the time when the president was to invoke an embargo, and a requirement that the president extend an arms embargo to other states that entered a war in progress, it did give the president authority to exempt short-term commercial credits from the loan ban, and the trade restrictions were dropped.

Administration forces in the House, relieved to find a way out, and the traditional neutrality forces, concerned about the approaching expiration date for the existing neutrality law, were ready to accept this bill. The disgruntled Maverick, however, protested bitterly against the passage under a gag rule that allowed only forty minutes of debate to a measure affecting the "lives of millions of our sons," while hours were wasted on matters of personalities and "home consumption speeches." He characterized the legislation as an inadequate "hodgepodge," grumbled that the Congress would apparently "pass up neutrality until after the war," and urged his colleagues to vote against the measure. It was passed by a vote of 353 to 27 on February 17.[10]

Professor Divine's conclusion was that the Maverick group prevented a potential majority for trade restrictions by its insistence on the rigid program of mandatory neutrality. The administration was bent upon getting the flexibility necessary to some passive cooperation with League of Nations sanctions against aggressors, and Nye, Maverick, Clark, and their supporters were determined to prevent all involvement in wars. As Divine put it, "These objectives were incompatible, and the result was an impasse which simply postponed the issue for another year."[11]

The debate on neutrality legislation was over, but shortly before it was concluded, Maverick indulged himself in one of his quixotic gestures by introducing a bill he no doubt knew had no chance of passage. It provided that all military training institutions have a required reading list to impress upon trainees the horrors of war. He recommended for the list *All Quiet on the Western Front* by Erich Remarque, *The Red Badge of Courage* by Stephen Crane, *The Road to War* and *The Martial Spirit* by Walter Millis, *Three*

Soldiers by John Dos Passos, *The First World War* by Lawrence Stallings, and *The Case of Sergeant Grischa* by Arnold Zweig.[12]

Maverick was more than ready to make war on the enemies of free expression in this second session, and he did not wait for the military disaffection bill or the Kramer antisubversive measure to come before the House. He published an article in January in which he combined his interests in neutrality legislation with his concern for the protection of civil liberties. He renewed his attack on both of the proposals and condemned the "false patriotism" of the American Liberty League and other "shirt front organizations." The way to secure liberty, he argued, is not through war, but by remaining "neutral abroad, but at home to wage a relentless campaign against all of those who stifle liberty—in the name of liberty—for the sake of profit."[13]

Shortly after the convening of the second session of the Seventy-fourth Congress, Maverick leaped to the attack in a speech to the Virginia Press Association and in other speeches to various audiences. He condemned the military disaffection bill and all types of gag laws. He told the newsmen that freedom of the press must be extended to all segments of opinion, and explained, "All this is based on the democratic concept of the preservation of society. We know that society cannot be held in concrete forms for all time. Society must and does change, and it is better that we do not let it crack up because of the violence against the rigidity of our forms, but that we let changes come gradually and easily by the freedom of expression with a certain flexibility of our institutions."[14] Here Maverick was arguing in favor of discussion for purposes of peaceful constitutional change, but he also extended his argument to a claim for the value of the making of the speech: permitting people to vent their spleen in violent speech may help to stave off the violent act. As he explained the point to fellow members of the American Civil Liberties Union: "The purpose of freedom of speech; the purpose of freedom of press, is to eliminate violence, destruction and revolution. By the use of freedom, by violent expression, we prevent the violent act. We must not, in our effort to destroy Fascism or Communism adopt their policy of the elimination of full, free, unhampered expression in every phase of life. Let us have our view of economics, but let us preserve democracy and freedom."[15]

On another occasion he said, "Let the public listen to us attack each other and read the war of words in the newspapers and then decide which is telling the truth, or more probably, decide that both of us are bores."[16] Finally, Maverick developed enough confidence in this notion to write, ". . . those who proposed the Bill of Rights, and who had recently endured a bitter revolution, had sense enough to know that the extremest type of speech, including all manner of violent talk and all manner of blowing off steam would help prevent a revolution, and help to maintain free and orderly government."[17]

In the early days of the 1936 session, Maverick warned that the Kramer bill and others like it in the Senate were not dead, and opposition against them should be kept up.[18] At one point, with tongue in cheek, he joined in an effort to block the teaching of the principles of the American Liberty League in Federal public schools only long enough to point out that the Liberty League's publications criticizing the Roosevelt administration were extreme enough to cause the League to be prosecuted under the proposed Kramer bill. He then insisted that the Liberty League had just as much right to have its views presented as anyone, even though he despised them.[19]

Maverick again attacked the disaffection law in the House on February 7, 1936, though the measure was not up for consideration. He told his colleagues, "I think the most fundamental thing for the country to know is that we do not approve of the Tydings-McCormack military disaffection bill. . . . These are peacetime sedition bills and are wholly unnecessary."[20]

Maverick could not have been more categorical about the permissible extent of freedom of expression than he was when he wrote that such guarantees were protected by the Constitution "with *no limitation and no exception.*" He said that he saw no limitations beyond the existing laws covering libel, slander, criminal conspiracy, treason, or "overt acts."[21] Though he seems to have never used the conventional expression "clear and present danger," he made a careful study and did some careful thinking about how far dissident political minorities could be permitted to go in their exercise of freedom of expression. He said that laws

Two Cowboys Are Better Than One 105

curbing their freedom were attempts to punish "constructive" treason as distinguished from actual treason and the fear of such laws was the reason for the adoption of a carefully drawn definition for treason in the Constitution. The provisions were designed, he said, "to prevent the adoption in this country of the doctrine of lese majesty—the chief characteristic of which has been said to be its 'juridic boundlessness.' "[22]

But what if the expression is an advocacy of overthrow of government? Maverick's argument was that *only* overt acts were subject to restraint. He said that the "general Anglo-American historical concept" was that there be no advance prohibition of any expression. Advocacy of the overthrow of government, "violent *talk, words*," was within the limitations of freedom; acts or criminal conspiracy, he said, "are all against the law NOW."[23] He presented the clearest delineation of his view and of the precise point at which words would become an offense, in a major address on March 4:

Now the reason advocacy is not made a crime, is because it is such a vague term. It is often confused with prophesy, with the expression of opinion and with hope. As such an utterance is entirely subjective, the law which cannot read what is in a man's mind, requires (in order that it be definite and clear) that it be accompanied by an overt act before it will punish the utterer. But, and this point cannot be emphasized too strongly, it does not punish the words, the speech—the advocacy, it punishes the act. If one "advocates" murder, unless some act is done in furtherance of the advocacy, or the people to whom were addressed the remarks do something about it, the utterer is guilty of no crime. But—get this—when the advocacy is such that anyone acts or makes the slightest move to carry out the suggestion, the one who causes it is clearly guilty with them, and responsible for their acts as an accessory.

For those persons who would ask why a virtually unlimited freedom of expression should be permitted in the area of dissident political expression, as well as all other areas, Maverick had an ample arsenal of answers. First, if one would accept the premise that democracy is "good" and desirable, Maverick would offer the logic that limitations of free expression are destructive of the meaning of democracy. He said, for example, "Communists have as little respect for free speech as they have for private property. Give them the power and they would abolish it forthwith. But democracy lives by the principle, and is under the obligation to assert it. Could there be a better demonstration of our confidence in our own philosophy and institutions.[24]

Maverick also warned of the dangers to all men of the prospective abuses inherent in the imprecise language of laws designed to curb dangerous utterances. For example, he singled out the word "advise," and explained that it meant "to view; observe; hence, to bring into view; consider, ponder, devise. To give advice to." In other words, a person could run afoul of this law by merely giving advice to another person that might lead him to disobey a law. After similarly treating words of the proposed disaffection measure such as "counsel," "urges," and "solicit," Maverick proceeded to support his argument with empirical evidence. He traced almost the entire history of sedition convictions and concluded that though such measures had been directed at those persons who advocate change by force and violence, they had been applied primarily to persons who had made relatively innocuous statements. For example, he said: "In the case of United States against Stokes, Rose Pastor Stokes was sentenced to 10 years in the Federal penitentiary for saying, 'I am for the people and the Government is for the profiteer.' Many of us have said worse than that.

"Here is what you would do, under the law proposed, to a Republican if he said the President is for communistic principles and putting us into bankruptcy. He (Mr. Maverick pointed to a Republican) would get 10 years for saying that. [Laughter]"[25]

Just as Maverick had begun his March 4 address, McCormack said that he did not have much hope that the disaffection bill would come up before the House. He reported that Secretary of War George H. Dern and the War Department were no longer supporting the legislation, and he sharply criticized Dern for having "shifted his position."[26] An earlier report of Dern's change of position stated that his original endorsement of the bill was "at the request of the Navy." He went on to say that there was no real danger from Communist literature and that suppression might only arouse curiosity—statements much like those advanced by Maverick in his attacks.[27]

On the same day, McCormack was still urging passage of the Kramer bill, which would make it a crime to urge or advocate overthrow of the government. In an exchange with him, Maverick restated his concept of the limits of free speech. He said, "Under our guaranty of freedom of speech one has a right to advocate the forceful overthrow of the Government. If anyone does anything about it, . . . however slight and be it ever so removed from the ultimate object . . . an overt act will have taken place and would be punished under laws on our statute books in existence for generations. Every conceivable danger to our Government is well covered now."[28] Despite a number of attempts, the Kramer bill was not cleared by the Rules Committee for floor discussion. The effectiveness of Maverick's opposition to this bill and the disaffection measure was indicated by the dozens of petitions against them received by the House Military Affairs Committee.[29]

Maverick's *bête noire* in this Congress was Representative Tom Blanton, a fellow Texan who supported most of the things Maverick opposed. Ten years after his first year in Congress, Maverick wrote in his own copy of the *Congressional Record* opposite Blanton's name, "A mean old bastard. I think this. Sept. 9, 1945—MM."[30] Blanton seemed to be intent upon putting this upstart freshman congressman in his place, but he picked the wrong man. In his major speech against the military disaffection bill and the Kramer bill, Maverick was chiding his colleagues for wasting time on personal attacks and the like. He said, "This kind of warfare is safe, for neither physical nor mental courage is needed, and all you need is lots of wind and good lungs," and he added that the Republicans had better sense than to get into intraparty squabbles. Blanton interrupted Maverick and made a slurring remark concerning Maverick's debt to his Mexican constituents, but the brash freshman cut Blanton off and said, "Now you gave me this time and you be quiet. I am going to answer that question. You gave me this time. Let me have it. I realize that the gentleman is going into the very thing I am talking about. He is trying to personally embarrass me. I want to tell you I have 90,000 Mexicans in my district and they are just as good as you are. [Laughter] They are decent American citizens. I do not consider that to be relevant to what I am talking about. I do not consider it fair in any way whatsoever."[31]

The next day Blanton tackled Maverick again. He had asked another member a question, but Blanton interrupted, gave the answer and then demanded the "regular order" when Maverick tried to protest. Maverick stormed back, "Mr. Chairman, I make a point of order. I asked a question according to parliamentary rules in a respectful and parliamentary manner. That was broken into by the gentleman from Texas [Mr. Blanton]. I did not push my question, but he broke into it. I am entitled to courtesy." Blanton interrupted again to say, "Mr. Chairman, that is not a point of order. I make a point of order." Maverick responded, "Just a minute. I am not through yet. Mr. Chairman, the gentlemen has no right to interrupt me. I am not going to be bullied off this floor. I am addressing the Chair, and I am not going to bullied off this floor." Blanton said no more, and Maverick made his point.[32]

Any threat to free expression that came to his attention was bound to bring Maverick into the controversy. While he was leading the struggle against the legislative threats early in 1936, he seized an opportunity to protest the banning of a "controversial" play in Washington. The Community Centre Department of the District of Columbia had banned the offering of a one-act play, *Private Hicks*, an antiwar drama by Albert Maltz. Maverick issued a sharp protest in which he said, "If a play doesn't cause 'controversial and acrimonious discussion,' it isn't worth listening to. . . . One of the complaints against the play was the language used by a soldier. Now does anybody think a soldier would say, 'Strike me pink! You must be illegitimate!' "[33]

In his fight against the military disaffection bill, Maverick advanced the thesis that the suppression or attempted suppression of printed material would bring about the opposite of the result desired. Greater attention would be attracted to the publications and this would bring about wider dissemination. The logical difficulty of such an argument is readily perceived. Let us, one might say, obtain the widest dissemination of ideas by suppressing them. But the idea is not as ridiculous as it may seem. Given a period of social and political unrest such as the 1930's, a system that offers any degree of facility of printing and distribution of literature, and a system that does not impose the severest penalties for violations, then the validity of the idea is apparent. Unless one is prepared to establish a complete and ruthless suppression, the approach is not a practical one.

Maverick could back up his point, at least to some degree, with empirical evidence. In April 1936 the Americanism Commission of the American Legion brought about the suppression, as far as its official endorsement was concerned, of a booklet on Americanism that had been prepared by the Americanism committee of the New York County American Legion organization.[34] Among the objections to the little book were such things as the use of "a cut that is supposed to resemble the American Legion emblem, and that done up in red rather than black or legitimate Legion color," and the use of a raised torch "with its striking similarity to the left wing socialist emblem."[35] When Maverick joined forces with the author and the New York Legion group to attempt to block the national Legion ban, the Texas congressman received requests for his House speech (which included the text of the booklet) from people throughout the United States, and one note came from Paris. The New York County Legion asked for one thousand copies, and O. Mykus Mehus, sociologist at Northwest Missouri State College, asked for five hundred copies.[36] As a result of the publicity, another publisher republished the booklet and Joseph V. McCabe, commander of the New York County American Legion group, reported that it was receiving wide distribution.[37] Thus it could be said, considering the printing in the *Congressional Record*, that the "suppressed" book received as much as ten times the attention that it normally would have.

The incident also furnished a prime example of Maverick's use of ridicule to fight suppression of publications. He wondered if the Legion objections to the flaming torch would lead it to sawing off the arm of the Statue of Liberty. Then, in a sardonic broadside, he wondered if the complaint against the "red" printing of the Legion symbol would result in the complete elimination of that color from American life. He then speculated as to the results of such a move:

Since red in itself is a sin, a logical dissertation on the effects is in order. If red should be entirely removed, however, there might be trouble. A study of the color red follows analytically for those who desire to be apprised of its evil character:

1. Congressman Sirovich, of New York, cannot wear his red carnation in the lapel of his coat. He will simply die. Florists will protest. . . .

3. Red wines prohibited. Discrimination as to white wines. No use

going to Italian restaurants. Grape growers will protest. People will get drunk, anyway.

4. Seeing "red" will also be abolished. In this many red baiters will suffer serious inhibitions and mental maladjustments.

5. Lure of the red-headed girls; handsomeness of red-headed boys to be eradicated by Federal law. Will cause importation of nonfading German dyes to make color of hair different. This will hurt "Buy American" campaign; besides, in this case, the importation will be a metamorphosis from communism to fascism.

6. Red herrings cannot be drawn across issues. This will also be a blow to red baiters. Old pals of Al Smith on Fulton Fish Market will protest. . . .

11. Red tape must be made blue; however, the change in colors will not affect red-tape psychology or human nature.

12. The high curtains in the Supreme Court, which are red, or near red, must be substituted at once. This would shock the Liberty Leaguers, the National Association of Manufacturers, and also the United States Chamber of Commerce, meeting in solemn conclave in this, our National Capital today.

13. Red ink will be abolished; and this is really good, for then there would be no depression. With only black ink the profit system would be assured ad infinitum.

14. Bulls will not get mad any more. This may cause serious difficulties in certain Latin American relations.[38]

Maverick did not spend all of his time merely meeting attacks on civil liberties; he devoted a major, though unsuccessful, effort to the passage of general civil-rights legislation that anticipated the successes of the 1960's. Maverick refused to accept the standard constitutional interpretation, derived from the *Civil Rights Cases*,[39] that the national government could not enforce a law providing protection of civil rights and civil liberties. He had begun to consider such a statute in 1934, but he did not pursue it actively until he received several prods from his friend, H. L. Mencken. In April 1935 Mencken told Maverick, "What we really need is a draconian statute making it a felony for any public official to violate the Constitution and especially the Bill of Rights. The day the first Federal judge was sent to Atlanta for neglecting the rights of citizens would be another 4th of July." Maverick said that he would make a trade; if Mencken would support Maverick's neutrality resolution then he would support an antilynching bill.[40] Mencken's

Two Cowboys Are Better Than One

rejoinder in this exchange of badinage was that he was astonished that such a man as Maverick was talking about a trade already. "I refuse absolutely," he said, but he would support a bill "penalizing violation of the Bill of Rights" for "a keg of beer down and another keg once a week."[41]

Apparently nothing more was said by either of the men until December 1936 when Mencken urged that Maverick seek either amendments to the Mann Act or its repeal, because it was "a fruitful source of blackmail," which "applies to simple fornications that are as free from white slavery as they are from piracy on the high seas." He then repeated his plea for an "act punishing violations of the Bill of Rights."[42] Maverick replied immediately, indicating that he was primarily interested in the Bill of Rights legislation. He said that he had been studying the matter for two years, but that he had been too busy and needed some professional help in drawing up such a statute.[43]

In little more than a week Mencken sent along his own draft of a civil-rights bill. He said that it probably violated "every article of the code for law drafters," but that the text of the measure was not so important. "There is very little chance that such a law will be passed the first time it is introduced. Almost any text will suffice to bring the business under debate, and so get some light on it." His proposal contained essentially these provisions:

1. Any person, including a public official of any government in the United States, who deprived a person of any rights and privileges guaranteed by the Constitution would be guilty of a felony.

2. It would be a felony to attempt or conspire to do the above.

3. "Mistaken understanding" or "excess of zeal" would not be a defense.

4. Those persons convicted under the law would be forever barred from holding office.

5. Negligence in enforcement of this act would be evidence for impeachment of officers "so subject."[44]

Maverick then enlisted the aid of the staff of the American Civil Liberties Union to assist him in drawing up a measure that could avoid constitutional pitfalls.[45] In order to get the matter before the House of Representatives as quickly as possible, he introduced a bill based on Mencken's draft. The essential difference was that violations had to be "willful," and an added provision was incorporated to require the Justice Department to investigate complaints and report to local Federal district attorneys, and to entitle offended persons to recovery of civil damages.[46] The measure met with virtually no support in Congress and Maverick became discouraged about its prospects. He had hoped to secure support of a measure that avoided the race question, but, if he wanted the support of the ACLU, it would have to be included.[47]

When Mencken asked Maverick to revive the bill in May 1938, he responded with a pessimistic statement about the "wide divergence of opinion" with respect to the interpretation of the Fourteenth Amendment and said that extremists wanted to "write a law which invites the colored cotton pickers into white people's drawing rooms." He told Mencken that any bill that gets into Jim Crowism was doomed and that the practical thing to do would be to confine the bill to the right of *all persons* to freedom of expression and procedural guarantees.[48] On this note the effort seemingly came to an end.

Consistent with his propensity for defending any type of underdog, Maverick endeared himself to many members of the Federal bureaucracy by championing them when they were under fire from congressional critics. Republican Representative Rich and others were attempting to make a major slash in appropriations for the Indian Bureau on the basis of contentions that there were bureaucratic abuses in the office. Maverick accused them of using "insinuation and innuendo" in "general and vague attacks" on the bureaucracy. He said that cutting the appropriations "without scientific consideration is just absolutely criminal foolishness." Maverick then proceeded to show how the facts had been distorted and urged that the amendment cutting Indian Bureau appropriations be defeated. It was, and Representative Rich apologized for his attack on the head of the bureau.[49]

On an earlier occasion Maverick demonstrated the consistency of his views with respect to free expression and elemental fairness to the opposition by defending the same Representative Rich, who had frequently tangled with him and who was then making the type of speech that Maverick deplored—railing at "Roosevelt the Socialist" and the like. Other Democrats objected to giving Rich more time when it had expired, but Maury persuaded them to give him more time and said, "That is fair; let him talk."[50]

Maverick ridiculed Republican attacks on brain trusters and charged that they were trying to find some of their own, "a new set of green academicians from north, south, east, west and from over the cuckoo's nest." He particularly defended Rexford G. Tugwell against criticisms of the Resettlement Administration activities. He said, "Tugwell has been mauled around so much that he sometimes snaps back. He would not be human if he did not. . . . He has learned to be a good administrator." Maverick argued further that all Americans should be proud of the work of the Resettlement Administration for "taking farm families off the dole and setting them up where they can make a respectable living."[51]

Maverick was strongly in favor of a law to regulate lobbyists when it came up in the Seventy-fourth Congress, because he said he came from a state where "the big corporations dominate" and "the lobbyists go unrestrained," but he objected strenuously to a proposed amendment to the measure that was designed to protect new congressmen from the influence of bureaucrats. He said, "Some gentlemen seem to think that the administrative branch of the United States Government are our enemies. . . . The answer is that we should cooperate with each other in giving people good government. Moreover, I consider myself intellectually able to withstand the political blandishments of a few men in any branch of the Government." When a colleague pointed out that speeches had been written for young members of Congress by bureaucrats, Maverick responded with a "why not," and added, "I have no contempt for knowledge and learning." He said he had used people in the bureaucracy so that he would know what he was talking about. The proposed amendment was defeated.[52]

In April 1936 Maury Maverick was given twenty minutes under special order of the House for a speech defending the WPA and PWA and Harold Ickes and Harry Hopkins, their administrators, against "unthinking criticism." He said that the criticism of brain trusters implied that it was "a sin to have knowledge, to know something, to have brains, to have been to college, or to have been a professor at one time; so the form of criticism which it takes is to make the same sort of banal, silly and idiotic statements which we have heard." The business community, he said, wanted "brainless, spineless people" in government.[53]

At the same time he was defending Ickes in Congress, Maverick took it upon himself to have a bit of sport with the "old curmudgeon" in an exchange with President Roosevelt:

17 April 1936

Dear Mr. President:

In days of old, young princes became famous for saving their King. My God. Ickes sent out a copy of your speech, which ended by saying that the celebration was a "good orgy." I caught it just as it was going to the printer, and I would not let my President have such words, but I found, of course, it was all Ickes' fault.

I immediately 'phoned the Department of Interior at six o'clock, and to my astonishment and shame, found Ickes had already left, and they said he would be back at seven. By seven-thirty that night he had not returned.

What would have happened if the word "orgy" had gone out to the public? I tremble with horror. If Ickes had not been out boon-doggling it would not have occurred. In fact, I understand that recently Ickes cut his work down from 18 to 16 hours a day, and boon-doggles every day for two hours.

I trust you will appreciate my correcting this error and will instruct Brother Ickes to quit boon-doggling.

Respectfully yours,
Maury Maverick

Roosevelt's return note was penned:

April 29, 1936

Personal

Dear Maury:

I thoroughly and completely disagree with you. If the public had known that at the corner-stone laying we all had "a good orgy" there would have been millions of votes in it. People love orgies. They don't give a continental about auguries. I suggest that Plank No. 1 of the Philadelphia Platform read as follows:

"We advocate bigger and better orgies."

I am speaking seriously to the Secretary of the Interior about cutting his work way down.

Run in and see me soon.

Always sincerely,
Franklin D. Roosevelt[54]

Ickes had written to Maverick a few days earlier to say that Roosevelt had told him that the Maverick letter was "the funniest he had ever received," and that he was sending it on to Ickes. The secretary of the interior said, "I suspect that when I read it I shall accuse you of being a plagiarist."[55]

"The Drama of Conservation" was the title Maury Maverick chose for a speech to the Virginia State Planning Board in May 1936. He told his audience that the natural resources of America were the "heritage of the whole nation," and, "I deny no man the right to his ambition, or his individuality. But I deny to every man in America any right to destroy his portion of the natural resources, or to so plan his business or industry as to be a danger to the health and lives of his fellow citizens."[56] The speech was a vehicle for a plea for Maverick's bill to establish a permanent National Resources Board to replace the existing National Resources Committee, which was based on an executive order. This agency was charged with the function of doing research concerning both natural and human resources in the United States and advising the president on the optimum use of such resources. Maverick called the agency one of the "finest organizations" of the New Deal.[57] It was first established as the National Planning Board in 1933 by Harold Ickes, head of the Public Works Administration. In 1934 it was made a presidential board, and then from 1935 to 1939 it was known as the National Resources Committee. Maverick's aim was to give the planning agency a more permanent status, and in a CBS network speech he said that he had a personal letter from FDR supporting the proposal.[58] Maverick was not successful, but his colleagues succeeded in establishing the National Resources Planning Board in 1939 after Maverick had left Congress.[59]

In March Maverick was characterized as a leader in conferences between members of Congress from southern states and federal officials to press for "economic rehabilitation of the South" by working for rural electrification and the Bankhead bill for loans to tenant farmers. Maverick said that the South had been exploited, but that the chief responsibility for remedying the conditions lay with the southern congressional representation.[60] When the Soil Conservation Act was under consideration, Maverick called for an amendment designed to require the secretary of agriculture to prescribe rules and regulations for equitable distribution of payments among tenants, sharecroppers, and farm workers as well as the landlords. He introduced information from Professor H. Clarence Nixon of Vanderbilt University and others of the Southern Policy Committee indicating that tenants and sharecroppers would be left out and benefits would go largely to the landlords. He later withdrew his amendment in favor of a similar one by Representative Tarver of Georgia.[61]

When legislation designed to make the Rural Electrification Administration an independent agency was before the House, Maverick urged its passage and gave his colleagues a learned lecture on rural electrification in Holland, Germany, Sweden, Canada, and Japan. He suggested that they should all read and study Marquis Child's "illuminating book on Sweden, which he aptly terms *The Middle Way.*" He also took the opportunity to thumb his nose at the private utilities that, according to him, "pretty well run the State of Texas." He added, "So far as utility legislation is concerned, we are probably the most primitive state in the United States of America."[62]

In January, Maverick had sent letters to members of the press asking for their ideas on the crucial issues of 1936 for use in a speech. The almost unanimous response was: "The reelection of Maverick."[63]

Maury's second congressional campaign opened with the announcement that his opponent in the Democratic primary would be Lamar Seeligson, former Bexar County district attorney and a machine candidate.[64] Maverick was to characterize him later as "a nice fellow and a schoolmate" who was a first cousin of John Dos Passos.[65] On the date of Seeligson's announcement, an article on Maverick appeared that hardly reflected the usual apprehensions of an incumbent representative facing his first attempt at reelection. Paul Y. Anderson quoted the "brilliant and promising young member of the House" as saying, "Well what did I find? I found that politics in Washington is no different than it is in Bexar County. There is the same trading, the same self-interest, the same pressure from minority groups, the same precinct psychology." Maverick added that great liberals had urged him not to stick his neck out, and thus he could be reelected. He said his response was, "I don't believe it is important to the liberal cause that I be reelected, but I know it is important to me that I say and do what I should."[66]

The indications are, however, that this was a bit of grandstanding on Maverick's part. He knew he was in for a tough campaign, and he set about doing something about it. In June he had several members of Congress prepare "plugs" for use in the coming campaign. Veteran Democratic Congressman A. J. Sabbath supplied: "I feel that if there is one member of Congress who merits renomination and reelection, it is you. I have been a member for nearly thirty years and I do not know of any new member of Congress during that time who has rendered as valuable services to the party and to the country as you have." Sabbath added a note saying, "I hurriedly dictated this. If you think it should be enlarged or changed in any particular, I will be glad to do it because I am sincere in my statement."[67]

Representative Herman P. Koppleman of Connecticut sent Maverick an unsolicited endorsement in which he said, "You have distinguished yourself as one of the outstanding liberals of the day with the added distinction that your liberal thought has sound foundation." Later he sent an editorial from the July 16 *Washington News* that read, "Maverick represents in a way, about the best type that comes to Washington. While mindful of the interests of his own district . . . he also is a national legislator. Few fought more effectively last session than he did in the causes of peace and neutrality, civil and religious liberty and freedom of speech. We hope to hear him answer the roll-call again in January."[68]

Senator Homer T. Bone used the privilege to extend his remarks in the *Congressional Record* to heap praise on Maverick's record as a first-term congressman. He pointed out that Maverick had been chosen Congressman of the Year by Drew Pearson and Robert S. Allen, listed a series of laudatory editorials, and said finally of Maverick, ". . . over 700 newspapers throughout the country commented favorably on his fight for civil, religious and academic liberties."[69]

A spot of trouble seemed to be in the making for Maverick when on March 16, 1936, Walter Tynan, former district attorney, Maverick's running mate on the 1930 Citizen's League slate, and a "power in the Citizens League Council," announced that he was supporting Seeligson. A few days later Tynan said he would support all of the League candidates except Maverick, after a split had developed in the League over the matter. The executive committee of the organization, however, endorsed Maverick and Tynan resigned.[70]

Maverick's fortunes took an upward turn in early June when he stood at President Roosevelt's side at the Alamo as thousands of San Antonians cheered. Roosevelt told newsmen that he felt "revived" by his visit to the city and that his reason for coming was that he had promised Maverick on several occasions that he would.[71] President Roosevelt wrote to Maverick later and expressed the "keenest delight" for his visit. He said, "I cannot restrain the impulse to write this note to tell you once more of the pleasure I derived from my trip into Texas and my visit to San Antonio."[72]

But a few days later Maverick learned that William F. Brogan, his campaign manager in his first congressional campaign, had accepted the position of campaign manager for Seeligson. Brogan had been closely associated with Maverick since 1929, had worked with him in the development of the Citizens League, and had served under Maverick for four years as head of the automobile license bureau of the county tax collectors office. Brogan gave as his reason for the break that he was no longer in accord with Maverick's "political views and some of his political associates." Maverick's succinct comment was, "Poor fellow."[73]

About the same time Maverick turned in desperation to other sources outside Texas for some help. He wrote to Tom Corcoran under the heading "personal and confidential" that Richard A. Tullis, director of the San Antonio division of the Federal Housing Administration, had come to Washington before the campaign and had agitated against him in the Texas delegation, saying that he was going to give Maverick "opposition from the Machine" and telling them that "nobody was for Maverick in Washington except that old bastard, Ickes." Now, Maverick said, Tullis was working with a "bunch here which is working up the money among oil men who are the enemies of the Administration, bitter enemies of Ickes and enemies of the President." He asked that Tullis be fired.[74] Three weeks later Corcoran wired, "Tullis resigned this morning. Tom." Drew Pearson wrote to Maverick, "Tom Corcoran tells me

Two Cowboys Are Better Than One 119

that he got Garner's nephew [an error, Tullis was not Garner's nephew] fired yesterday, and that the situation looks better."[75] The *San Antonio Evening News* simply reported that Tullis had resigned to campaign for Seeligson. In the scrapbook containing the clipping of this story, Mrs. Maverick heavily underlined the word "resigned" and wrote opposite it "Oh, Yeah!" and "Tut, Tut, Mr. Tullis."[76] Corcoran later wrote that he was sending some money for the campaign. He told Maverick he didn't see how he could lose and that Maverick should call "any time you need me."[77]

Maverick also had sought some help from his friend Ickes, but on June 29 Ickes wired, "Hoped until the last that I could somehow crawl under the tent but I have discovered no way," and pointed out that no member of the administration could take part in a primary contest.[78] Maverick indicated his concern by his somewhat angry response: "It would, of course, be crude for you to come and make a political speech for me in a primary, but any ordinary expression would certainly not be out of order. If I had asked you to do it in January you would have done it, so why not now? . . . As I said to you, nothing you can do will make me sore. You know the feeling that I have for you, and I am sure it's mutual. However, the attitude of "not taking part in the primary" is illogical and not according to any sensible rule."[79]

The secretary of the interior remained unmoved. His reply a week later read: "I appreciate the spirit in which you wrote your letter to me of June 30. The fact is that I am a member of the Administration, which means that I am a member of a team, so that I can't play solo. If I could I would. I really feel badly that I can't come to Texas to help you out because I want to do just that thing. I hope you will clean the other crowd up so that you will be in a position to thumb your nose at all of us who sat on the sidelines without lifting a hand to help the right kind of man when he was in a tight place."[80]

On July 9 Seeligson opened his campaign with charges that Maverick had opposed a bill that would "prevent any Tom, Dick and Harry from going about the country publicly advocating overthrow of the government by force and violence," which was true; and that Maverick had supported a bill that would permit the teaching of communism in the public schools, which was untrue.

He had opposed a law requiring teachers in the District of Columbia to sign an oath that they had not taught communism.[81] Seeligson concluded that Maverick was neither a Democrat nor a Republican and said that he should join William Lemke and Marion Zioncheck on the "Union Ticket."[82]

Two days later Seeligson again said that Maverick was a "Democrat in wolf's clothing," but he then provided Maverick with a piece of grist that he gleefully pounced upon. Seeligson said that Maverick lived in a brick house that was paid for, while he himself lived in a frame house that was not paid for.[83] Maverick said that his nervous supporters were worried, but he smugly assured them that he would make a "spectacular speech, destroying my opponent." In a speech at San Pedro Springs, Maverick made great sport of the brick-house charge in an exercise of self-confessed demagoguery. He asked how many persons in his audience would refuse to live in a good brick house, and when no one responded, he asked if it was all right for him to live in a brick house. They all agreed. Then he delivered the *coup de grâce*; his house was not brick but plaster. In his own words:

> Now, my fellow Americans, let us go into the matter. My statisticians and my great staff of brain-trusters have made a thorough study. My opponent lives three blocks from my house, much nearer the country club of which he is the revered vice-president, and in which great humanitarian institution I hope he will be appointed president, where he can get his promotion, so that I may return to Congress. (Mock interest shown by the audience.) But my statisticians have told me, fellow citizens, that my opponent has passed my house 7,862 times in the ten years he has lived near me. Every day as he passes my house (aside: for indeed it is a house where a sinner lives, since he aspires for office and he lives in a brick house) (laughter) he looks out. He looks at the plaster. He cranes his neck, like this. . . . And when he looks at the plaster, he sees brick, red brick, I presume.
>
> Now, my fellow citizens, I say to you that a man who has no better eyes than that, or that isn't smart enough to tell plaster from brick, hasn't got enough sense to go to Congress.[84]

In one of his major campaign speeches, Maverick made no effort to placate his critics, and he spoke with pride of his part in the defeat of the gag bills that would have limited free expression. In another Burkean thrust he said:

Two Cowboys Are Better Than One

I must follow two stars of duty, one, my country, and the other, my district. We must meet these problems, and silly talk about ladies not being allowed to carry flags—which is a lie anyway—and other puerile nonsense and bilge will get exactly nothing for the American people and not a single dime for Bexar County. . . .

No man who goes to Congress can use anybody else's head, brain or mouth. You must use your own eyes to see, and with those eyes you must have the power to observe, the power to see suffering, misery and hardship and to discern how to rectify it. . . . With your ears you must be able to hear, and with those ears you must transmit to both your heart and brain what is worth thinking about. . . . Congress is not a place for a man with a master. It is a place only for a man who is unfettered, free of the cogs of a machine, the leashes of his owners.[85]

But even Maverick was not candid enough to state publicly what he thought of the typical Texas campaigning that he had to do at this time. He complained to a friend of having to attend every barbecue that came along and having to subject his stomach to the punishment of Polish, German, and Mexican concoctions as he made the rounds in Bexar County. He lamented that much of campaigning in those hot, sweaty days was a test of how much barbecue you could eat and how many gallons of beer you could drink. On the brighter side, however, he was able to report in this communication to a friend that he had asked no one for money for the campaign and that contributions came to him from many parts of the United States.[86]

The campaign got rougher as it went on. The *San Antonio Light* reported on July 11 that an election investigating committee of the United States Senate was going to probe the padding of poll-tax lists in San Antonio. The *Light* said that the information came from authoritative sources, and that the move was seemingly designed to hurt Maverick and Senator Morris Sheppard,[87] but apparently nothing came of it. In fact, a few days later Maverick threw in some charges of his own. He said that the election had better be honest or "some G-Birds are going to fly over San Antonio and are going to put a bunch of thieves in the penitentiary if they don't watch out." At the same time he charged that Seeligson was a "big pal" of the Du Pont interests and that he had recently been conferring with the public relations director for Du Pont.[88]

Rodney Dutcher reported from Washington that utilities companies had Maverick marked for "political death" because of his work on the holding company bill. Dutcher said that Ralph W. Morrison, a Texas member of the Federal Reserve Board, was "reported to have expressed willingness to spend as much as $150,000 to defeat Maverick and is said already to have spent tens of thousands to elect Maverick's opponent in the primaries of July 25."[89] Five days before the election, Ruth Finney reported in the same newspaper that big business was out to get "a few outstanding spokesmen for the New Deal." She said that Representative Sam Rayburn and Maverick were among the marked men and repeated the estimate that much as $150,000 had been turned over to Morrison for the fight against Maverick.[90]

On the final canvass of returns for the July 25 first Democratic primary it was proved that Maverick's apprehensions were not groundless. He had 21,703 votes to Seeligson's 14,378, but R. S. Menefee, a third candidate, received 7,606 votes—Maverick lacked 281 votes of having the necessary majority for the Democratic nomination. He was relieved when Seeligson decided to withdraw from the runoff primary.[91] For all practical purposes, Maverick had retained his seat in the House of Representatives, but he could not afford to be too complacent in a district that was once part of a district that had elected a Republican representative for many years. Indeed, Maverick was to have some fairly strong Republican opposition in the general election.

Meanwhile, he was able to bask in the glow afforded by many messages of congratulations from across the nation. He was no doubt most pleased to receive this note:

Dear Maury:

Highly privately and extremely confidentially, I am told that I may send you my congratulations. (The etiquette arbiters who own Presidents would not let me publicly felicitate my own brother if he won a primary fight). You did a grand job and you can be of tremendous help in lots of states.

I am telling McDonald; Tullis no, West yes, and I will let you know what happens.

As ever yours,

Franklin D. Roosevelt[92]

Two Cowboys Are Better Than One 123

Maverick's success in the primary was applauded in newspaper editorials in many parts of the nation.[93] The *Baltimore Evening Sun* gave Texas "two cheers," one for the defeat of Congressman Blanton and one for the victory of Maverick, "a bold fellow with a sharp eye for reality and not much liking for hokum."[94] In Washington, Heywood Broun applauded Maverick's success and said that he was one of the few genuine liberals in that city.[95]

The evidence does not indicate that Maverick was called upon to render the help in the presidential campaign of which Roosevelt spoke in his letter of congratulation. Maverick wrote to James A. Farley, chairman of the Democratic National Committee, and gave him a prod on the matter. Farley assured the Texas representative that there were many places in the country where he could be of help and that he would be called upon for "real service."[96] But Farley and others had misgivings about Maverick's party regularity and his generally volatile nature. Whether the fears were justified or not, they were there. Maury had organized and worked with the Mavericks, he had expressed concern as to whether the New Deal was moving ahead as rapidly as it should,[97] and he was at this very time engaged in activities that would make the regulars nervous.

Sometime shortly after his primary victory, he received a penciled note of congratulation from Jerome Frank, who spoke of "a combination (after FDR is elected) of Bob La Follette and John Lewis as head of a farmer-labor group to begin things and get ready for 1938."[98] A month or so later and two months before the presidential election, Maverick attended a meeting of the National Conference of Progressives in Chicago, which held a four-hour secret session. Among the 116 Democrats, Republicans, Progressives, and Farmer-Laborites there were Senators Norris, La Follette, Edward F. Costigan, Hugo L. Black (the only other Southern Democrat in attendance), and Elmer Benson. Other leading figures were John L. Lewis, Sidney Hillman, Governor Phillip F. La Follette, Governor Hjalmar Petersen, and Mayor Fiorello H. LaGuardia. Maverick was chairman of the committee of the organization that drafted a telegram to FDR, assuring him of the support of the group.[99] Assurances aside, it was obvious that there was some cause for alarm among professional politicians, who probably remembered a report in 1935 of a meeting behind closed doors of "liberal groups" in and out of Congress "for the avowed purpose of formulating left wing policies on which perhaps a third or fusion party might be created for the 1936 election." Maverick did not participate in the latter meeting, but his close association with such people and such movements made him somewhat suspect.[100]

On the home front Maverick continued to seize every opportunity to jump into civil liberties controversies. He gained more national publicity when he joined a fray at the University of Texas concerning the censorship of the student newspaper, the *Daily Texan*, for which he had written in his student days.

At a meeting in Austin, July 27, 1936, the Board of Regents of the university added to its *Rules and Regulations* the establishment of an Editorial Advisory Committee for university publications and directed the committee to employ "an agent" to examine each issue of the *Texan* to guard against not only libelous statements but also "improper personal attacks, reckless accusations, opinion not based on fact, inaccurate statements, articles of national, state and local political questions, indecencies, material detrimental to the good conduct of the student body, and material prejudicial to the best interests of the University and any material in conflict with good taste or wise editorial management." Texan editor Ed Hodge was called to President H. Y. Benedict's office the next day, without having had any previous warning or reprimand, and told of the regents' decision. When Hodge asked what it was all about, Benedict's reply was, "Surely it was not unexpected." He explained that the *Texan* was not a regular newspaper, but an annex to the university. "We don't want the University to suffer when the paper forgets this," he said. Benedict also told Hodge that the paper should not be a "political journal of opinion." A few days later President Benedict told the *Austin Statesman* that the university wanted to give "all freedom possible. But we don't believe this freedom entitles the students to run a political newspaper."[101]

Hodge had assumed the editorship of the *Texan* on June 4, 1936, and he soon began writing strongly pro-FDR, pro–New Deal editorials. Probably the first editorial that caught the eye of the power

Two Cowboys Are Better Than One 125

structure of Texas appeared on June 21; it was based on an article written for *Nation* magazine by Maury Maverick. The editorial, "Pea Game Flourishes While Texas Is Choked," supported Maverick's thesis that the states of the South were struggling upward but that the people were being hoodwinked into the "old pea game, and the operator of the pea game with his smooth talk is the lobbyist of the special interests." Texans were "suckers" who were being used by the utilities interests, and there should be an adequate tax on Texas sulphur production to support the educational system. In a few days this final note inspired Hodge to write another editorial applauding an investigation of the Texas Gulf Sulphur Company's reported assets for the 1936 tax assessment.

Hodge was already stomping on some pretty sensitive toes, but he committed near-sacrilege in an editorial on July 9 in which he supported an investigation of the Austin-area Lower Colorado River Authority concerning allegations of pork-barrel deals and graft, involving the United States representative from that district, James P. Buchanan, who was chairman of the House Appropriations Committee. Hodge said that there should be probes into such allegations regardless of whether the people were on "our side" politically—a view shared by Maury Maverick.[102]

As soon as Maverick learned of the censorship he wired Hodge and urged him to make a "stiff fight," and then wrote to Benedict that, though they were long-time friends, this incident was the "most serious detriment the University has received in many years. It is on a par with the persecution you received several years ago." Maverick urged that the "illegal," "unconstitutional," and "unwise" action should be canceled. He directed similar communications to the veteran chairman of the Board of Regents, Lutcher Stark, and to Governor James V. Allred. He suggested to Dr. Robert Maynard Hutchins, president of the University of Chicago, that the matter should be taken up by national academic organizations and told Dr. J. W. Studebaker, national commissioner of education, "You have no jurisdiction in this matter, but for moral influence I am informing you of the situation."[103]

On August 3, 1936, Hodge received a call from Maverick advising him that he was coming down to Austin to make his own investigation and to see what could be done about the matter. Newsmen met the "square-jawed champion of civil liberties" when he arrived at the university the next day. Hodge reported that Maverick "snorted and frowned, barking charges and threats about the Board of Regents and all parties concerned." Among other things, he said that the regents were "nazifying the University. Their ukase sounds almost exactly like the press decrees of Hitler, Communist Russia and Fascist Italy." He concluded, "For the University to censor the *Daily Texan* in such a manner is for a father to choke his child. It is knowledge using its powers to destroy itself."[104]

The news of Maverick's blast spread over the state and the nation, and many editorials condemning the action began to appear. On August 8 the Intercity Council of the ex-students association, representing twenty-one Texas communities, including most of the large cities in the state, condemned the censorship. As time dragged on with no action by the regents and a refusal by Governor Allred to intervene, the *Texan* confined itself to such editorials as a tongue-in-cheek "Keep Off the Grass (A Model Editorial)," and the *Columbia* (University) *Spectator* sadly commented that the *Texan* had become "spineless and lifeless"—"typical of a shackled press."[105]

In the waning months of 1936, student groups worked out a compromise proposal that was adopted unanimously by the student assembly on December 10, but the regents remained unmoved. A few days later Chairman Stark voiced his concern with the hiring of a "big time" coach for the university and expressed his disapproval of President Benedict's view that the coach should not be paid more than the highest paid professor. The *Texan* carried in almost every issue a small standing editorial feature, "Which Is the American Way?" consisting of a quotation from the regulations of the University of Wisconsin concerning student newspapers. That is, a university ". . . should encourage the continual and fearless sifting and winnowing by which the truth can be found." Maverick played no further direct role in this controversy, but there seems to be little question that he could take some credit when the Board of Regents finally decided on March 7, 1937, to repeal the censorship regulation. Effective June 1, 1937, the *Texan* began to operate under a regulation stating merely that the editors should not "violate editorial propriety."[106]

Two Cowboys Are Better Than One

San Antonio was also the scene of a storm of protest from Maverick in 1936, when Herman G. Nami, district commander of the American Legion, tried to prevent Professor Robert M. Lovett of the University of Chicago and the Reverend James W. Workman of the Methodist Episcopal Church in Fayetteville, Arkansas, from speaking at San Antonio's Thomas Jefferson High School. Maverick said that he did not know the men, but that it was "ridiculous" and "childish" to bar them from speaking to the students. Nami had said that the speakers had "Communistic tendencies" and made references to their "records," but produced nothing definite. Superintendent J. C. Cochran had at first closed the auditorium to the two speakers, but Maverick was able to effect a compromise by which the two were permitted to speak at Wheatley High School, but students were not required to attend. Maverick introduced the speakers.[107] The speeches were pleas for neutrality and peace, and Dr. Lovett was quoted as saying, "Big business must pay the price if peace is to be maintained." Nami said, "The emergency peace campaign is just another plan of subversive activity," and, "My organization is against those birds." San Antonio Rabbi Ephraim Frisch called the charges "absurd."[108]

A week later Maverick was in Houston, where the same speakers had been banned. In announcing his forthcoming speech to the Houston Open Forum, the *Houston Post* told Houstonians that they were in for a "rare intellectual treat" from the "dynamic San Antonio congressman who has become a national figure." Though a "bit spectacular, . . . he is considered by his colleagues at Washington one of the ablest and most substantial members of the Texas Congressional delegation," the *Post* editorialized.[109] In his remarks, Maverick ridiculed those persons who had blocked the appearance of the speakers and told Houston citizens that when free speech was threatened, they should "stand up on their hind legs and raise hell." He also said that the Texas Legislature's conduct of a Red hunt was "the silliest thing I ever heard of." In an aside, Maverick told his Houston audience that President Roosevelt would easily defeat Governor Alfred Landon in the November election. He said that Landon was one of the weakest candidates that the Republicans had ever offered and predicted that FDR would carry at least thirty-five states.[110]

Maverick was not without his own problems in the November

general election. He had a vigorous and articulate Republican opponent, Ernest W. Clemens, a San Antonio attorney. Clemens won the support of a group of "Jeffersonian Democrats," one of whose major speakers was R. J. Boyle, who had been associated with Maverick in the old Citizens League. Boyle said that he was concerned about the trend toward "Socialism" in the New Deal programs.[111] Maverick was not in serious trouble, but regular Democrats were worried about a close race. Mayor C. K. Quin, normally a political enemy of Maverick, joined him to resist the Republican threat in Bexar County. Maverick urged a heavy vote so that "John Nance Garner won't say, 'What the hell is the matter with Bexar County.' "[112]

Clemens hammered away at Maverick's association with radical groups, his speeches in Congress and articles in "various radical magazines," and his unwillingness to express similar views at home. R. W. B. Terrell, speaking for a group known as the Constitution League, attacked Maverick for his association with the American Civil Liberties Union, which he characterized as "closely affiliated with the communistic movement in this country."[113]

At a major rally at Woodlawn Lake, featuring a six-ton elephant named Vera, Clemens ripped into the Tennessee Valley Authority and Maverick's association with it. He said that the TVA town of Norris, Tennessee, had no church, that in the regimented life there "a top sergeant tells them when to get up, and a corporal tells them when to go to bed. They can send their children to the government school to learn radical new deal doctrines, or not at all!" Maverick was said to consider this to be the ideal American town.[114]

The same day Secretary of War Harry Woodring made a speech in San Antonio urging the election of Maverick, and Maury told the crowd, "Turn out a large Democratic victory in Bexar County, and let me tell old man John Garner about it, and I will get you something for San Antonio."[115] Maverick defeated Clemens by a vote of almost three to one (34,478 to 12,056), but he was still about one thousand votes shy of Roosevelt's majority, and the issues and forces that arose in this campaign were to prove his undoing in the next.[116]

A letter of congratulation on his victory provided Maverick with an opportunity to have some private sport at the expense of Harvard law professor and FDR adviser Felix Frankfurter. In a handwritten note, Frankfurter said: "You certainly licked them. Of course you had a hard fight—but I feel you wouldn't want to win an easy battle. We need you badly in Washington—'We' means the country." The writing was almost indecipherable, and Maverick typed on the back of the letter that "secretaries and several handwriting experts attempted to decipher the handwriting to no avail." He then wrote beneath the statement, "I certify the above is correct. Maury Maverick, M.C."[117]

Maverick spent the rest of the year making speeches in Texas and the Southwest. He was the major speaker at the New Mexico Government and Business Conference at the University of New Mexico, December 1, 1936. In a lengthy interview after the speech, he blasted away at a number of sacred cows, including states' rights and the recent "Red hunt" at the University of Texas, which he said was instigated by a group of corporation and utility lawyers who wanted to oust several professors advocating fair regulation of utilities.[118] Most of the focus of this investigation was turned on economics professor Robert H. Montgomery, who was the key organizer of a student-faculty group called the Progressive Democrats. Montgomery and Maverick were friends, and Maverick was singled out as one of the people who had corresponded with this group, which was supposed to have principles that were basically communistic—according to the "Red hunters." In retrospect, Dr. Montgomery's chief offenses seem to have been that he knew what he was talking about when he criticized utility rates and the sulphur industry, and that he produced affidavits linking the investigation to a representative of the sulphur interests. The embarrassed Texas House committee, especially after finding that two of its members were using letters in the investigation that were almost certainly stolen from an ex-student of the university, dropped the entire inquiry and gave the university faculty a vote of confidence.[119]

Maverick capped his second year as a congressman by writing the kickoff article of a series entitled "The Next Four Years," for *New Republic* magazine. Subsequent articles in the series were written by Henry A. Wallace, Rexford Tugwell, Morris L. Cooke, John L. Lewis, Dr. Arthur E. Morgan, Thomas Reed Powell, Bruce Bliven, and George Soule. In his piece, Maverick said that the 1936 election was "the greatest revolution in our political history." He warned that the next session of Congress would see further efforts in behalf of bizarre—and dangerous—legislation that would threaten civil liberties. "Liberals and conservatives alike," he said, "should take the offensive for the Bill of Rights."[120]

Ever Insurgent Let Me Be

THERE WAS NO LETUP in the furious pace that the man who had been described as "a Texas norther in Congress"[1] set for himself in his second term in the House of Representatives. He was one of the most sought-after speakers in the country, and he was rarely able to decline invitations to appear at all sorts of speaking or discussion engagements. When he wasn't making speeches on the floor of the House, he was preparing articles for magazines or, as was the case in 1937, writing a book. He worked from twelve to fourteen hours a day, read voluminously and caused observers to wonder how he managed to keep going.[2]

Early in this second term Maverick had the following poem by Louis Untermeyer reprinted in the *Record* without comment:

PRAYER

God, though this life is but a wraith,
   Although we know not what we use,
Although we grope with little faith,
   Give me the heart to fight—and lose.

Ever insurgent let me be,
   Make me more daring than devout;

From sleek contentment keep me free,
And fill me with a buoyant doubt.
Open my eyes to visions girt
with beauty and wonder lit—
But let me always see the dirt
And all that spawn and die in it.
Open my ears to music; let
Me thrill with spring's first flutes and drums—
But never let me dare forget
The bitter ballads of the slums.
From compromise and things half done,
Keep me, with stern and stubborn pride,
And when at last the fight is won,
God, keep me still unsatisfied.[3]

Maverick did not like to lose, but he seemed to relish the unpopular fight, and he rarely felt uncomfortable as a member of the minority. When he read this poem into the *Record*, he was committed to the "wrong" side of one of the most bitter controversies of the New Deal era.

The most celebrated issue of the 1937 session of Congress was President Roosevelt's attempt to "pack" the United States Supreme Court. In February 1936 Maury Maverick had opened his long series of challenges to the Court's power to find acts of Congress unconstitutional, in response to the Court's decision that the first Agricultural Adjustment Act was unconstitutional, partly because the law violated states' rights.[4] In urging passage of the 1936 Soil Conservation Act, Maverick had said that though he realized that the argument was now academic, he believed that the first AAA had been constitutional. There was no implied power for the Supreme Court to declare acts of Congress unconstitutional, he maintained, and Congress could do what was not prohibited to it. That the Supreme Court should not bow to the "will of mobs, or temporary prejudices and passions" he recognized, but he also asserted that the Court should acknowledge "progress in the affairs of men."[5]

With the passage of time and more New Deal legislation being struck down or threatened in the courts, Maverick's criticisms became more pointed and his judgments more harsh. He told a Philadelphia audience a few weeks later: "The judges of the Supreme

Ever Insurgent Let Me Be 133

Court are human beings like you and me. If a member of this audience were appointed to the Supreme Court, his political viewpoint would probably not change at all; he would take his political viewpoints with him to the Supreme Court, just as the corporation lawyers who go there take their views with them. And remember, though courts are a necessary function of any government, times change, views change, and people have a right to adjust their own government to their own will."[6]

When Maverick was queried later in the year as to what he would propose for dealing with the Supreme Court, he said that he did not favor increasing the number of justices. "We are not being honest if we do this," he was quoted as saying. Rather, he preferred the approach of attaching provisions to major legislation, such as the proposed minimum-wage law, which would prohibit the Supreme Court from having appellate jurisdiction over that particular matter—the device advocated by equally unsuccessful critics of the Court in the late 1950's.[7]

When Congress convened in January, there were reports of an anti-Court bloc meeting in Washington in which Maverick participated with Senator Norris, John L. Lewis, Jerome Frank, Morris Ernst, Representative David J. Lewis (D.-Md.), and Frank R. McNinch, chairman of the Federal Power Commission.[8] Soon thereafter Maverick was questioning his solution to the problem. In a national radio speech, prepared with the assistance of Frank, he attempted to explain to the nation how the solution of many problems that were national in scope was being thwarted by rulings of the Supreme Court, and, after quoting Justice Harlan Stone as saying, "The Court gives effect to the economic predilections of the judges," Maverick admitted, "Just how we are going to get the judges out of their prejudices and predilections is far from clear."[9] He received hundreds of letters offering praise, advice, and criticism from lawyers and judges in all parts of the nation. About 90 percent of the letters were favorable to his position.

Other New Dealers, including FDR, had had their difficulties in deciding just what could be done about the Court,[10] but on February 5, 1937, Roosevelt sent his famous message to Congress. As Maverick described the scene, some fifty or sixty House members were on hand at the time, there was no air of tension, and the galleries were nearly empty. Only the occupants of the press gallery, who had advance notice of the president's message, seemed interested. According to Maverick, the telegraph companies in back of the gallery were "getting ready for a killing." He said they had ordered extra messengers to handle the "flood of exultation and execration" that would soon be on the wires. "The clerk, who has read thousands of messages, begins to read. A few representatives begin to listen. What's this?"[11]

"This" was Roosevelt's general proposal for reform of the Federal judiciary, which included the specific suggestion that the president could appoint additional Federal judges for each judge who failed to retire upon reaching the age of seventy, thus providing Roosevelt with the opportunity to swing the narrowly divided Supreme Court over to the New Deal side if the measure should be passed. Though the *Washington Star* depicted Democratic leaders as "stunned" by the proposal,[12] this seems unlikely in view of the fact that FDR had explained the bill to a meeting of leaders before presenting his message.[13] Whatever the case, Maverick "grabbed a mimeographed copy of the bill, scribbled his name on it, and threw it in the bill hopper."[14] Despite the fact that many Democrats in the Senate were reported to favor the move and legislative leaders generally predicted a hard-won victory, the quixotic Maverick had again taken a stand that was not likely to do him much good back home.

The Texas Senate passed a resolution against the measure, and Maverick told the body to mind its own business. He said, "I want it understood that I don't consider myself bound by the Senate of Texas even if their action is approved in Maine.... It may be the Senate of Texas will get down to attending to their own business and will take the responsibility of passing a good utilities law for that state, and take the crushing burden of taxation off the backs of the people of Texas, they will be better off."[15]

The San Antonio Bar Association overwhelmingly opposed the president's court plan. The association refused by a voice vote even to listen to a reading of the bill by H. P. Drought, state administrator for the WPA and "a prominent member of the bar." The leadership characterized the measure as "radical and dangerous" and then adjourned to head off any debate on the matter.[16] Maverick gave his Bar Association fellows a blunt reply in which he said that

Ever Insurgent Let Me Be 135

he didn't think that any of them had read the bill and that he would continue to fight for the measure and "look forward and not backward." "In doing so, I will be doing my duty, and consider myself as performing the best service for the people of my district and their children."[17]

A few days after he had introduced the president's proposal, Maverick and Senator Hugo L. Black appeared on the NBC Blue network radio program "Town Meeting of the Air" to debate the proposal with William H. King and Frederick H. Wood, the winning attorney in the NRA, Guffey coal, and Gold Clause cases. Maverick led off the discussion with the argument that the checks on the Supreme Court were inadequate for the occasion and that the framers of the Constitution had left the determination of the number of justices to the Congress and the president in order to provide adequate checks when they were needed. Maverick argued that the older justices would retire if they followed the best opinion of their own profession, and he cited historical examples to demonstrate that changes in the number of members of the Supreme Court had been made several times before. He also pointed out that since interpretation of the Constitution varies with the changes in the personnel of the Court, presidents and Senates have always concerned themselves with the general attitudes of men appointed to the Court. He concluded, "Such considerations are thoroughly moral, and thoroughly constitutional. And our traditions—largely established by Republican presidents—sanction it."[18] Again, Maverick may have been winning an argument, but he was not winning enough votes.

On February 19 he was reported to be a member of a seven-man steering committee of a twenty-seven–man special House Judiciary Reform Group.[19] Though he continued to make speeches in behalf of the measure through the next few months, the Southern Democrats prevented it from coming to the floor in the House. Despite the dim prospects, Maverick doggedly pursued the objective, and in May, when young Lyndon B. Johnson was sworn in to fill the seat from the Tenth Texas District, Maverick shouted, "Mr. Speaker, the gentleman just sworn in, Mr. Lyndon Johnson, supported the President's judiciary plan and was overwhelmingly elected."[20]

When the Senate Judiciary Committee reported unfavorably on

the bill on June 14 and Senate Majority Leader Joseph T. Robinson died the same day, the measure was for all practical purposes abandoned.

Though the Supreme Court soon began to sustain New Deal measures, and older members died or resigned, Maverick's enthusiasm was at best guarded. He continued to urge that the Supreme Court should "withdraw from the economic and legislative fields and confine itself to the protection of liberties of the people."[21] In a similar vein he wrote: "The reason I say this is that I believe this country is passing through a major institutional and constitutional phase, just as England has passed through several such major phases in its history. I do not pretend to give any absolute chart of what the future evolution should be; but I am quite certain that the Supreme Court should withdraw, or be forced to withdraw, from the field of legislative policy. That they should ever have declared the Agricultural Adjustment Act unconstitutional will someday be considered fantastic."[22]

Maverick himself reported that the story in Washington was that several senators had politely advised members of the Supreme Court that they had best change some of their opinions or the Court "would surely get packed." Though he would not vouch for such stories, Maverick noted that changes had taken place, and the president's fight had seemingly been won. On the other hand, he continued to have misgivings in 1939. He argued that the question had not been settled and that it should be. He wrote, "Therefore, the issue will inevitably bob up again. As the public forgets, the judges may change their opinions again, enter the field of legislation, and declare laws unconstitutional merely because they do not like them."[23]

Maverick should not be misunderstood. He opposed, almost exclusively, the power of the Court to find social and economic policies unconstitutional. When critics expressed fears that Congress would override personal liberties, Maverick said that he shared their fears, but then explained that in the first place the Court had been of little help: "The answer is . . . if you look at the cases on sedition, espionage and the rest, that the courts declared pretty nearly every silly law constitutional during and following the World War. There was not much protection of civil liberties in this country. . . . You might take the trouble to study the judicial system of England where no such powers are exercised and where the judiciary is held in equal if not superior respect to the judiciary of our country."[24]

Indeed, Maverick's argument was that the Supreme Court should confine itself to enforcing the "specific prohibitions" against violations of civil liberties. There were no such prohibitions, he said, *"against making legislation for economic and social ends."*[25] The Court should be the final arbiter of questions involving the "arbitrary use either of government or *private* power, for the protection of individuals." Striking down laws for "health, hours of labor, safety, unemployment insurance and Social Security" often "reverses the purpose of the Constitution." He concluded with the prediction that the Court's invalidating of laws regulating business in the public interest, under the guise of protecting individual rights or states' rights, would one day be looked upon as "an example of the curious perversions of logic of the Middle Ages."[26] Thus Maverick, in 1937, essentially anticipated the argument presented by two constitutional scholars who wrote in 1959: "It is still relevant to ask whether a politically irresponsible body, such as the Supreme Court, can block the will of the majority in the name of minorities and still remain a democratic institution. When the minority rights protected are those of property, the answer is probably 'no.' Between 1890 and 1937, the Supreme Court actually retarded the growth of democracy. When, on the other hand, judicial review serves to give a minority, otherwise barred, access to the political process, it implements rather than limits free government."[27]

In a speech in Boston in April, Maverick gave a detailed examination of all cases in which the Supreme Court had reviewed legislation that threatened or denied civil liberties. After the recital he said, "There is not a single case on record of the High Court knocking out a Federal law, or declaring it unconstitutional, on a basis of its violating civil and religious liberties."[28] In concluding his speech, Maverick indicated that he was not too sanguine about the prospects for passage of the Court reorganization bill by giving three things that he thought the "present controversy" would accomplish: first, it would "inform the American mind" and eliminate the tendency to make a taboo of the Supreme Court; second, it would remove from the judge's mind "his own taboo that he can settle social problems with pen and ink"; and third, "the Court will cease to become a super-Congress and a super-President, and will confine itself to judicial duties."[29] As Maverick defined the duties of the Supreme Court, this is essentially what has occurred.

In addition to the general civil rights measure that he had been working with for two years,[30] Maverick somehow found the time to fight a number of other battles in his personal war on behalf of civil rights and civil liberties. He had an early baptism in the struggle against loyalty oaths, which were to create such a furor in the 1950's. His encounter with what became known as the "red rider" began in 1935. The appropriation bill for the District of Columbia slipped through the House with such a provision that went unnoticed, though it was read by the clerk. This section of the bill stated that no money could be paid to persons who taught or advocated communism. In pursuance of this section, the comptroller general prescribed an oath to be taken by teachers on each pay day to ensure compliance with the terms of the law.[31]

Early in November 1935, before much notice had been given to the "red rider," Maverick sought the help of the Legislative Reference Service in the Library of Congress with some research into the matter.[32] He built up a file of materials against such a requirement and wrote letters to anyone who could help him to fight it.[33] The *New York Herald Tribune* soon lashed out editorially at this piece of "intellectual lynching" that had, the paper said, put an "appropriate seal of imbecility upon all this sort of heresy-hunting legislation."[34] At his first opportunity, Maverick demonstrated the "sense of strategy" and "canny estimate of the weak spots in the opposition" that Roger Baldwin had attributed to him in a speech to the Press Association of Virginia on January 17, 1936.[35] In this talk, which Maverick had printed in the *Congressional Record*, he adopted the practical approach of questioning the efficacy of oaths. He pointed out to his audience that our Revolutionary War leaders had taken oaths to support the king of England, that his own grandfather (Sam Maverick) had been pardoned for treason against the United States, and that Robert E. Lee had spent "40 years on the payroll of the United States," and had then "revolted!" He used these audacious, shrewdly chosen reminders to

Ever Insurgent Let Me Be

illustrate his sweeping contention that "oaths make no difference whatever" when it comes to maintaining loyalty.[36]

When the "red rider" was mentioned in debate on May 4, 1936, Maverick gave a scathing denunciation in which he said that he could not find an instance in the history of the world in which a person had to give "oath after oath that one has kept an oath. No parallel to 'red rider,' even in nations where liberty does not exist or in the most benighted nations on earth, can be found."[37] Maverick's chief opponent in his efforts to repeal the "red rider" was his enemy, Texas Representative Tom Blanton, and it was predicted that Blanton would use every parliamentary maneuver to block repeal efforts.[38] But Maverick did not have to worry about Blanton. When the time came to consider the District of Columbia appropriation measure in 1937, Blanton had been defeated in the 1936 primary.

Though Maverick might have been expected to introduce the measure to repeal the "red rider," the explanation as to why he did not was to be found in his letter to the *Baltimore Sun* saying that, though he would have been glad to do so, Representative Ambrose J. Kennedy of Maryland would introduce such a bill. Maverick said that Kennedy was "unassuming" and did not get much publicity, but that he should and this was his opportunity. Maverick said further: "In my district it was made an issue. I was accused of permitting the teaching of communism, and people paid no attention to it whatever. Inasmuch as the issue has been presented to my people, and they are ordinary, average Americans, it would seem to me that it more or less represents a mandate that the bill be repealed.... I suggest you call up Mr. Kennedy, because he is not given much to making statements unless they are pulled out of him."[39] In view of the fact that Maverick repeatedly denounced the "red rider," and no one would have ever accused him of being bashful, it would appear that he was genuinely interested in boosting a like-minded colleague.

The measure (H.R. 148) did not reach the floor of the House until February 8, 1937. Maury used this occasion to attack "fake, racketeering organizations in Washington" that had supported the oath requirement. He said, "You don't have to join a club or society that professes moral uplift or patriotism to be decent or patriotic."

He belonged to the Sons of the American Revolution himself, but he did not consider this fact to be of any relevance in questions of loyalty. The oath requirement, he told his colleagues, was "the most barbaric law that was ever instituted in the mind of man," and that if they did not vote to defeat it they would be "adopting the principles of communism and fascism to show that we are a democracy." The oath requirement was repealed,[40] but Maverick was not satisfied until he saw the final passage of the appropriations measure when it came from conference on May 24 without a "red rider" provision.[41]

Maury Maverick amazed and enraged Southern representatives and delighted northern liberals when, at the opening of his second term in Congress, he announced that he was strongly in favor of an antilynching law. The *New York Enquirer* called his stand a "commendable" one,[42] and the *Boston Chronicle* hailed him as one of the "enlightened minds of the South."[43] The *Amsterdam* (New York City) *News* featured an editorial cartoon depicting Maverick in cowboy garb putting the match to a trash can labeled "age-old lynch law."[44]

When the Gavagan Anti-Lynch bill came before the House in April, Maverick not only announced that he was going to vote for the measure, but he also made a lengthy speech in support of it. He told his colleagues that he did not expect to get any Negro votes as a result of his stand. "In my district the colored people do not vote (in the primary), and if they did they would probably vote against me. . . . I am doing it because I think it is right, and because it will take a stigma from the escutcheon of the United States of America." He argued that the measure was needed for all Americans, not merely Negroes. Then, after giving his fellow Congressmen a scholarly discourse on the history of slavery and the causes of the Civil War, he concluded, "Whereas we speak of States' rights and the Constitution, we must know that the Constitution was written by the people for all the people of the United States. We want everyone to get decent treatment. We want the Negro to have economic justice just as much as we want the white man to have justice."[45] Many years later he revealed that one of the authors of the bill told him at the time, "Vote against it—don't be a fool. (I represent Harlem)."[46]

Virginius Dabney hailed Maverick as courageous, the only

Ever Insurgent Let Me Be 141

Southern Democrat who voted for the measure as it went down to defeat by a vote of 277 to 119,[47] but Maverick later told an audience that it was not a matter of bravery—that he received only seven letters as a result of his action, one from a friend, "a colored mail clerk." He candidly stated that he did not think that the measure was workable and that he voted for the bill "as a gesture."[48] He then urged that his general civil rights measure would be more effective in dealing with the problem.[49] As he said in his first book: "It is then apparent that an act must be made to cover the whole subject of constitutional civil liberties. It should guarantee that no man, White or Negro, shall be lynched, or beaten to death by rangers, local police, sheriffs or 'special officers.' And we must have not merely a regional or state interpretation of the Constitution, but a national one. A right is a right, whether that citizen is blue, green, lavender, or even yellow."[50]

While he was fighting the "red rider" and supporting an antilynch bill, Maverick was also determined to head off the establishment of a Committee on Un-American Activities. While others questioned the legitimacy of purpose from the standpoint of the amount of legislation that such investigations had produced in the past, Maverick bluntly charged:

> This is nothing but a witch-hunt, that is all it is. The last time they were hunting Communists. This time they are going to hunt Fascists. . . .
> Mr. Speaker, seriously, this is a dangerous thing. The resolution goes on to say:
> "Slanderous or libelous un-American propaganda of religious, racial or subversive political prejudices."
> That covers everything on the face of the earth.
> Let the proponents of the bill beware. It may be a boomerang of intolerance, and return to curse those who favor it. Kill this resolution. Cut it down.

And kill it they did, by a vote of 184 to 38.[51]

Representative Samuel Dickstein (D.-N.Y.), who had sponsored the Un-American Activities Committee measure, also offered a bill designed to make subject to deportation any alien who used any "propaganda" critical of various races, religions, the United States government, or who tended to "foment political acrimony and business animosity in the United States." Maverick was appalled.

142   *Maury Maverick: A Political Biography*

After the Texan was joined by several conservative critics of the bill, Dickstein agreed to eliminate part of it, but Maverick said that was not enough; the whole bill should be defeated. Representative Rankin agreed that the measure was a "legislative monstrosity," and Maverick administered the *coup de grâce* with, "This is actually the worst bill that was ever introduced in any legislative body in the whole world [laughter and applause]." Dickstein himself asked that the bill be recommitteed![52]

No issue of individual rights was too small for Maverick's attention. On May 27 he brought about the defeat of two amendments to an appropriations bill by using one of his favorite weapons, ridicule. One of the amendments would have prohibited people on relief or WPA work from "parading" or criticizing Congress. Maury asked, "What are we? Are we a House of Lords, back in 1500, to tell people that they cannot parade, that they cannot strike? Are we the Lord High and Mighty of the Privy Council? We must be going crazy to even listen to things like that [laughter and applause]."[53] With that amendment safely out of the way, Maverick next tackled one designed to take resident aliens off the relief rolls or WPA employment. "Let us be sensible and humane," he said. "We take a condemned murderer and feed him well." The amendment was narrowly defeated by a vote of 116 to 112.[54]

No matter what the topic might be of the many public speeches that Maverick made in 1937, his eloquent pleas for the maximum defense of civil liberties would creep in. In November, the *Dallas News* reported a series of accusations of denials of civil liberties in Dallas that had been made by Maverick in a San Antonio speech. A man had been tarred and feathered for speaking on a "subject which may lawfully be discussed," several men had been beaten on the suspicion that they were CIO organizers, and a man had been "howled down from the platform" while under the "professed protection of the city police." The *Dallas News* said that Maverick's charges were substantially true and then concluded, "If you get any pride out of conditions in this connection, you are easily puffed up."[55]

In 1937 Maverick was for the first time, in his own apt phrase, "with book." In May the *Saturday Review of Literature* pictured two young authors lunching with Pascal Covici, their publisher—

Ever Insurgent Let Me Be 143

Maury Maverick and John Steinbeck. Maverick's *A Maverick American* was soon to be published, and Steinbeck was in New York to "dramatize" his book *Of Mice and Men*.[56]

Most reviewers of the work that tumbled out of the Texas congressman's churning brain in 1937 quickly gave up trying to find a label—it was no more susceptible of labeling than the man who wrote it. Maverick, in characteristic fashion, had started the book with a first chaper titled "Approximately a Preface," in which he freely admitted that he "got everybody's help, ranging from policemen and gas station operators up to—I almost said the Supreme Court." Among his major helpers were his "main braintruster," Leon Pearson, and Leon Henderson.[57] It *is* possible to describe the book, after a fashion. It is a semiautobiographical vehicle for the presentation of Maverick's hopes and prescriptions for a land where people work and play in freedom—freedom from want as well as the more conventional civil rights and civil liberties.

Time called the bestseller a "rambling, engaging, man-to-man discourse," written by a "literate legislator" who was the "most reconstructed Southerner in Congress."[58] Heywood Broun called it "one of the most engrossing books ever to come from a public figure." Though he did not feel that Maverick could qualify as a "prose master," Broun did say that his war chapters "remain with me as among the most vivid I know."[59] An unsigned *Washington Times* review said, "His descriptions would put *All Quiet on the Western Front* in the very deep shade."[60] Herbert Little said, "His description of the World War engagement in which he was wounded is a high point of descriptive writing. . . . The description of his own demagogic attack on a political opponent is a jewel in the Mark Twain tradition."[61]

The late Senator Richard L. Neuberger, then a journalist, called this maverick work "one of the most important books of the year,"[62] and an English reviewer referred to the author as a "clear-thinking, courageous man" who had written "an important book; one that I would recommend to anybody desiring to understand the conflicts, complexities, paradoxes, hopes and possibilities of America in the Nineteen-thirties." He said that Maury's passages on war were "well worth pondering for their philosophical overtones."[63]

A rare uncomplimentary review appeared in the *Washington*

Star. Mary Carter Roberts said that the book represented an "exposition of our political psychology," and that it was a "vivid demonstration of how Americans have trained their representatives in government to make profundities out of the obvious and to bring forth the platitude with all the triumph commonly appertaining to the epigram."[64] Perhaps the most complimentary remarks on the book (and something of an answer to Roberts' criticism) were written for the Book-of-the-Month Club's news sheet by Broun, who said, ". . . people may say he has done little more than accept many of the ideas of the old line radicals and put them into new terminology. But 'little' is hardly the appropriate word, for Maverick has gone a great distance in accomplishing the important task of stating age-old philosophies, sometimes called alien, in terms of the American language."[65]

Whatever the literary merits of Maverick's brainchild, the book was bound to be significant and influential. In addition to the reviews cited, it may be noted that the volume narrowly missed being a Book-of-the-Month selection and that it was serialized in the *Philadelphia Record* and the *New York Post* beginning September 13, 1937.[66] President Roosevelt thanked Maverick for sending him a copy and vowed that he would read it.[67]

The one legislative achievement of 1937 for which Maverick expressed the greatest pride involved little in the way of dramatic and bold speeches or parliamentary maneuvering, but there was opposition, and he was credited with carrying the day.

In June 1937 he offered a bill (H.R. 6767) to provide "cancer research, the training of technicians and the establishment of a central cancer clinic," and said, "If this bill is adopted we can truly say we have done a service to humanity."[68] Maury Maverick made no claim of originality in presenting the bill; he credited Dr. Dudley Jackson, a San Antonio surgeon, with interesting him in the matter and with providing him with information necessary to drawing up the bill. Newspapers referred to the measure as the Maverick Cancer Bill, but this was not strictly correct. Three measures had been introduced in all, but they seemed to have died in the Interstate Commerce Committee. Maverick's personal contribution was to wage a relentless publicity campaign, including a national network speech, in order to get some action. As a result of

Ever Insurgent Let Me Be 145

his pressures the chairman of the committee granted a hearing on the bills. Maverick then arranged for the appearances of various witnesses in behalf of the measure.

The bill eventually reported out of the committee bore the name of Representative Alfred L. Bulwinkle (D.-N.C.), and it did not include the hospital for which Maverick's measure had provided, but he urged passage anyway. When the victory came on July 23, it was Maverick who was credited with having "won a long and aggressive campaign" for a cancer research institute for the United States, the world-famous National Cancer Research Institute at Bethesda, Maryland.[69]

In this 1937 session, Maverick continued to champion the cause of labor, organized and unorganized. He was one of the most outspoken supporters of a minimum-wage law in the House, and he was particularly harsh in his judgments of Southern opposition to such legislation. He said that businessmen too often followed the philosophy that anyone is justified in doing whatever is not contrary to law—this was the reason minimum-wage laws were necessary. With uncommon daring for a Southern representative, he castigated a southern textile-mill operator, John E. Edgerton of Nashville, Tennessee, as one of "the worst labor haters in America." According to Maverick, Edgerton had told a House committee that the question as to whether a family could live on sixteen dollars a week was irrelevant to the minimum-wage bill. When the crowd laughed, said Maverick, Edgerton "smugged into a contemptuous smirk and spoke of his church work."[70]

Maverick's statements in behalf of minimum-wage legislation were like those he offered on other issues—carefully drawn and documented. He gave statistical comparisons of the executive salaries and the workers' wages in selected industries and said that he had found wages as low as four cents an hour. "I am not opposed to high salaries," he said. "I believe that people should be allowed to make money. But I also believe that there should be a minimum standard of decency."[71] In the final unsuccessful attempt to pass such a bill at the close of the 1937 special session, he told his Southern colleagues that "if a black man does the same work as a white man, he ought to receive the same pay." He said that the Texas AFL had wired him to support a substitute measure, but he was not going to do it. He called attention to the astonishingly low wages paid to pecan shellers in San Antonio—an average of $1.29 a week![72]

There were votes to be had in Maverick's support of a minimum-wage law, but relatively few could be expected from his support of organized labor. Circumspect politicians thought it foolhardy for Maverick to go all out for organized labor, particularly the CIO, but he did not care what they thought. He flaunted his labor associations and friendships before the people of his essentially anti-labor region, state, and district. He did not deny having said, "When I ran for Congress, I was opposed to lobbyists, and I still am opposed to them. But whenever a labor lobbyist comes into my office, I greet him with open arms."[73]

Maury Maverick's friendly associations with organized labor dated from his earliest days in politics, but in the 1937 session his stands in matters of labor strife focused greater attention upon his outspoken and daring position. In February he castigated General Motors for interfering with the activities of the National Labor Relations Board. He said that the company had used OGPU methods like the Russians and "spies with criminal records, rascals and racketeers to prevent the workers from even having an election to determine who is to represent them." "Like Bourbons who never learn anything, they add insult to injury and declare a dividend, when production has stopped . . . during the bitterest strike in American history." Maverick bluntly warned that if there was violence it would be the fault of industrial leaders and not labor.[74]

The speech that probably hurt Maverick most with his constituents was given on June 5, 1937, to the United Auto Workers in Detroit. He had a habit of pumping his right arm upward with his first clenched as he made a major point. A wire-service photographer caught him with the arm at full length in a Mussolini-like stance as he belabored big business and praised labor for creating the circumstances in which "free-born Americans . . . can live without fear of company police, spies, hired thugs, murderers and private armies." He told the cheering mass of auto workers, "I want you to know in the first place that down my way labor is not very well organized; labor is not very well organized anywhere in the South. But let us get organized North, South, East and West . . . for the purpose of preserving American liberty and the Ameri-

Ever Insurgent Let Me Be   147

can standard of living." When Maverick mentioned the name of William Green, leader of the rival AFL, the crowd booed, but he told them they had no business booing—"We are trying to build America" and are not "fighting any labor organization." The boos changed to loud applause.[75]

Maverick clearly did not want to be cast as an extremist in his support of organized labor. A student asked him in 1937 how long labor unrest would last. Maverick expressed the opinion that it would be four or five years. The student asked, "And who is going to protect capital when labor gets the upper hand?" "Labor," Maverick replied. "This may appear paradoxical, but the working people know that if they destroy the capitalists, they destroy themselves."[76]

The violence of which Maverick had spoken in the House was not long in coming, and when it did come, he leaped to the defense of the workers. Angry and truculent, he declared, "Over there in Chicago, nine men, something like six blocks from a steel plant, were attacked by the police and nine of them were murdered; and we stand here and not a soul has said a word about those nine freeborn Americans who were murdered out there in cold blood. All we do is to spend our time criticizing organized labor."[77] A week later he came back to the floor with the most scorching blast he had ever delivered there. He said he had seen the films of the violence in the Chicago strike and that he had learned that the police killed *ten* men, and he had watched a policeman beat one of the felled union pickets. This was the time of the highly controversial sitdown strikes, precursors of the sit-ins of the 1960's, and Maverick was referring to the notorious incident on Memorial Day of 1937 at the Republic Steel Plant.

Maverick singled out veteran Congressman Eugene Cox (D.-Ga.) for a tongue-lashing because of his "hysterical" and "provocative" statements against labor and for his "unfair" and "wholly unwarranted" attack on Secretary of Labor Frances Perkins. Maverick said, "Sometimes I am called a left-winger, sometimes a liberal, sometimes worse; but who is calling for blood and violence? Why, gentlemen, they are those who prate about the preservation of the Constitution, those who carry their patriotism on their sleeves, the ones who call themselves conservatives and wrap themselves in the flag." Seven of the ten men, he said, had been shot in the back. It was "one of the bloodiest and most shameful pages in American history," and no conservative had spoken out. "I am disappointed that a Democrat, a gentleman from the South, a conservative, should act in such a manner."

The acid response of Representative Cox was to the effect that he knew Maverick was patriotic and therefore the only conclusion he could draw was that the Texan was not serious but "interested only in provoking amusement by his extravagance and buffoonery." Maverick leaped to his feet and demanded that Cox's remark be "taken down" and thus stricken from the *Congressional Record*. The House voted against Maverick's motion, but Cox was not satisfied. He went on to express the hope that Maverick believed in some form of government and had not "become wholly Russianized, and that John L. Lewis is not in fact his candidate for the Presidency in 1940." When Maverick demanded that this statement be taken down, Cox laughed and withdrew it.

Cox then proceeded to taunt the angry Maverick with such questions as did he collaborate with John L. Lewis in shaping his official conduct in the House and was he in sympathy with the CIO and its effort to terrorize industry? Cox then implied that Maverick could not give an honest answer. When Maverick asked for time to answer, Republican Representative Rich, whom Maverick had once defended in his right to criticize Democrats, deferred time to the Texan. Maverick then told Cox that the questions were of the have-you-quit-beating-your-wife variety, and, turning Cox's original attack back upon him, Maverick said that the Georgia congressman did not seek answers to his questions, but had asked them for purposes of "insult and display" and his own "peculiar satisfaction." Turning to his colleagues, Maverick said, "We have heard enough of bitter personalities for the time being. The people of this country would rather see us do our duty and carry out the promises of the Democratic Party [applause]."[78]

Most newspapers gave the story straight treatment, and the worst one might have gathered from such stories was that House members thought that Maverick, in this instance, should have taken it as well as he dished it out. But he was given shabby treatment in the *San Antonio Express*, which headlined the affair on the front page, "Maury Buffoon, Congressmen's Votes Decide." Mrs. Maverick jotted above her clipping: "The following is an-

Ever Insurgent Let Me Be 149

other example of the loyalty the S.A. Express has to the home town boy. If they ever said anything good about us we might die with amazement. We've gotten along this far without 'em. O.K. by us."[79] William Allen White wrote that the "spanking" of Maverick was not justified and that the language of Cox was "intemperate." He said that the House had "rebuked and insulted a patriot. It should have granted to a young man the intemperance of his convictions. It might have tried moral suasion rather than a hot-handed spanking."[80] The *New York Times* simply called the action an "unnecessary insult."[81]

The most friendly supporter of Maverick, however, could not help but come to the conclusion, after a careful examination of his career, that his readiness to say what he thought on almost any subject would make him a likely candidate to write a book on how to lose friends and alienate people. His scrupulous honesty and fairness, on the other hand, could win many of them back. His activities in 1937 were replete with such examples, some of them already treated. Early in the year he said bluntly, "I see no reason to break precedent, and I am not for the President in 1940. There ought to be somewhere . . . a progressive, honest Democrat to lead the party next time."[82] As *Time* put it, Maverick was no sycophant either to Franklin Roosevelt or the C.I.O."[83]

Indeed, when either the AFL or CIO thought it had his uncritical support he would confound either of them. He had upbraided the United Auto Workers when they booed AFL's William Green, and when he saw a letter from the president of the Auto Workers, Homer Martin, which told Members of the House who voted against the wage and hour bill that their "unfavorable vote [would] not be forgotten next year," he said that Martin "had better learn a little manners," that his letter was "indiscreet" and that "information fairly presented is more effective."[84]

Maury's subsequent lecture to William Green, president of the AFL, was to plague the Texas congressman later. When he learned that every member of the House had received a wire from Green urging that they defeat the minimum wage law, he read the following response to Green into the *Record*, "Your attitude is taken upon the basis that the exact wording of the 'American Federation of Labor bill' has not been adopted by Congress. Where I must make a decision, even though I run the risk of the displeasure of the highest figures in America, I do it unhesitatingly." Maverick went on to tell Green that the AFL measure was too rigid and probably would be found unconstitutional. Moreover, Maverick said, the rank and file of labor was "deeply dissatisfied" by the split in organized labor and wanted unity. He concluded that members of Congress were expected "to do our duty according to our consciences and judgment. I have made my decision, believing it to be right, and will take the responsibility just as you will for yours."[85] Later events proved that Green never forgave Maverick for the lecture.

More of Maury's "winning ways" could be seen in his statement in support of the Wagner-Steagall housing bill in which he said, "The housing in my city in the slum areas is as bad as any city in the United States of America."[86] On the same subject, he commented that "two-thirds of the buildings" in Baltimore should be torn down.[87]

One of Maverick's favorite whipping boys at this time was the American Bar Association—and conservative lawyers generally. In various speeches he characterized the association as "a reactionary force in American life,"[88] and as "stupid, undemocratic and behind the times in its attitude toward social legislation." Interestingly enough, the conservative *Dallas News* commented that though Maury's attack was "something less than a reasoned and balanced appraisal, . . . if the bar associations, in their attitude on social legislation, represented the views of the average lawyer instead of those who are ultra-conservative, there probably would be little occasion for such attacks as that of Representative Maverick."[89] The *Literary Digest* also expressed the opinion that "probably there are few more conservative organizations than the A.B.A." in an article on the organization of the rival National Lawyers Guild on December 22, 1936. Maverick was pictured at the meeting as having "denounced the old order" and "doffed his hat to the head of the new group," John Patrick Devaney, former chief justice of Minnesota.[90]

Maverick managed to get himself into a major donnybrook when he took on the lawyers at a meeting of the Harvard Club in Washington. In his address entitled "College Men and Their Lack of Education," he said that all he had heard about liberty in Wash-

Ever Insurgent Let Me Be 151

ington had been said by high-priced lawyers who were promoting liberty for corporations. He wanted to hear some of them speak up for academic liberty or freedom of speech. "Lawyers," he said, "had expanded in influence only as corporations had grown in size."

Then the chairman, a Harvard law school graduate who practiced locally, arose, livid with rage.

Inasmuch as Maverick had criticized university men and suggested they were prejudiced, the chairman said, the usual period for questions to and answers from the speaker would be omitted.

Maverick stood up and said he didn't care what the club did, but if he were going to be treated with discourtesy, he wanted everyone to understand that he knew it.

The meeting then became a turmoil and the cry, "We want Maverick," was overwhelming.[91]

Maverick spoke again, questions were raised and answered, and the secretary of the club apologized to Maverick. Shortly thereafter, Frederick Delano and others got the chairman in a corner and made him apologize to Maverick.

Maverick's sheer audacity and candor were often captivating to audiences. On another occasion he was reported to have "held a large audience of hard-boiled businessmen spellbound" at the Economic Club of New York City. They insisted that the rules of the club be broken so that he could speak longer and then asked him to speak again.[92] Edwin C. Hill reported how he was charmed by Maverick's refreshing approach to a newsman: " 'I am a propagandist,' he said, 'and I want to put something over on you. I am Congressman Maury Maverick from Texas. I've got a bill here which I believe in, and I want to make you believe in it. Maybe you don't like it, but if you do, I want you to write it up and help me get it passed. When can I see you and tell you about it?' Maverick worked like that with newspapermen, never with a buried ace, and he got a full and friendly hearing for all his stuff."[93]

Humor as well as candor, or both combined, served to take some of the sting out of Maverick's barbs or to disarm some of his adversaries. He opened a speech in the House once with the remark that "anyone who wishes to sleep or rest during my address may do so. But I shall appreciate it if gentlemen who are talking loudly will go outside, so that the rest can sleep if they wish."[94] When military appropriations were under discussion he displayed some of the candor that endeared him to newsmen who were so accustomed to political pettifoggery. He said, ". . . if there is going to be any building I want to see some of the building in my own district, and you will understand this is the reason I am talking [laughter]."[95] Again, after a disjointed speech, he admitted by implication something that most congressmen would never admit when he said, "Mr. Speaker, I ask unanimous consent that I may revise, extend, illuminate and eliminate certain portions of my remarks [laughter]." The Speaker dropped the formalities long enough to agree that Maverick could indeed "eliminate" as well as "illuminate" certain of his remarks.[96] Many citizens are not aware of the fact that members of Congress are provided with transcripts of their remarks on the floor, and that the members are permitted to, as one writer put it, "sanitize" their remarks. Usually this procedure involves cleaning up the grammar and the like, but some members may indeed "eliminate" and "illuminate" parts of the substance of what they said before it is printed in the *Congressional Record*.

Maverick saw it as no breach of etiquette when he went over to Virginia one day and ridiculed the conservatism of both of its United States Senators, Glass and Byrd, before a meeting of the Jeffersonian Club of Elizabeth City County. A quotation from a local newspaper indicates that his audience enjoyed it as much as he did: "Pointing to the flag of Virginia, Representative Maverick remarked: 'I see that the man [fallen tyrant] lying there under the foot of the lady has curly hair. He looks like Senator Byrd.' There was an outburst of laughter."[97] Another Virginia paper praised Maverick for his "courageous bluntness" on this occasion and predicted that he would "achieve great heights in the American political scene."[98]

The press had a field day and the upper crust winced when Maury Maverick entered a contest sponsored by the "hors d'oeuvres reform committee," inspired by a midwestern hotel man who had put up a loving cup as a prize for the person who came up with the best name to replace the term *hors d'oeuvres*. Maverick seized the opportunity to attack French menus and to offer the suggestion that the appetizers be called "dingle doos." Newspapers as far away as Fargo, North Dakota, chortled editorially at this

Ever Insurgent Let Me Be 153

latest bit of Maverick antics.[99] But famed restaurateur George Rector had the last word when he wired to Maverick the suggestion that the new name be *mavericks*. He said, "A maverick is something that does not belong anywhere in particular and any man can put his brand on it if he can catch it. And that fits the old-time free lunch as well as the fancy appetizers in the fanciest hotel in the country. Well, why not?"[100] If Maverick responded, it has not come to light.

As someone once remarked, Maverick was not an insurgent Democrat, he was an insurgent insurgent. From the occasional digs and prods of 1936, he moved into mounting and increasingly sharp attacks on what he considered to be a flagging New Deal leadership in 1937.

In May 1937 Stanley High, a senior editor of the *Reader's Digest*, wrote an article for the *Saturday Evening Post* entitled, "The Neo-New Dealers," in which he asserted, "Undoubtedly, the moving spirit, guiding genius and general out-in-front man for this bloc is Maury Maverick."[101] Walter Lippmann, criticizing Maverick's attack on the Supreme Court, wrote, "Mr. Maverick is very representative indeed of the little group of bold and reckless men who have been setting the pace for the President in the past few months."[102]

Newspapers at the time referred to the organization of a Maverick group, but this was essentially the same group that Maverick had led from the 1935 session on—it was simply a matter of renewed interest and attention being directed toward it as it grew more critical of the lagging program of the New Deal. Estimates of the size of the group ranged from forty to a hundred, but this was usually based upon fluctuations in attendance at the meetings held in several Washington restaurants during the latter part of 1937. The best evidence indicates that there were about thirty to forty hard-core Mavericks who could rally additional support varying with the issue that was before the House. Maury Maverick was now the chairman and Thomas R. Amlie, Wisconsin Progressive, served as secretary.

What did these Mavericks want? Maury pushed for all kinds of remedial and reform legislation, but the program he announced as spokesman for his "colleagues" in April of 1937 included:

1. Every "willing worker" had a right to a job.
2. Public works projects of all kinds must be expedited.
3. A Department of Public Welfare should be established.
4. Low-cost housing must be provided.
5. Increased taxes based upon the ability to pay should be used to balance the budget.

Maverick told his House colleagues that the group had been meeting for some time to formulate their program, and, in the belief that the program represented the views of a hundred House members, he was submitting it to the public in their behalf.[103]

Most of the Maverick program was consistent with administration proposals, but Maverick and his crew felt that leaders were beginning to play it safe and drag their feet. In May he asked who would be the next candidate for the Democratic nomination for the presidency and then speculated that it might be Secretary of Agriculture Henry A. Wallace, because Wallace was "becoming very respectable of late. Where is the farm-tenancy bill? Where is essential legislation for the farmers?" After considering other presidential prospects, Maverick indicated that he might be doing no more than having a bit of sport, but he urged his fellow Democrats to get together, have a few caucuses, and get on with the needed legislation.[104]

Maverick caused Democratic leaders to shudder and confounded his critics when he called for an investigation of charges of political favoritism and excessive costs in the administration of the relief program and WPA. Though the resolution was defeated by a voice vote, Maverick received favorable editorial comment from papers across the nation. The *Peoria* (Ill.) *Journal Transcript*, after expressing astonishment that Maverick should have made such a proposal, said that Congress was "duty bound" to approve it.[105] The forthright Texan said later, in a second attempt to win support for his resolution, that the investigation was necessary to meet criticisms. He said he had been receiving letters concerning graft and the like in the programs.[106]

Maverick was increasingly becoming a thorn in the side of the leaders. On the day that the House voted on his resolution to investigate the relief program and WPA, Democratic leaders sought unanimous consent to expedite a measure sought by FDR, designed to establish a Joint Committee on Tax Evasion and Avoidance.

Ever Insurgent Let Me Be 155

Maverick exploded, "What is the hurry? . . . So far as I am concerned, I am tired of bills being presented with some mysterious reason why I should do something. I want to know the real reason. This is supposed to be a parliamentary body, not a door mat [applause]." The measure was temporarily blocked until it was given more conventional consideration.[107]

The defeat of his investigation resolution a few days earlier by a voice vote may have been the basis for another challenge to the leaders when Maverick proposed that a voting machine be installed in the House. He said that voting behavior would be liberalized if the members had to go on record when every vote was taken in the House. Again, he had no success, but newspapers throughout the United States applauded his attempt.[108]

The press gave the impression that some kind of a showdown was in the making between the Mavericks and FDR himself when the president invited Democratic congressmen to a weekend conference at a retreat called the Jefferson Island Rod and Gun Club, on a tiny island in the Chesapeake Bay about fifteen miles from Washington. Republican Representative Rich was somewhat closer to the truth when he kidded his Democratic colleagues about the invitations. He said that Roosevelt was going to get them down to Jefferson Island to tell them how he wanted them to be rubber stamps.[109]

The next day, June 22, the *Washington Herald* described a warm-up session: "Representative Maury Maverick is planning to discharge his Texan oratorical gunfire against those Democrats in Congress who have turned against the New Deal. Announcing his subject as 'Revolt of the Palace Guards,' with the subtitle of 'It Looks Like Landon Got Elected,' the fiery Texan will speak Thursday night at the Rockdale Restaurant, 1735 F Street, N.W., the only consumer cooperative restaurant in the East outside of New York City."[110]

Various reports during the next two days explained that the Jefferson Island meeting was being held because a number of Democrats in Congress had complained that Roosevelt was becoming aloof—he was not keeping proper liaison with his supporters on the Hill, and they were becoming restive at not being able to see him. Drew Pearson and Robert S. Allen gave as another related reason Maury Maverick's complaint about measures being tossed at congressmen without notice.[111] The preconference stories also pictured Maverick as prepared to talk turkey to Roosevelt concerning the need to forge ahead with the New Deal program. He was quoted as saying that he and thirty-nine Democrats in the House were going to urge the president to keep Congress in session "until January, if necessary" in order to get major bills passed. The insurgents were going on the trip not merely "for sociability or to get inspiration, but to tell the President just exactly what we think."[112] Maverick's aim was also "an effort to make the House leadership return to belligerency."[113]

The day before the island festivities the *Philadelphia Record* reprinted the program of the Mavericks and asserted that Harry Hopkins and Heywood Broun had met with them to "advise on policy and strategy." Maverick, chosen to head the delegation to speak to the president, said that Democrats opposing the New Deal should be "purged," or "kicked out." He not only called for giving Senator Carter Glass of Virginia the boot, calling him a "disagreeable old bore," but said that his own Senator Tom Connally of Texas was "no more liberal than Glass."[114]

On the day the conference opened, Friday, June 25, Raymond Clapper wrote that Maury Maverick, "leader of the New Dealers," had gone to the meeting to keep conservatives from persuading FDR to let his program go over to the next winter. Clapper predicted that Maverick would be unpopular at the meeting and that he would receive "dirty looks" from many Democrats.[115] With his bent for the use of symbolic gimmicks, Maverick had even secured Democratic badges from the Democratic National Committee that, he tartly said, he was going to pin on Roosevelt men, if he could find any on the island.[116]

But somewhere the fire and fervor died or at least was considerably dampened. The picture of the meeting was one of "good fellowship, feasting and song," of "fishing, swimming and good clean fun." The smiling chief was inducted into the mock Demagogues Club of Congress by Texas Representative Martin Dies. The president asked if this was Maverick's organization of House progressives. Dies quickly demonstrated that he had the proper credentials for the organization by responding that the Maverick group was a CIO outfit while the Demagogues believed in "craft labor."[117]

Ever Insurgent Let Me Be 157

In his own report of what he was able to accomplish at the meeting, Maverick said that it was not good manners to tell the whole story, but that amidst the jokes, beer, songs, and "jollification," "I slipped up to the President and mumbled our message and here is where I cannot violate good manners. I cannot say what the President said; but it seemed to me he mumbled, in fact said, something very encouraging."[118] But a bit of reflection must have given him some caution, for he had told reporters earlier that he had talked confidentially with the president and that his response was "we are going through." When reporters asked if that meant in the present session of Congress, Maverick replied, "The President is smart enough," and refused to discuss the matter further.[119]

Whatever the case, Maverick's disappointment and disgruntlement with the results of the encounter seemed clear. In his own report he said that everyone at the conference was "a perfect gentleman, so perfect indeed, that no one said what they really thought," and that the meeting should have been called Ostrich Island because most of the congressmen "had our heads in the sand, when we were not talking of the weather, or telling jokes."[120] One gathers that though the meeting was not a complete failure, Maverick got little support from his colleagues in attendance, he was himself not immune to the Roosevelt charm and the conviviality of the circumstances, and the encounter failed to live up to the advance billing of rebelliousness that newspapers had led the public, and perhaps Maverick himself, to expect. That this effort and others by Maverick was not a complete failure, however, is attested to by the fact that the Maverick bloc was able to win some victories and that a special session was called in November 1937 by Roosevelt.

The liberal press praised and encouraged Maverick's efforts to move the New Deal along. The *Progressive* said that he was one of the real leaders of the "progressive-liberal group," and that he filled the gap in the House "left vacant since former Representative Fiorello La Guardia retired."[121] The *Washington Daily News* said that the liberal bloc had a "possible balance of power on closely divided issues, and in other situations it has a nuisance value which sometimes forces consideration of its ideas." Of Maverick the paper said, "Now as in the past he roams restlessly through the halls of Congress, conferring, promoting, making radio speeches, urging action on the President's program. He interviews reporters as much as they interview him, and publicly criticizes his colleagues from the South who have blocked the New Deal's new drives for legislation."[122] And Jay Franklin wrote in the *Washington Star* that Congress had apparently become indifferent to farm legislation, which could cause a "CIO-like" movement among farmers, but "Southern statesmen like Hugo Black of Alabama and Maury Maverick of San Antonio sense the danger and are willing to take measures to combat it."[123] Before the session of Congress was over, *Time* magazine reported that the passage of the Third Deficiency Appropriation Bill "included a victory for the House Liberal bloc headed by Texas' noisy Maury Maverick, who wanted $20,000,000 for an experimental Government farm tenancy program, $1,800,-000 for the National Labor Relations Board, and got both."[124]

As the regular session drew to a close, Maverick delivered a national radio network speech, "Congress Must Not Go Home," in which he urged that the representatives should stay on the job and produce legislation necessary to deal with minimum wages, housing, the Supreme Court's powers, tax loopholes, and other pressing matters. He said that the Gallup Poll indicated that 63 percent of the people wanted Congress to do these things.[125] A few weeks later he launched a blistering attack upon the House Rules Committee for blocking key legislation, an attack that was to be expanded in the special session. He called the group the "dictator of the House," and declared, "It is grotesque and amazing for a civilized country that claims to have a democratic government" for the Rules Committee to exercise such power over the legislative process.[126] The *Philadelphia Record* charged that Maverick's Texas colleague, Martin Dies, had "organized the cabal of reactionary Southern Democrats on the House Rules Committee to block passage of wage-and-hour legislation," but that Maury Maverick had "fought tooth and nail" against the "reactionism of his Texas colleagues."[127]

No sooner had the special session of 1937 opened than Maverick was yelling again. He wondered at the strange goings on of the House of Representatives. He said that he had received no notification of a special session but had to read about it in the newspapers. He charged that the session was marked by no coordination, dilatory tactics, and unfair efforts to block Republicans from speaking,

Ever Insurgent Let Me Be

which he had voted against. He asked if this was to be known as the "great horseplay session of 1937." Again the Rules Committee was his prime target: "The Rules Committee is the Supreme Court in reverse. It is stronger than any dictator, and it tells us we cannot vote on a certain question. I talked to a friend of mine on the Rules Committee. He said, 'If you gentlemen will amend this bill, we will let it be brought to the floor and voted upon.' I ask you, is it the 'censor' committee or the Rules Committee? Has the Rules Committee any right to tell other committees how to write their bills?"

He argued that the Rules Committee, by virtue of a combination of Republicans and Southern Democrats, did not represent the Democratic party. He admitted that he had voted for the resolution providing for the difficult process of a petition of 218 signatures to force Rules Committee action, but he said, "To my shame and sorrow I did. . . . I now know better." He declared that there were too many gag rules in the House of Representatives, thereby diminishing its powers. He concluded, "To repeat, we must have party responsibility, must meet issues head-on—we Democrats. Else we get kicked out by the voters of America, which we would deserve [applause]."[128]

Maverick came back to the attack in December with what he called a nonpartisan speech on the lack of "responsibility" in the United States government. He proceeded to treat his colleagues to a long, scholarly discourse on the parliamentary system in Britain and various measures by which certain of its advantages might be achieved in our government. The speech elicited many serious questions from interested colleagues, but he could not win any support for his specific proposals. For example, he contended that since the Rules Committee's opposition to the wages and hours bill had been repudiated by the petition signed by 218 House members, the committee should resign as the British Cabinet would when its position was repudiated. He introduced resolutions to provide that only 145 signatures would be needed to discharge the committee of responsibility for a bill and to provide that the House emulate the House of Commons by having an interpellation or question period for members of the president's cabinet and other key officials to appear on the floor of Congress and answer questions put to them by the members.[129] Again, Maverick won the votes of the press, but not those of the House.[130]

Maverick saw a waning New Deal and appeared to be almost frantically trying to hold back the tide single-handedly. In another network radio address in November he charged the business community with the responsibility for bringing on a downturn in the economy through "Hoover talk." He said that when a little prosperity began to return the "monopolists raised prices, grabbed off unreasonable profits, and left the public to hold the bag. Indeed, what happened is simple: farm income, and city wages, industrial and white collar, were not sufficient to buy all the goods at these exorbitant prices." Hence inventories were up and the stock market was down. These were the results, too, of a failure to enact farm, and wage and hour legislation.[131]

As the special session came to an end, Maverick said that the failure to enact a wage and hour bill would be known as the Bull Run of the Democratic party. The Democrats had made "a mockery" of carrying out their pledges to the electorate. The major cause of defeat, according to Maverick, was the obstructionism of his Southern Democratic colleagues. He grimly told them that in their obstructionism and dereliction poor whites and Negroes were taught to hate each other—"a system of 'checks and balances' based on hate, helping to perpetuate a miserable system." He urged them to read Carpenter's *The South as a Conscious Minority* and said that they were not only a conscious minority, but a self-conscious minority, "an irritable, touchy, and ready-to-take-offense minority." They must come to realize, he said, the need for a farm tenancy bill, economic justice for the Negro, and minimum wage–maximum hours legislation.

Maverick was even able to find a parallel in the actions of the Supreme Court. He gave a lengthy comparative study to demonstrate that the Court was following the Constitution of the Confederate States of America more closely than the Constitution of the United States![132]

Maverick had been busy on so many fronts in the 1937 session that it strains credulity. Remarkably little attention was given then or in subsequent studies of a farm bill that Maverick introduced in February 1937 when Senator Guy M. Gillette (R.-Iowa) introduced its counterpart in the Senate. This measure, labeled the Gillette-Maverick bill by the press, was designed to provide for soil

Ever Insurgent Let Me Be 161

conservation, commodity loans, and disposal of excess production of agricultural products. In March a Republican newspaper in Iowa reported that a three-state conference of farmers had gone on record with the statement that the Gillette-Maverick bill was "more nearly approximating the legislation needed by American agriculture than any farm measure ever before proposed."[133] A Democratic paper, reporting on the same conference, gave strong support to the proposal and praised "Senator Guy Gillette and Congressman Maury Maverick who STAND FOR THE AMERICAN FARMER FIRST!"[134] In May the same paper said that the basic principle of the proposal was "so right and so sound that ultimately society must adopt it for its own self-preservation." The editorial declared that though it had not gained wide publicity, the Gillette-Maverick "nonpartisan" bill had great support in northwest Iowa. The problem was that Secretary of Agriculture Wallace had viewed the proposal unfavorably and was generally "gloomy" over new farm legislation.[135]

In April, in a brief note buried in a recital of congressional activities, the *New York Times* reported that a subcommittee of the Senate Agriculture Committee had voted to withhold action on the "pending Gillette-Maverick bill providing a far reaching farm-aid program." Senator Gillette said that in view of the developing economy drive at that time there would be "little or no chance of enacting a bill in the near future."[136] The particular bill was dead, but the second Agricultural Adjustment Act that was enacted in 1938 had many of the features of this measure.

Maverick also continued to push for mandatory neutrality legislation with embargoes on all shipments of munitions to all countries,[137] to say that President Roosevelt was "wrong" on neutrality,[138] and to argue that existing legislation, enacted in 1935 and 1936, was "hasty and ill-advised."[139]

Newspapers throughout the country gave favorable editorial comment to Maverick's proposal for a Congressional Medal of Honor for contributions in the arts and sciences,[140] and the self-trained scholar continued to give his colleagues the benefit of his spritely reviews of the books that they should be reading.[141] When Congress adjourned the regular session, he enrolled in courses in labor problems and transportation at San Antonio's Saint Mary's University and made the honor roll![142] Maverick also won praise for sponsoring legislation called the American Youth Act, which was to provide employment and scholarships for youths from sixteen to twenty-five years of age—not unlike the youth programs of the Great Society of the 1960's.[143]

At the American Political Science Association convention in Philadelphia in 1937, Maverick was photographed in an informal discussion with Thomas Reed Powell, president of the association and Charles A. Beard, famed historian and admirer of Maverick's neutrality policy. Maverick's friend, C. W. Ervin, sent him a clipping of the picture with the sly comment, "three lights of the literary firmament." Indeed, Maverick was there to lead a discussion entitled "The Constitution and Foreign Affairs," in the course of which he made a proposal remarkably akin to some of our hemispheric security arrangements with Latin America after World War II. He suggested that the countries of this hemisphere agree (1) never to take aggressive action against another member of the agreement; (2) never to fortify the boundaries separating member countries; and (3) to unite in defense of any member threatened by exterior aggression.[144]

Maury Maverick was riding the crest at the close of 1937. His first book was a best seller; the liberal press (and much of it that was not) was hailing him as a conquering hero. One writer speculated on his possible appointment to the Supreme Court,[145] and another placed him in a "Texas Dynasty" with John Garner, Sam Rayburn, and Jesse Jones, commenting, "Maury Maverick has carved a definite place for himself by his championship of progressive measures, his fresh viewpoint on national problems and his outspokenness on the floor."[146]

When Maverick's political foe, San Antonio's Mayor Quin, received a letter from someone in Louisiana requesting the name of the congressman from the Bexar County district, Quin replied, "I thought everybody could answer that question."[147]

Sultan of the Young Turks

THERE WERE FEW INDICATIONS that Maury Maverick was entering his last session of Congress in January of 1938. A Washington newspaper expressed the opinion that any well-informed citizen who might be asked to name "a few really important members of Congress, probably would list such men as Senators Norris, Borah, Glass, Wheeler, and Wagner or Representatives Maury Maverick and David J. Lewis." These men, the paper said, had in common the disposition to "legislate with the welfare of the whole country in mind."[1] The *New York Times* featured Maverick among eighteen leading members of Congress as it convened,[2] and in February he was among those persons mentioned by respondents to the Gallup Poll as possible presidential candidates if Roosevelt did not run again.[3] In San Antonio, young Maury Maverick, Jr., saw his famous father in a *March of Time* news film and was nearly thrown out of the theater when he yelled at the top of his lungs, "That's my Pop!"[4]

A few days after Congress convened, Maverick was the principal speaker at the Jackson Day dinner in Minneapolis. He told his audience that another Andrew Jackson was in the White House.

"Roosevelt is fighting like that mean-talking, hard-bitten old soldier . . . Andrew Jackson; although our FDR uses a little bit more graceful language."[5] It appears that Maverick was trying to convince himself or to smooth over some of his differences with FDR, but, whatever the case, he continued to oppose a number of Roosevelt's proposals and to make statements that were of little comfort to the man in the White House.

Roosevelt had his hands full. In the summer of 1937, conservative Democrats in Congress had begun to break away from his leadership and to slip into a coalition with Republicans to frustrate further New Deal measures. Fear of chaos no longer restrained the business community from attacks on the New Deal and conservative congressmen had little fear of reprisals from constituents. Conservative Democrats were already looking forward to gaining control of the 1940 Democratic Convention. The last thing Roosevelt needed was opposition from Maury Maverick and his group, with their pushing for more New Deal programs. On the other hand, as Maverick saw it, he was trying to fight the good fight for FDR's New Deal and the president would not cooperate.

FDR particularly resented Maverick's opposition to his proposed naval construction program. In mid-1937 Maverick had secured appointment to the aviation subcommittee of the House Military Affairs Committee. He was "an almost fanatical believer in aviation as the best instrument of national defense and as an efficient means of ordinary transportation." To him, "development of the air corps is the most economical defense this country can build."[6] As soon as Maverick had had time to study the president's message on rearmament, the salty Texan delivered a blistering attack on it. He declared that building battleships was about like the government "opening a rope factory and going out here and manufacturing rope in order to hang itself." He complained that "it sometimes looks as if the New Deal has abandoned all its economic and political ideals and that we are riding wild horses in all separate directions and not getting anywhere." He said that he did not know what the battleships were for. Japan was not bent upon conquering the world, and "I do not think it is any business of the American people whether the Germans have fascism or the Russians have communism [applause]."[7]

Republican Representative Charles L. Gifford (R.-Mass.), in an

Sultan of the Young Turks

exchange with Maverick concerning the latter's differences with the president, said, "I can visualize the gentleman himself may be President of the United States some day [applause]." Maverick replied that he would like to applaud the remark, thanked Gifford for a "vision that will never come true," and explained that he did not feel bound to do as Roosevelt wanted in all cases—that the president was usually right, "but not always, not always." The thought seemed to call up further criticisms; Maverick said that FDR was saying it was now time for legislation aimed at prevention of profiteering in war. Why now, asked Maverick. A 1935 measure was supposed to have done this, but "the bill stunk to the high clouds of heaven." Maverick concluded with the blunt observation that bills designed to give special powers to the president in time of war were a step toward "totalitarian or dictatorial government."[8]

Early in February Maverick joined with Senator William H. King (D.-Utah) to offer a resolution urging FDR to call a Washington arms-limitation conference. He cited an editorial of February 13 in the *Springfield Republican* expressing the opinion that Japan was acting in good faith in her stated desire for a meeting on disarmament.[9] Some members of the Japanese Diet were reported to be seeking at this time to form an "Allied Comrades on American Policy" to thank the United States for its position of neutrality and to promote the continuance of U.S. friendship. On this subject, the Japanese news agency, Domei, carried long reports of speeches by Maverick and others.[10]

Maverick also made another appearance on "America's Town Meeting of the Air" in February; this time he was taking the negative of the proposition "Should Congress Adopt the President's Armament Proposals?" He argued that studies had demonstrated the vulnerability of large ships and that they were thus outdated. What was needed was to modernize and expand the air service and to construct speedy tanks.[11] Later in the month Maverick delivered a speech in the House entitled "The War Scare and National Defense." It was a bitter indictment of Administration policies. He said:

Now we Democrats have got to admit that we are floundering.
The reason for all this battleship and war frenzy is coming out: We have pulled all the rabbits out of the hat, and there are no more rabbits.

The Republicans need not rejoice, because they never had any rabbits—or even ideas.

The truth of the matter is that at the present time we are a confused, bewildered group of people, and we are not delivering the goods. The Democratic administration is getting down to the condition in which Mr. Hoover found himself: it looks as though we are beginning to feel that the way to prosperity is to stop spending altogether, and that in some way, magic or otherwise, prosperity is going to pop up around the corner sooner or later.

He repeated his contention that it was not battleships that were needed, but planes.[12]

Representative Gifford again praised Maverick for his stand against the president and called him the great hope of the Republican party. Maverick asked that the statement be expunged from the *Congressional Record* lest it break his heart. Gifford replied, "Having done the damage, I am perfectly willing to withdraw it." He went on to praise Maverick for "not being afraid to speak out," and then read a report from an unidentified source, "It is understood that the 30 liberals who marched on the President so recently were so abrupt in their demands that no opportunity was given to the President to indulge in so-called silken language and the delightful amiability of which he is the greatest past master."[13]

Gifford referred to the recent visit of the regrouped Mavericks to the White House to renew their demands on the president. In January, Harlan Miller had written that all of the insiders knew about the group of thirty-four Young Turks from seventeen states who were now meeting every Wednesday evening at Renkel's Cafeteria, a block or so from the Capitol, where one could get "a square meal for 50 cents." Their views, he said, would have been labeled Bryanesque twenty-five years ago, but their ideas were "modernized and streamlined," and the group was "far from wild eyed." Maverick presided at the meetings, but did not want it said that he was the "sultan of the Young Turks," because they were all individualists.[14]

The first week in February, with Maverick as their spokesman, the group that was reputed to represent a liberal bloc of more than a hundred members called upon President Roosevelt and urged "immediate revival of a fighting New Deal." Among the specific measures they called for were a "push to enact the wage and hour

Sultan of the Young Turks

bill"; passage of a "cost-of-production agriculture measure"; "renewal of government spending on a large scale and a drastic increase in relief appropriations"; "a tax program based on the principle of ability to pay, plus retention of both the capital gains and undistributed profits taxes with modifications"; a nation-wide soil conservation bill; expansion of the social security system; simplification of government credit agencies to provide credit for secured loans for low-cost housing, agriculture, small business, and public works; a program for increasing and regulating industrial production; and the revival of a public-works program "on a permanent basis." Maverick said that FDR expressed "keen interest and sympathy" on all points.

When the group discussed the strategy for getting the wage and hour bill out for passage, however, Roosevelt counseled them to get a bill that could get the Rules Committee's approval rather than concentrating on how to get by the Rules Committee. In the course of the conversations, Roosevelt indicated that he was smarting from Maverick's attacks on the naval construction proposals. When Maverick referred to the durability of public-works projects, FDR shot at him, "And airplanes deteriorate more rapidly than battleships."[15] His anger was understandable—Maverick had even charged that the president was keeping secret information that would demonstrate the vulnerability of surface warships to airplane attack.[16]

But Maverick was angry too. In March he returned to the attack with the statement that the New Deal was being abandoned. The warships were not needed, he said, and, "May I say to the Democrats that for the first time since I have been a member of Congress the Republicans have put in a real, honest-to-God, sensible minority report." They were right, in short, in their argument that it was not necessary to appropriate "billions for lopsided, unreasonable national defense." One of the most bizarre turns that this debate took occurred when Earl Browder and the Communist party denounced Maverick for opposing the naval construction measure and said that he had been "poisoned" by isolationist doctrines![17] Maverick told the House that the reason for the Communist party's support of the bill was that "they think we are going to take our Navy over there and fight Japan and get Japan out of China, because that is a menace to Russia. But I am not getting up a new 'red' scare." The reckless Maverick also said that he was not going to be worried about being "put on the political scrap heap" for opposing the president.[18]

It was at this time that Joseph Alsop and Robert Kintner expressed the opinion that an anti-Roosevelt revolt by liberals was looming. Alsop and Kintner wrote, "There's no question that the Roosevelt depression has impaled Bob LaFollette, John L. Lewis, Representative Maury Maverick and all other liberal leaders who have flourished under the New Deal on the horns of an excessively painful dilemma." The contention was, in brief, that Roosevelt had deserted them, and that "the President, so far, has handled the depression as though he were Herbert Hoover on an off day."[19]

There was no evidence to suggest that Maverick was joining any revolt, but he would not let up in his broadsides at the president. On March 25 he complained that too much attention was being given to international affairs; too much attention was being given to the navy rather than the army. He said he saw too much of a parallel with Woodrow Wilson's administration, which had "started out with great reforms, bogged down, and muddled . . . into the World War."

We do nothing and "wait on the executive," Maverick said. Recently, the president had "made no effort whatever to guide or dominate Congress," of which he had earlier been charged. Congress was in a "sort of stupor," and responsible through its inaction for the increase in executive power. "I hear various fellow Democrats wondering what the President thinks of this and that, and we are told mysteriously that the White House wants this or that when there is absolutely no indication of it whatsoever. We had better learn to do something for ourselves," Maverick said.[20]

In April he complained that too many planes were going to the navy and not enough to the army and that seacoast and antiaircraft defenses were being neglected.[21] He had told a national network radio audience that the United States needed at least twenty thousand antiaircraft weapons, that the existing supply was scarcely adequate for the defense of New York City, and that Britain planned to use nine hundred such weapons to defend London.[22]

Maverick also told the House that the United States was "miserably behind every modern country in the world" in aviation and urged members to vote for his bill (H.R. 10350) designed to set up

Sultan of the Young Turks 169

a program for the training of aviation cadets at all of the land-grant colleges and universities, and the establishment of a United States Aeronautical Academy.[23] The *San Antonio Light* said that this would mean the training of "at least 100,000 pilots" at a "West Point of the Air" with branches at Kelly, Randolph, Duncan, and Brooks Fields in the San Antonio environs.[24] The proposal received editorial support throughout the nation. A Connecticut paper later said that Maury Maverick "may some day be hailed as the 'father' of the 'West Point of the Air,' just as the nation pays its homage to those forefathers who gave us the Military and Naval Academies at West Point and Annapolis."[25]

Two weeks later Maverick was calling for the establishment of a single civil aeronautics authority and expansion of the National Guard and reserve air arms, as well as the air academy.[26] Later in May, as he spoke proudly of securing passage of appropriations of $1,747,000 for improvements at San Antonio's Kelly Field, an advanced pilot training base, Maverick again urged passage of his air academy proposal, and a few days later he treated the nation and the Congress to some more of his engaging candor. In a discussion of possible sites for such an academy, he said:

> Mr. Speaker, I join in the praise of the gentleman from California [Mr. Dockweiler], who has the laudable ambition of being Governor of his State; he would make a good one, and we all wish him well. But I have an equally laudable ambition to be reelected to Congress—so listen to what I shall say about this appropriation for Kelly Field, which is in exactly the right place, my district [laughter], San Antonio, Texas. That is the place I want to get an aeronautical academy established, and I hope everybody will interest themselves in it, because it is the one and only advanced flying school of the Army.[27]

On another occasion, after asserting that his record would show that he had cast his votes for the "national welfare," he admitted that he had not "sprouted wings." "For, indeed, I am no bashful John Alden when it comes to getting appropriations for my district. And I think that is perfectly proper—a Congressman should be the business delegate of the people, whose conditions he knows and whose lives he understands, and at the same time he should be the Representative of his country."[28]

In his budget message of January 3, 1938, FDR had sought a

power that had long been advocated by reformers and still is—the power to veto items in appropriation measures comparable to that exercised by most state governors. Maverick agreed that the item veto could be used to stop pork-barrel projects, but he felt it would give too much power to the executive who could use it to "dominate Congress completely and more or less make us a sort of company union of messenger boys." Maury maintained that it could be used against individual members to the extent that "no Congressman would dare oppose the executive on anything." It was his contention, moreover, that the proposed device, an amendment to an appropriations bill, would be found unconstitutional—a constitutional amendment would be the only valid way to give the president item-veto power.[29]

Two days later Maverick attacked the irregular way in which the Appropriations Committee and Representative Clifton A. Woodrum (D.-Va.) had proceeded with the item-veto amendment. It specifically authorized the president to reduce by executive order the amounts authorized to be spent. Maury said that this approach was "worse than a veto," that it could be used to alter basic policies established by Congress. Maverick made no bones about the fact that he was concerned about the prospect that the president might eliminate appropriations for post offices, which were "perfectly proper" for congressmen to seek for their districts.[30] There was no doubt that this dollars and cents argument would strike a responsive chord, if not terror, in the hearts of fellow members of the House. Roosevelt, of course, was not extended this item veto, nor has it been extended to any other president.

As he had done with his proposal for an investigation of alleged irregularities in the administration of relief and WPA programs, ardent TVA supporter Maverick confounded the administration and his critics in 1938 by calling for an investigation to meet criticisms of the Tennessee Valley Authority. In support of his resolution for an investigation, he said that no friend of TVA should fear the results. He declared that there was some basis to the charges made by enemies of TVA, but gave them small comfort when he said that he was concerned about some of the power sales to great corporations, such as ALCOA. He said that there was a lack of frankness concerning TVA affairs on the part of Harcourt A. Mor-

Sultan of the Young Turks

gan and David E. Lilienthal, members of the Board of Directors of TVA, who had been accused of malfeasance by the chairman, Arthur E. Morgan. Maverick had once said that TVA officials seemed to think that they had "wings and work in Green Pastures,"[31] and now he said, "This lofty attitude is possessed by some of the high bojums and key cockalorums of the T.V.A. My idea is that all of them should be requested to dismount from their highhorses and talk with us poor, benighted fellows in order that we may be enlightened."[32]

Maverick repeated his call for an investigation on March 3, saying that Congress was becoming a "door mat." He urged fellow Democrats not to "evade responsibility" but to "get up and assert" themselves.[33] When he urged support of the investigation at the end of the month, Maverick got some more Republican support. Representative Harold Knutson of Minnesota quoted in praise of Maverick a line from the March 28 *New York Herald Tribune*, which stated that he had "led an open revolt against any whitewashing inquiry." Knutson said that Arthur Morgan had been put before a kangaroo court at the White House and praised Maverick as the "fearless Democrat who is never afraid to take the floor and express his honest convictions."[34] The kangaroo court was Knutson's description of the removal of Arthur Morgan by FDR for insubordination when the chairman refused to produce evidence of his charges against Harcourt Morgan and Lilienthal and called for an investigation instead. After he was fired, an investigation was made and it resulted in a majority finding that Lilienthal and Harcourt Morgan were guilty of nothing more than policy differences with Arthur Morgan, rather than the alleged malfeasance.[35]

Maverick was not always jousting with Roosevelt's positions and proposals in 1938. As an astute politician, FDR was well aware of this, and he valued Maverick's aid. For example, Maverick indicated privately sometime in the 1950's that FDR had asked him to help defeat the famous Ludlow amendment, which was designed to amend the Constitution to provide that popular approval in a national referendum would have to be obtained before the United States could go to war. In spite of the fact that Maverick was originally in favor of the amendment and that he was one of the bitter enders on neutrality legislation, FDR somehow persuaded him to make this switch. Maverick said no more than that he got enough liberals to change sides to bring about defeat of the proposed amendment.[36] The measure was rejected by a vote of 209 to 188.[37]

Maverick also gave staunch support to FDR's request for a bill giving him power to reorganize the Federal administrative structure based upon the study by the 1937 President's Committee on Administrative Management (Brownlow Committee), which preceded the Hoover Commission studies of the 1940's and 1950's. Maury said that big business yelled for more efficient government and then defeated the means to accomplish it. Its opposition he characterized as "a lot of platitudes, a lot of empty generalities, noise and wind and intellectual junk." Again, with reckless audacity, he said that the people who were sending him wires against the bill did not understand it, and, "I am not afraid to go back home to my district . . . and say that I voted for the reorganization bill."[38] Though the bill failed for that session of Congress, his speech evoked a letter of congratulation from Adolph A. Berle, Jr., then assistant secretary of state, who said that Maury had "stated the cold facts about the opposition" to the reorganization bill "amazingly well."[39] Maverick seized the opportunity to plead his usual case. He wrote to Berle:

> Now that we got whipped on the Reorganization Bill, I find your kind letter. It must be borne in mind [that it was] not on account of what was in the bill, but on account of our own bungling.
> Not for weeks has any New Dealer been permitted to get out in the front. Of course, one can get on the radio, if he has sufficient standing, and ask for time. But fighting these separate battles is getting tiresome. Concerning the Reorganization Bill, the tax bill and various others: not a single person has gotten on the air to give evidence of their worth. I made a speech on taxes with the help of Leon Henderson—I know of no others who did it. The tax bill is a monstrosity and should be repealed. Such a bill is "letting the people down." I could give example after example.
> It must be remembered that many of the Members of Congress have no convictions particularly, one way or the other. When Roosevelt slows down and doesn't take command of the battle, and when friends of Roosevelt are not even permitted to help, it is only natural that those without convictions turn against Roosevelt. Basically, Roosevelt is still as strong as ever—but he must get out in front.

Sultan of the Young Turks 173

In his conclusion Maverick urged that the reorganization bill be passed because its defeat would be a blow to FDR's prestige. He said that though Roosevelt might be a little unpopular at the moment, "deep down in the hearts of the American people they are for Franklin D. Roosevelt . . . the symbol of America."[40]

Maverick also endorsed the recommendation of the president's committee for the establishment of a welfare department. Indeed, Maverick had made such a recommendation before the committee had done so.[41]

Though Maverick could be outspoken in defense of seeking appropriations for his district, he thought that patronage was a pain in the neck. He supported Roosevelt's expansion of the civil service and said that members of Congress should bring all Federal jobs under civil service. He argued that congressmen would be better off "because then we would not have people worrying us about jobs and we would have decent, independent people on the payroll, neither enemies or friends."[42]

Maverick was always out in front in the fight for passage of the federal minimum-wage law, and he shared the credits for its passage in 1938 (the Fair Labor Standards Act). Only twenty-two southerners signed the petition to bring the measure to the floor of the House. The three Texas members were Lyndon Johnson, Maverick, and Sam Rayburn.[43] Maverick also took the lead in beating back attempts to make the minimum wage lower in Southern states, and criticized chambers of commerce in the South for advertising "cheap and docile labor."[44]

Maverick's references to a tax speech in his letter to Berle alluded to his effort to head off demands by businessmen for reductions in the profits taxes on corporations. In a defense of capital-gains taxes and undistributed-profits taxes Maverick, with the assistance of economist Leon Henderson, presented the following arguments to the nation. First, he said, in defense of capital-gains tax, those who are cut from seven million to five million dollars of "paper profits" complain of the government stealing their money —a notion based upon "some of the weirdest ideas ever thought up since people believed in spooks and goblins." What these people really meant, said Maverick, is that if they sold some major stock at a profit, they would buy another stock and sell it when it had "ballooned up" on the market. "That would not put one thin dime in the hands of the American people; it would start no new enterprise—in fact, it is this kind of practice that bids up stocks to artificially high prices." Tax relief, Maverick contended, did not cause business to expand; previous attempts in 1930, 1931, and 1932 proved that it did not. His studies showed, he said, that machinery was purchased only after consumer goods were being bought at a high rate. The focus of government action, in brief, should be in the area of increasing consumption. Maverick admonished:

Without defining capitalism, it certainly is not a condition of trade and commerce where a combine or organization dominates other business at will, fixes prices, evades taxes, and at will regulates what other persons or concerns do.
But many have been so twisted around by this modern-day propaganda that you actually see a man who is being destroyed by monopoly and big business, denouncing the Government for giving him a chance. In other words capitalism—free enterprise and free competition—[is] certainly not possible in an economy dominated by monopolies, combines, big family fortunes, or a combination of them.[45]

A week or so later Maverick told members of the Philadelphia Real Estate Board at their annual banquet that they had invited the wrong man to speak to them—and then he proved it. He told them that Philadelphia was the cradle of liberty but that it was also the cradle of poor housing and the cradle of crime. Big business had lost its influence, he said, and it would not be regained until "business itself cleans house; until it is fair to labor and to the public, and willingly pays the taxes that it owes the Government." Inadequate housing, he said, was a serious national problem and no one was doing anything about it. Maverick then gave them a short discourse on the economy that was remarkably like the one that A. A. Berle was to express in one of his books many years later. Maverick said, "Manufacturing is no little shoe cobbler's store, but a set of gigantic, Herculean ventures which trade not alone with every part of the Nation, but with all the world. . . . Believe me, physical science and industry have progressed so mightily, and so far ahead of political science, that we will have to stretch our brains to even begin to understand our problems today."[46]

Sultan of the Young Turks

Maverick had one more joust with the Congressional proponents of investigation of un-American activities, but this time he lost. In May 1937 his Texas colleague Martin Dies brought up a resolution for the establishment of the House Committee on Un-American Activities, arguing that it was now necessary to deal with the activities of the German-American Bund. Maverick said that though he despised the Bund and its activities, there were plenty of national and local laws to deal with the problem. "It is the same old stuff," he said, "pompous patriotism" as a substitute for getting things done. "In Greece, if someone expressed an unorthodox idea he was called a Persian; when Rome got to have hard times, they accused a man of being a Greek if he did not agree with orthodox opinions." It was all a fake side show, said Maverick. "We do not have to investigate to find out what we already know, and if we do investigate, the only reason . . . will be . . . to scare the people with exciting stories, making them suspicious of their fellow Americans, which will get the committee members headlines in the papers."[47]

Even in party politics, the professionals found Maverick to be painfully and distressingly honest. Though FDR could never bring himself to repudiate the support of the infamous Boss Frank Hague of Jersey City, Maverick called for an investigation of his denials of civil liberties in December 1937,[48] and when, in the political season of 1938, a Republican colleague questioned Democrats on their acceptance of Hague, Maverick rose to the occasion:

> I want to say that as a Democrat, I am not proud of Mayor Hague of Jersey City. I think it is a proper activity of the minority party to call attention to the faults of the majority party, whatever the motive, and I am glad the gentleman is doing it.
> I denounce Mayor Hague as a cheap, ignorant, tawdry, villainous little dictator who is a disgrace to his city, a disgrace to his state, and a disgrace to the United States of America. There is no excuse for his violent and brutal actions in a free country.

If that wasn't enough, Maverick said that Hague "should be viewed with contempt by all self-respecting Americans."[49]

While Maverick was making hay for national causes and speaking out on national politics in 1938, no one was minding the store back home. His old enemies and some new ones were determined to "get Maury" this time. In February 1938 the *San Antonio Express* made the straight-faced announcement that Mayor C. K. Quin had announced his intention to support San Antonio's "fiery chief of police," Owen Kilday, in the coming Democratic primary against Maverick. The *Express* said that this announcement constituted endorsement by the "city machine, the members of which hold a big majority of the offices in the city and county government."[50]

The first phase of the campaign against Maverick then took on a comic-opera note. The *San Antonio Light*'s "Don Politico" column said that the announcement was the "laugh of the week," and no one was "more dumfounded by this strange departure from political orthodoxy than the chief himself." "Don Politico" doubted that the mayor could be serious and wondered about the reason for the action.[51] It was just possible that Quin had his Kildays mixed up, for on March 13 "Don Politico" correctly predicted that Paul J. Kilday, Owen's brother and first assistant district attorney, was about to receive the nod from Mayor Quin.[52]

Further bizarre activities marked what appeared to be an unofficial kickoff of the campaign when, by an engineered coincidence, Elizabeth Dilling, author of *The Red Network* and *The Roosevelt Red Record and Its Background*, appeared in San Antonio on March 16. Maverick had been mentioned in the latter book as "Red Maury Maverick," the pet of the "Communist-aiding American Civil Liberties Union."[53] Inside the front cover of his own copy of the book, Maverick wrote a three-word review: "This obscene book."[54] The *San Antonio Evening News* objectively reported that Mrs. Dilling "spoke vibrantly and with much gesticulation at the interview . . . and the vigor of her manner was enhanced by a bright blue coatsuit that she wore." She told San Antonians, "I know he's a Red. He's Moscow's pet. Is he red? Baby he's their darling." Maury was for "the peace movement of revolution," and she did not know of a peace movement that was not designed for civil war.[55] No one lifted a pen to point out that Dilling's work was a mishmash of inaccuracies and innuendoes—that there was no credible basis for the charges against Maverick.

The following day, March 17, James E. Kilday, another brother of the San Antonio police chief, was quoted as having said, "Paul is going to oppose Maverick, and he is going to pitch the fight on the issue of Maverick's communistic affiliations."[56] On March 30 Paul Kilday announced his candidacy for Maverick's seat, saying that his object was "the elimination from Congress of one overwhelmingly shown to be the friend and ally of Communism."[57] He pointed out on another occasion that he had not said that Maverick was a Communist, but that he was a "friend and ally of Communism."[58]

The "evidence" was that Maverick had expressed admiration for Eugene V. Debs, had supported the CIO, had spoken favorably of John L. Lewis, had had a conference with the Russian ambassador, and had been praised by a Communist paper.[59] The "conference" was a social gathering at the Soviet Embassy during which Maverick, with his usual flair for diplomacy, had "twitted the Russians for wholesale purges." He is reported to have said to Ambassador Alexander Troyanovsky, "What can we think of a country which shoots half a dozen of its best generals and 20 of its top bureau officials at a volley?" Maverick then added a jolting, "They may get you next."[60] This was the "conference" that supposedly indicated Maverick's Communist sympathies!

The praise referred to was probably a review of *A Maverick American* in a leading article in a Communist periodical. It merely called him a "twentieth century Populist," and said, "Maverick has many shortcomings in his ideas when they are taken as a whole, but he is a progressive and stands out as such."[61] While Maverick was getting the red-paint treatment in San Antonio, the *Daily Worker* criticized him severely for being an isolationist and said that the only way to peace was through "collective security, a united front of the democracies"![62] Moreover, Earl Browder, head of the Communist party, had attacked Maverick and others who were fighting the naval expansion bill in Congress.[63]

Though there was no substance to the charges of communism, Maury Maverick was in trouble. The Citizens League had begun to disintegrate in 1937, and he had failed to do the needed fence mending in Bexar County.

Early in the 1938 campaign, Mayor Quin had charged that Maverick had written an article signed by Owen P. White for *Collier's* magazine.[64] The article was a hard-hitting indictment of the shortcomings of machine government in the Alamo city.[65] Maverick said that Quin's charge was "plain, unsupported falsehood," and countercharged on one of the issues discussed in the article that Quin had refused a personal offer of Dr. Thomas Parran, surgeon general of the United States, for a survey of public health conditions in San Antonio.[66] When queried on this matter by a reporter, Quin said that he did not care to say anything about it.[67]

Maverick might have been said to have won that round, but neither he nor Quin made any public statements at this time concerning other sensational revelations of the article. White had included an extensive exposé of the recently deceased Charles Bellinger and his relationship with prominent citizens of San Antonio. Bellinger, a handsome, intelligent Negro boss, was said to be able to deliver from five to eight thousand votes to the city-county machine. Gambling and vice were rampant in San Antonio in the twenties and thirties, and White charged that politicians would take 25 percent of the gross earnings of the gamblers, and that the City Health Department was used to shake down prostitutes by charging them two dollars a week for health cards. Bellinger's controlled vote was usually enough to swing city and county elections, and, White said, "It meant he could either open or close the channels of graft that we have just been talking about."

Bellinger was said to have started out as a small-time gambler and then had become the "boss gambler of Austin Street." He later moved into money lending and real estate and bought whole blocks of shacks. He would ask ministers of Negro churches to get the votes for him and he would see to it that streets to churches would be paved and that better parks and schools would be provided—and it all worked, because he delivered the goods.

When Bellinger was sent to prison for income-tax evasion, "prominent citizens" signed a petition for his pardon. In May 1937, the *San Antonio Light* reported that Mayor Quin and Phil Shook, Sr., the district attorney, had gone to Washington to "obtain a full pardon for Charles Bellinger, negro racketeer, gambler and political power." The account stated that Maverick had made appointments for the two and accompanied them to several conferences, but he "emphatically declared he took no part in the plea for Bellinger's pardon." Bellinger had been out on parole since President Roosevelt had commuted his sentence after the Negro leader suffered a heart attack. Shortly after the attempt to win him a full pardon, Bellinger died,[68] but his Harvard-educated son succeeded

Sultan of the Young Turks

to the empire, and he and Maverick were to lock horns in a later contest.

Throughout June 1938 Kilday kept hammering on charges of Maverick's alleged "communistic" associations. On June 28 Kilday said that Maverick had endorsed John L. Lewis for president in 1940, but that he (Kilday) would be a supporter of Roosevelt.[69] Maverick said Kilday's statement was a lie: "Now don't any of you newspaper boys say 'Maverick shouted that it was a lie.' Say in a quiet, unassuming way, 'Maverick said it was a dirty lie.' "[70]

Maverick was assisted by a "dozen timely bouquets" from Secretary of War Harry H. Woodring,[71] and Kilday's attacks seemed to become somewhat more temperate. As the election drew near he said, "There is one issue which no matter of shouting, no matter of irrelevant things can remove from this campaign—Maverick's radicalism." He went on to say that Maverick had been out gadding about and speaking to the CIO when he should have been looking out for the interests of San Antonio.[72] Maverick's reply to Kilday's earlier charges had been, "Anyone who criticizes those in power is a radical or communist in this town. Well, I say what I think and I'm going to continue to do so until some of these conditions are cleared up."[73]

Maverick was banking heavily on the support of FDR, in spite of their differences. He went to Fort Worth on July 10 to join the presidential train, and when he boarded it Roosevelt reportedly greeted him with, "Hello, Maury, glad to see you. How's the boy?"[74] Later in a speech at Amarillo, FDR had kind words for Representatives Marvin Jones, Lyndon Johnson, W. D. McFarlane, and Maury Maverick, referring to the latter as "my friend."[75] But Maverick wanted something stronger and had been led to expect he would get it. On June 25, in a confidential note to Tom Corcoran, Maverick said that, without any prompting on his part, FDR had invited him to come by for a visit. "He also promised to write me a letter extolling my virtues, my pious character—and also how much dough I got for San Antonio," Maverick said. He urged Corcoran to "do your stuff," and directed another letter to FDR aide Marvin McIntyre in which he made some suggestions as to the text of the letter. But there was no letter.[76]

A few days later, in one of his stump speeches, Kilday claimed the endorsement of Texas Representative Hatton W. Sumners and

Senator Tom Connally. Both of these men had locked horns with Maverick, particularly over the court-packing plan, and the endorsements seemed plausible enough. When queried by Maverick, however, Sumners wired that he had not endorsed Kilday, and Connally wrote from Marlin that he had not "either directly or indirectly" endorsed anyone.[77]

In April the astute (and usually correct) political reporter, Raymond Brooks, had written, "Congressman Maury Maverick took them to a major defeat two years ago, and he will win again easily against them this year,"[78] but on July 27 the official canvass of returns by the Democratic committee of Bexar County gave 24,822 votes for Kilday and 24,329 for Maverick—a difference of only 493 votes.[79]

Why did Maverick lose? Considering the small margin by which Kilday defeated him, almost any single reason given by the Monday morning quarterbacks could have been *the* reason. Maverick's first public reaction was to state that his defeat could be attributed to the "bankers and the wealthy" from the north side of San Antonio.[80] He also said that enemies of FDR had raised "huge sums of money" to defeat him and nine other House liberals. "It was amazing," he said. "I almost lost interest in my own race watching the slick way they beat me." He added that "scandal squads" were used against him in the campaign to brand him as a Communist and an atheist, and that votes were actually bought.[81] He added other factors in a prepared statement: (1) he was up against a machine like that of Jersey City; (2) more money was used against him than in any other Southern campaign; (3) he got off to a late start on campaign organization after the adjournment of Congress; and (4) he was hurt by the antilabor vote resulting from his CIO connections.[82]

The usually perceptive "Don Politico" column emphasized the antilabor factor, pointing out that Maverick's speech to the Auto Workers in Detroit and his attack on Henry Ford had hurt him in the rural precincts, which Kilday carried by a vote of 2,271 to 2,082. Had Maverick held them as he had in 1934 and 1936, he would have been reelected.[83] AFL leader William Green actually took credit for Maverick's defeat, lambasting him as an "ill-tempered, ill-informed, unstable and half-baked legislator." Maverick responded that Green had lied when he said that he had attacked

Sultan of the Young Turks

the AFL. It will be recalled that Maverick had defended Green when he was booed by the United Auto Workers, but that the Texas congressman had later lectured the labor leader for his stand with respect to the wage and hour legislation. Now, Maverick said, "The truth is, Mr. Green is himself entrenched in his job, and out of private spite and envy he is willing to betray labor. He is weak, stupid, vacillating and cowardly."[84] The *New York Post* quoted Green's boast of the defeat of Maverick and commented, "We feel sorry for Mr. Green."[85] Paul Y. Anderson called Green's statement incredible, and said that his rejoicing over the defeat of Maverick "was almost as if a man were to demand credit for shooting his best friend in the back."[86]

Green's contribution to the defeat of Maverick was not in taking AFL votes away from him, because the local AFL endorsed the congressman. Rather it was a matter of Green's endorsement of Kilday, lending support to the charges that Maverick was a CIO man and the consequent loss of the essentially anti-CIO rural vote in Bexar County.

Thirteen years later, as Maverick looked over his scrapbooks, he came to the newspaper photograph of Paul Kilday winking at the camera as he cast his vote in the 1938 primary. Maverick jotted next to the pictures, "He knew how to win that election, *one* box was held out several days (it had *over* 500 votes in it) there Maverick lost by about 480 votes. No wonder he winked."[87]

Then there was the story of the campaign train, reported by Pearson and Allen, Maverick's friends. They said that in defeat Maverick had the one consolation that his loss had "caused more bitter recrimination in the inner White House circle than anything since the loss of the Supreme Court reorganization bill." Pearson and Allen said that the "anguished partisans" of Maverick had made "scorching cracks" as they blamed his defeat on the White House. FDR was said to have promised Maury, in response to his request for help, "Maury, you write the prescription, and I'll fill it."

When Maverick boarded the train at Fort Worth in July, White House secretaries Marvin McIntyre and Stephen Early gave him the run-around. McIntyre let Maverick see the president only briefly, and Early refused to issue a statement to the effect that FDR hoped Maury would be reelected, which the president had directed Maverick to tell Early to give to the press. Roosevelt was considered to be sincere in his wish to help Maverick, but his aides felt that the Texas whirlwind was too militant and outspoken. Insult was added to injury when Maverick found that his opponent's campaign manager was "comfortably ensconced in the lounge car of the Presidential special." At that time, Pearson and Allen said, "how he got on the train is still a mystery."[88]

Months later Pearson and Allen were able to clear up the mystery. Maverick visited FDR in late November, and the two journalists said that he as good as told the president that his son Elliott was a "meddling carpetbagger." The "budding Texas radio magnate" from Houston was flatly accused of helping Maverick's opponent by employing Kilday's campaign manager on one of the radio stations and also of getting him on the president's special train. Maury asked Roosevelt to give his son a "good bawling out," and FDR excused his son as being "young and inexperienced." Maverick is said to have responded that he had a seventeen-year-old son who had "better sense than that."[89]

These specific factors might serve to explain Maverick's narrow defeat, but the explanation as to how he dropped from a majority of more than three thousand votes in his first primary victory for a seat in Congress and a plurality of about seven thousand votes in his second success lies in the general causes underlying the specifics. "Don Politico" captured it neatly in a quotation from "one wire story," which read, "He took too many liberties with a normally conservative constituency."[90] A Negro paper said that Maury was "trounced at the polls because he talked too much and too unguardedly."[91] The paper used as an example the remark attributed to Maverick as he opposed voting in the District of Columbia, "Hell! We got to have slaves somewhere. It might as well be in Washington."[92] In August, more than a week after the damage was done, Maverick wrote to Eleanor Patterson of the *Washington Herald*, the source of the story, to protest that he did not make the remark attributed to him. He said, "Either the man who gave the story was lying, or I am lying. . . . I said nothing like the statement that was attributed to me." The response was, "We have been unable to find any evidence to contradict the story which we ran."[93]

The *Baltimore Sun* saw Maverick's troubles in the fact that he

Sultan of the Young Turks

was more "Roosevelt than Roosevelt": "Mr. Maverick was not only a New Dealer. He was not only the leader of the bloc in the House on which the more strident manipulators in Washington depended to scare the regular leadership whenever it showed signs of stopping, looking or listening. Mr. Maverick also specialized, in his hearty and engaging manner, in private roars because Mr. Roosevelt was not taking the Government into things right and left at an even faster pace."[94]

Finally, Maverick was caught in the general swing toward conservatism and opposition to the New Deal in Texas and, though less pronounced, in the nation. Many of the Mavericks lost their seats in November, and one analyst concluded that Maury's defeat was the key one. He had "rallied the lads of radical ideas," and "his little band of zealots, through the strength of organization, became a power in the House. . . . They were pledged to work for reforms in the next Congress. Now Maverick is gone. Others of the little 'sworn to die' band, in Wisconsin, Minnesota and Pennsylvania, who hang to their seats by small majorities, are slated for the November ax. Maury was the vital force. And a likeable fellow he is, too."[95] Maverick apparently saw all of this himself when he wrote the following for the *Philadelphia Record*: "Stop your telegrams telling me how sad it was that I got beat! It was a miracle that I got elected in the first place!"[96]

Maury Maverick looked well in defeat, both because of his reaction to it and that of newspapers throughout the nation. He told the *New York Times*: "I voted nationally always and for progress, I never cast a sectional vote. I never demagogued on our serious questions and stood for civil liberties. I have no regrets. . . . Whatever happens, nothing will dim my spirit and I will stand by the people, for civil liberty and economic justice."[97] He told another newspaper, "The personal problem of any man who was beaten unfairly is to refuse to succumb to bitterness, and refuse to become a baiter of racial and religious minorities in order to get back. That has happened to some of our best Southerners. It will not happen to me."[98]

Editorial comment deploring the defeat of Maverick was nation wide. The *Portland Oregonian* wondered, "Just what the democrats of his district hope to gain by displacing him is not easy to perceive,"[99] and the *San Francisco News* declared, "Perhaps the one result of greatest concern to non-Texans was the defeat of Maury Maverick in the Texas primary election."[100] In an editorial headed, "A Loss to the Nation," the *Saint Louis Star-Times* said that it was "a genuine minor tragedy" that Maverick had been denied renomination,[101] and the *Philadelphia Record* expressed dismay at the loss of "one of the ablest and most courageous of national liberal leaders."[102]

Seldom has a single representative's race received such national publicity and attention. The most significant editorial for Maverick came from the pen of William Allen White, who said, "If the present progressive wave in the Democratic party has produced one honest, intelligent, courageous man, that man is Maury Maverick, congressman from Texas, who Saturday went down to defeat under the maledictions of the local Democratic organization—the local Tammany—of San Antonio. . . . The first thing they do when he [FDR] is looking the other way is to crack down on a brave, wise, honest man like Maury Maverick." White went on to discuss the prospects for a third-party movement and then concluded, "In the meantime, here is a silent tear for Maury Maverick—and not so terribly silent either!"[103]

The conservative and influential *Dallas News*, a paper that practically never agreed with Maverick but usually treated him fairly, said, "Congress will miss Maury Maverick, bull ways and all. Maverick's independence commands respect even when his theories may be disapproved or disbelieved. He is sold on new deal legislation, but no one could mistake him possibly for a subservient yes-man. He would certainly support no Roosevelt program with which he does disagree."[104] There were, of course, a number of conservative newspapers that rejoiced in the defeat of the nettlesome Maverick.[105] As one writer put it, "nervous tories" thought he was "the Robespierre from the Rio Grande."[106]

Representative Thomas R. Amlie, Progressive representative from the First District of Wisconsin and a coleader of the Mavericks in the House, wrote to tell Maverick that he regarded his defeat as the "most serious setback that the liberal cause has received," and said that he had tried to get some money into Maverick's district to help him.[107] In November, Amlie wrote an article

Sultan of the Young Turks

for the *Progressive*, "Two More Years," in which he said that Maverick's defeat was "nothing less than a national calamity," and that he was "the most significant member of either House of Congress."[108] Amlie himself was defeated shortly after the article was published.

Maverick's supporters persuaded him to try to run in November as an independent candidate with the expectation of picking up part of the votes of Bexar County Negroes (who could vote in the general election) on the basis of his support for antilynching legislation. Governor James Allred and Texas Secretary of State Edward Clark had both encouraged Maverick to make such an attempt, but after studying the matter the secretary of state ruled that a candidate for the Democratic nomination could not run as an independent in the general election.[109] Had this approach been legal, the prospects for its success were dubious. Though many Negroes signed the petition to get Maverick on the ticket as an independent, most of the rank and file were bound to be confused as to where they stood with Maverick.

Voters of whatever color could not be expected to appreciate the subtleties of Maverick's relationship to the Negro voter. In the 1932 primary he had unsuccessfully attempted to secure an injunction to prevent Negroes from voting and had stigmatized Charles Bellinger as a "certain negro gambler, a vicious overlord of vice and crime," and even warned Negroes not to "do anything to cause hate, revenge or destruction to your people."[110] In 1934 he had been able to prevent Negroes from voting in the primary.[111] National Negro leaders later told Maverick, in effect, that they recognized that most of the San Antonio Negro vote was machine controlled and that they knew what a dilemma it posed for him.[112] Thus one might conclude that Maverick was not opposed to Negroes voting but that his complaint was that Negro votes were being delivered to the opposition. On the other hand, Negroes were not sure what his motivation was. Also, though Maverick had voted for the antilynch bill and had sought general civil-rights legislation, he made no secret of the fact that he did not believe in social equality for the Negro.[113]

Maverick later secured an investigation of the primary, with a particular eye to campaign contributions to Kilday and possible "violations of election laws," but nothing came of it at that time.[114] It was later reported however that city employees and officials were "visibly worried" at the prospect of a grand-jury investigation of the padding of city payrolls in the last election.[115]

What would Maverick do now? Most observers agreed that he would not be down very long. Some thought he would wait to return to Washington in 1941;[116] others saw him in line for an appointment to some administrative post in the New Deal administration.[117] One paper reported speculation that he was to become successor to General Blanton Winship, governor of Puerto Rico.[118] But the "Don Politico" column had the inside information, predicting on October 12 that Maury Maverick would build a city organization and seek the office of mayor of San Antonio the following May. The "Don" said that Maverick had declined offers of "federal preferment" and wanted no federal appointive job.[119] Maverick tipped his hand when in October 1938 he announced with his usual subtlety, "San Antonio has the sorriest city government in the United States, so far as I have been able to ascertain."[120]

Later in the year, Maverick was making a swing through the country, speaking at colleges, universities, Rotary Clubs, and open forums.[121] He delivered his final admonitions in a parting shot to FDR and the New Dealers when he stopped off in Washington. He said that Roosevelt should get rid of Jim Farley because he did not represent what the president stood for and that FDR should take a strong stand against Mayor Hague and other corrupt Democratic bosses. "The people aren't fooled. You can't talk idealism on one hand and not do anything about the Hagues on the other. . . . Liberals must realize that they cannot compromise with corrupt machines."[122]

If Maverick needed any encouragement for his next plunge into politics, he had it in full measure, but he particularly prized the following letter from Supreme Court Justice Hugo Black:

Dear Maury:
   Your published statement indicates that you accept the recent results in your district as a *skirmish* only, and that you are now preparing for the *battle*—Your friends and admirers throughout the

country will welcome the Maverick spirit of your promise to *carry on*. The *Public* needs you. I have no doubt that you will come back stronger than ever—you are *right*, and that will triumph.

When you come to Washington be certain to come to see me. My wife and I both want you to come out and visit us. We have to leave for Washington tomorrow—

With my good wishes and genuine *admiration*, I am

Sincerely your friend,
Hugo L. Black[123]

A Texas La Guardia

EARLY IN DECEMBER 1938 a series of sordid revelations began to emerge, indicating that the San Antonio mayor's office was going to be ripe, or perhaps rotten, for the plucking.

The story broke with a controversy between Bexar County district attorney John R. Shook and the Criminal District Court grand jurors. Members of the grand jury had excluded the district attorney, for what turned out to be obvious reasons, from their sessions. After a heated clash, the irate Shook attempted to get Judge W. W. McCrory to "inform the probing body of the statutory rights of the district attorney's office."[1] What the grand jury was looking into, among other things, was the hiring of hundreds of city workers at the time of the Democratic primary in which Maverick lost his seat in Congress. Shook was himself a member of the machine that profited from the "political work" of those persons hired. Joe Diaz, one of the witnesses who appeared before the grand jury, told newsmen, "I've always been a friend of Johnny Shook. I promised Kilday I would help him and I wanted to help out Judge McCrory. About a week after the election I got $4 from the city."[2] There was small comfort, but some humor, in the possibility that some payoffs

A Texas La Guardia 189

did not work too well. Juan Flores told the *San Antonio Express* that he had received four dollars from the city to work for Sheriff Will W. Wood at the same time he was "doing a little precinct work for Albert West," Wood's opponent.[3]

But the grand jury was not amused. It returned indictments against Mayor Quin and two of his aides. Some five hundred citizens were listed in the *San Antonio Light*, the amounts paid to each of them ranging from four to forty dollars for "working around the polls." The indictments were drawn under Article 95 of the penal code of Texas, making misapplication of public funds a criminal offense, rather than Article 188, which covered bribery in elections. When the indictments were returned, Judge W. W. McCrory disqualified himself and called in Judge R. D. Wright of Laredo to hear the cases. Judge McCrory said, "During the time the grand jury was investigating the cases, it was generally understood that the witnesses were working for me, Paul Kilday and other members of the ticket."

The *San Antonio Light* accurately predicted that the indictments would be quashed because the money had not been "appropriated to their own use and benefit," as had been charged. Rather, said "Don Politico," the money "was spent to aid the political ambitions of District Attorney John R. Shook, Congressman Paul J. Kilday, defeated County Judge Egbert Schweppe, defeated candidate for sheriff Albert W. West, Jr., Bob Uhr, and the others who ran for office on the machine ticket." The "Don" now said that Maverick's defeat in the primary had been due to the "smart political maneuvers" of the chief of police, Owen Kilday. The *Light* stated in a front-page story two days before that the money spent by the city officials could account for at least one thousand votes.

The grand jury investigation, however, continued. In an editorial January 2, the *San Antonio Light* charged that a "personal property assessment racket" existed in Bexar County and urged the grand jury to continue its probe into general corruption in local government. The grand jury declared, "We deplore and condemn a political set-up which deprives all the people of adequate, effective and safe protection, as well as efficient and well-managed administration." When the indictment against Quin was actually dropped in February and Shook proceeded to dismiss the indictments against "other politicians," the *Light* indignantly editorialized:

> Let's review THE FACTS.
> Some 500 persons were put on the city payroll on or about the date of the Democratic primary last July.
> This is NOT hearsay or idle speculation.
> Scores of these "workers" were called before the Criminal District Court grand jury, which in turn indicted Mayor Quin and two of his aides. . . .
> "I have committed no offense," [Mayor Quin] said, "I have violated no law. Neither have my two employees who were indicted with me."
> "IS IT AN INDICTABLE OFFENCE TO FEED A FEW SCORE HUNGRY PEOPLE IF AT THE TIME OF EMPLOYMENT THERE IS PERCHANCE A DEMOCRATIC CAMPAIGN BEING WAGED?"
> Note carefully, the mayor DID NOT DENY the city's payrolls had been padded at election time.
> Rather, he asked, in effect: "What are you going to do about it?"

No one was fooled by the brazen action, and there were persons who were prepared to "do something about it." Maverick had again hinted at running for mayor on December 21, saying he had been approached by a number of people. Later it was reported that he had, without success, asked each of seven prominent San Antonians to run for Mayor. In a later discussion of Maury's efforts to get someone to run, "Don Politico" said that he was certain that Maverick had a federal appointment "in the bag." "The nature of this position would be such that it would pay him handsomely, yet allow him sufficient time to participate in politics," declared the "Don." But on February 2, the recently defeated congressman made the formal announcement that he would be a candidate for mayor of San Antonio. He confirmed that he had been offered a federal appointment, but said, "I am not going to desert San Antonio and leave it to the wolves. . . . I want to make this a fit place in which to live!"

A week later a crowd of fifteen hundred aroused citizens met on Saturday night at the Municipal Auditorium at the call of Charles M. Dickson. Dickson declared that the meeting was called to oppose the mayor and his machine, and that it offered "the first real opportunity . . . in many years to elect real representatives of the

A Texas La Guardia 191

people to public office." Grover C. Morris, a Maverick worker, demanded the election of a permanent chairman for the meeting. Dickson tried to rule him and those who seconded the motion out of order. Morris then nominated J. J. ("Jack") Patterson for chairman. The latter was elected, and Morris "clambered over the orchestra pit" and took the microphone. Maverick and his Fusion Ticket were endorsed. Dickson then said that he had attended a meeting at which the majority view was that Maverick could not be a successful candidate for mayor. Amid outcries from the audience, Dickson retired behind the stage curtains, and Maverick was called to the auditorium.

Dickson was reported to have "mourned" the action and said, "The Maverick forces would have helped themselves more if they had been more orderly. We have failed tonight to bring the opposition forces together."[4] The *San Antonio Express* reported substantially the same set of events, but characterized the Maverick movement as a steamroller and said that Dickson had been routed by the shouting crowd as he attempted to get a committee to choose a slate.[5]

That same day Quin improved the chances of his opponents by flaying each of the city commissioners serving with him, blaming them for the problems of the city. All four of the commissioners suggested that the mayor resign.[6] Later in the month the commissioners took action to remove Quin's "political employees" from the payroll, reducing city expenditures by about $90,000 for that year. "The commissioners' move, it was considered at city hall, would practically demolish the mayor's personal political organization and obliterate that group of employees usually described as his braintrust."[7]

As Dickson had predicted, the mayor's race was wide open—four different tickets were framed to contest in the May election. Maverick headed the Fusion Ticket, which he patterned and named after Mayor La Guardia's comparable movement in New York. Indeed, Maverick wrote to La Guardia as the campaign got under way and asked for all the information the New York Mayor could send him that would be helpful. La Guardia complied and asked, "Why in hell do you want to be Mayor?" Maverick's response was, "God knows. . . . Maybe I am crazy."[8] Quin was running on the People's Ticket, Leroy Jeffers headed a Young Men's Ticket and Theo M. Plummer, Quin's tax commissioner, ran on the Economy Ticket.[9]

The campaign followed predictable lines. The Fusion Ticket, it was said, would "wipe out the Machine and give San Antonio good government,"[10] while Quin branded Maverick as a "Communist, CIO-lover, rabble rouser." Jeffers also smeared him with the red brush.[11] The *San Antonio Express* opposed Maverick in a front-page editorial on May 7 for his radio speeches "defaming" San Antonio, the "cleanest" city in Texas, and on election day the paper called attention to his "dangerous radicalism."[12] Maverick pitched his campaign on the clean, efficient government theme, and when the returns were in on May 9, he had the needed plurality of 18,445 votes to 15,441 for Quin and 11,172 for Jeffers.[13] All but one of the Fusion party candidates were elected.[14] Quin's comment was that he had been "run over by a herd of stampeding Mavericks."[15]

A journalist friend may have saved Maverick from disaster in this campaign. Radical Representative Vito Marcantonio had vowed several times during the course of the campaign that he was going down to San Antonio to "help Maury." Maverick's friend said that he "assiduously pointed out" to Marcantonio that his services were too badly needed in Washington to help out that "punk" in San Antonio. The correspondent added, "I've been aiming to write you for some time to tell you that all efforts to rejuvenate the remnants of your liberal bloc failed miserably. It seemed that they couldn't decide who was going to be leader—everybody thought he ought to be it."[16]

The reaction of the *San Antonio Express* to Maverick's victory was an editorial informing him that he had better not forget his campaign promises, because the *Express* was not going to forget them.[17] But Maury was back on the front pages and the editorial pages of the nation. Favorable comment came in from far and wide—even from some conservative journals that had criticized the Maverick philosophy. Henry Ehrlich reported in the *Boston Herald* that President Roosevelt had been "glued to the radio until 1 A.M. listening to the returns the night Maury Maverick was elected Mayor of San Antonio," and that FDR had wired his congratulations to Maverick immediately.[18] The wire read simply, "GOOD BOY, FDR."[19] Thurman Arnold penned a note to say, "You

A Texas La Guardia 193

make me hopeful that they can't keep a real scrapper down. I'm always a thousand per cent for you. You have not only my admiration but also my affection."[20] Josephus Daniels wrote from Mexico City, "I watched the contest in your city with deep interest and am gratified at your victory and wish you the largest measure of success and satisfaction."[21] Hugo Black said that he wanted to congratulate San Antonio for having elected Maverick, and Dr. Harvey Cushing of the Yale University Medical School sent his congratulations on this "highly deserved election," and penned a postscript, "Power to your elbow!"[22]

From his close vantage point in Austin, Texas, newsman Raymond Brooks saw Maverick's victory as the elimination of the "boss of bosses." He said that the real "maker" of bosses in San Antonio was Jacob Rubiola, commissioner of parks and city property, who kept mayors and other officials waiting "hat in hand" until Rubiola got ready to see them. Now, Brooks said, there was an opportunity to bring back efficient, democratic government to San Antonio and to clean up the mess. "San Antonio," said Brooks, "is a supreme example that democracy can right conditions, no matter how vicious they get."[23]

Henry Ehrlich, Washington correspondent for the *Boston Herald*, saw a broader significance to Maverick's comeback. He said it was "like the hoisting of a huge red sign which said 'STOP' to those plotting control of the Democratic party in 1940."[24] Subsequent events tended to demonstrate that there was some validity to this evaluation.

On May 13, one hundred years from the date his grandfather, Sam Maverick, had become mayor of San Antonio, Maury Maverick was sworn in by his father, Albert Maverick.[25]

When Maury assumed the office he was quoted as having croaked, "I'm going to be a stuffed shirt. I got beat for Congress for not being one."[26] It is doubtful that anyone, including Maverick, believed this statement. The *Sacramento Bee* said of the remark, "It is about as much in character as if Franklin Delano Roosevelt proclaimed he was an economic royalist from now on or Herbert Hoover announced his conversion to Communism."[27] Another paper gave some proof of the *Bee*'s contention when it praised Maverick for his "refreshing frankness" when he dismissed hundreds of city employees and announced, "I am a professional politician and am going to give my friends jobs, but the jobs will go on a merit basis."[28]

Mayor Maverick was warmly congratulated on his victory by Mayor La Guardia, who later repeated his congratulations in a lengthier message of counsel and commiseration. He told Maverick that his troubles were just beginning, but, on a more encouraging note, said that Maverick's victory showed "that although politicians try to kick us around, the people will stand by us if we play it straight and fight with both fists. . . . Give the city of San Antonio a good, clean, honest administration, and you'll be all right." La Guardia added that he was looking forward to welcoming Maverick's daughter, Terrelita, when she came to the New York World's Fair with the Texas Lasso Girls, but she was not able to make the trip.[29]

Mayor Maverick continued to seek the aid and counsel of Mayor La Guardia. He visited the New Yorker several times in the months immediately after the 1939 election and was shown the various components of effective city government, including some of La Guardia's prized new garbage trucks. On one occasion Maverick was stumped on the radio show "Information Please" by a set of questions on city government posed by La Guardia. Maverick did not know that the "Holman rule" was a rule of parliamentary procedure relating to limitations on appropriations bills or that the "activated sludge process" was a method of treating sewage. Then Maverick struck back when he caught La Guardia with reporters at the World's Fair and asked him who named the city of New York. La Guardia said he didn't know, and Maverick crowed that it was none other than one of his ancestors, a Sam Maverick who in 1664 was a member of the three-man royal commission with the duke of York when the city was taken from the Dutch.[30] Two years later Maverick caught La Guardia again. The Little Flower missed a question on "Information Please" on how many mayors New York City had had. His answer was 99, but he learned that he was mayor number 103 and that twenty-five dollars and a set of encyclopedias were being sent to the person who had provided the question, Maury Maverick of San Antonio.[31]

Many observers had from time to time pointed to the parallels

A Texas La Guardia 195

between Maverick and La Guardia. Both were short and squat; both were of the "stormy petrel" type;[32] both had been heroes in World War I, La Guardia in the air and Maverick on the ground; both had led liberal blocs in the U.S. House of Representatives; and both had been defeated for Congress only to emerge as cleanup mayors of their home cities. The *New York Daily News* said in 1939 that "Maverick talks like La Guardia and thinks like him," and wondered "whether this is a Texas La Guardia or La Guardia is a New York Maverick."[33] As might have been anticipated, Maverick had the answer. Felix R. McKnight reported that when someone referred to Maverick as a "La Guardia of the South," Maverick snapped back, "Don't you mean La Guardia is the Maverick of the North?"[34]

La Guardia and Maverick saw one another from time to time during World War II, but the relationship had cooled somewhat, probably because of an incident related by Maury Maverick, Jr. At the beginning of the war, La Guardia sent Maverick an example of the hate propaganda used by the Nazis. The leaflet carried La Guardia's picture juxtaposed with that of a baboon, and the caption read, "Which is the baboon?" When Maverick received the leaflet, he couldn't resist wiring back to La Guardia, "Which *is* the baboon?" According to Maury, Jr., La Guardia called Maverick and cussed him out in three languages.[35]

Maverick had some interesting insights into the problems of municipal reform. Six months after his "new broom" administration was under way, he told a reporter: "Yes, I know the job is a big one. I think that nearly 90 per cent of American cities today are poorly governed, that what Lincoln Steffens showed up in his *Shame of the Cities* 30 years ago is generally true today, although today there has been a democratization of corruption. What do I mean by that? Why, that in the past generation a few bosses got all the money, now it is spread around more. The coppers on the beat get some."[36]

To the surprise of no one, Maverick programs and policies began to flow from the office of the mayor just as they had from that of the congressman. He applied a vigorous broom to corruption, gambling and prostitution, but waved aside the label of moralist. "I love sinners," he said as a preface to his argument that the whirlwind cleanup was needed to prevent vice from corrupting the city government.[37] The police department got the broom next; many members were fired, merit examinations were instituted, and Ray Ashworth, a *northern* police specialist who had graduated from the police training school in Wichita, Kansas, was brought in as chief of police! A new health department was established, the "fix" was taken out of the city traffic courts, the increased revenues being used to build parks and swimming pools. A vocational guidance program was instituted, and the budgetary process and other administrative routines were improved.[38]

The machine could not wait for the next election to get rid of Maverick; they were after him before he could get comfortable in the mayor's chair. According to his account, it all started when he gave $250 to the International Ladies Garment Workers Union for a poll-tax campaign. Maverick had a falling out with the union's lawyer over a patronage matter, and, said Maverick, the lawyer sold him "down the river." Information concerning the contribution had provided his political foe, District Attorney Shook, with some sort of pretext for criminal charges. Shook was able to secure twenty-six indictments against Maverick for allegedly having bought the poll-tax receipts (a criminal offense) of a like number of voters. There was little doubt that the charges were politically inspired.[39]

Twenty of the twenty-six counts in the original indictment were quashed at the opening of the trial. After the packed courtroom had heard the witnesses, "defense counsel Carl Wright Johnson, one of Texas' most eloquent bull-roarers, snorted that conspiracy testimony was stronger against Shook. . . ."[40] The jury quickly agreed, and the courtroom crowd broke into a burst of cheers despite a warning by the judge. Shook dropped the remaining indictments. FDR broke a foreign policy conference with Secretary of State Hull to telephone his congratulations to Maverick,[41] and other notables joined in with their notes. Harold Ickes called the acquittal a victory for democracy, Thurman Arnold said he had "no doubt of the outcome," Norman Thomas wrote, "Texas has some sense," and Josephus Daniels, ambassador to Mexico, offered the following lines, referring to Shook:

> He digged a ditch
> He digged it for his brother
> To punish his sin he did fall in
> The pit he digged for t'other.[42]

When his friend Sherwood Anderson asked Maverick if he had been scared, Maverick replied, "Hell, yes. I didn't think I'd look good in a cell."[43]

Anderson was one of Mayor Maverick's most sympathetic visitors to San Antonio. A rather close relationship had ripened between politician and novelist during Maverick's first term in Congress. The two most likely became acquainted when Maverick was making speeches in support of civil liberties in Virginia, where Anderson had edited the *Marion Democrat* and *Smyth County News* in Marion, Virginia. He had turned the papers over to his son, Robert Lane Anderson, in about 1929, but the elder Anderson was in and out of the operation from time to time. Sherwood and his son were both Maverick admirers, and Sherwood not only wrote Maverick chatty letters but also did a certain amount of confiding in him concerning his literary projects. The novelist and playwright even did a bit of soul baring in one letter to Maverick. Anderson was ruminating over the social obligations of the storyteller to do "something decent." He said, "There can be as much crookedness and dodging the real issue in the imaginative world as in the so-called Real World. And our writers constantly sell it out, just as the real world is sold out in politics. What else Maury can you say of the man who takes on the Hollywood thing nowdays, knowing the set-up. I just point this out to indicate to you a realization that we writers have our own mess to clean up."[44]

Anderson visited Maverick in San Antonio on more than one occasion. His last visit, in 1939, moved him to write an article titled "Maury Maverick in San Antonio." He found that Maverick had lost none of his "magnificent swagger." "He takes you around, proudly, swaggeringly.... He is working, half playing, full of energy, a real Texan, not wanting to be a stuffed shirt, not, it seems, revengeful for what they tried to do to him, trying to keep his head."[45]

Maverick also added some swagger to the office of mayor. "He liked to put on the dog," said one friend, as he described encountering Mayor Maverick in the first chauffeur-driven limousine provided for that office. Maverick's rationale was that the mayor's office needed to be given some dignity and "class." He also took boyish delight, as Anderson implied, in carrying off some piece of contrived gimmickry. When Maverick learned that H. G. Wells and Orson Welles were scheduled for engagements in San Antonio on the same evening, he arranged to have the two men, who were arriving separately, to be met by police cars and conveyed to their respective engagements. Maverick was acquainted with both of these men, but they did not know one another, and he deemed it a must that they meet. When he learned that their schedules would not permit them to get together, he proudly demonstrated the effectiveness of the two-way radio system in San Antonio police cars by having Wells and Welles "meet" over the radio waves between the two cars in which they were riding.[46]

Perhaps it was nostalgia for his boyhood days in San Antonio that gave Maverick his motivation for restoring the chili and tamale "queens" to the plazas of the city, but he had a thoroughly modern concern for the progressive sanitary measures he required of the Mexican-American women who vended the Mexican foods. He also wanted the color of the original Spanish atmosphere to be "jazzed up" a bit.

Walter Prescott Webb told the delightful tale of Mayor Maverick's encounter with one of the members of a Mexican strolling band that was part of the color he introduced. Maverick had insisted that the musicians wear the picturesque Mexican regalia for such occasions, and he checked up on them from time to time to see that it was being done. On one such tour Maverick viewed with satisfaction the "glowing braziers" and sniffed the "tangy odor of tamales and chili" on the night air, but then he spotted a handsome guitar player who was "out of uniform." The irate mayor asked, "What the hell are you doin' out here without a uniform?" "I," said the Mexican in broken English, "am exercising my constitutional rights." Maverick was floored—the redoubtable defender of constitutional rights hoist by his own petard—but he recovered quickly and demanded in emphatic terms, as only he could do, that the musician change his garb. Thirty minutes later the guitarist returned in full regalia and remarked to his companions, "The Mayor he like me; he joke with me."[47]

The Mexican-Americans liked Maverick, and with good reason. Sherwood Anderson said that the San Antonio mayor had bought their votes in a "new and legal way." In addition to the many pieces of evidence of his great interest in their heritage, Maverick had fought the "pecan kings" to secure better wages for Mexican-American pecan shellers, who were getting as little as $1.75 a week —a plight Anderson called one of the "ugliest messes in the U.S.A." after he had attended a National Labor Relations Board hearing on the pecan-shelling industry during one of his visits to San Antonio. Perhaps of equal impact on this ethnic group was the fact that Mayor Maverick had brought about the classification of Mexican-Americans as "white" on census and other records in San Antonio.[48]

Early in his administration, Mayor Maverick began one of the projects of which he was most proud—one of the few achievements of which he would boast—the restoration of the historic Spanish village, or La Villita ("The Little Town"), in the heart of San Antonio.[49] On August 3, 1939, twenty-five youths, supported by a grant from the National Youth Administration, began to clean up the area that was to become the now-famous tourist attraction and center of San Antonio's festive and cultural activities.

Maverick said that he conceived of the project when he visited the area one moonlit night in 1939 and decided that it could be a "symbol and monument to those simple people who had made possible the great city which had grown up around it." La Villita was the civil settlement, founded in 1718, that was attached to Mission San Antonio de Valero, known today simply as the Alamo. San Antonio had grown up and around a largely forgotten clump of eight adobe huts, one of which (dating from 1722) had been the site in 1835 of the signing of the capitulation of General Martín Perfecto Cos after the battle of San Antonio in the series of events leading to the independence of Texas. In addition to restoration of the Cos House, there were plans for the establishment of the Bolivar Building (library-museum) through a gift from the Carnegie

Foundation, and a central square to be named Juarez Plaza, in honor of the great Mexican leader.

Maverick traded other city property to the local public service company for the La Villita site, and on October 12 secured adoption of the Villita Ordinance, which declared among its high purposes "the promotion of peace, friendship and justice between the United States of America and all other nations in the Western Hemisphere."[50] With the ordinance as a basis, the National Youth Administration put up $100,000, the city its share of $10,000, and 110 youths were employed in the restoration work. Maverick said that they cleaned out "tons of filth" from what had become a slum. A WPA project prepared *Old Villita*, a complete history of the original settlement, and, as Maverick put it, the area was "restored to what it always was—a village of plain simple people, with architecture indigenous to the soil of San Antonio and Texas."[51] Programs for training youths in arts and crafts were incorporated in the project, and George Biddle, Philadelphia art authority and Maverick's friend, was retained to direct art activities.

Maverick said that his project was known throughout Latin America. It also attracted considerable attention in the United States as it neared completion. The *Chicago News* carried a major spread in February 1941 with pictures of La Villita and a feature article by Lucia Lewis. She said it was an idea "of which even his bitter opponents approve," and marveled at the work of youths who had been taught to make pottery, tiles, and textiles and to craft other articles from salvaged materials and just plain junk.[52] The *Dallas News* also treated the La Villita project to a major rotogravure feature headed, "Out of a Texas Rubbish Heap Comes the Symbol of Peace."[53] Maverick was well known and admired in Mexico for this and other efforts toward improvement of United States–Latin American relations. In November 1940 the Mexican government expressly requested that Mayor Maverick be included in the group to accompany Vice President Elect Henry Wallace to the inauguration of President Avila Camacho.[54]

Today La Villita is the hub of most of San Antonio's festive activities. There in Casa Villita is housed the San Antonio Conservation Society, a moving force behind such festivals and the organization responsible for many improvements in and programs for La Villita. "The Little Town" is the scene of "A Night in Old San

Fontaine Maury Maverick at the age of five months, March 1896. His mother, Mrs. Albert Maverick, wrote on the back of the photograph, "Susie (& No. 11)."

Maverick's birthplace, 218 Avenue E, San Antonio.

Maury Maverick, age three.

Maverick at about the age of thirteen.

Lieutenant Maury Maverick, 1917.

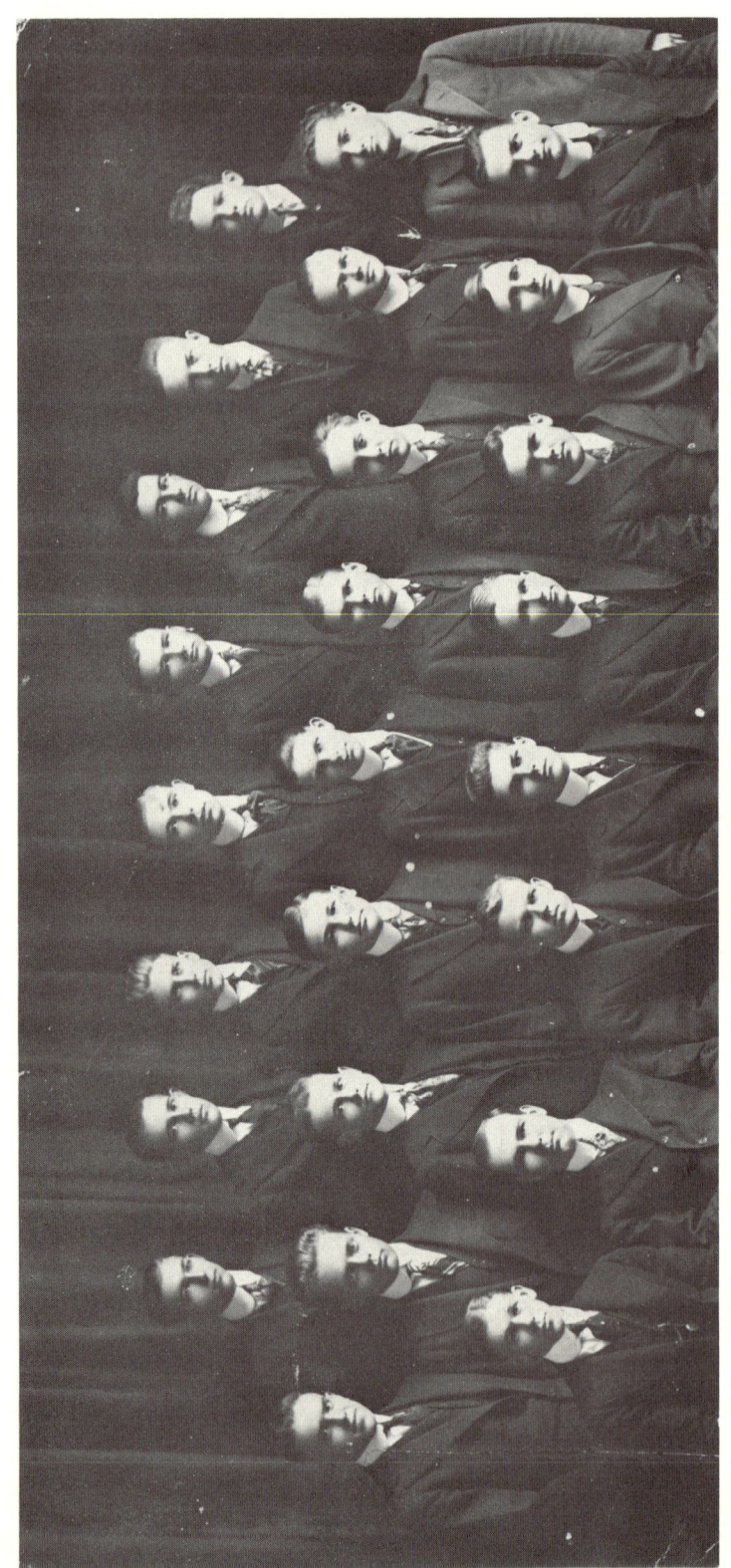

Maverick (second from left, second row) with his fellow Sigma Chi's at the University of Texas, Austin, 1914.

Maury Maverick and Terrell Dobbs in their courting days on the beach at Port Aransas, Texas, in 1919.

Another glimpse of the courtship of Maverick and Terrell Dobbs—Sunshine Ranch, 1919 or 1920.

In 1932 Pat Jefferson, Maury Maverick, and Harry Futrell donned hobo garb to "ride the rods" and sleep in hobo jungles in order to learn firsthand the plight of the migrant unemployed. (Photo by Jensen Studio, Austin, Texas.)

Maverick with his two pet javelinas (peccaries) "Anthony" and "Cleopatra" in 1934.

Three generations of Mavericks: Maury, more trim than usual; his father, Albert Maverick; and Maury, Jr., at Sunshine Ranch about 1939.

Congressman Maury Maverick commented on this 1936 penciled caricature by his friend Washington correspondent Walter Karig, "This is really great, aggressive art. He told me off."

Maverick is bombarded with some of the "gobbledygook" he deplored in his famous memorandum in 1944 as chairman of the Smaller War Plants Corporation. (© 1944 by The New York Times Company. Reprinted by permission.)

Freshman Congressman Maverick drives home a point on the floor of the House of Representatives in 1936. (Photo by Acme News Photos.)

Mrs. Maverick samples an apple supplied by Pennsylvania admirers of her husband.

An intent Congressman Maverick puts a query to one of his colleagues, 1937. (Photo by Thos. D. McAvoy, Washington, D.C.)

Maverick notes an engagement on his office blackboard in 1937. The picture above the blackboard is of his idol, Senator George W. Norris.

Congressman Maverick on his way to his office in the House Office Building on a cold Washington day in 1936. (Photo by Acme News Photos.)

Maverick and five other congressmen vie for FDR's attention and support at Amarillo, Texas, in July 1938. Left to right are FDR, Elliott Roosevelt, Governor James Allred, and Congressmen Maverick, Fritz Lanham, and Marvin Jones. Congressman Lyndon B. Johnson is behind Lanham, and Congressman W. D. McFarlane is over Maverick's right shoulder. (Photo by Acme News Photos.)

Maverick speaks to the crowd that turned out to greet him on his return to San Antonio from his second term in Congress in 1938.

Mayor Maverick discusses the model for the restoration of San Antonio's La Villita, one of his proudest achievements. (Photo by King Tomlinson, San Antonio.)

Mayor Maverick describes some of the points of interest in La Villita to his guest, H. G. Wells. (Photo by H. G. Summerville, San Antonio.)

Rioters, one with brick in hand, climb over stacked folding chairs in violent protest against the Communist meeting in the San Antonio Auditorium.

A mob presses in to prevent the Communist party meeting in San Antonio's Municipal Auditorium—a meeting authorized by Mayor Maverick in 1939.

Mayor Maverick speaks from a terrace next to one of the restored buildings of La Villita. (Photo by Harvey Pattison, San Antonio.)

Mayor Maverick speaking at a groundbreaking ceremony for a slum clearance project in San Antonio. (Photo by Studer Photo Company, San Antonio.)

A busy Mayor Maverick looks up from his desk at city hall. (Photo by C. S. Urton, San Antonio.)

Mayor Maverick, speaking at La Villita in 1940, uses the characteristic raised fist gesture that brought him trouble when he spoke before the United Auto Workers in Detroit in 1937. (Photo by Zintgraff Photographers, San Antonio.)

Mayor Maverick, with Mrs. Maverick at his side, prepares to make a network radio address in January 1940.

The Texas delegation to the 1940 Democratic National Convention in Chicago. Left to right are Maverick, Sam Rayburn, R. L. Bobbitt, Sam Fore, Jr., Myron Blalock, Mrs. Maverick, and Mrs. Fore. (Photo by Acme News Photos.)

Wartime administrator Maverick at his desk in the Office of Production Management in 1941.

As chief of the Bureau of Government Requirements, War Production Board, 1942–1943, Maverick inspects the fabrication of submarine nets at San Quentin prison.

Maverick accompanied Eleanor Roosevelt on a number of wartime tours of major prisons. Here they begin an inspection of the Maryland Penitentiary in 1943. (Photo by Hughes Company, Baltimore.)

Maverick is sworn in as chairman of the Smaller War Plants Corporation in 1944 by District of Columbia Court of Appeals Associate Justice Thurman W. Arnold as Speaker Sam Rayburn (right) and Majority Leader John W. McCormack look on.

Congressman Maverick points out the new San Antonio Post Office to FDR during the president's visit to San Antonio in 1936.

Maverick arrives at Atsugi Airfield, Tokyo, November 21, 1945, on one leg of his World War II Pacific tour. (Photo by U.S. Army Signal Corps, Kazimer, photographer.)

Maverick and Paul V. McNutt, chairman of the War Manpower Commission (center, in trench coat) on the 1944 inspection tour of European battlefronts.

SWPC chairman Maverick chats with Korean leader Dr. Syngman Rhee at lunch at the Chosen Hotel, Seoul, Korea, in November 1945.

Maverick and his aides leave their plane at Guam on the Pacific trip in 1945.

Archbishop Lucey with President Truman on the occasion of a visit to San Antonio by President

A Texas La Guardia

Antonio," a part of the famed Fiesta San Jacinto, which runs for a week every April. Visitors can stroll by the picturesque restored buildings of the village and booths featuring traditional Mexican wares and foods, while watching San Antonians dance on Juarez Plaza to the Mexican and German music that is a part of the city's unusual and colorful background.

Another related project that came to fruition in Mayor Maverick's administration was the conversion of the untidy and neglected San Antonio River, which winds through the downtown area near La Villita, into what one writer called "a winding waterway the counterpart of which can be found only in the canals of Venice." Enhancement of the natural beauty of the spring-fed river had long been the dream of Robert H. Hugman, a San Antonio architect who had spent years drafting plans for such a project. Conditions favorable to carrying out these plans arose in 1939. Jack White, a hotel executive, and Tom McNamara, an advertising man, formed an improvement district along the river that voted $75,000 in bonds. Maverick was instrumental in getting a $450,000 allocation from the WPA and in getting the project under way.[55]

Visitors to San Antonio today can walk down from the bridges crossing the deepened stream and stroll along shaded walks at the river's edge past well-tended flowers and shrubs set off by well-planned rock walls and bank reinforcements. At a bend in the river near La Villita is Arneson River Theatre, with its rock seats set into the river bank. This beautiful spot adjoining the site of San Antonio's 1968 HemisFair is the scene on Easter Sundays of the annual Starving Artists Show. Thousands of people crowd the banks to get an early view of the colorful displays of oil paintings, water colors, and various other works of art that sell for ten dollars or less. Visitors can also view the scene from boats and gondolas that ply the narrow river. It was in an artificial canal with water diverted from this river that HemisFair visitors took the boat tour of the fair. San Antonio's Summer Festival, which began in 1958, features the Fiesta Noche del Rio, involving gondola rides down the river to the theater area where visitors can listen to Mexican music and watch Mexican dances staged on the other side of the river.[56]

Sherwood Anderson's visit to San Antonio also gave rise to an unusual story that related to Maverick's efforts in behalf of the restoration of parts of the historic grandeur of old San Antonio.

After some reflection on the historic sites and background of San Antonio, which Maverick had shown and explained to him during the 1939 visit, Anderson wrote Mayor Maverick an enthusiastic letter in which he proposed "a sort of Oberammergau idea" for the dramatic presentation of the city's rich heritage. He said that he knew of no other city in America with such "grand dramatic material," and he specifically suggested a play to be presented for about two weeks each year that would bring back the early life and the creation of the state of Texas—featuring the Alamo, Santa Anna, and other people and places of early Texas. "It could, it seems to me, so easily be built up into an institution, an annual affair, a real part of the city's life," Anderson told Maverick. The playwright first said that he was not suggesting himself as the writer of the play, but, on second thought, he added in a postscript, "At that I'd like to try it. Maybe because I like San Antonio and get excited every time I think of the dramatic material right at hand there." In spite of the enthusiasm of both Maverick and Anderson for projects of this type, there is no indication that either of them followed through on the idea.[57]

Thirteen or fourteen years later, a then little-known Texas playwright—steeped in the literature and lore of the Texas that he loves—began to work on *A Cloud of Witnesses: The Drama of the Alamo*. When Ramsey Yelvington, now playwright in residence at Southwest Texas State University, completed this play, his friend Paul Baker, then director of the Baylor University Theatre, and the San Antonio Conservation Society and other interested groups, joined in setting in motion almost the exact project Sherwood Anderson had outlined in his 1940 letter! Nearly every year since 1958 the drama has been presented at what is now the Texas State Historical Theatre at Mission San José (San José de San Miguel de Aguayo). Below the old San José mill an amphitheater was built in the 1930's, in part because Maury Maverick was instrumental in securing federal funds for assistance in the project. The amphitheater was completely reconstructed in 1958 to make adequate provisions for the *Drama of the Alamo* production. The production has been directed in recent years by James Barton, professor of speech and drama direction at Southwest Texas State University.

A Texas La Guardia

City beautification and cultural projects were not the only projects on Maverick's mind. As had been forecast, he soon became committed to a major political project.

No sooner was he elected than the pundits began to look for the broader implications in Maverick's victory. The *New York Post* dubbed him "Man of the Week" and said that he could be expected to run for Tom Connally's seat in the United States Senate.[58] R. M. Fritz, a *New York Times* reporter, saw the beginning of a "Maverick-Garner War," and this one hit the mark. Fritz pointed out that about twenty representatives and two senators known to be anti-Garner people had congratulated Maverick warmly and said that his friends construed this as the basis for an anti-Garner movement in Texas, with Maverick "possibly serving as the spearhead." At the time, Maverick would not discuss these speculations.[59]

There were frequent references to the animosity between Maverick and Cactus Jack. Reporting on Maverick's 1938 defeat, Jay Franklin wrote that "large sums of money were shipped down to San Antonio to defeat Rep. Maury Maverick for the greater glory of Jack Garner and the remains of the Insull empire."[60] Heywood Broun also said that the fundamental reason why Maverick lost in 1938 was that "every businessman in San Antonio knew what Garner wanted." Now, said Broun, "The New Deal marches and Maury Maverick rides again and offers leadership to those who will never heed the cactus call of retreat."[61]

During his first term in Congress, Maverick's relationship with John Nance Garner had been good enough to place him among the privileged few who drank bourbon out of the "big glass" in the vice-president's office. The symbolic measure of a man's standing with Garner was whether he was offered the "big glass" or the "little glass" when the bourbon was poured.[62] When the court-packing plan and sit-down strikes came along, however, Garner's native, old-school conservatism turned him away from the New Deal and the Mavericks, making him the rallying point of worried Southern Bourbons and their fellows in other parts of the country. Though Garner did not formally announce his candidacy for the presidency until December of 1939, friends had gathered with him in Uvalde a year earlier to get the Garner-for-president boom under way.[63]

On May 20, 1939, a *Dallas News* editorial discussed an Austin speech to the Young Democrats Club in which Maverick had "damned with faint praise" the Texas Garner-for-president movement and had expressed the opinion that the speech corroborated "the view taken at Washington that Maverick intends to use the San Antonio election as a springboard for an anti-Garner and pro-Roosevelt third term election." Maverick's position was attributed to the bitter memory of the campaign train incident of 1938,[64] reflected in the speech by his raising the question as to whether certain members of the Roosevelt family were "more loyal to Mr. Garner."[65] The next day famed cartoonist Jim Berryman depicted Garner saying to Sam Rayburn, "Something tells me we should adjourn as quickly as possible and get back home." An inset in the front-page cartoon showed Maverick saying in Texas, "Garner's too old to run! Roosevelt's too reticent to run!"[66]

Maverick really opened fire on Garner when interviewed by reporters as he attended the New York World's Fair in July 1939. He said the boom for Garner was being promoted by lobbyists for big business "whose primary interest was in the election of a reactionary as the next President." He particularly singled out Roy Miller, lobbyist for Texas Gulf Sulphur, as the man behind the Garner-for-president move in Texas. Maverick said these forces did not think Garner could win but that his candidacy would bring about the nomination of an even more conservative Republican. Garner had "lived in a vacuum for the past thirty years," said Maverick, who indicated that he was prepared to support the squire of Uvalde for president of the pecan growers association. "Garner is a myth," Maverick said, as he explained to reporters that in his view all Garner had ever done was to keep quiet and get elected. "He's been a deaf and dumb politician all his life."

A week or so later Maverick said in Milwaukee that the Democrats had better nominate FDR again if they wanted to win. He said that he had been by to see the president and that he had talked to him like a candidate. Maverick's original opposition to a third term had been completely reversed. On September 20, 1939, he declared after another meeting with FDR that "Garner's future is behind him" and that the party would win "1,000 per cent" with FDR. Maverick's remarks to reporters at this time were slightly more temperate than those of earlier interviews. When they re-

A Texas La Guardia 205

minded him of John L. Lewis' classic description of Garner as a "labor-baiting, poker-playing, whiskey-drinking, evil old man," the San Antonio mayor said with surprising mildness, that Garner was a "fine, water-drinking, Christian gentleman, with a fine past," but that he was too old to be president.[67]

In the spring of 1940, FDR told Young Democrats that a "pair of liberals" should be nominated by the Democrats in 1940. He mentioned himself and, among others, Henry Wallace and Maury Maverick.[68] Though Maverick was recognized as a leader of Texans working to block Garner's attempt to stop the FDR third-term movement,[69] he must have been still troubled about the president's "reticence," because he wrote to A. A. Berle two weeks before the Texas Democratic Convention to see if he knew anything about Roosevelt's intentions. Berle responded, "I really think the question of whether Mr. Roosevelt will run or not is being settled somewhere on the banks of the Meuse River. You know my private theory. It is that he did not want to run, does not want to run, and will not want to run, unless circumstances are so grave that he considers it essential for the country's safety...."[70] This meant, of course, that Roosevelt would run.

A major struggle was shaping up in Texas between the Garner-for-president element and the Roosevelt third-termers, and Garner was going great guns. National polls showed that he was the choice of Democrats if FDR did not choose to run, and his campaign was assuming major national proportions. On March 9 he learned that he had been endorsed by the Texas State Democratic Executive Committee. A week later, however, the Roosevelt third-term organization was set up in Austin. The leaders at this time were Mayor Tom Miller of Austin, who had discussed the move with Maverick; former Governor James E. Ferguson; and Edward Clark, Texas secretary of state under Governor James V. Allred. Garner people said that Lyndon B. Johnson was also active in the movement. By early April the third-termers had a campaign under way in precincts and counties throughout the state. Maury Maverick was the San Antonio leader.

By mid-April both Maverick and LBJ were viewed as leaders in the state third-term draft activities in a report of efforts by Miller and Clark to find out where Sam Rayburn and Jesse H. Jones, federal loan administrator, stood on the fight. Rayburn counseled compromise. He was loyal to FDR and wanted resolutions endorsing the administration and its accomplishments, but he saw no reason why a loyal Democrat like Garner should not be given the favorite-son nod. Later in April a showdown between the two forces appeared to be inevitable. E. B. Germany, Texas steel executive and a Garner manager, had angered Roosevelt men when he said that the third-term movement was dead, and Maverick's friend, Harold Ickes, seemed to be determined to force the issue from the other side. He wrote to Amon G. Carter, publisher of the *Fort Worth Star-Telegram* and a "warm Garner supporter," challenging the Garner men to submit their cause to the people. Ickes told Carter that when Roosevelt was reelected in November, "You and other 'leaders' will be the first to hie you to the pie counter." Ickes was said to be smarting from a reference in Carter's newspaper to certain "carpetbaggers" coming into Texas.

Other leaders, however, were bent on compromise. Three days after the Ickes statement, Rayburn wired the Garner forces and Lyndon Johnson sent the same message to the FDR group, urging them to agree that Garner would get the Texas delegation to the national convention in exchange for his agreement to abandon the stop Roosevelt movement. The deal was accepted by Myron G. Blalock, campaign manager for Garner and for the Roosevelt men by Undersecretary of the Interior Alvin J. Wirtz, who had recently conferred with FDR and had come back to Texas to drum up support for the third-term movement.

Garner won most of the county conventions handily on May 7 after this deal had been made, and he seemed to have everything in the bag for the Texas Democratic Convention, scheduled for May 27 in Waco. But Maury Maverick had not been consulted, and he and a few others were in no mood for compromise. Sunday afternoon, the day before the convention, he presided over a caucus of about fifty other delegates who wore ribbons proclaiming "Roosevelt Again" and "Draft Roosevelt" in the Roosevelt Hotel (named for FDR). They joined Maverick in a telegram to Roosevelt endorsing Jesse Jones for vice-president and Maverick for national committeeman. Maverick said that he was instructed to support Garner by his Bexar County convention, but on the basis of discussions with some early arrivals, he thought there might be a stampede to FDR. He added that he thought Garner should withdraw.

Blalock said that this was "ridiculous and wishful thinking on the part of some."

Before the business of the convention got under way, Maverick got into a rhubarb with one of the members of the credentials committee, who was also one of his fellow delegates from San Antonio. Fred Rucker, a state committeeman who had announced as a candidate against Senator Tom Connally, charged that Maverick was the "no. 1 Communist of Texas" and said he had a "bagful" of proof for the credentials committee. When the committee met he withdrew his protest, giving as his reason his realization that since there was no contesting delegation from Bexar County, the matter was moot! Maverick was not there, but when he learned of the charge, he stormed, "I want to denounce as an infamous liar and coward anyone who made the statement that I am a Communist. . . . I am an ex-soldier. The matter was wholly irrelevant and had no place at the session of the state executive committee. It was done with the hope that it would hurt and discredit me." There was no reply from Rucker, but several delegates hotly defended Maverick.

Before the main meeting of the convention on Wednesday, May 29, Maverick also got into a fracas at the entrance to the hall. Mayor Miller, a big, heavy man, threw a punch at Mayor Maverick and hit Floyd McGown, Maverick's executive assistant. Maverick claimed that Miller had started the row, and Miller said that Maverick had made an insulting remark to him. What happened was that Maverick—holding out to the bitter end for an FDR endorsement and viewing Miller as one who had "sold out"—was arguing with Miller as they approached the hall. In the tense atmosphere Maverick made what he thought was a commonplace remark that Miller interpreted as a deliberate insult.

In the convention it was clear that the compromise forces would easily have their way. Lynn Landrum of the *Dallas News* said that the convention was a managed "steamroller." These forces overwhelmed the "vociferous minority" led by Maverick and Oscar F. Holcombe, mayor of Houston. Garnercrats were after Maverick's scalp and they nearly got it. They charged Maverick with "blitzkrieg tactics," and they were almost successful in an attempt to eliminate his name from the list of delegates to the Democratic National Convention and the list of presidential electors. In fact, he might have been saved only by the action of a loyal little woman on the floor who rose as the standing vote was taken, turned to the delegates near her with her arms outstretched and said, "Come on, get up—support this man." Many responded to the plea, and most of them did not know that she was Mrs. Maury Maverick, who laughs heartily today at having carried off this minor coup.[71]

Garner won only sixty-one votes at the national convention and Maverick figured that he had had the last word. In later years, going over his clippings, he came to one stating that in December 1939 it was doubtful whether he would be able to keep the Texas delegation from voting for Garner in the next Democratic Convention. Maverick jotted on the clipping, "Garner didn't get it."[72]

Unlikely as it may seem for a man who was so much involved in running a major city and engaged in the turmoil of state and national politics, Maverick was again "with book" in 1939, two years after his first book was published. *In Blood and Ink* attracted much less attention than his first effort. The book contained 189 pages of analysis by Maverick in Book I, "From Runneymede to Roosevelt," and 51 pages of documents illustrative of the development of rights and liberties in Book II, "Documents Tell the Tale." His aim was to bring the story of constitutional liberty to ordinary people in a seventy-five cent paperback volume; he said in an "Advertisement" inside the front cover that he should have dubbed it *The Grocery Man's Constitution*.

Parts of this book were overdramatic, but a great deal of it showed a better understanding of American constitutional history than many textbooks of the time, and some of the documents analyzed and reproduced had usually been ignored by historians and political scientists. The flamboyant title, format, and style belied the solid work that went into the book.

Though reviewers did not know it, Maverick had a rather distinguished research staff, including Charles A. Beard, Leon Henderson, Leon Pearson, and Thurman Arnold. Maverick said that Beard helped him eliminate some historical inaccuracies, and his research file reveals that Leon Henderson prepared the basic data on monopoly power. Arnold assisted the Texas mayor with the Bill of Rights section, and Pearson and Herbert C. Henderson, an Austin writer, helped him with the general editing.[73] Maverick had a

A Texas La Guardia

knack for getting help out of subordinates, friends, and associates on anything he was writing. He would turn out a quick draft and then send it off with the question, "Tell me what's wrong with this," and, more often than not, he would add, "Get it back in a hurry."

Though scholars paid little heed to the book, it did not go unnoticed. Arthur Griffith, in the *Miami Herald*, called it a "well-written digest of what has gone into the life and documents of American democracy."[74] The *New York Times* found it to be a valuable consideration of little-known historical documents with "vigorous and sometimes dramatic turn of phrase."[75] It was praised by the *Richmond Times-Dispatch* for the analysis of the concept of economic liberty,[76] and the *Durham* (N.C.) *Herald* also called attention to the exposition of economic liberty and said that Maverick had demonstrated "his complete knowledge of the Constitution."[77] Herbert Agar wrote, "His book is not a brief history. It is a series of brief and vital essays on the aspects of our history which seem to the author to be most important. . . . It is a comment by one of the most enlightened and experienced of American liberals on the whole course of our history."[78] In October 1939 Maury received a letter from C. R. Wasson, Mayor of Saint John, New Brunswick, Canada, saying, "No book has ever made such an impression on me as your 'In Blood and Ink.' I have read and re-read it, and now am circulating it amongst my fellow townsmen."[79]

In Blood and Ink was reprinted in the *Guardian*, monthly paper of the Building Service Employees International Union,[80] and in 1948, Bert Masterson, then head of the Chicago office of United Press, urged Maverick to revise the book. He wrote, "I believe there is great need of its clarity in statement of the real liberties, and that you would help many as you have helped me," and asked for two copies for friends.[81] The *Nation* styled Maverick's work as "in the fine pamphleteering tradition of Tom Paine,"[82] and the *Cleveland* (Ohio) *Plaindealer* reviewer said, "I think the volume should be adopted as a textbook in our public schools."[83]

In the book Maverick developed a highly sophisticated treatment of the theory of constitutions and U.S. constitutional development,[84] but the chief significance of the work lay in his final articulation of the concept of economic rights or "freedom from want" that was one of the major contributions of New Deal ideology—an idea that Maverick had been advancing since before the New Deal. Indeed, he dedicated this book to the concept of freedom from want. On the front cover, with his signature, is the paragraph, "Democracy, to me, is liberty plus economic security. To put it in plain language, we Americans want to talk, pray, think as we please—and eat regular. I say this because there is a lot of nonsense in talk about liberty. You cannot fill the baby's bottle with liberty."[85] Max Lerner has described modern liberalism as embodying the idea of "freedom of the person, higher living standards and a more spacious way of life." He added, "As Maury Maverick phrased it with a perhaps oversimplified pungency, liberalism has always meant 'freedom plus groceries'—not only (one may add) for some of the people, but for all, not only sometimes but all the time."[86]

Maverick sent a copy of *In Blood and Ink*, with its emphasis upon economic freedom, to Roosevelt, and the president responded, "Ever so many thanks for the new book. Keep on writing them—for it is worthwhile for the good people of the U.S.A. for you to do it. I am taking this one with me for a few days on a cruiser in northern latitude [sic] after that august body, of which you were once a member, decides that it is tired of fraticide [sic] and goes home!"[87] In his message to Congress on January 6, 1941, the president urged that there were four essential freedoms of democracy —among them "freedom from want."[88] Later in the year, the Atlantic Charter voiced the same message.[89] Finally, his message to Congress on January 11, 1944,[90] contained an elaboration of the concept that is striking in its resemblance to the first three pages of Maverick's chapter entitled "What's Liberty if You Don't Eat?" from *In Blood and Ink*. Maverick presented what he called a "Charter of True Liberty," and Roosevelt a "second Bill of Rights"; the lists of provisions are quite similar.[91]

There is no proof that Roosevelt took his statement or his ideas from Maverick's writings, but it is not necessary to prove anything of the sort to demonstrate the significance of Maverick's contribution. Roosevelt's statement has been hailed as an important articulation of the ideology of the welfare state, and Merle Curti calls it the arrival of "an up-to-date democratic ideology"—the concept of a "right to work usefully and creatively for pay sufficient to command the necessities and amenities," which represented a "far-

A Texas La Guardia 211

reaching shift in public attitude." Maverick had been advancing these principles before the inception of the New Deal. Curti points briefly to their origin in the writings of "[Henry] Wallace and other leading liberals," and in the report of the National Resources and Planning Board of 1942.[92] But these ideas were well developed in Maverick's speeches in 1932 and perhaps earlier, and Henry Wallace's first treatment of the subject was not published until 1934.[93]

Nor is any claim made that this idea was completely new. Maverick had so steeped himself in the literature of natural rights, social justice, and democratic socialism before he began to work with such ideas that *he* probably could not have told what was original with him and what was derived from the ideas of others. In 1939 he did pen a private note on a copy of one of his 1932 speeches: "Nov. 12, 1939: This is interesting to me in that many of the things I here suggested were adopted by the Roosevelt Administration. Some of my views are changed, indeed, and I hope I write them better, but I am a little proud that I knew as much as I did, and *before* Roosevelt suggested any of this. M."[94]

Maverick's thesis concerning economic liberty could have been the basis of a falling out between him and H. L. Mencken. After the sage of Baltimore had read *In Blood and Ink*, he sent the following caustic critique to Maverick:

> I read the book with great pleasure, and I agree with at least nine-tenths of it. It seems to me, however, that you greatly exaggerated the conflict between property rights and personal rights. After all, property rights are themselves personal rights. I see no reason why a man who has honestly earned a thousand dollars should be forced to hand it over to someone who was loafing all the while. The idea that every person who is dead broke is the victim of Wall Street is sheer nonsense. Nine-tenths of them are victims of defective germ cells. What we need in this country is a wholesale sterilization of the unfit.
>
> It seems to me that Hugo Black's view of the 14th Amendment is completely cuckoo. Carried out to its logical conclusion, it holds that persons organized into corporations have no human rights whatsoever. I see no essential difference between them and other persons. If I have rights as a private man, I have the same rights as a stockholder in a corporation. I can see little in Black save a Cracker demagogue. The idea that he is a master-mind is complete nonsense.[95]

Maury Maverick could take criticism of the ideas he shared with Black and probably could have given a good rebuttal to Mencken's views, but he must not have been able to take the "Cracker demagogue" comment about a man whom he greatly admired, because there was no further correspondence between Maverick and Mencken in the Maverick papers.

He Stirreth Up the People

ASK SOME PEOPLE of Maury Maverick's generation in central Texas or even in San Antonio itself what they remember about him, and likely as not you will get such benighted comments as, "Yeah, he was that crooked mayor" (remembering only his politically inspired indictment and trial, forgetting his acquittal), or "He was the guy who let the commies use the San Antonio Auditorium."

Maverick was not one to count such costs, however, and he was just as determined to fight for civil liberties for political dissidents as mayor of San Antonio as he had been as representative of the Bexar County district in Congress.

In one of his best speeches, he told the San Antonio Library Board in 1939 that Socrates had died because "he kept his own mind free and would have mankind free also. . . . He did not cry out, nor beg, nor listen to those weak friends of his who would have him *recant* so to speak, and, to use modern language, lay down the liberties of the people." Mayor Maverick urged his listeners to read, as he had, "Erasmus, Spinoza, and many others who belong to that deathless class of high-souled men who were soldiers in the upward path of man and in his forward march of human liberty."[1]

One of the functions of the mayor's office in which Maverick took obvious delight was the issuance of proclamations. He issued a great many during his two-year term, all of them festooned with ribbons and seals. Many of them were vehicles for his pronouncements on civil liberties and civil rights. He chose Good Friday as the occasion to preach a sermon on tolerance and free expression to San Antonians. He said that Christ was charged with sedition: "He stirreth up the people. . . . His freedom to preach The Word had been denied, His liberty blotted out, and He suffered death by crucifixion. . . . And the INTOLERANT of his day exulted and thought they had put an end to this humble carpenter who dared raise his voice against injustice and intolerance. But as the MAN died, scorned and unknown, HIS SPIRIT rose to lead and guide mankind to Truth and along the path of Justice."[2]

As Maverick carried out these views, it is ironic that his defense of freedom of assembly should have provided the basis for some of the greatest editorial acclaim that he ever received, and that soon thereafter, his failure to extend this guarantee should have brought about the temporary denigration of his reputation as a champion of civil liberties.

A small sheet of cheap note paper that landed on the Mayor's desk about August 2, 1939, proved to be as explosive as any bomb. The penned note read:

Mayor Maverick,
 The Communist Party requests the use of the East Wing of the city auditorium for Friday August 25.
 The original date of the meeting was the 24th, but since the city is planning a meeting for the 24th, we are perfectly willing to change the date of our meeting.

Sincerely yours,

(Signed) Emma Tenayuca[3]

The permit was issued, and when its approval was made known, Catholic Archbishop Arthur Drossaerts issued a prepared statement urging that the permit be revoked. "San Antonio," he said, "boasts of having within its walls the Cradle of Texas' Liberty: The Alamo. It should be the very last of all our cities to admit a

He Stirreth Up the People

bold and brazen harangue of Communism from the platform of our auditorium."[4] While veterans organizations were preparing further protests against Maverick's decision, he issued another of his proclamations, "Civil Liberties in San Antonio," in which he stated, "No amount of pressure will force me to violate my oath to support the Constitution nor force me to fail to carry out the principles of democracy. . . . The right of assembly, and the expression of unpopular belief, are the bases for the preservation of democracy."[5]

Maverick was sustained in his position by a wire from Grenville Clark, chairman of the Committee on the Bill of Rights of the American Bar Association, which read in part, "Perhaps when subject is further discussed your opponents will come to see themselves that their demand that you flout the constitutional guarantees of free speech and assembly as so recently upheld by the Supreme Court is wholly inconsistent with the Americanism they profess."[6] But Clark was wrong.

Protests from veterans groups and churches in and around San Antonio mounted as the time for the Communist party meeting drew near. The day before the meeting, however, the American Legion declared that it would take no part in any violence at the auditorium. Mayor Maverick then expressed the belief that the meeting would be held without incident, but he took the precaution of ordering most of the police force to be on hand for possible trouble.[7]

As the one hundred Communists, led by tiny Mrs. Emma Tenayuca Brooks, attempted to begin the meeting, the scene erupted into a riot, as described by a *San Antonio Express* reporter: "A screaming, angry, stone-hurling crowd of 5,000, completely out of hand and ignoring volleys of tear gas and streams of water directed at them by police, broke up the Communist rally in the Municipal Auditorium Friday night."[8] Maverick and his wife were at home at 339 Mary Louise Drive when they began to hear dimly the noise of the mob two miles away. Maury, Jr., called to report on events at the scene, and he told them that people had even come by bus from nearby towns to join in the fracas. Maverick was heartsick to find that this course had been taken by that many people, and he even began to doubt that he had done the right thing. He walked slowly out of the house and over to his wife as she stood watering the flowers. He moved closer to her as though he were seeking to draw some added strength from her, and as he touched her, he said with tears in his eyes, "I couldn't do it [revoke the Communists' permit]—I'd be going against everything I've stood for all my life." Today his wife says ruefully, "They wouldn't understand."[9]

The Communists fled out a rear door under police protection while the mob broke nearly every window in the building and committed other acts of outright vandalism, such as ripping open the upholstery of the auditorium seats in their rage at not being able to get their hands on the Communists. Some members of the berserk mob even cut the fire hoses. More than a score of persons were injured before the fury of the mob abated. Chief of Police Ray Ashworth and fourteen other policemen were hurt in the melee, and Maverick was hanged in effigy by the mob. Though the *Express* characterized the crowd as mainly "teen-age hoodlums," Maverick's collection of photographs of the incident shows that more than a few adult and even middle-aged faces were among the leading elements of the mob.[10]

All of the San Antonio newspapers joined in deploring the resort to mob action. The *Light* was moved to refer to the performance as "jungle savagery."[11] After styling the excesses of the mob as "shameful," "deplorable," and "despicable," the *Express*, however, devoted most of its editorial to an attack upon Maverick for provoking the incident by issuing the permit. His grounds for rejecting the protests were "utter poppycock." He had no right to "subject San Antonio's name and interests to the risk and the occasion of the miserable performance brought on by the Auditorium permit granted the Communists."[12]

On the eve of the meeting, Maverick had delivered a radio address, "Communism, Common Sense and the Constitution," that represents some of his best oratory. He urged his listeners to look to the lessons of history—to the "obscene display of folly" of the "Great Delusion of Salem," when innocent people were burned as witches. He warned his audience to "beware of modern witch hunts," and suggested that they follow the philosophy of Jefferson, who wanted "absolute freedom of spirit, not only for himself, but for those whose principles he utterly abhorred."[13]

After the incident, he wrote to a friend, "The riot was probably the worst exhibition of Nazi activities that has ever taken place in the United States. I do not think the reaction has been good politi-

He Stirreth Up the People

cally; however, I have no regrets. If I had it to do again, I would do it again."[14] A few weeks later he told his friend George Biddle, "I literally get sick when I think of the intolerance of human beings who can't even let somebody talk in peace. Today I am writing a proclamation on *Dog Week*: the sons of bitches are on my mind, and I am trying to write a metaphorical story about how dogs will at least let each other bark."[15]

Maverick's stand produced a torrent of favorable editorial comment in newspapers throughout the United States. Virginius Dabney sent Maverick a copy of the *Richmond Times-Dispatch* editorial with the penciled notation, "Give 'em hell, Maury!" Under the heading, "San Antonio's Shame," Dabney had written, "We suggest that these overexcited ladies and gentlemen address themselves to some of the manifest shortcomings of San Antonio, as described in 'San Antonio: The Shame of Texas,' appearing in the August *Forum and Century*, instead of seeking the scalp of a man who is manifestly trying to uphold the Constitution, and to bring some meaning to its guarantee of speech and assembly."[16] The usually conservative *Dallas News* said that Maverick "did the right thing," and that his aim to permit "every reformer a soapbox" had worked well in England and should work here.[17]

The auditorium incident also set two powerful egos on a collision course. Eddie Cantor, the famous comedian and showman, was performing in San Antonio at the time, and he made some general remarks as a part of a patriotic piece that he characteristically included in his act. These remarks could have been interpreted as directed at Maverick—at least that is the way the mayor viewed the matter. Maverick called the Jewish comedian to tell him that "his people" certainly ought to be the first to defend minority rights instead of stirring people up on such issues. The mayor suggested that Cantor include in his stock statement of opposition to "all isms but Americanism" a more positive statement in behalf of free speech and the Bill of Rights. Cantor repeatedly told Maverick that he had never heard of him, probably the most devastating thing anyone could say, adding that he would not change his lines for anybody. Maverick's friends, Pearson and Allen, reported this incident and generally gave Cantor "the works" in their syndicated column. Cantor threatened to sue them, but in a few months all of the principals cooled down, and Cantor apparently dropped his suit. Months later, however, Maverick still could not refrain from commenting acidly to Morris Ernst concerning Cantor, "No doubt he has good qualities—he told me about them himself."[18]

There was a much less publicized reversal in Maverick's stand on freedom of expression before another year had passed. When Maverick was confronted with an application from the Jehovah's Witnesses for use of the auditorium in June 1940, he flatly rejected it. In August 1939 Maverick had viewed the Bill of Rights as extending to every group, regardless of its views, the right to hold a meeting in a public facility, but just as he had been able then to rely on the ruling of the Supreme Court in the *Hague* case,[19] he was now afforded the ruling in *Minersville School District* v. *Gobitis* as a rationalization for his refusal of a permit to the Jehovah's Witnesses. Justice Felix Frankfurter's majority opinion had affirmed that the state could require the flag salute of children of Witnesses, despite their religious scruples against it.[20] Maverick extended this argument to the assertion that the Jehovah's Witnesses' refusal to salute the flag or "recognize any civil authority" constituted overt acts. In a press release he explained:

> Society cannot exist without authority. The United States cannot so exist. In our hour of grave peril, even though offenders may be considered mere members of eccentric religious cults, such cults cannot be permitted to deny authority upon the false refuge of God.
> I have always believed that any man can say anything without previous censorship, being responsible for his acts. However, the incitement to riot, or overt act, are both illegal. Admittedly such a meeting by its own acts, is incitement to flout civil authority, and thereby force and violence against the government. The physical defiance of the flag, even though passive, may be in its nature, and by the reasoning of the Supreme Court, an overt act.
> We note deep convulsion and change in this world. It is a world to break men's hearts, mine as well as yours. . . .[21]

In a rough draft of the press release, he had also said: "Personally, I am frank to say that I am neither neutral nor impartial in the present crisis. We are not in a state of war, but we are in a grave emergency. . . . Religious liberty should be strained to its utmost, because if one is denied freedom for even what appears to be great extremes, it may lead to other extremes against other religions. But though organized religion may by precept follow God,

He Stirreth Up the People 219

its secular organization is composed of men, and men must recognize civil authority, whatever their religious belief."[22]

Three months later Maverick rejected a second application from the Communist party for permission to use the auditorium. His blunt press release explained:

Independence of this country is more important than the liberty of an individual to overthrow that independence. In such case we would lose both independence and liberty.

A year ago I would have granted a permit to anyone. But now the world is turned up-side-down, and it is the duty of our people to first learn and then observe unity. . . .

The Communists who want the permit are of the dominant faction of Russia, and do not even tolerate difference of opinion of other Communists. Last night, the papers show, this faction had a 'pick-axe driven into the head of Trotsky,' which is of no concern to our democracy. But it is of grave concern to our democracy that no pick-axe be driven into the head of our country.

Because of the present impropriety of it, the granting of a permit is postponed to such a time as will appear more appropriate.[23]

Maverick was sensitive to criticism of his inconsistency. Despite his attempt to demonstrate that the Jehovah's Witnesses matter was different from the Communist application of September 1939, the subsequent refusal of the second Communist application indicated clearly that he, like the United States Supreme Court, "was at the moment deeply affected by the wave of patriotism and nationalism then sweeping the nation as the United States prepared to battle for its life against Germany and Japan."[24] When he refused the permit to the Jehovah's Witnesses, there had been a Dunkerque, and France fell to the Nazis the day after his press release. The air assault on Britain had begun when Maverick refused the second Communist permit.

In 1938 Maverick had stated explicitly, "We should be careful not to lose our heads and ourselves violate democratic rights. Nazis should be given the right of full expression." But on July 2, 1944, he penciled a marginal note opposite this statement, saying, "Soon after, I changed my mind. It is now violently opposite."[25]

These incidents illustrate how persuasive is the "exigencies of war" argument that Holmes used in the *Schenck* case and other World War I sedition cases.[26] Maverick himself had said that his study of these cases had convinced him that the basic reason for the rulings had been a doctrine of "emergency" powers, which he then deplored.[27] Professor Samuel J. Konefsky says that Holmes failed to make clear what the controlling factor was in the *Schenck* case, despite his assertion of the "clear and present danger" doctrine. Konefsky concluded: "Holmes may have revealed, perhaps unwittingly, the really controlling consideration when he declared—'When a nation is at war many things that might be said in time of peace are such a hindrance to its effort that their utterance will not be endured so long as men fight and that no Court could regard them as protected by any constitutional right.' "[28]

During World War II, despite the reversal of the *Gobitis* ruling,[29] a unanimous Supreme Court refused to question the curfew law directed at all persons of Japanese ancestry,[30] and the relocation of American citizens of Japanese ancestry on our West Coast (despite the fact that these measures violated nearly all of the fundamental rights) was upheld by a six-to-three majority of the Court. Libertarian Black wrote the opinion, and he was supported by a libertarian Douglas.[31] In the case of *Ex parte Endo*, a Japanese-American woman was granted a writ of habeas corpus, but Justice Douglas' opinion did not question the constitutionality of the detention and relocation program.[32] There is nothing to indicate that Maverick ever commented on these decisions. They are cited here to demonstrate that in one instance a unanimous Supreme Court and in another a majority of the court would go so far as to sustain *actions* in violation of fundamental liberties during prosecution of a war. There is no explaining away Maverick's inconsistency, but it may be appropriate to point out that at least he was "postponing" the use of a facility rather than supporting an *action* against basic rights.

War seems to have a corrosive effect upon even the stoutest of defenders of civil liberties. As one writer succinctly put it, "Like a party that comes to power and takes over the government, war brings in its own virtues and values to supplant those that rule during peace."[33]

Maverick was also ambivalent in his position on the Negro question, and much of his feeling could be traced to what he considered to be the ingratitude of San Antonio Negroes. He was as much a

He Stirreth Up the People 221

maverick on this subject as on any other; over the span of most of his life, he was not a liberal champion of integration and complete Negro suffrage, nor was he clearly in the southern "gradualist" school of Hodding Carter.[34] Rather he seemed to be standing between the two positions—pushing the gradualist and restraining what he conceived to be the liberal extremist.

In Maverick's first recorded statement on this issue, he set down the kernel of the view that was to dominate his thinking throughout most of his career. In 1929 he wrote to a friend that he had been studying some books on the Negro problem and that he had concluded that social equality for the Negro would come only when he had "more than enough" of the world's goods. "Recognition in any line comes from Power," Maverick concluded.[35] In 1937 he wrote "The Negro must have full economic justice. This alone will satisfy most of his problems. And this will be such a Herculean job that we need carry the discussion no further here, except to say that the low economic status of the white man in the South has given him a new viewpoint on the Negro problem."[36]

In *A Maverick American* he said, "The first thing to do about the question is to see [that] the colored people eat and have jobs. Let them have a wage scale equal to white people if they do equal work. If economic opportunities are fair, and the different races show restraint, other questions will work themselves out."[37]

Maverick joined this argument more fully to the "freedom from want" idea as a means for solving the Negro problem when he wrote:

The Negro stands like a Black Colossus in the middle of every Southern, and hence every American, problem. He is both a symbol and an excuse for reactionary voting. But there is not much use in setting out problems unless we try to do something about them. So as a starter, certainly a unanimity of opinion should demand that the Negro obtain economic justice, that he should have the right to jobs, the right to own homes and farms, to have food and education. More, since the Negro is greatly subject to disease, he certainly should have the opportunity of benefiting by preventive medicine and public health measures.[38]

Again Maverick used his shrewdly pragmatic arguments to sell decent treatment of the Negro to his Southern brethren. It was not necessarily a matter of being "charitable or humanitarian," and such an approach was "not altogether" for the Negro's benefit, but, "If the Negro's economic status is improved it will solve many other serious and complicated problems concerning the races."[39] He also used his approach of appeals to self interests of whites. He said, "Today the low wages, long hours, working conditions, the rotten conditions of the share-croppers, both black and white, *are still a menace to the nation.*"[40]

Then in his Proclamation of Interracial Sunday, February 11, 1940, Mayor Maverick told San Antonians, "Lynching, fighting, exploitation, settle nothing. Negroes have a higher rate of disease, are ignorant, say some—then give them the opportunity of good health and education. The Negro is entitled to full economic justice —jobs, education, homes, the right to lead a Christian life. He is also entitled to due process of law under our Constitutional democracy."[41]

Maverick joined his views on the various phases of the Negro problem in a major address to his fellow members of the Southern Conference on Human Welfare on April 16, 1940, in which he presented his general prescription for the solution of that problem. He said that "economic justice" was the most important objective for the Negro and that the Negro did not even want social equality. He then urged upon his fellow delegates:

Let's free our minds from prejudices as much as we can and have the courage to think;—and let's preserve constitutional democracy, civil rights for all. . . . We of the South must get over the idea that the man who spits tobacco juice, has a big bat, and carries a six-gun, is thereby an intelligent peace officer. We need men . . . who have been trained, who are reasonably well-educated, and who are honest, decent and humane. . . . Should lawlessness reach a point where life is in danger and EQUAL PROTECTION of the law breaks down, then the Federal government under the Constitution has a perfect right to provide protection, and SHOULD give protection.[42]

Maverick had voiced virtually the same views in a speech to students at Georgia Tech in January 1940.[43] His assessment of the Negro problem and his proffered solution must have represented some fairly acute perception of what it was that the Southern Negro wanted at that time. One of the Texan's files is filled with

He Stirreth Up the People

letters and telegrams from Negroes in various parts of Texas and the United States, warmly commending him for his statements. Many of the correspondents quoted excerpts from the speeches as accurate reflections of their aims. A Houston Negro, who did not sign his name, commented on the January speech, "You said right when you said: 'As for social equality, Negroes do not even talk about it.' And I will go one step further, Mr. Mayor, we do not even think about it."[44] In February 1940, moreover, Maverick was one of five white persons among fifteen men and women cited for "distinguished achievement in the improvement of race relations" as a result of a nation-wide poll conducted by the Schomburg Collection of the New York Public Library and the Association for the Study of Negro Life and History.[45]

In his key speeches, Maverick did not deal with the Negro suffrage question, but he was at this time in the process of waging a fight for the elimination of the poll tax as a prerequisite to voting. He was the first witness sent by the Southern Conference on Human Welfare to testify in behalf of the Geyer anti-poll-tax bill,[46] in March 1940.[47] The San Antonio mayor said that the poll tax created in the South a "sort of piece-meal, part-time, fractional, divided democracy," but he also argued that it was not merely a Negro problem—that the number of whites enfranchised by a lifting of the poll-tax requirement would be "something like eight times the number of colored people."[48] He contended that Congress probably had the authority to eliminate the poll tax for all elections, but certainly for national elections.[49] He based this argument upon the provision of Section 4 of Article I of the Constitution, which provides that Congress may "alter" state regulations of the "manner" of holding elections of members of Congress.[50]

Maverick was sharply critical of the opponents of the measure, characterizing them as advocates of white supremacy, and ridiculing them as "good, highly virtuous, conservative citizens who fear the black menace, the Pope's Navy or are just employed by the economic groups that exploit the South." "In general," he said, "they are a group out to get a Roosevelt, a Maverick, or anybody else who won't do his bit to keep the colored people, the white share-croppers, the whole lowest third down in the dirt. . . ."[51]

As had been the case with his efforts in behalf of general civil-rights legislation, Maverick wanted the fight against the poll tax pitched on the level that it was fundamentally undemocratic,[52] and he pointed out long before the late V. O. Key, Jr., that, as Key put it, "the poll tax, insofar as it has deterred voting, has operated primarily to keep whites away from the polls."[53] In other words, Maverick again did not want the anti-poll-tax measure put forth as a bill to give Negroes the suffrage. He was being intensely practical (some might say politic) when he said that he was not "out on a reforming tour to help the poor, persecuted black man." In Maverick's mind, freeing the poll-tax fight from the Negro question might be the measure of its success.

Maverick did not oppose the white primary. In fact, he said in 1940 that he favored the white primary as long as it was judged lawful.[54] There is no indication that Maverick gave any justification for his position or that he expressed any views on the demise of the white primary.[55] The reason for his position, however, is not difficult to discover. Most of the time he had the frustrating experience of trying to help the Negro cause only to see their votes go to the local machine that shrewdly gave them short-run local favors and inducements.

Maverick's plight was attested to by national Negro leaders, but one of them, finding that Maverick would not oppose the white primary, told him that they would "part company." John P. Davis, secretary of the National Negro Congress, told Maverick, "We knew that most of the Negro vote was in the hands of certain corrupt politicians." Davis also said he was willing to overlook Maverick's efforts to prevent Negroes from voting in primaries, and had done everything he could to persuade San Antonio Negroes to vote for Maverick, but he could not continue as long as Maverick favored the white primary.[56]

Walter White, head of the National Association for the Advancement of Colored People, seemed to have a better understanding of and a different attitude toward Maverick's situation. When Maverick complained of the lack of Negro support in the mayor's race in 1939, White wrote that he recognized the machine control of the vote. He explained that many Negroes found it expedient to vote against Maverick, because, "they do not dare sometimes to turn the old machine loose, lest the new machine fail and leave them high and dry." He added that the "colored citizens of San Antonio"

He Stirreth Up the People 225

would no doubt say privately that they are "for the new Mayor of San Antonio, who stood so bravely for all of us in the United States Congress."[57] White voiced no criticism of Maverick. In fact, in a later letter he commended the San Antonio mayor for his "superb" article in *Nation*,[58] and said he would be honored to have a statement from Maverick for the next conference of the NAACP.[59]

Maverick was often irritated by northerners' attacks on "Southern justice." He felt that he knew what was wrong with Southern justice and attacked many aspects of it himself, but he wanted his Northern brethren to concern themselves with the "starving industrial piece-workers of New York," "the Negroes of Harlem," and the "poor whites." He said, "There is likely more sectional prejudice in Manhattan than there is in the South."[60]

He was obviously irked by a letter from White in 1940 asking him to assist in securing witnesses for an antilynch measure then under consideration in Congress. White said that he feared that Texas Senator Tom Connally would probably get some "Uncle Tom Negroes" as witnesses against the need for such a bill. Maverick penciled a curt note on the letter: "No answer."[61]

Even in the Conference on Human Welfare speech, which won so much Negro support and approval, Maverick complained that he was being damned by whites for urging rights for the Negro and damned by Negroes for admitting his prejudices, and that "liberals and progressives" should not fall out over "picayunish differences." "Some of the things we talk about are not problems as such, but problems merely as symbols . . . used to excite minds on both sides." On this point he concluded, "I refuse to discuss symbols except as symbols. I refuse to slobber and fawn over racial and religious minorities; I refuse to wave the bloody shirt and refuse to let one be waved at me."[62] Thus Maverick indicated that he was chafing under the assumption of some Negroes that he was a *completely* reconstructed southerner—he was not, he still had some native prejudices, and it embarrassed and irritated him to be reminded of it. He was not to alter these views significantly until after World War II.

Perhaps the energetic mayor should have spent more time at home in 1939 and 1940, rather than making these speeches in Chattanooga and points east. His traditional foes were preparing for him the roughest of his rough campaigns, with C. K. Quin again the opponent. Maverick was running on the Greater San Antonio Ticket, which he said had "started San Antonio's march of progress."[63] Quin opened his campaign on April 29, 1941, in a speech to "anti-Maverick forces." The *San Antonio Express* said, "Significant was the attendance of Sheriff Owen Kilday." Maverick was hit for what might be called his "un-San Antonian" activities. He had hired experts from out of the city for important posts, he had used an out-of-the-city firm for tax appraisals, and he had been out of the city too much himself. Kilday reportedly told the crowd that he was "still after that man."[64]

Maverick responded with a sober recital of his record and boasted of the achievement of a modern administrative system for the city of San Antonio. He defended his trips out of the state as the means for getting things for the city. He also claimed credit for keeping "crooks" out of San Antonio.[65]

The campaign dirt was largely confined to broadsides. Mrs. Maverick wrote the note, "This is a mild sample of the stuff we had to fight," on a copy of one entitled "Is This a Coincidence???" which had been signed by "The Citizen's Committee." The sheet charged that Maverick had used tax money to finance his 1934 campaign and that "David Dubinsky, CIO head," had helped to finance his campaign in 1938. The handout rehashed the old charges that Maverick had purchased poll taxes for members of the CIO Garment Workers' Union. Maverick had "control of the Tax Payers money." "Will he use it for political purposes as he did in 1934? Is your money being used to satisfy Maury Maverick's political greed?"[66]

About two weeks before the election the anti-Maverick forces said they had "found" a campaign handout outside a meeting of Communists on El Paso Street. The sheet contained the message:

Workers unite! Hurl the chains!
Forward with Maverick for a greater San Antonio!
    Municipal Committee of San Antonio

Maverick's reaction was, "Cheap stuff like this has been pulled on me before. . . . I am sending this to the FBI and it will turn up as having come from the stooges of the 'anti-ticket.' "[67] The authors of the handbill were not found, but a few days later the "Don

He Stirreth Up the People

Politico" column said that such circulars were "not unexpected." Except for the appearance of this item, there were "no new issues to lend excitement to the race." The principle issues boiled down to (1) The Maverick: "I am the greatest mayor San Antonio has ever had." (2) The Anti-Mavericks: "Maverick is the worst mayor San Antonio has ever had."[68]

Just before the election Maverick charged the opposition with conducting a completely negative campaign. He said he had called their election headquarters without identifying himself and asked what their program was. A woman who answered said she didn't know and then put someone on the phone who said the only aim was "to get Maverick out of office."[69] The next day he charged that Quin was conducting a whispering campaign among the various minority groups in the city.[70]

May 13 was an unlucky day for Maverick. Quin polled 17,347 votes to 16,142 for Maverick, and 2,000 votes went to the also rans. Now a runoff was required. Maverick noted that Quin had carried the Negro boxes by overwhelming margins, so he directed his attention primarily to the northside middle-class white supporters. He opened the runoff campaign with a speech to a large crowd at Denver Heights Park on May 17. He said that his chances had been "wrecked" by the Negro voters, and fixed the blame on the Harvard-educated Negro boss, Valmo Bellinger, who had fallen heir to the kingdom and subjects of his father, Charles Bellinger. In his desperation, Maverick called Bellinger a "black baboon," and warned, "If Quin wins, Bellinger will get the lottery racket."[71]

Maverick's fortunes were boosted a bit when Representative Fagan Dickson announced that he and his Better Government organization would support the mayor. Dickson said, "I have no love for Maverick but my civic pride prevents me from being a silent supporter of ex-Mayor Quin. His previous administration was marked by under-world domination of municipal affairs."[72] Dickson was rapped by Owen Kilday for turning against those who helped him. Kilday said, "There is some loyalty in politics, believe it or not. . . . If I scratch his back, I think he ought to scratch mine. But I'm marking him down in my little black book for next summer."[73]

When Maverick learned that Congressman Paul Kilday was coming to San Antonio to speak for Quin, the mayor declared that "pygmy politicians" should stay out of the race and attend to their business. Then, turning to some of the devices that had been used against him Maverick said, "I don't think Quin is a thief or racketeer, but he is a fellow-traveler of thieves and murderers." Maverick said that the names of some of the people who had signed petitions for Quin were in FBI records as gangsters and racketeers.[74]

But whatever tack Maverick took, it was to no avail. On May 27 he was narrowly defeated in the runoff by a vote of 20,982 to 19,799.[75] The next day Maverick stunned his most hardened adversaries when he appeared before the city council with Quin, offered him "sincere congratulations," and said, "I wish you a successful administration. I hope you have a really fine administration." The *San Antonio Evening News*, which usually had nothing good to say about Maverick said, "The gesture by Maverick was termed by city and county politicians as one of the finest they had ever seen a losing candidate in any election make."[76]

Why did Maverick lose again? As before, he carried too many burdens into the contest. There was the auditorium row, his poll-tax trial, the inevitable toes he trod upon in a reform administration, and again his failure, despite an avowal to the contrary, to keep his fences mended. Maverick, of course, fully understood the function of patronage in the successful political operation, but, as had been the case when he was in Congress, he had little real taste or feel for it. His files indicate that he failed to politic with some of his supporters, avoided job-seekers, and was generally pretty difficult to see.[77] His impatience with such matters is revealed in his response to a query from his assistant, Floyd McGown, concerning three job-seekers. Maverick dashed off a terse memorandum reading, "———— is no good—to hell with him. However, ———— is O.K. But all ————'s should be shot."[78] These files do show, however, that he was earnestly trying to correct these shortcomings by improvements in his staff communications system. Even these efforts were not likely to be too successful, because he was on the go so much.

It does not seem too likely that his reference to Valmo Bellinger as a "black baboon" cost him many votes, because the machine had most of the Negro votes. On the other hand, Maverick did not need too many more votes, and there is some indication that he might

He Stirreth Up the People

have had some sort of chance at some fence-mending with Bellinger. The Negro leader seemed to be in the mood for something of the sort when he made an unsolicited call to Maverick's office early in his mayorality to let him know that he was taking no part "officially or otherwise" in the recall petitions being circulated at that time with the hope of ousting Maverick after the auditorium incident.[79]

Postelection commentaries heaped unstinting praise upon Maverick's accomplishments as a mayor, upbraiding San Antonio voters for their "political ingratitude" and for repudiating "one of the best administrations any American city has known."[80] A liberal Texas weekly repeated this judgment and said the ex-mayor was "quixotic" and "his own worst political enemy," because he was willing to risk all on "doing what is right and honest and brave."[81] *Business Week* commented that despite his defeat, Maverick could derive satisfaction from "one of the most significant civic improvements which any American city can boast."[82] The *Dallas News*, editorializing on a later contest, said of his administration: "Whether San Antonio has voted wisely time will have to tell. In a previous mayorality incarnation, the doughty Maverick is generally credited with having been a good administrator. His personal integrity is beyond question. He had a healthier respect for sumptuary law than can be discerned in administrations under which the Bexar capital has operated as a wide-open town. The inference may be that the San Antonians like it that way. At any rate, the dominant machine does, and in the duel of Maverick the man versus the machine, the machine won."[83] Five years after the contest, John Gunther said that Maverick was "incontestably the best mayor San Antonio ever had."[84]

The *San Antonio Light* gave a "factual survey" of Maverick's administration on June 1 in pursuance of its "established policy" of reporting on every city administration in San Antonio at its closing. The report listed at least eighteen categories of improvement in San Antonio government during the Maverick administration:

1. The Health Department was recognized by the U.S. Public Health Service for the first time.
2. "Strict enforcement of a meat inspection ordinance has brought about much-needed sanitation in local packing plants."

3. Other ordinances on inspection and grading of milk and eggs were better enforced and better scientific equipment introduced.

4. Improvements were made in sewage disposal and a mosquito control program was established.

5. Consolidation and more efficient operation of city inspection offices were achieved.

6. First effective enforcement of zoning ordinances.

7. New system of weights and measures established.

8. La Villita virtually completed—"the pride and joy of Maury Maverick."

9. Secured $3,000,000 for the municipal airport.

10. "Return of chili queens to Haymarket Plaza."

11. "Major advances" in the parks department and improvements to the zoo.

12. Modernization of garbage collection and equipment.

13. New street-sweeping equipment that saved the city $135 every 24 hours.

14. New flood gates at Mitchell Lake.

15. Construction of the reptile garden and landscaping of Witte Museum.

16. Many improvements in tax commissioner's office: new records system, new evaluations by experts, inequities removed in real property evaluation.

17. Best percentage of tax collection in San Antonio history, at lower rates for most property owners.

18. Complete streamlining of fire and police departments, modernization of records division, first full-time traffic engineer, cadet training for police recruits inaugurated, and "ticket fixing" out and corporation court revenues up.[85]

A month after Quin took office the *Light* said that the new administration seemed to be "determined to wipe out every vestige of the preceding administration." The police department had been "wrecked" and a "police court that had been an effective arm of law enforcement was converted into a travesty and a farce."[86] Earlier, immediately after Quin took office, "Don Politico" had called attention to a purge in the police department which, he said, all agreed was Maverick's greatest achievement. "Perhaps," said the columnist, "it was too great an achievement."[87] Even the *Ex-*

press joined in to report that Quin was apparently bent on wrecking the Health Department. He had gone through a two-phase shake-up, with new people he had just hired being fired in the second phase. The *Express* also noted an increase in non-civil-service personnel.[88] Perhaps, as the *Dallas News* suggested, a majority of San Antonians did not want good government.

Again, Maverick did not lack encouragement in his second defeat. His son, Maury Maverick, Jr., had written to President Roosevelt to complain about his father's defeat at the hands of those people who had benefited from a good administration. FDR responded:

I am not quite sure I should answer you because your father once told me that you opposed me as a well as him during the Supreme Court reorganization battle. I am not being too serious because he told me that when you heard the reasons on our side you changed your point of view. . . .

When the people, in Texas or the United States, are told the truth long enough and often enough you do not have to fear that they will not do the right thing. Your father and my friend was defeated for reelection after he had given the City of San Antonio intelligent and good government which is all too rare in municipal affairs. I know he feels badly about it but I also know, because I know him, that he is quietly sure his point of view will prevail in the long run.

The same thing is true about Lyndon Johnson. I hope he will win but even if he does not the things for which he stands will eventually win. He will tell you that, your father will tell you and I also tell you. You may have forgotten but I once ran for Vice President at a time when I thought I was right and received a thorough defeat.

I hope this does not sound too much like a lecture, but do not forget that temporary defeats mean nothing as long as our side wins the last battle. That is what counts.

> Very sincerely yours,
> Franklin D. Roosevelt[89]

An Isolationist's Change of Heart

MAVERICK'S VIEW OF WAR was undergoing a profound change in 1940. Until that time he had clung fiercely to his neutrality and antiwar views. Oswald Garrison Villard had characterized the patriotic Maverick pretty well in 1936, however, when he said that the Texas congressman was not a complete pacifist and "if the drums were to beat and the troopships were on the tide once more, Maverick would be just inconsistent enough to volunteer again."[1] He did just that, *before* the troopships were on the tide. In the fall of 1940, he said that war was coming, and the much-wounded war hero tried to get a commission but was rejected for physical reasons.[2]

Turner Catledge of the *New York Times* wrote from the Democratic National Convention on July 13, 1940, that the "liveliest episode of the day" came when Mayor Maury Maverick stared across the green-topped table in the Blackstone Hotel and told the platform committee of his conversion "from the virtual pacifist to a practical militarist." He called for the utmost in preparedness and said he wanted a rebirth of the attitude in which his forefathers "went across the river into Texas . . . with a bottle of whiskey in one hand, a gun in the other and a prayer on their lips." Maverick also confided that he had resumed praying, and, finding her usually irreverent husband in prayer, Mrs. Maverick had joyfully concluded that he was praying for their draft-aged son. "I'm sorry to disappoint you, honey," he said he replied, "but I'm praying for the British Navy and the Bank of England." Maverick had watched with growing alarm as Nazi legions drove British forces into the sea at Dunkerque and then turned toward Paris, bringing France to her knees. To him, embattled Britain was the last great hope.

Swinging the pendulum all the way back never bothered Maury Maverick very much, and this time he had some good company when he did it. In January 1940 he told an audience in Fort Worth that he feared democracy was dead because leading democracies had "lost their courage,"[3] and later in the year he was one of the key people, along with Adlai E. Stevenson and William Allen White, in the organization of the Committee to Defend America by Aiding the Allies.[4] In September he told a Committee-sponsored meeting at the Chicago Coliseum that England was the source of constitutional rights and that it must be saved: "WE SHALL NOT PERMIT THESE SPARKS OF LIBERTY TO BE WIPED FROM THIS EARTH."[5] That same month he appeared in New York to deliver a great speech, "An Isolationist's Change of Heart," which should have been called "A Pacifist's Change of Heart," for Maverick was never a typical isolationist. His tentative draft of this talk was even superior to the version delivered and represents some of his best writing:

The change came to me in the spring of this year. Not China nor Ethiopia nor Spain moved me from my isolationism. I was even able to watch the murder of Poland with the feeling that this tragedy was not our fight. But in May two things happened. First, the news began to leak out of how the Germans dealt with the conquered Poles—by killing the possible leaders of Polish life, and by enslaving (literally enslaving) those who could not be expected to lead themselves. Second, the rapid and ruthless destruction of four of the most harmless, neutral, democratic, isolationist nations in the world convinced me that not only did Hitler deal with his conquered enemies as the Romans dealt with Carthage, but that all free men, all neutral men, all men who are not actively serving his cause, are classified as enemies, and marked down as victims. . . .

Suddenly I realized that *Mein Kampf* meant what it said. What I had taken to be another splurge of rhetoric, no more meaningful than the Kellogg pact, became a sinister blueprint for the decline and fall of man. Every hour since the dreadful month of May has confirmed the view that was forced upon me. The news of the last few days has been the most terrible news of all [the bombing of Britain]. . . .

I saw for the first time the meaning of Hitler—something which a man who had tried to fight the fight of liberalism at home was perhaps best qualified to see. No tragedy such as this could happen, no such revolution of nihilism and destruction could conquer the home continent of the civilization of the West, unless that civilization had first betrayed itself from within. The battle we liberals have supported here at home, the battle for the rights of man, was never successfully fought anywhere but in the small and defenseless countries Hitler has recently murdered. In the great and powerful nations the rights of man were applauded but they were not served. Hitler is the product of our failure to live up to our own ideals. If we had done our job there would be no Hitler. Unless we remove Hitler there will be no second chance to do our job. . . .

Hitler, by taking a world view while the rest of us were still tied to parochial views, had made an ally of time and space. The deadly combination of the first man in modern times to take a world view and the first man since the end of Rome to say out of the depths of nihilism that there are no rules of conduct, makes nonsense of the thought that oceans or miles or bigness can save us.[6]

In the following months, Maverick delivered a set of speeches to San Antonians comparing the perils of 1940 to those of Demosthenes' Athens and casting Hitler in the role of Phillip of Macedon. He cited Demosthenes' urging for preparedness and quoted, "For the war with the Dictator is a war for no other stake than OUR COUNTRY, our *life*, our *habits*, our Freedom *and all that we value.*"[7] In November Maverick spoke again for the Committee in Saint Louis. He urged that "America should quadruple its output of planes and turn at least half of them over to England." If the United States could produce one million automobiles, he argued, there was no reason why it could not produce fifty thousand airplanes.[8]

In 1941 Maverick was back on the "Forum of the Air," this time to reverse his earlier arguments on that same program.[9] The Japanese, he said, were "getting too big for their britches." It was time to stop sending oil, steel, and scrap to Japan and to turn to a policy of firmness in the Pacific and aid to China. Congressman Hamilton Fish told Maverick that Congress would not consent to a war against Japan unless the United States was attacked, and, he said, "Japan hasn't the slightest idea of attacking us"—a view Maverick had himself expressed a few years before when opposing the armaments program. Now Maverick expressed the opinion that Japan would attack in order to take the strategically important Philippines.[10]

Maverick continued his efforts to arouse the nation to the time of the December 7 Japanese attack on Pearl Harbor. In November he was the principal speaker for a mass meeting at the Lyric Theater in Baltimore on the occasion of the establishment by the mayor of National Defense and Fight for Freedom Week. Urging support of President Roosevelt's foreign policy, Maverick had come full circle.[11]

Maverick was, in fact, an internationalist ready for some kind of United Nations even before Pearl Harbor. One October evening in 1941 he chatted with Justice Felix Frankfurter concerning the role of the United States in world affairs. The next day Frankfurter carried on the discussion in a letter: "All I wanted to convey last night regarding American relations to the world, is that we should be concerned with our responsibility, not with our power. Unfortunately, power does not carry with it wisdom in its use, and the beginning of wisdom is humility. Preoccupation with power tends toward domination; preoccupation with responsibility makes for civilization. If you tell me this is merely a difference in emphasis, I can only say that the emphasis makes the song."[12]

The next day Maverick said that he too wanted to make his position better understood. He said, "I do not think the United States should be the big boss but I do think we should take heavy responsibilities. I do think also that there should be some sort of league of English-speaking democracies as well as such democracies as France, Czechoslovakia and the Scandinavian countries."[13]

Though he could not get into the armed services, there was other war work to be done, and Maverick was bound to be in on it. When he was defeated for mayor of San Antonio, the *New York Herald Tribune* suggested editorially that, as a friend of the president, excellent use could be made of the versatile gifts of the "La Guardia of the cow country."[14] Maverick's friend Ickes had expressed some doubts about this; in his *Diary* he had written that Maury Maverisk was "too volatile to be entrusted with an important administrative job."[15] But another friend, Harry Hopkins, had written to Maverick that he hoped that FDR would appoint the defeated mayor to "one of these important commissions."[16] The latter counsel eventually prevailed.

On September 11, 1941, Maverick was made assistant to his old friend, Leon Henderson, federal price administrator. At first it was not too clear just what he was to do, but he was soon given responsibility for reviewing the application of price administration to insular territories and possessions of the United States. In another month, in the rapid shifting of prewar agencies and posts, he was with Henderson in the Office of Production Management, as head of the division that handled applications of state and local governments for priorities on critical materials. He presided over a staff of eighty people in one of the wooden, barnlike structures on Washington's Maryland Avenue. He vowed that he was impartial in the handing out of priorities, and said, "I don't hate anybody but Hitler."[17]

In a few days he was headed west on what one reporter called "the unenviable mission of telling State and municipal officials how little they can get of the much they think they should get under the defense restrictions." Maury was depicted as having a knack for telling a person unpleasant things "in a blunt and final way," and winning their "cooperation and esteem."[18] Maury also provided some graphic illustrations of the difficulty of securing scarce goods. In one of his early conferences with purchasing officers from large cities, when he was not able to furnish them with chairs in his office, he had one of them sit on an upturned waste basket and the other on his desk.[19]

When the War Production Board was established on January 13, 1942, Maverick was made chief of the Bureau of Government Requirements, with essentially the same tasks he had had under the Office of Production Management.[20] After two months in this position, he predictably began to "maverick" again. Monsignor Cletus A. Miller and Dr. George S. Sperti came to him to discuss some priorities for chemicals for public health purposes. Both men were associated with the Institutum Divi Thomae, a Catholic institution for scientific research. In the course of a conversation, Maverick

An Isolationist's Change of Heart

and the two men did some thinking out loud about making science, particularly research, serve not only the large concerns but also small business (and the war effort) through a government office that would make discoveries available to all industries rather than having them monopolized by the large ones.

Though this proposal was outside Maverick's formal responsibilities, after some careful research and study by the three men, he submitted a memorandum to Donald M. Nelson, chairman of the WPB, recommending the establishment of an office to coordinate the scientific research laboratories of the United States in a "cooperative research program to meet the problems of shortages of materials and to assist industry and government in war production."[21] (The office of Scientific Research and Development, headed by Dr. Vannevar Bush, was devoted to weapons development.) Nelson was impressed by the proposal and appointed a five-man committee, including Maverick, to study the matter further. Dissension in the committee was acute, centering primarily on approval or disapproval of the "revolutionary" idea of making optimum use of scientific research and development for the war effort, with the determining factor to be whether developments were desirable for the country as a whole, rather than "whether they are desirable for making money."[22]

The three-to-two vote in the committee enabled Maverick to recommend an Office of Technical Development to Nelson. The plan was championed by Robert Nathan, head of Nelson's Planning Committee, which recommended the establishment of the Office and a War Research Development Corporation with a capitalization of $100,000,000. Bruce Catton said of this plan, "For what this proposal actually said was substantially this: If there is, or by any exertion of our best intelligence can be, any technical means whatever for increasing the productivity of our industry, then our government is going to see to it that it is used to the absolute maximum no matter what this does to competitive relationships, profit-and-loss statements, or who-owns-what."[23]

Nelson and the Planning Committee prepared to put the plan into effect. It was even endorsed by Fred Searls, Jr., "a crusty gentleman of the Republican persuasion," who was on the Planning Committee. In the course of a search for the man to head the program, opposition developed in the War Department and the sweeping proposal was watered down to a small committee of scientists and technicians, the Office of Production Research and Development, which "did a considerable amount of useful work before the war ended, and disturbed nobody."[24]

It was surprising to no one that the peripatetic Maverick was also dashing about the country, making speeches to all types of audiences, giving advice here and there, writing articles for the "think" magazines, and usually evoking favorable responses from the newspapers.[25] The *Salt Lake City Tribune* commended him for an "inspiring address" on the war effort,[26] and the *San Francisco Examiner* praised him for his work in aiding slum clearance in that city.[27] In Chicago he told Mayor Edward Kelly that he should keep in touch with his voters. "I didn't have time to do enough of it back home. But you should do it, Ed."[28]

One of Maverick's responsibilities was the supervision of prison industries engaged in war production. He accompanied Eleanor Roosevelt on tours of prisons,[29] and became sufficiently interested in the plight of prisoners to urge in an article and a speech a sort of Bill of Rights for prisoners. A *New Republic* editor called his article "one of the meatiest articles we have had in a good while."[30] Maverick urged in the article that "morally, a prisoner, like any other human being, is entitled to work. Indeed, he is sentenced to 'hard labor.' He is also entitled to good food, a clean bed, recreation and medical attention. Since he must work, it should be productive and educative labor, and not of the humiliating type which breeds only hate, and then vomits him out penniless and friendless on the sidewalk of society to renew his criminal career."

He proposed as the most basic reform an effort to keep as many people as possible out of prison by the use of pretrial examination to see if a defendant "might be adjusted to society by probation. All this requires an informed community to back up thoughtful judges and prosecuting attorneys, well-trained psychiatrists and common-sense social workers." Wages, however small, should be paid to prisoners for purposes of boosting their morale and improving chances for rehabilitation. Prison stripes should be abolished, and there should be more use of honor farms, cottages, and prisons-without-walls instead of the brutalizing and degrading jails that had become "grammar schools of crime."[31] Again Maverick won favorable comment from newspapers throughout the nation.[32]

An Isolationist's Change of Heart

Chairman Nelson indicated in December 1943 that Maverick was his choice to fill the vacancy created by the retirement of Robert W. Johnson from the chairmanship of the Smaller War Plants Corporation. The House and Senate Small Business Committees were said to be irate at the choice of the volatile Texan,[33] but Nelson said Maverick was "an able, vigorous administrator,"[34] and many businessmen with the WPB agreed. Republican Senator Kenneth S. Wherry said it would help his party if the Democrats put a "parlor pink" like Maverick in such a job.[35] But Nelson disagreed, and he went to Roosevelt and secured the appointment of Maverick. *Business Week* reported that Maverick had won Nelson's confidence by his handling of municipal supply problems and his stepping up of prison production for war. Nelson thought Maverick could be "counted on to fight for small business in the hurly-burly of industrial demobilization and conversion to peacetime operations."[36]

One writer, I. F. Stone, said that he knew Maury had "spunk," but did not know he was intrepid enough to take this position. He said, "The job has been the graveyard of reputations and not a few likely candidates have hurried past it, whistling, since Brig. Gen. Robert W. Johnson resigned the post in October." Maverick's task was pictured as being "harder than his predecessors," because of his reputation for radicalism.[37] When Maverick took the job on January 12, 1944, he received stacks of congratulatory letters from congressmen, governors, and mayors. Adlai E. Stevenson, then special assistant to the secretary of the navy, told him that his appointment was "the first good home front news I have heard in a long while."[38]

As chairman of the Smaller War Plants Corporation, Maverick's assignment was to bring smaller businesses more into defense production that was dominated by big business while aiding development of plans for the postwar role of small business. He did what was expected of him and more. *Fortune* magazine said that while "big name executives tried to solve the problem without success," Maverick had brought about a "real increase (perhaps even double) in contracts to small business."[39]

It was while serving as the SWPC chairman that Maverick's longstanding interest in promoting the cause of clear writing and speaking gave rise to the contribution for which he has probably been best known, the coinage of the word *gobbledygook* and the elaboration of his argument for terse, lucid prose. On March 24, 1944, he dashed off a brief memorandum to his SWPC employees:

Be SHORT and use Plain English.
Memoranda should be as short as clearness will allow. The Naval officer who wired "Sighted Sub—Sank Same" told the whole story.
Put the real subject matter—the *point*—and even the conclusion, in the opening paragraph and the whole story on one page. Period! If a lengthy explanation, statistical matter, or such is necessary, use attachments.
Stay off gobbledygook language. It only fouls people up. For the Lord's sake, be short and say what you're talking about. Let's stop "pointing up" programs, "finalizing" contracts that "stem from" district, regional or Washington "levels." There are no "levels"—local government is as high as Washington Government. No more patterns, effectuating, dynamics. Anyone using the words "activation" or "implementation" will be shot.[40]

Maverick's memorandum attracted immediate and widespread attention. He was asked to write an elaboration of this argument (gobbledygook about gobbledygook?) for the *New York Times*, and the piece was also printed in the *Reader's Digest*.[41] Jerry Klutz, writer of "The Federal Diary," said of the original memorandum, "The most refreshing—and effective, I predict—memo ever written in the Federal service was handed out yesterday."[42] Senator William Benton called the longer article "one of the best pieces the Sunday Times will ever publish."[43]

Since that time, Maverick's famous memorandum has been reprinted in textbooks and journals on public administration and English composition, provoking a considerable literature on the subject.[44] The Bureau of Land Management of the U.S. Department of the Interior has recently published a 113 page booklet on gobbledygook that strangely has no mention of Maverick in it![45]

Maverick often said that he would take a back seat to no one when it came to patriotism; he had a very strong sentimental attachment to the symbols of this nation's heritage. While serving as chairman of the Smaller War Plants Corporation, he began a one-man campaign in mid-1944 to bring about the opening of the United States Capitol on Sundays for servicemen's visits and the

An Isolationist's Change of Heart 241

public display of the original copies of the Declaration of Independence, the Constitution, and the Bill of Rights in the Library of Congress. He said that he wanted young men and women to have a "thrilling memory of their Capitol," but he was also interested in making people conscious of the legislative process in a time of executive ascendency. President Roosevelt responded to Maverick's proposal: "I think you are right about your subject, 'Capitol Hill is a deadly place on Sunday.' Why did you put 'on Sunday'! I am asking McReynolds and Harold Smith to look into it and see if we cannot do something about it. Capitol Hill certainly needs some good advertising and its own music is often so out of tune that it would be marvelous to have a real band play there! [Maverick had also suggested this.] Please burn this! I want no one to see it because some of the people on Capitol Hill are touchy and they might not appreciate your sense of humor."[46]

All of these measures sought by Maverick were accomplished on August 27, 1944.[47] Also, "The Flag of Liberation" was preserved through the efforts of Maury Maverick. When the Japanese attacked Pearl Harbor, he had the flag then flying over the Capitol taken down. Next he persuaded FDR to take the flag to Casablanca, and later it flew from the balcony of Mussolini's Palazzo Venezia in Rome after the Italian defeat. Truman took the flag with him to Potsdam, and on its return to the United States, Maverick had it flown to Pearl Harbor, Guam, Iwo Jima, and Okinawa where it was raised at those historic Pacific battle sites. It was on the battleship *Missouri* when the Japanese surrender was concluded, and on September 17, 1945, it was raised over the American Embassy in Tokyo by General MacArthur before its return to the United States.[48]

As far as the future of small business was concerned, Maverick first aided Nelson in drafting reconversion plans that were partly responsible for the WPB chief being eased out in favor of Charles E. Wilson (of General Electric).[49] Fighting a developing conservative swing in the country and in the government, Maverick took the campaign for small business to the Congress and to the people —he wrote articles, testified, made speeches to groups and on the radio, and did whatever else could be done to further the interests of small business during the reconversion period.[50]

Allan Drury saw Maury in those days as the "short, stocky, bull-necked, frog-faced Texan" who was making an "uphill fight" for small business as he gave his "blunt, honest testimony" to a Senate Small Business Complaints Committee. Maverick told senators that the conventional attitude toward reconversion held by most of the seven hundred War Production Board advisory committees was going to lead to even greater concentration of American business than that existing at the time. "Consequently, little business, and little business friends, stood in grave danger of 'taking a hell of a beating.'" Drury's entry of August 16, 1944, in his *Senate Journal* again depicted the "bluntly honest Maury, fighting his battle for little business like a Texas Tantalus who can never quite slake his all-consuming thirst," as Maverick attempted to persuade Congress to pass a surplus-disposal measure that would benefit little as well as big business.[51]

Maverick sometimes sounded like an echo of Justice Louis D. Brandeis as he extolled the virtues of small business, but, unlike Brandeis, Maverick said he was mainly interested in promoting what he called "real" competition. He explained to a reporter who had called him the most articulate and sincere champion of small business: "I am not against big business as such. It is not inherently bad, any more than little business is inherently good because it is little. But I have no patience with those who always talk about the efficiency of big business. It is and can be efficient only if there is an absolutely free economic opportunity for small business to challenge the leaders. It is efficient in a real sense only if there is opportunity for new energy and new methods to move in and challenge any existing business."[52]

Essentially, what Maverick wanted the administration and Congress to do in the coming reconversion period was to give some advantage to small business in the disposal of surplus equipment and plants, and to provide loans to enable small business firms to get established or to grow. Not only should small business be given priority in acquisition of surplus machine tools, but also large plants that had been created largely at public expense should be made available on a "multiple rental system" (individual small industries using parts of a large plant) to small business. This interesting idea, said Maverick, had already been used by private business, but he wanted

An Isolationist's Change of Heart

to have the government make the surplus plants available in the same fashion.

Maverick had an ideological justification for his position. He explained that the public domain in the early years of the United States had been used to "carry out the inspiring principles of the Declaration of Independence."

But now the land is taken up. We face new and heavy problems. We are now a nation of cities, an industrial nation, the kind of nation Jefferson hoped we wouldn't be. That cannot be helped. . . .

And as far as that is concerned, an industrial civilization *can be JUST* as free, and even more so than an agricultural civilization. The Declaration of Independence can be fused into an industrial society too.

The answer is simple. Give little business a chance. Guarantee small business opportunity and you will have competition. Remove undue and unjust burdens from small business and then—and only then— will there be full production and full employment.[53]

Maverick was successful in some measure. He received the plaudits of many newspapers and other publications, including some quite conservative ones,[54] and Congress adopted some of his proposals, but by and large his aims were not achieved. As Catton put it, the fight from "Nelson's dismissal down to VE-Day" waged by Maverick and two labor members of the WPB was a steady but "unavailing" one.[55] The general failure could, of course, be attributed to the swing, late in the war, to "business as usual" and the attendant pressures on President Truman and the Congress. But Maverick may have contributed to the failure to some degree himself. No one ever had to enjoin him to "think big," and he wanted to internationalize the small-business fight. In the fall of 1944 he approached Lauchlin Currie, deputy administrator of the Foreign Economic Administration, with the idea of going to England, France, and the Soviet Union to discuss plans for reconversion and thus get ideas for "developing plans and programs for encouragement and stimulation of small business after the war."[56] Currie thought the trip was worthwhile as did J. A. Krug, acting chairman of the WPB.[57] With this encouragement, Maverick prepared a long justification of his proposal, had Assistant Secretary of State A. A. Berle look it over, and then sent it to Cordell Hull for approval.[58]

After the trip (to Britain only) was approved, Maverick set

about getting letters of introduction to members of the British Board of Trade, members of Parliament, and other influential people. He prepared a "confidential memo" for himself with notes on the various people he would be meeting, with some amusing results. For example:

> Rt. Honorable Hugh Dalton
> President, Board of Trade
> London, England
> Professor. Loquacious to extreme. Talkativeness but will not commit himself except on generalities.
> Viscountess Astor
> Attractive, noisy, demagogic. Was Miss Langhome of Charlottesville. "Cleveden [sic] set."

And another, best unnamed: "One quart per diem. Arrives office 11 A.M. Rotarianesque."[59]

Maverick and his assistant, A. B. Wacker, landed in London on October 3, 1944. The first day they toured the House of Lords and the House of Commons, the next day it was lunch with Lady Astor, but the rest of the slightly more than two weeks was spent in a series of conferences with British officials. Maverick met and discussed postwar reconversion problems with Lionel Robbins, economist in the War Cabinet; Hugh Dalton, president of the Board of Trade; Oliver Lyttleton, Minister of Production; H. T. M. Gaitskell, price administrator, and a number of others, including British businessmen.[60] The impression one gets from Maverick's notes and subsequent correspondence with many of these people is that the trip was not productive. Most of the Britishers were interested, but seemed to feel that in their country there was not much of a problem between small and big business—small business had been in on war production from the outset.[61]

When the BBC learned that Maverick was going to make the trip, he was asked to make a speech. When he supplied a draft copy of his proposed speech, certain "corrections" were made by a member of the BBC staff. Maverick yelled "censorship," and said that what they were concerned about was his references to "cartels" as he spoke of future air-travel situations, saying that "if we divide up territories for monopolies, the prices of travel will stay up, a few, a very few, people will make a lot of money. . . ." Maverick later said, "I refused to change it and did not deliver the speech." He wrote a letter of protest to Lord Halifax, the British ambassador to the United States, and Halifax replied that he felt that the BBC was only suggesting and editing. Maury insisted, ". . . they *did* censor my speech," and that apparently was the end of the matter.[62]

Maverick returned to Washington on October 23, but he had been there little more than a month when he was invited by the War Department to join other "key officials" in an inspection tour of England, France, Luxembourg, and Belgium, including the war front. Maverick described the party as "Paul McNutt, Chairman of the War Manpower Commission—Harold Boeschenstein (Toledo-Glass), Dr. William Y. Elliott (Harvard), Jim Folger (San Francisco-Coffee), Joe Keenan (Chicago-Labor)—all vice-chairmen of the War Production Board."

Maverick prepared a manuscript from a set of notebooks that he kept during the trip.[63] This discursive account tells first of Maverick's return trip to England where he was violently ill for several days with an ear ailment. During several days in the hospital at Prestwyck, Scotland, and in London, he set down his thoughts on socialized medicine. His view was that some "compromise" type of socialized medicine was inevitable in the United States and that Morris Fishbein of the American Medical Association would some day be known as the "Father of Socialized Medicine" because "he has indoctrinated his club so fiercely and he makes so many people sore, that he hastens the day of change, the opposite of what he teaches."[64]

After he left the hospital, Maverick joined Professor Elliott for another conference with Oliver Lyttleton, British minister of production. Later Maverick joined his friend Leon Henderson for an evening of dinner and conversation with Lord Beaverbrook that turned into something of a shouting match. Henderson and Maverick raged at British war policies that had resulted in the shooting of Greeks as British forces moved into Greece. Beaverbrook shot back that the United States had taken Panama when it wanted to build the Panama Canal, and Maverick said, "What? Compare the history and civilization of Greece and that of the Panama Canal?" In this exchange, which Maverick styled as "magnificent incoherence," Beaverbrook seemed to be rather pleased "to have someone talk back to him every now and then," according to Maverick.[65]

The party went on to Cherbourg on December 30, 1944, where Maverick indulged in some nostalgic reminiscences about his landing there in 1918 as the band played the "Marseillaise" and the mayor made "a hot speech for liberty." After a complete briefing on the tactical situation, proximity of the enemy, and matters of ordnance, quartermaster, medical, and transportation, they were off to Paris as the Battle of the Bulge was being fought. Maverick found Paris to be beautiful, but cold and dead. There was a problem of literal cold because of the shortage of coal in France, and Maverick worried about the shivering performers at the Folies Bergère, where the audience sat in overcoats and gloves.

Maverick could not resist inserting one of his Rabelaisian asides on the state of French heating and plumbing. He told of sitting in his "freezing bathroom" with his overcoat about his shoulders as he scribbled in his diary: "Because of reasons which must ever remain what we armchair strategists call *un secrete militaire*, I pull the string. I go on writing, so absorbed am I in French industry, but the throne had become in a state of estoppel, and, like a tree in the Mississippi, I am washed away; yea, verily, the toilet is brimming over, sevenfold; behold, I am but flotsam and jetsam, and jump across the room ere I drown."[66]

A few days later Maverick visited General Dwight D. Eisenhower at his Versailles headquarters. The SWPC chairman pictured Eisenhower as working day and night—a "reasonable and intelligent man" who was concerned about the effects of German V-2 rockets and who was "fully conscious" of the total situation of the war.[67]

After a secret briefing by high-ranking officers on January 3, Maverick and his party were off to Rheims and on through the places where Maverick was wounded and hospitalized in World War I, to Verdun and down the Meuse River to Saint-Mihiel. A few days later they were off to Luxembourg while the Battle of the Bulge was at its height.

Maverick obviously viewed his meeting with General George S. Patton as one of the highlights of the inspection tour. He found the controversial Patton to be "much too respectable." He saw no pearl-handled revolvers and found the General to be "modest and polite." He discussed with Patton the famous Drew Pearson account of Patton's alleged slapping of a soldier who was a victim of

An Isolationist's Change of Heart 247

battle fatigue. Patton simply said that he thought "Bob" was a fine fellow, referring to Robert S. Allen, Pearson's partner. Maverick said that he got the implication, but, "What the hell are you kicking about? Drew Pearson made you the most popular man in America!" Patton merely smiled.[68]

Next, Maverick went on to Belgium on January 9 and watched American, British, and Belgian troops move up to the front as buzz bombs spluttered through the air on their way to Antwerp. He arrived at a hospital immediately after such a bomb had struck it and saw a man with twenty-seven wounds die. He drove by a cemetery where a buzz bomb had ripped up graves and scattered coffins and bodies over the snow. As he left Namur, Belgium, for Paris on January 11, Maverick wrote that he had learned from an English officer that Liege and Namur were in danger of being retaken by the Germans and if the Germans had known that they were within twelve hundred yards of the U.S. gasoline supply they might well have been successful. Maverick then added the wry note that military historians would no doubt find that this was not the case.[69]

Back in Paris, Maverick told a press conference that the United States must extend aid to French, Belgian, and Luxembourg industries, remarking prophetically that the United States must "accept our responsibilities in the world, right from today into an endless tomorrow." After the press conference he heard an unnamed general speak of the policy of "unconditional surrender" toward the Germans, and Maverick wrote that this was a mistake—such a policy would only stir the Germans to keep up the fighting.[70]

It has been noted before that Maverick often used his toughness and, on occasion, even coarseness to cover up his sentimentality. As he prepared to leave his cold hotel room on January 12, a servant named Jacques ("Jock" to him, Maverick said) came to straighten the room. Maverick impulsively gave the servant his best suit and some long underwear. Other servants came and they were given shirts, ties, socks, candy, and cigarettes. When Maverick turned to leave they all stood by expectantly, and he asked the interpreter to find out how much of a tip they wanted. He reported, "They want nothing but to wish you well on your journey to America." Then Maverick said:

I call them in and hand them tips anyway. As we do in Southwest

Texas and in Mexico, we embrace. I see Jock is weeping. Tell him, I said to the translator, as follows, "Cut out that crying, you little son of a bitch."

At this delicate bon mot of mine we all laugh merrily, and it breaks the tension.

Then we become serious.

I say: "Pour La France."

They said something but I did not understand the words. But I understood.[71]

On his return to Washington, Maverick prepared his formal report on the trip, which repeated many of the things he had been saying and writing before. Essentially, he said, we needed to help France get back on her feet by providing her with raw materials, aid to industrial rehabilitation, and U.S. purchases of her goods.[72] In press interviews Maverick deplored the excessive amount of secrecy and classification of information. He argued that if the American people were given more "facts" about the war they would "understand" and work harder on the war effort.[73]

A month after his return from Europe, Maverick learned of the resignation of one of the directors of the SWPC, A. Abbot Smith, a wallpaper manufacturer, who charged that the agency was beset with "confusion and inefficiency." He criticized Maverick's trip to England and said, "Too much attention is being paid to getting headlines—too little to doing the job." He also charged that Maverick was paying "little attention" to the opinions of the directors.[74] In May it was reported that one group of regional SWPC "governors" had resigned, charging that Maverick was not heeding their advice and was trying to run things himself too much.[75] On the other hand, when Nelson had decided that he was "leaving the Government," he had written to Maverick from the White House to praise him for his "able leadership" and to ask him for his autographed picture.[76]

Though adverse reports were balanced with praise for the achievements of the SWPC under Maverick's leadership, they were bound to lend support to the opposition to his proposals for small business in the reconversion period and his hope for extension of the life of the Smaller War Plants Corporation. In the late summer of 1945 the SWPC was being "counted out"; Secretary of Commerce

Henry Wallace talked of integrating it into the Department of Commerce, but President Truman wanted to see the wartime agencies liquidated as their usefulness, as the administration saw it, ended. Maverick's friends were saying that, though he wanted the agency continued, he would not openly oppose its demise if he lost the "tug-of-war going on behind the scenes."[77] He was vigorously supported by Edward A. Harris in a lengthy article in the essentially conservative *Washington Star*. Harris declared that the proposal for a postwar small-business lending role for the SWPC was being blocked by the American Bankers Association.[78]

Though President Truman did not make public the abolishment of the agency (Effective January 28, 1946) until December 27, 1945, Maverick knew that its days were numbered nearly two months before. It was implicit in a letter in which Truman congratulated him for his work as head of the SWPC and said he wanted Maverick to do "one more job" for him. The job was a trip to the Pacific and Far East. As Truman put it, "The purpose of the Mission was to make a report to me concerning the development of small business in these countries and the possibility of stimulating international trade between them and small business at home. Particularly, I am interested in the development of American small business in the field of international trade."[79]

This letter gave no clue to it, but the whole idea was Maverick's, not the president's. The ambitious Texan had begun a campaign to get such a trip approved on June 29. At that time he wrote a set of memoranda to his assistant explaining the difficulties of convincing Truman that the SWPC chairman should go on a Pacific trip for small business. He said that if there should be any serious objection to the trip, he would not go.[80]

Maverick worked through Edwin A. Locke, "Personal Representative of the President," and W. S. Youngman, Jr., president of China Defense Supplies, Inc., who was also in Tom Corcoran's office. Locke told Maverick to clear the idea through John C. Vincent, chief of the China Division in the State Department. Youngman helped Maverick get Dr. Wong Wen-Hao (vice-premier of China, minister of economic affairs, and head of the Chinese War Production Board) to send a wire to Maverick urging him to visit China on his trip and affirming that it would "well serve Sino-American cooperation." Maverick also got a lengthy endorsement of the importance of such a mission from the delegation at the United Nations Conference on International Organization at San Francisco, signed by Dr. Chun-Mai Carsun Chang. Maury also secured an invitation from Secretary of the Navy James Forrestal to visit the battle areas of the Pacific. At first William M. Thorp, deputy to the assistant secretary of state for economic affairs, indicated that he was dubious about the value of the trip, but after the surrender of Japan he gave his approval.[81] Maverick's careful engineering was successful when Truman gave his approval on November 1. On November 10, 1945, the Texan left San Francisco for another Maverick adventure.

Asia — "Our Biggest Problem"

MAURY MAVERICK OBVIOUSLY had another book—a book that was never written—in mind when he boarded the plane in San Francisco for his tour of the Pacific and the Far East in November of 1945. He began at that time the first in a set of nine notebooks, plus a special one on Japan, in which he scribbled an account of his journey, anecdotes, descriptions of sunsets and native customs, bits of philosophizing, and anything else that fell within his scope of interests. The itinerary included stops at Hawaii, Iwo Jima, Saipan, Okinawa, the Philippines, China, Japan, New Zealand, Australia, the Fijis, and other islands and atolls.

The first stop was Hawaii. Maverick, at the age of fifty, still could not resist playing the bad boy. He was invited to dinner at a Marine general's home in Honolulu, and he jotted this "Secret!" in his notes: "When at General Geiger's, I got a dirty fork full of eggs, frogs and everything from the shores of Tripoli out. So I slipped the dirty fork to the General when he was not looking. Later—in late Jan., 1947, the General died. He was a great fellow, very courteous. Now I am sorry! MM. 2/9/47"[1]

As he continued his island hopping, Maverick found more serious matters to comment on. At Okinawa he made extensive notes on the people, their customs and burial places, even including diagrams of the tombs. As his plane took him to Japan, he jotted down his reflections on what he had seen: "We Americans have a duty to perform. It is global . . . geopolitical, and in detail for every village, every human being. This is not some spirit of doing good. But the 'savages' everywhere know, through seeing our bulldozers, our gigantic physical, mechanical and individual power, our moves. So the World Revolution has not yet begun. What Russia started is only a tiny beginning. The human race is in the mightiest ferment since man first breathed. As the engines roar I hear the roar and thunder of world revolution."[2]

As he viewed the destruction of Japanese cities, Maverick was moved to compose a prayer: "Almighty God, give me the strength to think highly, with clear mind, and without stupidity, naivete or hate. Almighty God, give Americans all the same: give us WISDOM, courage, discretion, insight and foresight. Let us use our powers fairly, for a good U.S.A. and a good world."[3]

In Tokyo on November 22, Maury bought another notebook and began, "In this I hope to place some ideas—not too many—and references to books and sources of information." As it turned out, he did incorporate some bibliographical data, but the "ideas" by far predominated. He first expressed dismay at the conduct of a drunken U.S. Navy commander who made many "fighting" remarks about "Japs" in a Tokyo bar as five Japanese waiters stood by. He said that such "bar-room and whiskey bravery" was undignified and a reflection on the United States. "The Japanese deserve to be punished. . . . But stupid, silly and slobbering remarks made by men who never risked their skins is morally bad and can do only harm."

Maverick went on to state that he did not believe in a "hard peace," but he thought that the United States was making a serious mistake in reducing its armed forces around the world at that time. He felt that the United States, as the most prosperous nation, was most likely to be "the target of attack from much larger forces, or political alignments of most of the rest of the world." The United States must provide leadership and a dignified example to the rest of the world. He said that Asia was "our biggest problem," and

Asia—"Our Biggest Problem" 253

that American diplomacy with respect to that area was "vague," while Russia's was clear.

After a luncheon with General Douglas MacArthur, Maverick expressed the view that MacArthur was doing an excellent job of governing the defeated Japanese, and he commended the general for comporting himself "without ostentation." Turning to a conversation concerning war-crimes trials, Maverick said that MacArthur had expressed doubt "that trying men in contravention of our Anglo-Saxon constitutional ideals and procedures would be a very good idea." Maverick agreed that "this will create a precedent to get our people tried and killed should we lose a war. Also, it is doubtful to me if we should violate our own precepts—this for our own sake."

Maverick also said MacArthur opposed the universal military training program that had been recently supported by General George C. Marshall. "He said things have now changed entirely where large masses of men may not be the determining factor. Industry and science, he said, were as much a factor in winning this war as anything else, indeed, were basic and essential. He said: 'A thousand planes based out of the U.S.A., and the same number out of England, could win a war in a week, with atomic bombs.'"

Turning to his own reflections after observing the Japanese people and the countryside of Japan, Maverick demonstrated the depth and prescience of his thought:

The world revolution keeps on. The children already begin to want to be in on the world. The women will see movies from Hollywood, and won't like working in the fields. People sitting and sleeping on floors will want beds, shower baths, stoves of modern design, chairs—everything we Americans have.

At one time, we of the North and the South hated each other. But unity came and we stick together to become the greatest people in the world. Why? A constitution providing no trade barriers, one money system and a Bill of Rights. We work toward these ends if it takes all eternity. We will not win the peace unless we begin to correct the causes of conflict. Increasingly, men will want higher living standards, dignity, freedom.

A visit to a Shinto temple prompted Maverick to write: *"What comes to my mind is that no one can change this culture of thou-*

sands of years in a few years. It would be impossible. Thousands of people came and departed in perfect reverence. Therefore, we Americans must appreciate this practical fact. We must know the cultural stream of the Japanese."

Maverick toured the railroad station and surrounding area in Tokyo as many American soldiers did after World War II, and he was astounded at the filth and squalor. He wrote:

I do not record this for reasons of sympathy or humanitarian impulse, although I have sympathy for these people who themselves did not start this war; and all this, too, in spite of the brutality.

It is aside from sympathy that I must record we cannot win this peace and ignore these human forces. I am sure China is worse. Humanity is miserable everywhere in the Orient. Will they continue to live in misery without rising?

No.

And the real point is that we are handling the problem NOW—but ... if we go isolationist at home, and don't get these people to work—then anything can happen.

What I mean is, we have got to wake up, to save ourselves in the future. We must be strong, able to fight, but we must also be humane, and decent, even though the Japanese have not been.

Weary at the end of a day of touring various shrines, Maverick looked out over Nikko (a national park) and wrote, "Everywhere I have been where there are many shrines there is much poverty. *Religion* is necessary for the people; I feel the need to pray. But where a priesthood flourishes with unbelievable extremities of religion, there is no doubt the people hunger, live in poverty and go without the advances of science."

On November 27 a Japanese newspaper reporter tried to interview Maverick, but he decided that it would be best if he refrained from comments on what should be done in Japan. He did, however, record what he *would* have said:

1. Eliminate monopolies and cartels, actually break the "Zibats." (Zibatsu—of the Four Big Families).

2. It must establish a government agency similar to the S.W.P.C. . . . to finance, give scientific and managerial aid.

3. It must greatly develop science and as a measure of faith keep open all information to the Allied Powers.

There are a hundred other things Japan ought to do, but there are

Asia—"Our Biggest Problem" 255

three of which I think. Shinto-ism ought to go, but to attempt to suppress it may make it worse.

The United States, Maverick said, should send ten thousand young boys and girls "of say 2 years of college" to Japan to learn the language and customs "at once."

The same day Maverick wrote these words he was off to Korea. There he wrote in his notebook that the ouster of the Japanese from that country had left a vacuum in the areas of politics and business management. The division of Korea at the 38th parallel should never have been agreed upon at Potsdam. "This split-up," he wrote, "must be corrected. It is not right; either we both should move out, or Korea, somehow, should be permitted to begin its reorganization, based on unification." He pictured the situation as one of great danger, and said, ". . . we Americans are in for bad trouble if we don't use our heads and soon." He again deplored the demobilization of U.S. forces while the Soviet Union was not doing so.

Maverick saw little hope for sound leadership from Syngman Rhee. He said that the Korean strong man proved to be "rabid" on the subject of communism, even "wild and nuts" on the subject, as the two lunched together. He said further that Rhee simply wanted everything for "his crowd." Paradoxically, he quoted Rhee as saying that Korea had plenty of money and needed no help. Maverick commented, "All the Koreans are unrealistic, and to me indicate no ability to govern themselves. Certainly they cannot possibly have the technical, legal, medical, or any other knowledge sufficient to run this country. They say it is none of our business. To me it probably is, because if they don't govern themselves fairly well, a stronger force will move in."

The last entry in Maverick's "Notes, Thoughts on Japan" was concerned with Taiwan, where he stopped on December 7, 1945, on his way to Chungking. He said that the people of the island were in serious difficulties because during the long occupation by the Japanese they were not permitted to be technicians, engineers or bankers. He felt that the United States should "have a big naval base there, airports, and some troops—and stay there."[4] At another point he discussed a strange Taiwan funeral, and in commenting on the public baths and other manners and mores he said, ". . .

here and elsewhere many, male and female, get in (without clothes, my Baptist friends) together."[5]

In one of his regular notebooks Maverick recorded other observations on Korea, including extensive notes on the resources and industries of the two "Koreas." At supper with General John R. Hodge, "a good soldier," he discussed the foolishness of the division of Korea and its various ramifications. Maverick even incorporated in his notes the basic alphabet of Korean, diagrams of the heating system in Korean homes, and a bibliography.[6]

The first week in December 1945, Maverick was carrying on discussions with various lesser foreign diplomats and other foreign residents, including a German couple in Shanghai. The impression of China's political climate that he drew from these conversations was:

Consensus—
No difference between Central & Communist government in ideals.
Chiang Kai Shek has not, or has not been able to put into effect reforms.
Chiang strongest, has more territory, therefore should be supported.
Communists not as big grafters, largely because no supplies from America and no money in international transactions.
Chiang's crowd, they say, are full-fleldged grafters in the old sense.
Foregoing opinions to be taken with grain of salt, because if Chiang gets in he may put Germans out. It may be Germans want confusion in which case they can or may hang on. The Germans & most conservative Americans say all the Russians want is confusion.[7]

Then, in this disjointed account, Maverick turned to comments on the Soviet Union and our political relations with that country. He said that the only nation we needed to worry about getting along with was Russia, and he wondered if the United States was blameless in its relations with the USSR. He wrote:

Teddie Roosevelt gave the Russians a dirty deal at the Treaty of Portsmouth. After the Russians held the Germans in World War I we sent troops overseas to "fight the Bolsheviks." We failed to recognize ... Russia for years.
Preceding this war we snubbed Russia, the allies rejected her aid against the Germans and took Munich instead.
It is my belief the British welcomed a possible attack by Germany

on Russia. Even after the Russians joined our side many of our American businessmen openly stated they hoped Russia and Germany would "wipe each other out."

During this war anti-Russian propaganda, willful, hateful, and unkind, continues.

We demand part control of Balkans, say the government is not democratic—and yet we demand sole control of Japan, sole "sphere of influence" in Western Hemisphere.

1. We are inconsistent.
2. Our own attitude is smug, impolite.
3. We talk too much against the Russians—
But—
We are *not* prepared.
We are demobilizing too fast.
The Russians are not.[8]

On November 30 or December 1, 1945 (Maverick was unsure of the date), he had a conversation with General Albert C. Wedemeyer, U.S. wartime commander in China, in which the General explained that his instructions were "1. To support central government firmly. 2. Not to use force in fratricidal warfare. 3. To keep a strong, unbroken military force. 4. To send the boys home." Maverick continued, quoting Wedemeyer indirectly, "That, he said, is impossible. You can't do it all. The State Department has been informed." Maverick told Wedemeyer that he should communicate directly with the president on the matter. Wedemeyer said that President Truman had encouraged him to do so, but he thought it best to work with the State Department. Maverick said that Wedemeyer emphasized the absolute necessity of a "firm policy" in China, but Maverick did not explain what he meant. He did say that Wedemeyer "talked more sensibly than any general I have seen," and followed that impression with the following quotation from Wedemeyer:

I don't blame the Russians for protecting themselves. Were I a Russian, I too would be suspicious. They are looking out for their country, etc.—
Q. by Maverick "Do you believe in a joint trusteeship?"
A. "Yes."
Q. "Who?"
A. "The Americans, Russians, English, French."[9]

Maverick was greatly disturbed by the boorish attitude of one of his aides in conversation with the Chinese, and it turned him to some reflections on his own shortcomings. He wrote, "My father, now 91, is dignified, and realizing his memory is probably not as good, keeps quiet. He has always been a modest, shy man; I, loud and talkative. I hope I can think of my father, and honor him by modeling a little after him. However, I have no wish to change my fundamental nature of talking some, but let me keep my big mouth shut more and listen more."[10]

At this stage in his journey, and at this point in his journal, Maverick wrote a fairly lengthy critique with the title, "Appointment of General Marshall as Ambassador." It follows in its entirety:

He was apparently appointed [ambassador to China] because of his vast prestige. Because a 5-star general can do business with the Russians or probably impress them. One paper says it is to back up the views of General Stillwell, who clashed with the Gissimo.

But my definite opinion is that Marshall can do nothing unless Wedemeyer's position is clarified, unless the American people stop the mad rush of demobilization and unless he gets full backing.

At this point, without knowing the details, I think, apparently in a minority, that the appointment is a bad one. It is piling a 5-star general on a 3-star general. Wed. knows the problems and appears to know China and his subject. The appointment of many generals is bad.

I predicted it would be bad in Germany where jobs were doled out in size and importance by number of stars. That has proved bad. Patton, but not alone, was a flop, and worse.

In America we pick a 3-star general to be Veterans Administrator (Gen. Omar Bradley) a fine soldier.

In Korea a general and a good one (Gen. Hodges) but he is not firmly backed, he has not sufficient troops—and, moreover, NOT ENOUGH civilians.

In France I predicted the elections would go left, and the Generals laughed at me. They refused, in what I believe a contemptuous manner, the aid of civilians. They refused the aid of civilian shipping experts, and I believe an investigation will show it caused a bad condition. . . . My opinion is that in America

(1.) We should slow down on generals in civil positions—but also back them in military assignments.

(2.) We should build up our military forces.

Asia—"Our Biggest Problem" 259

(3.) In 'unifying' our forces—*look out*: It should not be all military control—
(4.) Our State Department should be fully reorganized:
(1) To make it possible for people to see the Sec. of State, Ass't. Sec's. of State. This will require much greater personnel.
(2) Get rid of their snooty & snotty and 'exclusive' attitude.
(3) Develop consistent policies.
(4) Have overseas service like OWI [Office of War Information] —straight out, and big and strong.
(5) Like England, when going into a country to make a plan, include (a) political (b) economic (c) military.
(6) Fully inform American public of facts in international affairs. This should be pushed to the utmost and the truth should be told.[11]

Maverick pasted some clippings in his notebook on foreign aid, particularly the United Nations Relief and Rehabilitation Agency (UNRRA), and commented, "O.K., lend the money. But we should not throw it away. Concerning UNRRA—who gets it? Who gets tractors? Do we know they won't end up in the hands of speculators? . . . Also—in lending money, it should be policed. If little business bank is set up—after we lend China money and give technicians, WE SHOULD POLICE the operations."[12] When proposals for aid to China were being formulated in Congress in 1948, there were efforts to incorporate notions like those advanced by Maverick concerning conditions to be met by China, but the China Aid Act of 1948 did not contain such conditions, largely because of the objections raised by Sun Fo, president of China's Legislative Yüan.[13]

When Maverick noted his reflections on the relationship of the United States to the Far East, again he saw people-to-people understanding as the best prospect for improving that relationship. He wrote:

1. Much more news of the Orient should be given American people.
2. Piling stars on stars will no more solve our domestic or international problems than piling Pelion on Ossa.
3. . . . Thousands of American students should be given scholarships to study in the Orient.
4. Our foreign policies should be firm and polite—this requires a strong Army and Navy.
5. The American people must wake up to the fact that the world is around us—we're in it whether we like it or not.[14]

Maverick began his fifth notebook in Chungking on December 7. He said it was impossible for Americans to comprehend the poverty-stricken population that "infests" the land. Inadequate transportation and primitive communication, he said, made a high standard of living impossible. Chungking's only major means of transportation, for example, was by river.

Maverick's words best describe his encounters with Chinese officialdom in Chungking, as he attempted to sound them out on a program of small business aid:

Today, December 8, I visited Dr. T. V. Soong [foreign minister of China].

Famous man, rich, powerful. Brother of "Soong Sisters." Madame Chiang Kai Shek ("loves power") over Sun Yat Sen (loves China) and Madame Kung ("loves money.")

He is "Dr." Soong, apparently a Ph.D., but speaks with a fairly heavy Chinese accent.

He is affable. Whether he is interested or not I do not know. What puzzles me is that if China made a good case on this they could get 50–100–150 million dollars. They are either not interested or lack the perspicacity to see.

Mr. T. L. Chao, Bank of Communications, thinks little business good idea. Not too much comprehension and his main idea was textiles. I was later told that Chinese businessmen are expecting great profit out of getting hold of the Jap spindles.

Mr. Pei Tsu Yi, Bank of China.

Tubercular. Enthusiastic. Says work slow. I told him we have $350,000,000 capital. Said, huge! Finally said if SWPC started here should be for 5 million dollars. Should be done slowly, *gradually*.

Dr. Wong Wen-Hao [the man who had sent a wire in support of Maverick's mission], Minister of Economic Affairs. Was chairman War Production Board. Friend of Nelson. Did not respond. Apparently did not care. Said to be a great geologist.

These Chinese affect me as being polite, of course. Whether they give a damn I don't know. Or maybe they have been flooded with "missions" from America and are tired of them. In any event, my implications that the *Government* of China might possibly get this started with private profit eliminated does not strike a responsive cord [*sic*]. Maybe they are just bankers—ours were never for the SWPC

Asia—"Our Biggest Problem" 261

except when they could get something. But this technical aid is lacking in China and vital to their lives—and their response is not much.
Thought
During the war we were *interested*. Soldiers in their business, war. We had unity.
NOW—we relax. We are disunited—lazy—*What* should we do?

T. N. Lee. Bank of Communications in Shanghai—Very enthusiastic O.K. . . . Seems to clearly understand needs of developing small industry in China.[15]

Next Maverick wanted to find out what the Communists were saying and thinking. He had one of their number, Han-fu Chang of the *New China Daily News*, Chungking, to write a statement in his notebook. Chang said that his paper had no freedom and was under constant harassment by the Koumintang government. "Every day our deliverers are beaten or arrested," and mailed copies were confiscated at the post office "by government special service men," he wrote. Maverick then noted that a single tax on the income of land was being used in Communist-controlled territory, and he was astonished to find that there was a Communist headquarters "200 yards from Chiang Kai Shek's office."[16]

Naturally, Maverick was determined to go there. He first went to the office of the *Daily News* with Dr. John K. Fairbank, professor of Chinese history at Harvard and then head of the OWI. There Maverick was given a number of books written by Mao Tze-tung. He made careful bibliographical entries in his notes on all of the books, such as " 'On Coalition Government,' by Mao Tze-tung—pronounced MAH-O-ZEE-DUNG (Leader of Communists; said to be a very able man with ideals and sincerity.) Lib. China Series. New Chi. News, August, 1945."[17]

Maverick was intrigued and excited by this episode. He wrote:

Going to the Headquarters was more than an "exciting adventure." We pass Chiang Kai Shek's Headquarters. About 200 yards beyond we roll around into a cul-de-sac where we get out.
We then go into much narrower streets. Little businesses, "doctors" (one working on a horrible boil of a young man with a dirty knife, . . .), little artisans' plants, tea shops, restaurants, food shops, many with cooked foods. Above all heavy crowding of people, cold, wet, no sanitation, children shit in the streets.
We go into a sort of "compound," or more like a courtyard as in

Mexican cities. Finally, winding around, we come to a room with not even a hole in the wall; much less a stove, for heat.

One comes and hands us tea, and it always happens. Finally, one by one, the four come in. The editor, Han Yu Chang, is smart—The girl is smart, too, and pretty. She is not *too* intense, like some Commy-girls back home, she does not wear horn rimmed glasses or unusual dress. She is at ease, has bearing.

We go to lunch and the food tastes good. I have some misgivings, having just seen the unsanitary goods on the street. But I heave-to with a Merry-O with my chopsticks, and do better.

I ask Chang if he and his party are Communists, as called by name, or was it true that there was little difference in the two groups [Kuomintang and Communists].

He said, "I am a Communist. Our Party is Communist. There is much difference or we would not fight."

I said, "When can you establish Communism?"

"Not now," he said.

He then explained that the situation in China in agriculture, transportation, industry, etc.—would not permit Communism any time soon. That some reforms would take many years.

The girl, Mrs. Chow Kang P'en, broke in to say that the platform of the Communists is the full economic and technical development of China through little industries and the full use of the competitive system.

Further, she said the central government favored either private monopolies or government monopolies, plus strict government regulation. That they did not favor cooperatives, or little industries of the people. Thus, she said the Central Government did not have a competitive free economy nor did they have communism.

In response to the implications of some questions from Maverick, Mrs. P'en said that it was not characteristic of the Chinese to engage in graft and the like. It was "looked down on by the people," and "Chinese literature, ethics and public opinion did not approve it." Maverick said, "I gathered from here that she did not like the patronizing and somewhat insulting attitude of Americans that dishonesty is a part of accepted Chinese ethics."

Maverick went on to describe battle maps on the walls of the meeting rooms that showed the relative positions of the central government forces and Communist forces, "like the 'Briefing Rooms' over in France." He said, after sketching the maps and the arrows

Asia—"Our Biggest Problem" 263

which indicated deployment of forces, "Apparently the Communists are mainly in the field and do not possess too many villages." He said that he asked for a comment on General Patrick J. Hurley's famous statement that there was no more difference between parties in China than Republicans and Democrats in Oklahoma except that the Communists are armed. Chang's somewhat cryptic reply was, "The Chiang Kai Shek group is armed."[18]

Maverick's next visit was with Sun Fo, president of the Legislative Yüan and son of Sun Yat Sen. The Chinese leader said that he disapproved of the civil war; there should be no more fighting, and the people should "get together." Maverick commented, "He expresses interest in 'little business,' but I have no idea he expects to do anything about it. He is said to be a cagy fellow."

The most sympathetic reaction to Maverick's mission came from Tingfu F. Tsiang, director-general of Chinese National Relief and Rehabilitation Administration. Tsiang said that some two thousand tractors were needed in farming areas of northern China and Manchuria where there were large farms. He suggested that Maverick contact P. S. Ho of the Bank of China, but Maverick apparently was not able to do so. When Maverick asked Tsiang if the Chinese had to fight out the civil war, he responded, "In China we are different—we fight, we negotiate, we negotiate and fight." He concluded, "We must make a war on poverty!"[19]

Maverick's next conference was with Chiang Kai Shek, on which he reported as follows:

Chiang looks to weigh 125 to 130 pounds. He wore no ribbons, and as far as I could see, no insignia of rank. His personality is good, neither too effusive nor too unassuming. Although thin and almost drawn in countenance he has no lines in his face. There is not an inch of fat.

The conversation was not worth recording.

I make my talk on little business to which he responds as well as an American general, and better than an American businessman. Generally, he says he recognizes importance and wished to encourage it. Whether he understands it or not I cannot tell, but he is no worse than the average American. I cannot find fault with him for not putting in the kind of institution I suggest inasmuch as the SWPC is to be abolished in the U.S.A.

His advisor, moreover, is Soong, his rich brother-in-law. Soong was not enthusiastic about an industrio-technico-little bank. So why would a general be?

I compliment his wife; she likes it. I said, truthfully, she had spoken better than Churchill and Roosevelt in the U.S. Congress.

Returning to Chiang, Maverick commented:

It is notable that although he spoke with kindness, some warmth and ability, he did not mention social progress as Roosevelt would have done, except he did say that by industrialization and improved agricultural methods, the standard of living of the Chinese people would be raised.

I asked no questions about the Civil War, and he offered no information about it or about the usual charges of "squeeze" in high places, and the failure to institute reforms [Maverick had intended to ask questions about these things, but an adviser persuaded him otherwise].

NOTE—Everyone says Communists are good fighters, honest and able, and have ideals.

The Communists seem to have a social program or at least tell about it. No Central Government man has even intimated a social program.[20]

As he departed from China by plane, Maverick ruminated on various problems. Specifically, as the plane flew over the Yellow River and the mountains, he wrote that international air travel and "Freedom of the Air" would be impossible without international organization and efficient weather stations throughout the world— his pilot had taken off without any weather advisory.[21]

Returning to General Marshall's mission as President Truman's special envoy to attempt some resolution of the civil strife in China, Maverick expressed the view that it was probably doomed to failure because of demobilization and a "lack of desire" on the part of the United States government. Maverick quoted a young American foreign-service man in the American Embassy in Peiping as saying, "We are supposed to support a strong—united—and democratic China—but we are supporting a weak, disunited, undemocratic China."[22] On foreign aid Maverick reiterated his stand that it should be extended only to promote American interests and that some ways should be found to prevent graft and misapplication of materials.[23]

Finally, Maverick set down some "conclusions about Chinese character":

Asia—"Our Biggest Problem"

Opposite of violence.
Don't look like first rate soldiers.
Generally
   A. Indifferent.
   B. Conservative

Sharp traders and no more dishonest than any other racial group.
Personally kind; Americans say "house boys" loyal friends.

But—they want their cake and eat it, too. They want us to loan money, blind, we not to police it.

Their indifference runs into indifference about an industrio-technical bank, but this also because it is misguided shrewdness where they think they will make higher rates without government competition.

[Penciled note, added Nov. 12, 1949] Thoughts later—These were Nationalists, Chiang's crowd. As for the Communists, I never saw enough of them to judge them as a part of major Chinese character.[24]

Certainly no Maverick junket would be complete without some horseplay. In Peiping Maverick's chief aide "got somewhat tight" and decided to realize a long-nursed ambition. He hired a rickshaw and then insisted that the coolie change places with him so that he could give the coolie a ride. He was so inspired by the cheers of other coolies as he galloped up to the front of the hotel that he turned round and repeated the entire performance again around the block. He told Maverick, "I can leave China now. I have taken a rickshaw boy for a ride."

A day or so later the same aide spotted what he thought was some authentic Johnny Walker scotch in an obscure Peiping shop. As any good aide would do, he reported this find to his chief. Maverick expressed strong doubts as to the authenticity of the scotch, but eventually he was convinced and bought eight bottles of the stuff for eight dollars a bottle. "It was no good," said Maverick, and he required his aide to write in the notebook, "According to Mr. Maverick, I, Conrad A. Pearson, Capt., USMCR, am a goddam dumb Swede. As an aide should, (the Swede gets smug. MM) I advised him to buy one bottle which we could test, and if the reputed Scotch were really Scotch, we would back up a truck to buy out the store."

Roaming around a shrine in Peiping, Maverick encountered a priest with a "shifty look" who was willing to break the rules and sell him a figure of Buddha. Maverick concluded that he had been "taken," but he was philosophical about the respective roles that he and the priest had played. Maverick commented:

> A robber, a thief, a citizen of low standing—induced to thievery and disrespect by *me.*
> In any event we both walk off with cock strides—
> Later I found, that by meticulous shopping I might have done better —BUT I got it at the Lama Shrine, in Peiping, MYSELF.[25]

Next stop, the Philippine Islands. There Maverick toured most of the islands and visited with many guerrilla leaders. He had one of them, a Colonel Umali, write an account in the notebook of his activities during World War II, fighting the Japanese on Luzon. Maverick also incorporated a brief account of the wartime activities of Colonel Wendell W. Fertig, who led the guerrillas, and who established and maintained contact with U.S. and Australian forces in the Pacific. In his notes Maverick expressed the view that the Filipinos were "stupid" to leave the United States. He marveled at the untapped resources that could be exploited to sustain a large population, and deplored the fact that a diseased, lethargic people were not prepared to take advantage of these great resources. In Manila, he jotted some brief notes on his observations of the trial of Japanese General Homma. He described Homma as "dignified" as he rose quietly to waive the translation as the trial began. Maverick's terse notes read, "Travesty of justice. No time granted. Unfair. Americans should be ashamed."[26]

On the way to Australia and the Admiralties Maverick jotted, "Thought—Australia, New Zealand, white. Rest of Pacific and Orient, yellow. If China becomes militarized or Japan recuperates or China builds out, Australia-N.Z. can be wiped out, as their population is comparatively very small." On Manus Island Maverick wrote "very many beautiful girls," and then scrawled, "We drink MINT Juleps—(too many). Pearson fears I will make an ass of myself & so I will."

The party made brief stops at New Britain, Ferguson, and New Guinea, going on to Brisbane, Australia, on December 21, 1945. There Maverick learned from an American consul that American business was "hamstrung" by trade restrictions. He put down the thought that perhaps he should be just as concerned about big business as small business. All American business he said was having

Asia—"Our Biggest Problem" 267

its "throat cut in the Far East." He said the United States should emulate the English who were publishing a business paper, *Great Britain and the East*, in which there were advertisements extolling the virtues of British machines and equipment and their uses in the Far East. He also commended them for using the Chinese language in advertisements and for not taking sides in the political controversy in China.

On the Australians Maverick commented:

Australians not Anti-American but—fully as arrogant, smug, independent and thoughtless as we.

Talked to Brian Penton who wrote "Advance Australia." He reminded me that we *had* to have Australia on our side, etc.—bright fellow (see his book) many good ideas—but, like all active men, he is as arrogant per capita as one of a nation of 134,000,000; wants cake, eat it too; wants complete independence *and* our Army & Navy; they cannot protect their 'mandates'—many islands—willing for us to do it.

So—we protect England and Australia but are kept out by TRADE RESTRICTIONS.

Australians are ISOLATIONISTS (for themselves) and internationalists for the U.S.A.

Later he commented, "Australians with their isolationism, arrogance, anti-yellow race complex, refusal to co-operate with anybody MAY GET US IN A WAR—worse, and get us *Beat*.[27]

It was Maverick's judgment that Australia's economy and society was becoming stagnant. He said they lacked adequate science and military power. They were "Reactionary in both LABOR & CAPITAL. People not like their tough grandparents. SELF-SATISFIED." Maverick further charged that the Australians were parochial and childish in their "flat refusal to co-operate commercially." Moreover, he said: "[Australians] will continue to be King-wavers, i.e., love the King because he keeps His Royal Mouth Shut, a form of American flag-waving, this King Waving. Also an escape complex not to really co-operate in a sensible Far East policy, fair to Yellow Races and to continue mumbo-humbo about 'White Australia' 'High Standard of Living' UNTIL IT IS TOO LATE. Will put off to last all commercial, economic, racial problems, 'hoping for the best.' "[28]

In New Zealand a few days later, Maverick was writing much the same things. In Wellington, December 27, he got extensive and favorable press coverage for his "ADA" (Anglo, Dominions, American) idea. He explained the concept in his notes: "If ADA doesn't combine, trade freely with each other, adopt single financial unit for all, and in multiple ways trade with the world, and drops its racial arrogance we will be beat in 25 years and be a broken down slave race." Turning to the other side of the coin, Maverick wrote, "I have been lecturing Australia and N.Z. Now, we cannot complain about their isolationism—we are TARIFF CRAZY—WE MUST LEAD THE WAY. I mean—Australia has 7½ million, N.Z. 1.6 million people. If China is to be reduced as a future menace, we MUST NOT LET THE BRITISH HOG IT ALL—We must be fair, firm and offer N.Z.-Australia INDUCEMENT FOR FREER TRADE."[29]

The last leg of this Maverick excursion began in Auckland, New Zealand, on December 30. On the way home, stops were made at Samoa and at Suva in the Fiji Islands. The Fiji islanders invited him to a "Ceremony of Kava," where, after preparation of a drink in a ceremonial bowl and appropriate songs, he was offered a coconut shell with the drink made from the roots of the "Kava or Cava." As he recorded the event, "You *must* drink. I choke down a little; it has a piquant taste of horse piss (Although I never drank it before)."[30]

As he left Samoa on December 31, Maverick observed, "Here is where Somerset Maugham wrote 'Rain.' The hotel—a barn, or 2-story frame shack is known as 'Sadie Thompson hotel.' How there was ever any romance around the place I can't figure."[31] Here, as was the case in all of the places he visited, Maverick gleaned as much as he could of information on population, local customs and laws, economic conditions, and bibliographical data.

As Maverick flew over the Pacific on January 1, 1946, on the way to Honolulu, he mused:

And I am 50 years old. . . . I have some "jobs" or nibbles offered me but no assured prospect of a living. I have a wife, son, daughter, mother-in-law (wholly dependent on us) mother and father and many responsibilities.

I am 40 pounds overweight, eat too much and have coronary thrombosis. Many ex-congressmen either flop into a government job, live off somebody else or die. Or worse, take a job as a "lawyer," which is really a lobbyist. Such offers I have turned down.

My intention is to be as courageous as a youngster, and take a chance. In San Antonio we Mavericks have lived honorably since 1835 —110 years. But the place is isolated, has limited possibilities.

I can make a living there, but for the future of my children it is not so good—in fact, bad. So I think I'll meander away. I am a member of the California Bar in addition to Texas and Supreme Court of U.S.

On this trip I became a member of the Bar of Korea, Formosa (Taiwan), Philippines ($25.00 Am.) and American Samoa. I have studied the Pacific and Eastern politics, but have really known very little.

This has opened my eyes wide as saucers. Here lies the chance of America—her chance of existence. As I have said in previous notes, we must have a strong and generous policy in the Pacific; . . . we must be fair to China and all Eastern countries, and HELP THEM industrialize. We cannot hold back the progress of the world. England cannot win by her Empire preferences, her sterling bloc, holding companies, banks, insurance companies—and antiquated methods. She must get right and compete.

But here I am thinking of the world and now it is time I think of this old fat man of fifty. I must resign, of course, because I do not want to be a "career man" and furthermore cannot. Other career men will not let you succeed. They either look down upon, fear you, or regard you outside their pale. The politicians *like* you and keep you but they resent the fact that you haven't the guts to starve it out and fight it out like them. My heart is with these "politicians."

So—at 50 I've got to get to it—as do millions of others. The horrible thing of having been a congressman is the ego. A M.C. is really a big shot. He hates to get beat. I did. But if this was ever in me it's out now —and one thing, I must not be sorry for myself, vain, or egotistical about my past.

It was some accomplishment, but there was much of headlines and vanity in it. It is time to forget these things. It is time for humility.

At the same time there is no time for so much humility that I pass out. In 15 years of public experience I have had probably the best opportunity to learn government, business, world politics than any person in America. It is now necessary to "make money"—since now what money I had is gone. But I believe I can make the money, and have some leadership. I believe that with a degree of humility I need not take anything off anybody. So—as we fly along, so I think now— I will get out of the Government and be an independent "working stiff," and/or politician, citizen, etc. Maybe the influence will be greater. Many men who have no money have influence. Many members of the Cabinet—BIG SHOTS—have no INFLUENCE. They can get fired at the whim, caprice, or nod of the President.

It is time to get a little house. A yard in the back with some turnips. Some sunshine. And just thinking, the sun hits squarely to our right which means we must be going straight north into Honolulu—"The New Year."[32]

In his last entry in the ninth Pacific Notebook, Maury waxed eloquent and sentimental over the beautiful sunrise as his plane approached San Francisco—"beautiful because we near the mainland of the U.S.A."—the end of what he called "the greatest trip of my life."

Like Ripples on a Pond

Maury Maverick returned to Washington in January 1946, offered his recommendations for liberal small business aid in the Far East, and, on January 15, gave the final report of the accomplishments of the SWPC. His career in public office was over. President Truman, responding to Maverick's resignation, said, "Your years of service in the Government, both as a legislator and as an Executive, have been of outstanding benefit to the country and will, I am confident, be remembered by a grateful nation."[1]

It occurred to me that perhaps Truman had been influenced by Maverick's suggestions of technical aid to foreign countries when the former president had asked Congress to enact legislation to establish his famous Point Four program. When asked about this, Truman flashed back, "Oh, no! Point Four was me." But then, after a pause, he said, "Well, Maury's ideas were like ripples on a pond—everyone around was influenced to some degree by him."[2]

Much of Maverick's last seven or eight years were spent in making as many ripples on the pond as he could. He became a sort of Tom Paine of San Antonio—issuing sporadic blasts in letters, press statements, and memoranda that told us how to solve the problems of a muddled post–World War II America. These efforts were not those of a bitter, defeated "crank" who had lost a place of power and prestige from which he could hold forth. The cries were strident at times, but he knew what he was talking about—frequently more so than those important people to whom his remarks were primarily addressed.

Before Maverick settled down to this role, however, he was lured away for about one year to what seemed at the time to be greener pastures. As he had indicated in his "Pacific Notebooks," he had it in mind to "meander away" from San Antonio. The implication was that he would meander to California, and that proved to be his destination. Disillusioned by the failure of his fight for small business and skeptical about a political future in San Antonio, he decided to follow the advice of friends and associates who wanted him to practice law and seek a new political fortune in California. In late January of 1946, he went to Los Angeles alone and joined the law firm of Cohn and Robert Kenny. Morris E. Cohn had come to know Maverick as chairman of the SWPC and had urged him to join his law firm after the war.

Maverick plunged into a law practice, made speeches, took refresher courses at the University of Southern California, and even found time to coauthor with Robert E. G. Harris a chapter, "Los Angeles—Rainbow's End," for a book on cities of the United States.[3] Chester Bowles urged Maverick to seek political office in California and told him, "People like you are badly needed [in Congress]."[4] But Maverick was homesick and "lonesome as hell,"[5] a real maverick, far from the home spread. Even after his family joined him and they entered into a social life, particularly with the Melvyn Douglases, Maverick was still lonesome, even for his old political enemies. He could not understand why "if you call somebody a son of a bitch out here, he thinks you are insulting him!" He was delighted when old friends and even a few old enemies began to call him in Los Angeles, urging him to come home and run for mayor. The city administration had fallen into a state of sad disrepair, as had the city and its facilities.[6] After he had to go back to San Antonio in January of 1947 for the funeral of his ninety-three-year-old father and had had an opportunity to scout the situation a bit, Maverick decided to head for home and seek the

Like Ripples on a Pond

San Antonio mayor's chair once more, though Mrs. Maverick tried to talk him out of it.[7]

When he returned to San Antonio, Maverick pulled together his old organization, now called the Maverickos, and headed a Harmony-Progress ticket with Louis Lipscomb, Paul B. Blunt, C. Ray Davis, and James W. Knight. In all there were six candidates for mayor, including the incumbent Gus B. Mauermann, who headed the Greater San Antonio ticket, and Alfred Callaghan, who headed the Economy Ticket. In the campaign Maverick was "unusually unobtrusive," while his long-time aide, Malcolm Bardwell, and West Side manager Johnny Sánchez, organized the precincts.[8] Under the heading, "Maury's Back," a breezy *Time* magazine article captured the temporarily mellowed Maverick neatly. It told of Maury being approached by a businessman and being treated to the provocative statement, "I never voted for you in my life." As *Time* put it, "In the old days Maury Maverick would have said, 'No, you son-of-a-bitch, and I don't want you to vote for me now.'" But this time he said, "Maybe you are right. I made a lot of mistakes. . . . But now I'm for what it takes."[9]

Maverick pitched his campaign around two basic themes: there was disunity in the city administration that his "harmony" ticket would eliminate, and there was an overdue need for attention to flood control, expansion of the sewage system, and a general cleanup of the city, all of which would attract new industry to San Antonio. For the most part, his opponents refrained from the usual mudslinging, but the old charges of red associations were aired. Mayor Mauermann said to a group of American Legionnaires at the Saint Anthony Hotel, "I did not go to New York and make a speech for Representative Marcantonio." Maverick leaped to his feet at the speaker's table and said, "I did not either, and any one who says I did is a liar!" Mayor Mauermann rejoined, "I did not SAY you had. I said I did not make such a speech."[10] Charles W. Carroll, a bookbindery president who said he favored no particular candidate, brought up the 1939 riot at the Municipal Auditorium involving the Communist party and said that if Maverick should be elected, "Pravda would say that San Antonio . . . has repudiated democracy in its very citadel and elected one of Russia's fellow travelers to be its mayor."[11]

One of the minor candidates challenged the validity of Maverick's residence in San Antonio and secured copies of radio speeches the former mayor had made in Los Angeles in which he had made references to himself as a Californian.[12] State Senator Walter Tynan, a friend of Maverick's from the Citizens League days and the best man at his wedding, was pictured as the man behind the Mauermann organization. This new political enmity was traced back to the time when Tynan and Maverick had run together on the Citizens League ticket in 1930. Tynan as district attorney and Maverick as tax collector had vowed that they would seek no more than two terms. When the offices of county and district attorney were combined, and tax collector and tax assessor were combined in 1934, Tynan thought this absolved him from his pledge. He ran again and was defeated as Maverick went on to Congress and national fame. Tynan then slipped into relative political obscurity until he was elected to the state Senate in 1946. He was said to be determined to build a political machine, and Maverick stood in the way.[13]

But in the first phase of this election, Mauermann was eliminated, and Maverick entered a runoff campaign against Alfred Callaghan. Maverick said that he had no real differences with Mauermann's program, but that Callaghan had no program "except to organize a political machine."[14] Mauermann apparently did not accept Maverick's small peace offering, for he charged after his defeat that Maverick was not a resident and attempted to get the city council to keep his name off the runoff ballot, which the council refused to do.[15] "Don Politico" expressed the opinion that the real issue in the runoff campaign was "whether the electorate wants a Mavericko or a Callahando machine."[16] They preferred the latter by a vote of 25,362 to 22,435.[17] Again, as the *Dallas News* put it, Maverick "had a healthier respect for sumptuary law than can be discerned in administrations under which the Bexar capital has operated as a wide-open town. The inference may be that the San Antonians like it that way."[18]

Maury Maverick's career in active politics was essentially over, but he did not know it. In September of 1951 he announced his candidacy for the new post of Texas congressman-at-large and began to make extensive preparations for his campaign. After making several speaking trips and writing thousands of letters, he suffered

Like Ripples on a Pond

a severe heart attack and his doctor told him that he had to withdraw from the contest.[19] This disappointment marked his last attempt at public office.

Though he played no significant role in the 1948 contest, the 1952 Democratic presidential nomination provided Maverick's last splash on the national political scene. In the Texas struggle between the Loyalists and the Shivercrats, Maverick was styled as the "guiding genius" who won Bexar County for the Loyalist cause, while most of the remainder of the state was being swept by the anti-Truman, anti-administration Shivercrat forces of Governor Allan Shivers, who later supported the Republican nominee, Dwight D. Eisenhower. When on May 26, 1952, the Shivers-dominated state convention in San Antonio rejected Maverick's demand of a pledge of loyalty to the national party and its nominees, he rose with a dramatic flourish, echoing old Ben Milam's cry of the Texas Revolution ("Who'll go with me into San Antonio?") and said, "Who'll go with me to La Villita?" Bolting delegates followed him through a drizzling rain down the street to the La Villita assembly hall where they held a rump convention and selected a Loyalist delegation to the Democratic National Convention.

Maverick and Major J. R. Parten of Houston headed the pro-administration delegation that went to Chicago to contest the Shivercrats before the credentials committee of the convention in July. On July 18 three hours of the hotly contested Texas case was carried on NBC television as Maverick and others charged that Wright Morrow, national committeeman and chief advocate of the Shivercrat case, would have the Democratic party return to the platform of 1840 and support white supremacy and human slavery. The Maverick group offered at this time to drop the contest and go home to watch the proceedings on television if the Shivers group would only sign a pledge to support the nominees of the convention and see to it that their names were on the ballot in the general election, but Shivers ignored Maverick's evangelistic appeal for a "declaration of faith in the national party."

Morrow argued that if Maverick had his way the Texas Democratic party "would be a more exclusive club than the Old Guard Republican faction." For several days the hearings before the credentials committee wore on while the Loyalists sat in the gallery with "Seat Texas Mavericks" badges pinned on them, and the

Shivercrats "sat on their hands" on the floor of the convention rather than applaud national party figures. Television viewers saw Maverick on the floor from time to time, because he was able to borrow press passes from his friend Edward R. Murrow and other newsmen.

While the struggle was going on, Mrs. Maverick rode a Chicago bus to the convention in the company of a number of Alabama and Oklahoma delegates who did not know her. She heard Maury Maverick discussed as an "enemy of Democratic harmony" and a "politician who stirred up and thrived upon party strife." The pert little lady sat through all of it without saying a word, but as she left the bus, she extended her hand to one of the men, smiled sweetly and said, "I'm Mrs. Maury Maverick. I enjoyed the discussion very much."

On July 23 the *New York Times* pictured attorney John D. Cofer, chief counsel for the Loyalist cause before the credentials committee, waving a fist at Morrow as he attempted to drive home a point in favor of the Loyalist cause, but it was all to no avail. On that day the committee voted 36 to 13 to seat the regular Shivers delegation, whose members did agree that they would use all honorable means to assure that the nominees of the convention would be placed on the ballot in Texas in November. The full convention, whose leaders were fearful of a Southern bolt, ratified the committee's decision two days later. It would appear, then, as Governor Shivers had said, that the Maverick group had been beaten at every convention level and that they should have recognized that they did not represent the desires of the Democrats of Texas.

Subsequent events, on the other hand, could be interpreted as a demonstration that bitter-ender Maverick and his cohorts were right all along and should have been seated. When the Texas Democratic "governors" convention met in Amarillo in September, Shivers guided the delegates through the formal motions of living up to the pledge by putting the Stevenson-Sparkman ticket on the ballot, and then he led the convention in an overwhelming voice vote endorsement of the Eisenhower-Nixon ticket and, moreover, urged his fellow "Democrats" to work for that ticket! The disgruntled Maverick still thought Stevenson would carry Texas in November, but he underestimated the strength of the Shivercrats-become-"Eisencrats."[20]

Like Ripples on a Pond 277

Maverick out of office was not Maverick out of action, as one writer would have us believe.[21] His remaining years were not the idyllic days of the political war-horse out to pasture, musing over the times of victory and fame. Rather, he turned to an almost exhausting pursuit of all sorts of activities, among which his law practice became almost a sideline. He plunged into a study of the Far East that would do credit to any scholar and accumulated a private library on the subject that would rival any in the United States.[22] He assembled voluminous scrapbooks on world politics, with a special set on General MacArthur and the Korean War. A notebook in his papers revealed that he was teaching himself Chinese, and he was doing a remarkably thorough job of it. His published writings in this period were few, but, as has been indicated, he drafted all sorts of letters and memoranda on international problems (particularly those concerning the Far East) and bombarded the Truman and Eisenhower administrations with them.

In his "Pacific Notebooks," Maverick had introduced some adumbrations on a general theory of what was happening in the broad sweep of international politics. A number of times in the past he had speculated on the classification of different types of revolutions. He had dealt with this subject most extensively in a 1935 civil liberties speech, in which he characterized revolutions as being of three major types: radical, reactionary, and peaceful (or "constitutional"). The radical revolution was described as a "violent general rising of the people, similar to a *levee en masse*," and the reactionary revolution as one which "goes backward . . . and takes away the . . . ordinary democratic liberties."[23] Pursuing this line of thought, Maverick wrote inside the front cover of Laski's *Where Do We Go From Here* in June 1941 that it was an illusion to think that "Nazi-ism is the *world revolution.*" Rather, Maverick thought, "It is we who must offer revolution—a revolution for freedom, liberty, justice to and for all; including the German people."[24] He felt that there was a world "radical revolution" coming into being, and that the Second World War, acting as a catalyst, would stimulate action. He gave this prescient glimpse into the future to an audience in April, 1945, *before* his Pacific trip: "This war will *never* end. . . . This war will be followed by widespread psychological revolutions, global in character. . . . In the Orient, nations we scarcely heard of before, will demand independence."[25]

As early as 1946 Maverick had anticipated George Kennan's thesis concerning over-moralization in American foreign policy.[26] At that time Maverick spoke bluntly of a "long distance saviorism" on the part of both East and West, which could force the domination of one or the other.[27] He prepared an article in 1949 in which he compared the unrelenting name-calling of the present with the similar situation in the United States prior to the Civil War. As he trenchantly put it, the practice had reached such a peak in the pre–Civil War period that "it would have been indecent not to have gone to killing each other in a war."[28] Maverick began to tell the State Department and President Truman that moralization and a "fear complex" (both fear of communism and fear of treating it unemotionally) were preventing any realistic approach to the China problem. He counseled them to forget about incidents of "improper conduct" and to recognize Communist China as the only sensible move.[29] Truman wrote Maverick, November 22, 1949, and told him that his letter of November 19 was "the most sensible" he had seen on the China situation. The president added that it was a pleasure to hear from someone who had some common sense about such matters, because there were so many "crackpots" who thought they knew what to do, but did not.[30]

But nothing happened. Throughout 1950 Maverick wrote letters and memoranda to officials, publishers and professors—repeating his warnings on the crisis in the Far East. He sent a "Memorial and Memorandum" of April 1950 to President Truman and Secretary of State Dean Acheson, telling them that recognition of China was "urgent," if peace was to be maintained in the area.[31] Maverick said that he warned the State Department of what was going to happen in Korea six months before the Korean War began.[32] Professor John K. Fairbank, associate chairman of the Committee on International and Regional Studies at Harvard University, wrote Maverick that he was "very much impressed" with the memorandum. He added:

> I would be delighted if one of our Ph.D. men working here had an equally trenchant approach. I do not mean this as soft soap either. . . . We are just trying to set up here a seminar on "Chinese Ideological Change" and already have projects going on the ideological development of Chinese Communism and the history of China's ideological

Like Ripples on a Pond 279

response to the West. All these things refer to the realm of religion and attitude with which you are dealing, so I hope we can send you some interesting research papers from time to time. Your approach by way of the missionary record in China is also fundamental and I wish we had someone working on it here.[33]

Maury's "Memorandum," which he revised several times, was a quite carefully drawn research paper, generously sprinkled with the scholarly footnotes he had once derided and deplored. Many of the people who received copies of the paper probably had no idea of his extensive knowledge of the Far East—China in particular. He had had book dealers in the United States, Japan, and China combing the lists and back rooms for every book he could find out about, and he got most of them. He subscribed to and read Chinese periodicals and debated broad questions of East-West relations in correspondence with a Chinese Communist book dealer in Hong Kong.[34] An extract from this thirteen-page, single-spaced memorandum may indicate something of the caliber of the study and thinking that went into it:

The unitary force now developing in China has a strong element of mass emotion or, as some say, "religion" . . . under strong and disciplined leadership. This mass force is likely to develop the strong propulsive and aggressive characteristics which have predominated in Christian nations in centuries past. Such, for instance, as of Spain in conquering the New World, and of Western Europe in the Crusades— and of the Missionaries and Merchants who operated in the Far East roughly from 1850 to 1950. Historical analysis of . . . mass movements indicates similar patterns have occurred over and over in widely separated areas and altogether dissimilar races.

All of the aggressive Christian factors of the West which created "movements," crusades or conquests, whether "good" or "bad," were *strong*, combining military, economic, commercial and organizational powers. Whole masses of people, not necessarily of any different personal morals than of the "Pagans," "heathens," or Saracens, were motivated, directly or indirectly, by *mass religious zeal*, and organized by shrewd military and business leaders whose personal motives might have been entirely different.

In China today, Communism is taking on characteristics of emotional religion, and with unified, disciplined, aggressive motive power.[35]

In April 1950 Maverick displayed his prescience again when he told the Texas State Historical Association, "No longer will gunboats, airplanes or all the atomic and H. bombs in the world control in Asia. The people will not be destroyed by the H. Bomb. The people will destroy the H. Bomb. Thoughts and truth and humanity over in Asia cannot be controlled by our force any longer. We are faced with a problem of such magnitude as will determine whether our form of government and our civilization will exist or not."[36]

On through 1951 and 1952 Maverick continued to study, write, and make speeches on the religio-political character of the world revolution of the cold war. He came to the conclusion that the real basis of the "world revolution" was to be found in the Western concepts of the rights of man, spread in large part by Christian missionaries. He argued that the Soviet Union had "barged in on *our* revolution," and that the United States should make it known that it had accomplished the greatest revolution and preserved liberty, though not to the extent that might be wished.[37] He urged that a more objective consideration of communism and its meaning be made by people in the United States.

He probably shocked some of his Texas listeners when he pointed out that the Texas Constitutions of 1836 and 1845 had "beaten Marx to several provisions" of the *Communist Manifesto* of 1848. He cited a constitutional provision for an income tax that was not to be applied to people in "agricultural and mechanical pursuits" —"the proletariat of the day," as he put it. Banking by anyone other than the state was prohibited, there were to be no monopolies, and provision was made for public support of education. Maverick argued, moreover, that most of the objectives of the *Manifesto*, with the exceptions of the abolition of private property and the "dictatorship of the proletariat" had been eventually accomplished by both Republicans and Democrats in the United States. "The tragedy is," he said, "that the Marxist complaint of injustices has generated inflexible rules, cruelties and injustices far worse than those Marx challenged." Maverick ridiculed the loose use of the word "communism" by most Americans, and concluded, "We merely state a conclusion [in condemning communism] and forget that what has happened is the torturing of a utopian dream and many accepted

Like Ripples on a Pond 281

ideals, and we have run out of our own ideals. Russia has attained SOCIALIZATION, BUT NOT FREEDOM AND LIBERTY—a perversion of dictatorship of the proletariat—rise of a party elite—the class system."[38]

Toward the end of his life (1952–1954), Maverick was engaged in the process of pulling together some conclusions he had reached with respect to the prospects for world peace. He saw the United Nations and proposals for world government as progressive steps, but he felt that the real possibilities for world peace lay in the development of a "mutual repentance" among nations. He said that he had borrowed the term from Charles Malik, Lebanese delegate to the United Nations.[39] As Maverick reread his Jefferson and Thucydides, he jotted such remarks as, "It is unfortunate we cannot be placed in a position of being detached in viewpoint so we can judge ourselves—in times of stress nations and peoples [are] always suspicious and one blames the other";[40] and "The way that most men deal with traditions, even traditions of their own country, is to receive them all alike as they are delivered, without applying any critical test whatever."[41] He deplored the tendency of the people of the United States to think in terms of their own virtue while attributing "fraud, deceit and sorcery to the others."[42] In 1951 he picked up a little book on Russia which had been written in 1671. After reading this twenty-five dollar collector's item, he wrote inside the front cover: "Value of this book—principally that viewpoints about Russians began with idea they are inclined to buggery, sodomy; won't keep treaties; truce breakers; people afraid to talk; 'eat like swine'—etc. Chances are, not more inclined to buggery & sodomy than even perfect people, i.e., Texans—and all people, being human, are about the same; at least, an attitude of friendship for other races and regarding all people as human beings is more conducive to peace."[43]

Returning to this theme of the dangers of self-righteousness and over-moralizing, Maverick said that no nation is "wholly god-like," and one of the "paradoxes of life" is that "trusting one unworthy of trust may in the end be a moral victory."[44] As a parting shot to those persons who would, in the light of these views, question his patriotism, he wrote, "The greatest patriotism and courage is to be patriotic enough to be called otherwise, and courageous enough to be said to lack it; face the mob if your mind and soul say so!"[45]

Still another of Maverick's postwar interests and areas of activity derived from his experiences on the Pacific trip. In his Los Angeles and San Antonio law practice, he took up the unprofitable defense of the procedural rights of aliens and became a bitter critic of United States immigration laws. Most of a key chapter in J. Campbell Bruce's *The Golden Door: The Irony of Our Immigration Policy* was drawn from materials furnished by Maverick. His copy in the University of Texas Library is inscribed "To Maury Maverick, a bold leader in a noble cause—justice. 'Mil Gracias' for the wonderful help on Chapter 19."[46]

Charging no fee, Maverick came to the aid of several aliens who were caught in a fantastic web of denials of the most basic procedural rights. One Zygmunt Adamusia, a Polish refugee, was found to have been held in county jail on a "technical hold-for-immigration charge," for thirteen months. He was discovered by a Polish priest, Julius Dworaczyk, in 1949, and the only explanation Maverick was ever able to obtain was that the immigration officials had "forgotten" the man."[47] In 1953 Maverick was unable to stop the deportation of Pasquale Sciortino, who was later tried in Italy on charges made by Commissioner of Immigration Argyle R. Mackey and "acquitted on all accounts." In defense of Sciortino, Maverick had said that Mackey had issued "lurid, inflammatory, and prejudicial" statements to the press, styling the immigrant as a "bandit." In his brief to the Board of Immigration Appeals, Maverick said that these tactics were poisoning the "pool of justice" in this country. No other part of the administrative machinery of our government had such powers as those exercised by immigration officials. "Do you," Maverick asked, "when settling a strike, keep people in jail with the Labor Department prosecuting inside the jail?" In his conclusion, Maverick wrote, "Eventually, if the process continues, it will be decided that the usual courts are outmoded, as they are in the Iron Curtain countries—then nobody will have a chance—just as Sciortino hasn't had a chance from the start."[48]

Apparently Maverick had reached the point where he did not mind exposing his erudition, for he explained to Bruce that the problem was that immigration officials were not bad men, but they were "simply Javerts—like Javert in *Les Misérables*, who always got his man." Maverick referred here to Inspector Javert, the char-

Like Ripples on a Pond 283

acter who was more of a type than a man—indicated by Hugo's failure to assign him a first name. Javert had no vices, and he was the epitome of impersonal, inexorable law.[49]

In the 1950's Maverick took a number of immigration cases, which he pursued with unflagging zeal, involving Americans of Chinese extraction who were attempting to validate their claims to United States citizenship and return to this country. One of these cases provided a heartwarming story with an unusual happy ending. Maury Maverick was able to convince U.S. immigration officials in the 1950's that the alleged son of San Antonio Chinese restaurant proprietor K. A. Huey was indeed his son and thus was eligible to come to the United States from China. When the grateful son arrived in San Antonio, he took the name of Maury Maverick Huey and later even named his own son, Maury Maverick Huey, Jr. More than a decade later, in 1967, the family circle was completed when Maury Maverick, Jr., following in his father's footsteps, brought about the entry into this country of the mother of Maury Maverick Huey, Mrs. K. A. Huey.[50]

But many cases did not have happy endings. Maverick said that they were being delayed in the Hong Kong consulate for interminable periods of time. He wrote a memorandum concerning a series of such cases and directed it to President Truman and most of the major officials of his administration. In this document Maverick charged: "The conduct of and by the State Department in connection with entries of citizens overseas at the Hong Kong Consulate is excessively obstructive, uncooperative, brutal and cruel, and an outrage to common fairness and due process of law under the Constitution. . . . Stiffly and self-righteously adamant, afraid of criticism, they will never budge in their position, nor take the chance of acting in a kind, humanitarian or democratic manner; nor will they act efficiently."

Maverick complained that some persons had waited years for clearances which should not take "over an hour." In deploring such policies, he said: "The State Department, fighting for liberty on a great and global scale, is guilty of thousands of petty tyrannies, carried out by an apparently unsympathetic and personally contemptuous attitude *that ruins and destroys all the Department's major objects.* . . . Furthermore, ordinary justice to individuals, especially of Americans of certain racial backgrounds, is unavailable; there is no time for it. I protest this on humanitarian grounds, but also upon grounds of practicality, for the results will prove disastrous."[51]

The memorandum provoked a lengthy reply from President Truman. He said that Maverick's examples were "just samples of what I hear every day." Truman placed the responsibility upon people on the "third and fourth levels" in the State Department who were "still living in the time when Great Britain represented us in world affairs. . . ." Moreover, Truman explained, the McCarran-Walter immigration law had aggravated the situation by validating all of the past errors. He angrily charged Democrats as well as Republicans with voting to override his veto of the law, and concluded that he, as well as Maverick, felt "stymied at every turn of the road."[52]

When Maverick also tried to enlist the aid of the then Senator Lyndon B. Johnson, he received this response: "The situation you mention is not a new one. Actually it has been going on for a number of years. The only difference is that it appears to be reaching a climax. The difficulty is that it is impossible to pin-point the situation specifically. Practically every case becomes lost in a mass of regulations, red tape and bureaucratic unwillingness to act." Johnson concluded that nothing would be done about the problem until "the American people as a whole have voiced their dissatisfaction."[53]

This situation points up a very critical problem in the protection of rights. One may complacently point to some Supreme Court rulings (there are not many of them) protecting human rights in immigration and naturalization matters, but all this is unavailing when people are caught up in a maze of bureaucratic denials of rights; far removed by ignorance, distances and time from the courts. Maverick and others who have criticized such procedures drove home the point that due process has no meaning unless it is insured in the administrative operations of such programs.[54] Maverick contended further that, on humanitarian and practical grounds, due process should be extended to all human beings, much as the late Justice Frank Murphy had put it in his dissent in the case of *in re Yamashita* in 1946.[55]

When Hitler began to overrun Europe in 1939, Maverick's concern for the future of democratic states had caused him to relent

Like Ripples on a Pond 285

in his vehement criticisms of the House Committee on Un-American Activities. In addition to his denials of permits to Jehovah's Witnesses and Communists after the 1939 riot at the auditorium, he wrote to Martin Dies, chairman of the committee, and offered his cooperation in possible investigations in the south Texas area. Maury said that he was concerned with "*real* Fifth Column" activities along the Mexican–United States border. He told Dies that he had not recently spoken out against the Committee because he thought it had done "some" things of value, and "anyhow you have the committee and it will go on whether I favor it or not."[56]

The next year Maverick wrote Dies and told him that his committee should concern itself with Nazi use of money to "have good, patriotic citizens" branded as Communists in order to break down morale. "Also," he said, "both you and your Committee should be very careful in calling people Communists unless they really are." By this time (November 1940) Maverick was alarmed enough by events in Europe to say, "Conditions are changed entirely now and much worse than when I was in Congress. The extreme liberties of speech and press should no longer be allowed when they involve the safety of this country."[57] Maverick did not explain here or elsewhere what he meant by "extreme liberties." Though nothing developed from this tentative rapprochement with Dies, it did coincide with the beginning of Maverick's wartime departure from his position of defense of a near-absolute freedom of expression.

When World War II was over, Maverick resumed his attack on the investigators. He wrote in 1949 that the publications of the House Committee on Un-American Activities were "disgusting and puerile trash,"[58] and warned young congressmen against becoming a "punkin chaser."[59] One might judge that he had developed an even more liberal attitude out of his reflections on his World War II position, for he wrote George E. Sokolsky in 1951 that "every tolerant man knows that tolerance includes toleration of intolerance."[60] Marginal notations and tipped-in sheets indicated that Maverick was much influenced by his reading of a work on the Albigensian inquisition. He wrote that the inquisitors, "like Joe McCarthy," had "decreed that the adverse testimony of witnesses should be regarded as conclusive, in spite of the most strenuous denials on the part of the accused. It further decreed that convicted criminals and other scoundrels should be admitted as hostile witnesses."[61]

Consistent with his repeated urgings that positive action should be taken in behalf of civil liberties, Maverick joined with Marie S. Halpenny, a San Antonio writer, in the organization of an "American Activities Committee" in June, 1953. Mrs. Halpenny said that the name was taken from remarks made by Maury Maverick, Jr., in the Texas House of Representatives in opposition to a proposal for a Texas Un-American Activities Committee.[62] At first the Texas secretary of state refused to grant a charter to the organization,[63] but finally decided to do so on September 17, 1953,[64] after Maverick had repeatedly protested the refusal.

The organization had its inception primarily as a result of the attempted "red-stamping" of books in the San Antonio Public Library. In May 1951 Mayor Jack White suggested that a selected list of books should be stamped as "Communist-written volumes." The acting city manager, Wylie Johnson, urged that the books be burned. The list, which was presented to the city by the right-wing Minute Women organization, contained such works as Einstein's *Theory of Relativity* and Herman Melville's *Moby Dick* (because the illustrations were done by Rockwell Kent). The Library Board stood firm against the proposal, and the city officials soon indicated that they would prefer to let the matter drop. No books were burned —or stamped—but the American Activities Committee was organized because of fears raised by the attempt.[65]

The major purpose of the organization was "to uphold and defend, and to encourage the study and research of the Constitution and the Bill of Rights of the United States; to promote and defend the study, research and understanding of freedom of speech, press, conscience, religion and the freedom of information."[66] A set of bylaws set down as "imperative necessities" that investigating committees should not transcend limits of fair play and should adopt procedural rules like those of courts. The organization pledged "whole hearted opposition" to any form of book stamping and the like.[67]

The American Activities Committee actually did not do much of anything in the way of direct action. It did not conduct any studies or foster any research. In spite of the fact that it was virtually ignored by the San Antonio newspapers, however, it attracted the attention of and gave encouragement to liberal groups throughout the nation.[68] Another organizer of the group wrote, "Mr. Maverick rallied the forces of conscientious citizens who were interested in maintaining democratic principles at a time when the disease of McCarthyism was at epidemic level. In so doing, Mr. Maverick stemmed the tide of Fascist forces in our community."[69]

Maverick was never among those people who were daunted by Senator Joe McCarthy or his supporters. In February 1954 he was asked to make suggestions on a copy of a speech, "Will McCarthyism Be Fatal," to be given to the Army and Navy Club of Houston by Paul E. Daugherty. In some jottings he advised Daugherty:

Bear in mind these things: McCarthyism, insofar as McCarthy is concerned, is not necessarily the whole thing. He took advantage of a disease of fear and gave it a name. The people were already afraid, and he took advantage of the fear.

McCarthy was not the *inception*; he was the aggravator and organizer of fear. . . .

Do not forget big lies have always worked everywhere. Look up Titus Oates, Horatio Bottomley, etc. Also Guy Fawkes if you think it worthwhile. . . .

Progress is stopped by diverting ourselves, and McCarthy's work constitutes diversionary tactics. He has picked up the fear of the people and has used it for destruction just as Lenin.[70]

Maverick gave his most searching indictment of inquisitors and inquisitions at this time in a speech he regarded as one of his best.[71] He said in part:

The urge to persecute, to make inquisitions, to punish, to make people squirm, to find out everybody else's business or sex life, and to humiliate, may seem strange, but it is strong in some. Throughout history these Inquisitors want to force one to break silence, to confess publicly, and thus embarrass, persecute, cause public pain, torture and hurt,—and this country is passing through such a phase now. . . .

History repeats itself. My ancestors fled from the religious persecution of Louis the XIV in France, some from England. Now we all live in what amounts to civil persecution, fear, malice, Romanesque T.V. circuses and Modern electronic Inquisitions. . . .

I ask you, do women and men have to be brought before legislative committees to give affidavits as to whether they slept with certain people? Do you get brought before the city council or a Committee of the City Council to be asked whether you were drunk and disorderly on a certain night? The City Council, a legislative body, has as much right to do that within its own sphere, according to present day theories, as Congress has to put you before inquisitorial procedures. Imagine your Mayor and City Council calling you and questioning you on your sex life . . . and then asking you who were the participants of these drinking parties, sex offenses or other misdemeanors. This sounds ridiculous, of course, but if Congress has such rights, so have other bodies within their own spheres.[72]

Maverick argued in this speech that the Ninth Amendment[73] of the Bill of Rights should protect people from "illegal punishment by legislative committees . . . or unfair newspaper publicity or the remarks of bulldozing Senators or Congressmen." His view was that if no other part of the Constitution would afford protection against investigations and eavesdropping, the Ninth Amendment would give "a guarantee of human dignity, self-respect and personal honor" to protect a person's "security and privacy." In other words, this right was among the "others retained," when the list of specific guarantees was set forth in the preceding eight amendments of the Bill of Rights.

Maverick's invoking of the Ninth Amendment was something of a curiosity. Until that time it had been almost completely neglected in American constitutional law and commentaries thereon. The late Justice Robert H. Jackson, a friend of Maverick, confessed in 1955 that when "a lawyer friend" asked him what he thought about the Ninth Amendment, he could not remember what its provisions were, and after he found out, he said that what rights it protected were a mystery to him.[74] Most well-known source books on the Constitution either omitted or scarcely mentioned interpretations of the Ninth Amendment.

By a curious coincidence, at the same time that Maverick was giving his interpretation of the Ninth Amendment in Houston, a scholarly Texas lawyer, Bennett B. Patterson, was writing a book on *The Forgotten Ninth Amendment*. Patterson was not acquainted with Maverick and did not hear his speech, and Maverick seems to have had no knowledge of the Houston lawyer's work.[75] Apparently the two men, working independently, came to much the same conclusions regarding the Ninth Amendment's protection of a right of privacy.[76] Though the Supreme Court has still not used the Ninth Amendment for protection against investigations and the like, a considerable stir was created in 1965 when seven Supreme

Like Ripples on a Pond 289

Court Justices used it as the basis for throwing out Connecticut's anti-birth-control statute.[77] It is remarkable how often Maverick's restless, probing intellect was ahead of even the experts.

Maverick also made vigorous, well-reasoned and well-researched attacks on the tendency in the investigations of the 1950's to question the use of the Fifth Amendment's guarantee against self-incrimination. When he considered the question as to whether the Fifth Amendment's guarantee was being abused, he wrote, "If the Constitution says you don't have to testify, and you follow and use the Constitution, how is that a misuse? . . . To stamp out totalitarianism, should we adopt a policy of saying the use of certain parts of our Constitution is a *mis*-use; thereby adopting the thought control of totalitarianism?"[78] Maverick cleverly appealed to the self-interests of conservatives who might be most likely to favor a dilution of the Fifth Amendment. He told them that they were foolish for launching attacks upon the amendment that contained the "very core" of the American system of private property and competitive capitalism: the guarantee of due process of law and just compensation for property taken by government.[79] He also warned that the acceptance of the presumptive-guilt namecalling of "Fifth Amendment Communists" (that is, those persons who invoke the privilege to avoid answering questions concerning Communist party membership or activities *must be* Communists) might become "Fifth Amendment Property Owner." The government would take such a person's property without due process or just compensation on the basis that he does not need it, or ". . . you are too rich (or politically undesirable) or have too much property."[80]

When the Justice Department was seeking legislation in 1954 to grant immunity to uncooperative witnesses in order to remove the basis for the plea of the Fifth Amendment guarantee against self-incrimination, Maverick said, "As to the granting of immunity, also proposed by Mr. Brownell. This, in my opinion, will produce a crop of fast-talking liars and perjurers who will, out of profit, fear, malice or publicity-seeking exhibitionism, save their own skins and help to persecute others. The practice will get innocent people convicted because a promise of immunity can and will obtain convictions of innocent men and let liars, perjurers, traitors and criminals go free."[81]

Another of Maverick's areas of agitation in civil liberties in the 1950's involved a personal problem resulting from his efforts to get all of the information he could on political events in the Far East. He had always contended that the First Amendment guarantee of freedom of speech and press implied the freedom to listen and read —a freedom of information. He had said in 1935, "There is one point of freedom of speech which has not been covered; that is, that whenever a man says something, however tiresome or violent as it may appear to someone else, ... I have a right to listen to him."[82]

Maverick was equally insistent on protecting the right of access to the printed word. Again, he employed pragmatic arguments to support his position. He told a San Antonio audience, "The idea that one should not read Communist information has no more sense to it than that a doctor should not get a blood test or any pathological test if it is going to show something that is distasteful. In our intellectual pursuits we are proceeding on the theory that the way to win is to be ignorant of the competitors, ... and to stand off and call them names."[83] Maverick constantly urged anyone who would listen to him to read "whatever you damn please."[84] He sent letters and memoranda to J. Edgar Hoover, the Post Office Department, the Customs Bureau, and the State Department protesting interference with the transmission of publications from Communist countries and patiently hammering away at the importance of reading such literature. He told D. B. Strubinger, of the U.S. Bureau of Customs: "The point is that I am *a reader*. I am not any foreign agent and I do not 'disseminate propaganda.' If I stated that I am or ever was a foreign agent, I would be committing perjury and this I naturally will not do. ... It is hoped that your organization—although you do not make the top policy—will consider the lack of wisdom of this policy. You might also consider the work that you are put to for ferreting out matter which is the mass printing of propaganda information."[85]

Maverick's correspondence indicated that, with no explanation, several issues of Chinese Communist periodicals to which he had subscribed did not reach him, only to resume arriving and then, with equal mysteriousness, to be cut off for another period. In a letter to M. P. Chiles, Federal Bureau of Investigation agent in San Antonio, Maverick wrote:

Like Ripples on a Pond 291

What I want to get you interested in is this: That the reading of "Communist literature" is no indication that a man is a Communist. The reading of ordinary journals out of Hong Kong could have foreseen the Chinese attack, but the people were afraid to read them—even the State Department was afraid to act on clear evidence.

I receive the "Digest of the Soviet Press" and I challenge you to find more than a handful of Americans who would pay any attention to it. Without expressing any "high patriotism" to show my "Americanism" —the Soviet stuff is so tiresome that I nearly have to beat myself to death to get myself to read it. Nevertheless, to some extent it familiarizes me with the thinking of Russian Communists.[86]

Maverick used his pragmatic arguments again in a similar letter to J. Edgar Hoover during the Korean War. He said that he knew about the germ-warfare charges leveled against the United States "months" before they appeared in the newspapers in this country because he had read copies of *People's Monthly*, published in Hong Kong.[87] Hoover's responses to Maverick's letters were usually of the tongue-clucking variety; his essential point being that there was not much he could do about the situation.

When the famous Jelke case[88] was being heard in the New York courts in 1953, Maverick urged the American Civil Liberties Union to take action against the threat to freedom of information involved in the barring of reporters from access to the court proceedings. He told the ACLU:

But after all if courts can be closed on so-called "moral issues" because it might ruin the minds of our youth, they will be doing it on other issues soon enough. Young Jelke curdles my blood, and, of course, I think he is guilty. But if they begin having press excluded in any type of case they will begin to do it in others. Next it will be [Owen] Lattimore and then any kind of purge trial can come off, the judge sagely announcing that the wickedness of the case is such that it might destroy "the security of the nation." Vishinsky always bellows that they have more liberty of press and speech in Russia than in the United States—but he always adds in cases involving security it is necessary to act quickly without search warrants or publicity. I hope the Civil Liberties Union does not get sanctimonious. I am a little worried that Morris Ernst and several others will sit solemnly holding their hands like church steeples and saying my God we can't help a procurer of cafe society! What the hell is "cafe society"? . . .

I have never been a pimp or card-carrying pimp either and there has been no "guilt by association" for nearly 40 years.[89]

The gravity of the threat to freedom of information and the press at this time was dramatically illustrated by Maverick with some empirical evidence in a letter to Michael Straight, editor of the *New Republic*. The San Antonio lawyer reported this account of his defense of a civil-service employee who was in the process of being dismissed as a security risk:

QUESTION: Did you subscribe to the magazine known as the New Republic which is listed by a large number of government agencies as a Communist publication?

OBJECTION by Mr. Maverick: I subscribe to the New Republic and it is not a Communist publication and has never been listed as such.

Counsel of the Government: It is so listed by numerous governmental organizations.

Mr. Maverick: I demand to know what they are.

(The question was allowed.)

It was later developed that Mr. Tenney of California had alleged that the New Republic was communistic, but the Government counsel never was able to give any other such listing.

Succinctly, if not very delicately, Maverick concluded his letter with the statement, "This is the God damndest thing I ever heard of and there should be a national furor about it."[90]

After he had defended several such Federal employees who were being suspended or dismissed on charges of disloyalty, Maverick wrote to Senator Lyndon Johnson to tell him that many people were being fired for indiscretions of "five years past." "At Kelly Field they fired a young man who has an honorable discharge because he had a job with a Communist on return after discharge and his stepfather voted for [Henry A.] Wallace."[91] Apparently Maverick received no response or what he considered to be an unsatisfactory one, for he angrily wrote again, "*My* liberties and the liberties of the American people are at stake. *Nobody*, as far as I know, will take up for them at Washington—certainly not the Democratic Party." He went on to chide Johnson and asked if he was going to "come out for the Constitution" after he had been elected.[92]

Maverick also attempted to bring his influence to bear to reverse the war-crimes trials in Japan. He had thought from his conversa-

Like Ripples on a Pond 293

tion with General MacArthur immediately after World War II that there would be no such trials.[93] In June 1948 Maverick wrote to MacArthur:

> It is my opinion that we are abandoning our principles of constitutional government. The Nuremberg trials in many aspects were serious mistakes. In spite of the serious situation existing in the world today, we cannot afford to abandon our constitutional principles. If, as a great American [MacArthur] once said to me, we adopt the policy of the Orientals to kill our enemies on capture, we thereby adopt the Oriental principle ourselves. This means an abandonment of the principles for which we fought, and the establishment of principles gravely dangerous to our system of government.

Maverick offered to appear without pay to file a brief as *amicus curiae* and make a motion for a new trial or motion for dismissal of charges. MacArthur's reply was discouraging; he told Maverick that such a proposal would have to be presented to the Far Eastern Commission and that he was "highly doubtful" that anything would be done about it.[94]

Maverick did not pursue the particular case any further, but he later complained to his friend, Justice Jackson, who had been chief of the Nuremberg War Crimes Trials, that the whole concept was wrong and dangerous. Jackson sent him some explanatory materials and said, "You don't indicate what you would have done, and I would be interested to know." Maverick studied the materials and replied to Jackson:

> In your letter you indicated you would like to know what I would have done to the Nazi officials. In the absence of any Western precedent I am forced to make a rather clumsy answer, and that is, as far as incarceration or hanging, nothing. I might have hedged them about upon some principle of what the British did to Napoleon.
> My belief is we have our own constitutional precepts and ideals. I believed at the time of the trial that these various big Nazis were getting old and would be symbols of defeat while alive.

Maverick further argued that the trial of Nazi leaders was "bad psychology," and used the American Civil War to illustrate his point. He said that the United States could not have achieved unity out of the Civil War strife if Jefferson Davis and others had been hanged, and declared, "I think it could have been clearly established from a juridical viewpoint that he was guilty of treason." Finally, Maverick said that "strictly confidentially" he had gotten the idea for opposition to war-crimes trials from MacArthur, but "now he says from Japan that all the Korean war criminals will be punished." Maverick despairingly concluded that it was impossible for people to abandon an "emotional" approach to such problems, and that he would undoubtedly be charged with "favoring bad men."[95]

It is difficult to tell exactly why or when Maverick changed his view to one of virtually complete support for an end to segregation and discrimination against racial minorities. There are some indications, however, that his Pacific trip[96] and his subsequent program of self-education on the Far East and its problems influenced him in this respect as well as others. Though he did not say when he had read the book, he indicated in 1953[97] that he had been influenced by *Conflict of Colour*, a book that had as its general thesis the argument that there must be greater understanding of the growing conflict of races in the world—the black, yellow, and brown peoples were heading for a world revolution of color against white supremacy.[98] In my encounter with Maverick in 1952, he clearly indicated the influence of this book when he expounded the view that the people of the United States had to face up to the fact that there was a "world revolution" of color, and that we were going to have to adjust our thinking to it. He said with a grin, "This world revolution is here; it runs right through my kitchen and I see it when I ask the maid to fix me a sandwich and she says, 'Fix it yourself.' "

As early as 1951 Maverick was prepared to say privately, "Times, however, are changing in a big way. Somebody said to me the other day, 'You're certainly getting to be a broadminded son-of-a-bitch—you don't even say nigger in private.' Colored people are elected to school boards and the like, and as a people vote as intelligently as any other people. Nor is the Negro vote any longer a controlled vote; they enter colleges and nobody pays any attention."[99] In a 1953 speech he attributed this "conversion" on the rights of the Negro, at least in part, to his constant recollection of a statement Franklin Roosevelt had made to him in the 1940's: "Maury, I would like to interest you in the Black Man's burden.

Don't worry too much about the White Man's burden—just look out for the human race."[100]

Maverick first discussed the change in his views with a group of students at Brandeis University in 1952. With his usual candor, he traced the phases in his thinking from the time when as a young man he saw a statue of a Negro soldier on Boston Common. He said that his prejudice was such that the sight angered him—he did not believe that a "Negro could be a Soldier." He then used his attitude toward John Brown to illustrate the outline of his shifts in thinking about the Negro question. When Maverick was a boy, John Brown was "a dirty bum"; in the brief period at Virginia Military Institute, "a wicked character"; during his studies of radical literature in the 1920's, "a noble gentleman"; and finally, in what Maverick considered to be his maturity on the subject, "*now*, a fanatic, one-minded man, one idea, who brought something to the public—a tragic character—a trouble maker—agitator back in Kansas." Maverick then reiterated his point that abolitionists were sometimes as bad as the slave owners and that extremists generally do more harm than good. He then spoke with pride of having Negroes in his home and said that they had made great advances and were reaching "political maturity."[101] A few months earlier Maverick had even made the flat statement to a Houston audience, "I do not believe in segregation."[102] The next year he wrote with pride of the housing of Negroes in a San Antonio hotel in defiance of "Jim Crow."[103] In July 1953 Maverick wrote on the question of Negro teachers entering the Texas State Historical Association, ". . . why should there be any argument about that question at all? Teachers are teachers and they do not have to be Anglo-Saxon blonds to teach, and certainly in professional matters there should be no discrimination whatsoever."[104]

In 1954 Maverick wrote with pride to Thurgood Marshall, then chief counsel for the NAACP, about his son, Maury, Jr., winning an attack on a Texas law barring boxing matches between Negroes and whites. Maverick hailed it as a "great victory" for equal rights.[105] A month later he wrote to Marshall and chided him for not stopping by to see him in San Antonio and said, "I trust you will understand that I am completely emancipated (or so believe) from what they call prejudices."[106] In his final words on such matters, Maverick told San Antonio Young Democrats, "A democrat is one who believes in *all* Constitutional liberties—in *freedom*—in economic independence. DIGNITY—for everybody including Negroes, Chinese everywhere—English-French-Mongolians—and —EVEN—Russians."[107]

Maverick had come to a categorical endorsement of equal rights of all sorts for all people. He had started out in the 1920's and 1930's several steps ahead of the thinking in his South, and then by the time some of the Southern leadership began to draw abreast of him, he typically had to go out in front again.

I Am That Gadfly

MAURY MAVERICK was out of the political limelight and out of the national news columns in his last few years, but his voluminous files reflect his continuing influence and importance among "upper bracket" and "middle bracket" opinion leaders of the South and the United States—here a professor, there a labor leader, lawyer, editor, minister, public school teacher, member of the Texas Legislature, or garden-variety politician.

Something of his impact may be gathered from the results of his "holding forth" at considerable length during the 1952 Brookings Institution five-day conference on problems in international affairs in San Antonio, where I became acquainted with him. Despite the fact that Maverick had leveled some blistering broadsides at the State Department and its fear of Senator Joe McCarthy, a member of the State Department policy planning staff wrote this unsolicited note to him: "I have most pleasant recollections of our association at the Brookings seminar. You contributed greatly to the vitality and good sense of the meeting. I am enclosing a reprint in the Department of State Bulletin of some observations of mine on the nature of foreign policy. It is a part of an address which I made at the University of Chicago on February 4, 1952. I hope you will do me the honor of reading it."[1] The late Professor Sam B. McAlister, who was head of the Department of Government at North Texas State University, said of Maverick's participation in the Brookings seminar, "Everyone from Washington to Texas will profit from your contribution."[2]

There had always been ample testimony to Maverick's influence in the academic sphere; many examples can be found in his papers and books. Charles E. Merriam, the distinguished American political scientist, inscribed one of his books "To Maury Maverick, Honorable in title and fact—A Maverick American and a Real American—with the sincere regards of Charles E. Merriam."[3] Political scientist J. T. Salter selected Maverick from among the members of the House of Representatives for his book of portraits of the most significant American politicians in 1938.[4] In that book Maverick was given the highest praise by Robert C. Brooks, who soon thereafter became president of the American Political Science Association. Maverick's copy of David Mitrany's *The Progress of International Government* bears this flattering inscription:

Dear Maverick,
  You are doing what C.P.H. pleaded for in the fine passage which I quoted in my dedication. So I feel that I could almost re-dedicate this book to you.
                                            Devotedly yours,
                                            D. Mitrany

Mitrany referred to his dedication of the book to the late Charles P. Howland and the quotation, "There can be no sincerity in a tribute to the dead without a silent promise that their deaths will have been more than a splendid gesture of futility. The truest commemoration will be the vigorous enlistment of our own lives and capacities in the struggle between good and evil that continues in peace as in war."[5]

Arthur M. Schlesinger wrote to Maverick in 1943 and said that he had been "watching and cheering your public career from my ivory tower and hoping that sometime I might be able to meet you in person," and that he was delighted to know that "young Arthur" was working with Maverick.[6] Arthur, Jr., had helped Maverick with a number of speeches during the SWPC days. In a conversation a few years ago, Schlesinger told me that Maverick "worked the hell out of" him and called him at all hours about the speeches. Julian P. Boyd, the Princeton Jefferson scholar, once wrote to express his regrets at not being able to meet Maverick for a discussion in 1947, and then proceeded to "share" a scholarly discovery with Maverick concerning a discussion the two had had over Benjamin Franklin's annotation of one of the rare drafts of the Declaration of Independence.[7]

In 1951 Guy Stanton Ford, then editor of the *American Historical Review*, wrote in response to a Maverick criticism, "As an ordinary garden variety of American citizen, I have found myself so often in agreement with your views that I am almost ready to go along with you as a critic of medieval scholarship."[8] Professor of political science H. C. Nixon wrote from Vanderbilt University in 1952 that he was sending Maverick an article in which he might be interested, but, Professor Nixon said, "It may be taking coals to Newcastle to give you a piece on 'Ethics and Politics,' but the coals are meant to be a warm compliment."[9] Similarly, Professor Paul F. Boller, Jr., of Southern Methodist University, sent Maverick a copy of an article he had written on the New Deal and said, "I felt greatly honored to hear from you. Ever since my undergraduate days in the late thirties I have admired your work and have, indeed, quoted some of your witty and illuminating remarks on more than one occasion."[10] In his last year, Maverick received this flattering note from William W. Crosskey, author of a monumental and controversial study of the United States Constitution: "I remember reading many years ago a speech of yours in the Congressional Record. It was at the time when the Supreme Court was throwing out various pieces of New Deal Legislation. You said the trouble with the Supreme Court was that they had got ahold of the wrong Constitution, that they thought they were interpreting the Constitution of the United States, but in fact they were interpreting the constitution of the Confederate States of America. I thought of that many times in the years I was writing the book."[11]

The academic world also sought out Maverick in the later years. For example, in 1952 he was invited to Brandeis University "to meet with the senior class and to discuss with them some of your experiences and what working philosophy you have been able to fashion." More explicitly, Max Lerner and President A. L. Sachar were conducting a special seminar for senior students and they wanted Maverick to help the students to "face some of the intellectual and moral choices they will have to make when they get out of college."[12] After the visit, Sachar wrote: "I had enthusiastic reports of the impact which you made upon our youngsters. I only wish that the college generation could be more frequently brought together with spirits like yours. We could break down the sterility and the stodginess which has crept into so much of contemporary education. I know Max Lerner joins me in this expression of thanks to you and in the hope that we may have you back."[13]

Several years later Lerner appraised Maverick as a man with an "extraordinary combination of personality, insight and talent." He was "shrewdly pragmatic," and, "while he always dealt with the realm of the possible, he stretched the limits of possibility as far as they could stretch and was never content with an easy compromise either with vested interests or vested ideas."[14]

Maverick did not fare quite so well at the hands of one famous scholar. During the week of April 7, 1953, British historian Arnold J. Toynbee was being squired about central Texas by Professors Walter P. Webb and Joe B. Frantz of the University of Texas history department. The hosts for a visit to San Antonio were R. L. Bobbitt and Maury Maverick. After Maverick had given Toynbee and his wife the complete tour of San Antonio's historic landmarks, the group fell to discussing politics. Someone remarked on the anti-Americanism of "Nye" [Aneurin] Bevan, the maverick British Labor party leader, and Maverick contradicted the assertion with an offer to Toynbee that he would trade Senator Joe McCarthy "any day" for Bevan. Toynbee merely smiled, but Maverick kept at him with "periodic grunts" to the effect that he would "throw in" Congressman Harold H. Velde, chairman of the House Committee on Un-American Activities, General Douglas MacArthur, and "a few Texans I'd be glad to name." Toynbee finally yielded to Maverick's insistence that he agree to the mock deal, and later remarked, "He is rather like a bull, you know," and he chuckled, ". . . a nice bull of course. . . . Seriously," he continued, "Mr. Maverick is rather typically American . . . a buffoon, and a bit of the fool, don't you know, but beneath there is quite a concern for his fellow man, a deep human sympathy. I rather think that many men in their 30's and 40's must be much better men for the aid he gave them in the depression."[15] This damning with faint praise indicated that Toynbee did not see much beyond the obvious and that he may well have been a victim of what Maverick once aptly characterized as "reverse provincialism."

Maverick sought out and befriended foreign students and other visitors to this country in the 1950's, and they rarely failed to respond with praise of Maverick and the ideas for which he stood. In 1950 a German group studying civil liberties in the United States was shown around San Antonio by Maverick. One of the members of the party, after his return to Germany, wrote to him, "We are both too old to make or receive compliments; so you may believe in the sincerity of my words: it was my best day in America to meet you."[16] Another German wrote, "I was strongly touched by your personality, your sense of humor and your humanity. I can say you belong to the people I would wish to meet again."[17] In 1954 Dr. S. S. Nehru, then president of the International Union of Lawyers Associations, wrote from Allahbad, India, to commend Maverick for one of his articles: "Here in India we are deeply responsive to the stimulus we get from your activities and the feeling that the America you represent is 100 per cent with us in our efforts to create and strengthen a real basic peace on the model of the Sermon on the Mount."[18]

The list of people that Maverick was associated with or corresponded with would make up a national or international who's who. In addition to the many people already noted, he discussed public affairs with such prominent figures as Thomas Mann, Harold J. Laski, and H. G. Wells. Out of Maverick's limited encounters with Carl Sandburg came this inscription in the copy of *Abraham Lincoln: The Prairie Years* that Sandburg sent to Maverick: "For Maury Maverick, who is familiar with some of the loneliness and laughter herein—with respect and affection."[19] The late J. Frank Dobie recounted a meeting between Maverick and Sandburg in which, said Dobie, Sandburg was "deeply impressed" by Maverick. Dobie said that he viewed Maverick as one of the "few public figures Texas has produced who did have taste"—a rebuttal to the views of people who saw only the rough exterior of Maverick. On the other hand, kindred spirit Dobie did say that he and Maverick had some different ideas about education that emerged when Maverick asked the Texas folklorist to raise a grade that Maury, Jr., had received in one of his courses at the University of Texas.[20]

Novelist Lewis Browne once wrote to Maverick, "I have been following your career with interest and admiration. I have a feeling that you are one of the few genuinely significant figures in American public life."[21] In 1952, William T. Evjue, editor and publisher of the *Capitol Times* (Madison, Wisconsin), wrote to Maverick, "I am sorry that I have never had the pleasure of meeting you. However, your name has long been familiar to me as one of those in public life who believes that government should function for the public welfare instead of for private interests. You have made a long and honorable fight for the contention."[22]

Considering the fights that he did make and the time he needed for the mundane business of earning a living, it is remarkable that Maverick had any time for hobbies. He nearly "went broke" in his later years as he turned his seemingly endless energies and his limited funds to a set of expensive and sometimes eccentric hobbies that had long claimed a part of his attention. Some of these hobbies, however, turned out to be long-term investments. He was a serious and knowledgeable book collector and had a number of volumes on the subject. He accumulated a good many rare volumes, most of which have since been sold to collectors, dealers, and libraries. He also had extravagant, embossed bindings put on some of his prized volumes and even sent some of them to bookbinders in England for that purpose.

Maverick had an enviable stamp collection consisting mainly of plate blocks and first-day covers, some of them autographed by famous national and international figures. He also kept an impressive autograph collection containing the signatures, most of them on letters, of nearly every important political figure of his time. He had a richly-bound volume of autographs, again frequently on letters, of every president of the United States down to Eisenhower.

Incredible as it may seem, there were other hobbies. Maverick designed and had struck various commemorative medallions. One set, made up of the portraits of four great presidents, he had set into the corners of a desk in his home—others were placed in the hearth of his fireplace. He also designed silver pillboxes for gifts to friends and a set of miniature silver books, which he sent to Presi-

I Am That Gadfly

dent Truman for the Truman Library (for which, incidentally, Maverick was a major fund raiser).[23] The veteran Texas liberal Democrat, District Judge James C. ("Jim") Sewell of Corsicana, said that his most prized possession was a cane designed for him in 1951 by Maury Maverick. The cane bore the inscription *Illigitimi non carborundum*, which in Maverick Latin means, "Don't let the bastards grind you down."[24] This was the motto that Maverick frequently sent to fellow liberals who were facing a tough battle or who were simply down on their luck.

Maverick was also interested in heraldry, and he owned some of the classical studies in the field. He engaged in extensive research concerning the origin and significance of the design of the Great Seal of the United States and became a recognized authority on that subject. Reprints of his article on the Great Seal, written in 1952, are still sent to interested persons by the United States Treasury Department.[25]

Maverick was fascinated by symbols and symbolism. He bought or had made tiny silver figures (of the size commonly seen on charm bracelets) which symbolized the various aspects of life, and he carried them in his pocket in a small round silver box. He acquired such items as an ancient coffee mill or an antique silver vessel and covered them with a somewhat bizarre collection of coins, tiny flags and other emblems, and words clipped from printed materials. He then treated the entire creation with clear lacquer. He gave similar treatment to wooden boxes and even to the covers of certain books—much like the currently popular découpage. Most of these curious creations carried out some theme such as inter-American friendship, patriotism, peace, or simply the good life. The devices on the books were designed to convey something about the ideas or characters in the books or perhaps events to which the books related.

Why did Maverick do these things? Those of us who have no credentials probably have no business psychoanalyzing our subjects, and, for that matter, the explanation is probably simpler than one might think. Maverick's father had been a tinkerer with somewhat eccentric hobbies. Also, Maverick had a restless, creative mind and had developed a set of habits during the period of suffering from his war wounds. He had to be doing something constantly, and the time to do these things was during his many sleepless nights. He read, wrote, or tinkered with his hobbies into the early morning hours. These hobbies, however, did not provide him with relaxation, because he pursued them with the same zeal and intensity that he exhibited in his political and legal work. The late Professor Brooks wrote prophetically in 1938, "Obviously this is a pace that cannot be kept up indefinitely. It is true that political work is always fascinating and frequently amusing to the Congressman; in a sense he makes play out of it. On the other hand, the word 'recreation' is simply not in his vocabulary, a dangerous oversight. . . ."[26]

In my encounter with Maverick at the Brookings Institution conference in April of 1952, it was apparent that this bustling, dynamic man was not well. Before each meal he was popping the tiny nitroglycerin pellets into his mouth to treat the heart ailment that had recently wrecked his plans to run for congressman-at-large. He was obviously overweight, and at times his face was gray and drawn. He seemed never to relax. After rapidly consuming his meals, he fidgeted in his chair and moved things about on the table —anxious to be up and going.

Given the basis of Brooks' prophecy, it was ironic that it was while spending a few leisurely days in the country with his wife on May 25, 1954, that Maverick was stricken with another heart attack. As he lay dying in the hospital, his ebullient spirit never deserted him. A week or so after he had been there, he was writing Lawrence Bertetti, then chairman of the Bexar County Democratic Committee, asking for a list of names which he might use in writing letters in behalf of "Little Maury's" third campaign for the Texas House of Representatives. He spoke then of "things beginning to look good," though he figured he would have to lose about twenty-five pounds before he could get out of the hospital.[27] Three days later, June 7, 1954, he was gone.

Messages of condolence came from all over the nation, while "the longest funeral cortege in recent years" paid its respects to Maury Maverick.[28] As Alistair Cooke, the British journalist said, "In the beginning and the end, he was nothing but a maverick."[29] Indeed, Maverick had once said, as he discussed his determination to be an independent thinker, "I figure on trouble with my undertaker who will probably try to bury me in a dress suit."[30] A maverick to the end, he was buried in an ordinary business suit that

I Am That Gadfly

his wife took from the closet. As the remarkable Mrs. Webb, twice widowed by the deaths of famous husbands, discussed the death of her first husband and her reactions, she said of Maverick, "I never knew whether he was roughly gentle or gently rough," and then with captivating aplomb she prompted, "Take that down—that's a good quote!" She then explained more soberly that this is why the marker on Maverick's grave is half rough, half smooth.[31]

A little more than a year before his death, Maverick wrote to a friend concerning his contribution of the word and idea of *gobbledygook*: "I do hope that when I kick the bucket that they will do something else than say I originated that one word."[32] Perhaps he would have been satisfied with this "something else" from a man with whom he was not closely associated:

Maury Maverick was a man of great vision and understanding. He was far in front of most of his native Texans. He was a pioneer whose real fame will grow with the passing years. Then he will receive the recognition due one who has been in the vanguard of the forces which pave the way for human progress.

His untiring efforts in a righteous cause have not been in vain. Time and history are on his side. Future generations will honor and respect the name of Maury Maverick and the memory of his fighting spirit.[33]

No one has built a monument to Maury Maverick, but he unwittingly—or perhaps knowingly—built one himself. On a hillside overlooking the skyline of San Antonio there is a three-acre bit of what he called "worthless" land with three small cottages scattered about, and, in the center, a house made from a streetcar. He named this "piece of vanity and egotism," "The Maverick." While he was serving in Congress, Maverick had bought a derelict streetcar from the San Antonio Public Service Company for twenty-five dollars and had it hauled to the rugged hillside plot that had once been a part of the old Sunshine Ranch. A rock apron was placed around the base of the car, a door was cut in the side facing downtown San Antonio and the interior was converted into surprisingly livable quarters. Later an Army "hutment" was added to the back of the streetcar to provide a living room. Where the motorman stood is a tiny kitchen and in the conductor's compartment, a small bathroom. Near the center door there is a rock fireplace with a collection of great keys hanging to one side and a set of branding irons on the other.

A broad, rustic flagstone veranda with a roof supported by rough cedar posts was built along the side of the car facing San Antonio. Most of the grounds are covered with native trees and shrubbery. The leaves are usually stirred by the prevailing southeast breeze, and it is quiet there. Occasionally a cottontail, unafraid, plops through the dusty grass around the cactus, sotol, cenizo, and agarita (agrito), or a mockingbird flits through the trees. Here and there is a redbud tree, some mountain laurel, or a bright-blooming lantana. One end of the streetcar is shaded by some pecan trees Maverick planted in holes blasted in the rocky hillside. This place is Maury Maverick—rough, tough, eccentric, and Texan.

Great ribbons of expressways slash through this part of San Antonio; suburbia with its sameness of split levels, green lawns, and barbecue pits has crept up to the fence of "The Maverick," and a shopping center is a block away; but this piece of rough Texas hillside survives. Down the slope from the motorman's window of the streetcar is the modest home of Santos Rodríguez, the caretaker who used to make Maverick feel himself a "baron" as he strolled about the place and told Santos what to do in a "quite baronial manner." The baron is gone, but Santos continues to care for the manor.

San Antonians and people elsewhere may see other monuments to Maverick in the restoration of La Villita and the beautiful downtown river development, but Maverick probably would have been equally concerned about monuments of another sort that will also endure. A San Antonio newspaper that had rarely said anything good about Maverick during his public career, editorialized on the occasion of his death, "Not alone in fairness, but in genuine appreciation let it be said that some of Maury's arbitrary doings which provoked sharp controversy actually redounded to the public benefit. Often excoriated as a 'leftist,' he died at a time that found the President and Chief Justice of the United States holding forth as Maury had been holding forth for years."[34]

One of the reasons why the president and the Supreme Court were "holding forth" as they did in 1954 and moved on to an even

I Am That Gadfly 307

more libertarian position in the 1960's was the effort put forth by Maury Maverick and men like him through the preceding decades. Maverick was an outstanding member of what Professor John P. Roche called the "great legal migration" to Washington in the 1930's, which produced the essentially new doctrine of a near-absolute freedom of expression as well as other libertarian positions.[35]

This view, now the majority view of the Supreme Court, is consistent with the position Maury Maverick took throughout his career in Congress and most of his life as well. Aside from his writing, speaking, and acting on the subject, Maverick was closely associated with both of the men who are considered to be chiefly responsible for bringing about this trend. Justice William O. Douglas wrote, "I knew Maury Maverick well and admired him greatly. He was a stout defender of the rights of man. . . . I was never associated with him on any civil liberties project, so I never saw him in action, but I felt the importance and power of his ideas in that field."[36] And Justice Hugo Black said: "I knew the late Maury Maverick intimately and he was one of my favorite people. His public service in Washington manifested at all times an extraordinary loyalty to the principles of civil liberties, particularly the liberties which the Bill of Rights was designed to protect. He was a courageous exponent of these principles and had little sympathy or patience with governmental intrusion upon individual rights. His views on these matters were expressed in speeches, articles and books."[37] Both of these men, of course, had their own ideas, but they needed the encouragement and stimulation of men like Maverick; one had "felt the importance and power" of his ideas and the other knew him "intimately" and was familiar with his "speeches, articles and books" on the subject.[38]

Such views were never popular with a majority of the Texas electorate, or with much of any other electorate for that matter. Socrates, so Plato tells us, said, "I am that gadfly which God has attached to the state, and all day long and in all places am always fastening upon you, arousing and persuading and reproaching you. You will not easily find another like me. . . ."[39] Maury Maverick might well have said the same. Had he been willing to trim, to adjust his views to those predominant among the Texas electorate, he could have written his ticket for anything political the state had to offer. He had all of the assets, including what one might call "protective coloration"—a son of the American and Texas Revolutions and a wounded and decorated war hero. But instead he chose to follow the trail of the maverick through political thickets that were as thorny as any of the wild Texas brush country that he loved.

It was for this reason that Maverick was the rallying point of liberal political thought in Texas in the 1940's and 1950's. His dogged courage and sincerity earned him the respect of even many conservatives, though Jesse Jones probably expressed their deepest sentiments when he said, "I like Maury Maverick a lot, but always thanked God he never became President."[40] On the other hand, it was almost impossible for anyone of liberal or radical inclinations to avoid being drawn to Maverick and his ideas. His intelligence, earthy humor, and enthusiastic ripping of sacred cows delighted liberals who looked upon him as the man they would be if they but dared. When the spirits of some Texas liberals began to flag during the period of McCarthyism, Maverick kept going loud and strong. When Willie Morris made his journey to Texas in those days, he found that Maverick was the "spiritual leader of the tiny group of liberals in the Texas legislature,"[41] and Lyndon Johnson said, "Certainly, Maury was an outspoken, uncompromising advocate of the ideas he expounded. Certainly, he was a force in the community. Certainly, he served as a rallying point for many others who agreed with his ideas but who needed a center for expression."[42]

Professor Webb remembered Maverick as a man of "character and unflinching integrity." Webb said, "This fact was recognized and proclaimed after his voice was stilled by the voluntary and unstinted tribute poured out for him not only in Texas but all over the nation." Webb reported that a conservative friend had put his finger on Maverick's most "subtle" and perhaps most important contribution when he told the historian that Maverick had "steadfastly and courageously 'reminded us of things we ought to be thinking about.' "[43] New Dealer Benjamin Cohen called Maverick a "true Jeffersonian" who was among the first "to sense the dangers to our civil liberties in the roving investigations of the early un-American Activities Committee," and a man who had "resisted the growing tendencies toward dull conformity" in American life.[44]

I Am That Gadfly

Robert Maynard Hutchins called Maverick a "classical 18th Century civil libertarian,"[45] and Senator William Benton saw him as a "formidable fighting liberal" and a "great leader in the field of civil liberty—for Texas and thus for the United States."[46]

There was also eloquent testimony over the years to Maverick's place in the leadership of liberalism in the South, but perhaps the most eloquent came from the pen of Harry S. Ashmore, famed editor of the *Arkansas Gazette*. As he speculated on the type of man needed for a new liberal Southern leadership in 1958, his thoughts turned to Maury Maverick. In his Pulitzer Prize–winning *An Epitaph for Dixie*, Ashmore wrote, "It is even possible that we may see a hell-roaring political liberal with a Texas-size bank account—something that has been conspicuous by its absence since Maury Maverick joined the riders in the sky."[47]

He was a hell-roarer, all right, and most people chose up sides on that basis. Several years ago I was involved in something of a confrontation that neatly demonstrated how the lines were drawn. An anti-Maverick professor who had known this provocative character, and had apparently been provoked by him, listened to my speech and then asked, "Why did Maury have to be so irreverent, blunt and coarse." I congratulated myself on my reply to the effect that bread did not have much savor without the salt, but I was demolished with the quick retort, "But *rock* salt?!"

Maury Maverick was a man of great contradictions—a political radical who was a passionate patriot, a rough-spoken man of action who was no mean scholar, and a tough-minded man who could be uncommonly sentimental. Given the importance he attached to the latter quality, it might be said that he carried on a sort of all-encompassing love affair with *his* land, *his* people, and *his* Texas heritage. It was a tempestuous affair, because many people were just wrongheaded enough not to want to go his way—but when he died he was certain that one day they would.

NOTES

CHAPTER 1. A MAVERICK AMERICAN

1. Expressions found in the order given in: *Manchester Guardian*, June 9, 1954, p. 10; *San Antonio Express*, June 8, 1954, p. 1; *Dallas News*, June 8, 1954, sec. III, p. 2 and sec. I, p. 1; *Express*, June 10, 1954, 4; June 8, 1954; ibid.; *Time* 63 (June 14, 1954): 104.
2. *New York Times*, June 8, 1954, p. 27.
3. In the order given: Representatives Paul J. Kilday, Sam Rayburn, Wright Patman, John E. Lyle, Jr. (all Democrats of Texas), and George M. Rhodes (D.-Penn.); *Congressional Record*, 83rd Cong., 2nd sess. (June 8, 1954): 7844–7845; Rhodes in ibid. (June 16, 1954): A4453.
4. The best biographical sketch of Maverick is Robert C. Brooks' "One of the Four Hundred and Thirty-Five: Maury Maverick, of Texas," in J. T. Salter, ed., *The American Politician*, pp. 150–174. Maverick's *A Maverick American* contains a wealth of information to that date, but it is widely scattered through the unusual book. See also pamphlet by F. C. Chabot, *The Mavericks*; Oswald Garrison Villard, "Pillar of Government: Maury Maverick," *Forum* 95 (June 1936): 295; Hamilton Basso, "Maury Maverick: A Portrait," *New Republic* 90 (April 21, 1937): 315; Stanley High, "The Neo-New Dealers," *Saturday Evening Post* 209 (May 22, 1937): 10; Audrey Granneberg, "Maury Maverick's San Antonio," *Survey Graphic* 28 (July 1939): 420; "Fortune Faces," *Fortune* 32 (Oct. 1945): 274; Anna Rothe, ed., *Current Biography*, pp. 454–458; Green Peyton, *San Antonio: City in the Sun*, pp. 31 and 164–193.
5. See Mary A. Maverick, *Memoirs*, p. 123, for the "true account" of the origin of the term.
6. Rena Maverick Green, ed., *Samuel Maverick, Texan: 1803–1870*, pp. 9–19.
7. Ibid., pp. 18–20.
8. Ibid., pp. 21–45.
9. Ibid., pp. 48–49.
10. John Mason Brown, "Samuel Augustus Maverick," *Encyclopedia of the New West*, ed. William S. Speer, p. 237. See also George Cupples, *Eulogy on the Life and Character of Hon. Samuel A. Maverick*.
11. See "Historical Letter Written by a Texan in Chains," with additional remarks and research notes by MM, *Congressional Record*, 75th Cong., 3rd sess., 1199–1202.
12. Waddy Thompson, *Recollections of Mexico*, p. 96.
13. MM to Albert Maverick, March 25, 1936, "General Correspondence, 1936," Maury Maverick Papers (hereafter referred to as MMP). After some investigation at Yale University, Maury Maverick was reporting that his grand-

father, like his father and himself, was a poor student but a "colorful" man. See also *A Maverick American*, p. 24.

14. I am indebted for most of the account of Albert's youth to Albert S. Maverick, *A Maverick Abroad*, ed. James S. Maverick, pp. ix–xx, 30–50 and Epilogue, no pagination. See also *A Maverick American*, pp. 22–23, 89; account of Maury family under "Dabney H. Maury," *Dictionary of American Biography*, ed. Dumas Malone, XII, 427 and Chabot, *The Mavericks*, p. 8.

15. John W. Wayland, *The Pathfinder of the Seas: The Life of Matthew Fontaine Maury*, p. 33.

16. *Dictionary of American Biography*, XII, 427.

17. Albert S. Maverick, *A Maverick Abroad*, Epilogue; interviews with Mrs. Walter Prescott Webb (formerly Mrs. Maury Maverick) and Palmer Giles, boyhood friend of MM and rancher near Comfort, Texas.

18. Chabot, *The Mavericks*, p. 8.

19. Mrs. Webb, interview.

20. *A Maverick American*, p. 75.

21. Ibid., p. 20.

22. Notes on the family on a fragment of a book cover, dated Oct. 3, 1896, "Maury-Slayden-Maverick Family Papers," MMP.

23. *A Maverick American*, pp. 50–57.

24. Thus Ellen Maury Slayden, Jane Maverick's sister and a frequent visitor to Sunshine Ranch, described a morning view from the gallery, July 20, 1914, in *Washington Wife*, p. 242.

25. Mrs. Webb, interview.

26. Biographical notes prepared for a newspaper reporter, Feb. 3, 1936, "Gen. Corr., 1936," MMP and Mrs. Webb, interview.

27. *A Maverick American*, p. 50.

28. "Gen. Corr., 1912–1918," MMP.

29. In a political advertisement in *The Bexar Facts*, San Antonio, July 11, 1930.

30. Palmer Giles, interview.

31. Ibid.

32. Albert Maverick to MM, Aug. 29, 1918, "Gen. Corr., 1912–1918," MMP.

33. *A Maverick American*, pp. 74–75.

34. MM to Jane Maverick, Aug. 13, 1935 and Jane Maverick to MM, Aug. 16, 1935, "Gen. Corr., 1932–1935," MMP.

35. He made this remark to me during the association at the Brookings Institution conference described in the Preface. See also, Brooks, "Maury Maverick," p. 153.

36. Quoted by Felix R. McKnight, *Houston Post*, March 30, 1941.

37. *A Maverick American*, p. 58.

38. Ibid.

39. MM so wrote in his copy of Frederick Lewis Allen's *The Big Change*, The University of Texas Library.

40 Robert Hunter, *Poverty*, p. viii.

41. Ibid., pp. 325, 318.

A Maverick American 313

42. Charles Carver, *Brann and the Iconoclast*, p. xi.
43. W. C. Brann, *Brann, the Iconoclast*, ed. J. D. Shaw, I, 3–6.
44. Carver, "Introduction," *Brann*, p. xvii.
45. W. C. Brann, *The Complete Works of Brann, the Iconoclast*, ed. J. D. Shaw, XII, 45.
46. Ibid., pp. 50–79, for reproductions of editorials. The demise of this extraordinary man was more sensational than his life and matches anything concocted by the writers of television westerns. One of Brann's more irate readers, Tom E. Davis, shot him in the back on the streets of Waco in 1898. Brann whirled, drew his gun, and as the two men fired repeatedly, he emptied his six-gun into his assailant. Both men died soon after the shooting; ibid., pp. 4, 33.
47. Brann, *Brann, the Iconoclast*.
48. Letter to George Henry Shoaf, Sept. 23, 1953, "Gen. Corr., Aug.–Dec., 1953," MMP.
49. Brann, *Complete Works*, I, 152–153; Brann blisters the Philadelphia schools for the banning of Victor Hugo's *Les Misérables* on grounds of obscenity.
50. MM's copy of Shaw, ed., *Brann, the Iconoclast*, I, 176.
51. Carver, *Brann*, pp. 43–44.
52. Ibid., pp. xvi, 44–45.
53. *Brann, the Iconoclast*, I, 179, MM's copy in the University of Texas Library.
54. "Books I Have Read," "School Papers: University of Texas," MMP.
55. Ibid.
56. Mrs. Webb, interview.
57. *A Maverick American*, p. 75 and Herbert C. Henderson, "Unbranded Maverick," *Today*, Nov. 21, 1936 (bound copy in University of Texas Library).
58. *A Maverick American*, p. 75.
59. "Private Notes of Albert Maverick," "Maury-Slayden-Maverick Family Papers, Albert Maverick: Notes & Memoranda," MMP.
60. AM to MM, Nov. 19, 1917, "Gen. Corr., 1912–1918," MMP.
61. Henderson, "Unbranded Maverick."
62. *A Maverick American*, p. 28.
63. Vic Niemeyer, "Frustrated Invasion: The Revolutionary Attempt of General Bernardo Reyes from San Antonio in 1911," *Southwestern Historical Quarterly* 67, no. 2 (Oct. 1963): 213.
64. See complete account in letter to the editor by Hobart Huson, Refugio, Texas, *Southwestern Historical Quarterly* 68, no. 3 (Jan. 1964): 435.
65. *A Maverick American*, p. 59.
66. *Who Was Who in America*, I, 1133; see also Walter P. Webb's "Introduction" in Slayden, *Washington Wife*, p. x.
67. *A Maverick American*, pp. 63–64.
68. "Maury Maverick Memory Book," "Scrapbooks: VMI, 1912–1913," MMP.
69. *A Maverick American*, p. 65.
70. Files of the *Daily Texan*, The University of Texas, 1913–1915.
71. Registrar's Office, The University of Texas.

72. Brooks, "Maury Maverick," pp. 153-154.
73. Palmer Giles, interview.
74. *A Maverick American*, ch. IX, p. 68.
75. Walter P. Webb, interview.
76. Letter to the writer, June 22, 1958.
77. *The Blunderbuss*, April 1, 1915, p. 3.
78. Letter to the writer, June 22, 1958.
79. *A Maverick American*, p. 71.
80. Ibid., pp. 66-69.
81. Letter to the writer, Aug. 3, 1958.
82. Wire to MM from Eli Ammons and reply, Aug. 18, 1915, "Gen. Corr., 1912-1918," MMP.
83. Copy of application for a reporter's job with A. H. Belo Company, Dallas, Oct. 8, 1915, "Gen. Corr., 1912-1918," MMP.
84. Vaughn Brant to MM, Sept. 30, 1915, "Gen. Corr., 1912-1918," MMP.
85. See pp. 19-21.
86. Quoted in Mrs. Albert Maverick to MM, September 1916, "Gen. Corr., 1912-1918," MMP.
87. Ellen Slayden to MM, Sept. 9, 1915, "Gen. Corr., 1912-1918," MMP.
88. Mrs. Albert Maverick to MM, Sept. 8 and Oct. 15, 1915, "Gen. Corr., 1912-1918," MMP.
89. Ellen Slayden to MM, Oct. 10, 1915, "Gen. Corr., 1912-1918," MMP.
90. A receipt indicates that he paid his fees on Oct. 19, 1915, "Misc. Notebooks and Diaries—Receipts," MMP.
91. *A Maverick American*, p. 67.
92. Interview with Dr. Green, June 20, 1958.
93. Letter to the writer from Dr. Green, June 16, 1958; he is a former dean of several law schools and the author of such works as *The Rationale of Proximate Cause* and *Judge and Jury*.
94. Brooks, "Maury Maverick," p. 154.
95. Webb, *Washington Wife*, pp. x-xiii.
96. Ellen Slayden to MM, July 23, 1916, "Gen. Corr., Jan.-Dec., 1916," MMP.
97. Slayden to MM, March 20 and May 13, 18, 1916; Sheppard to MM, March 20, 22, 1916, "Gen. Corr., Jan.-Dec., 1916," MMP.
98. Palmer Giles, interview.
99. *San Antonio Express*, June 8, 1954, p. 1.
100. Correspondence and military records of MM, "Military Papers: 1917-1920," MMP.
101. Slayden to MM, May 30, 1917, "Gen. Corr., 1912-1918," MMP.
102. *A Maverick American*, p. 116.
103. Order of the Division Commander of the 157th Infantry, Jan. 29, 1918, copy in "Military Papers, 1917-1920," MMP.
104. *A Maverick American*, p. 122.
105. *A Maverick American*, p. 123. See also the typed statement, dated Dec. 30, 1918, which MM apparently dictated while he was recovering from his

wounds, "Narrative of Lieutenant Maury Maverick," "Military Papers, 1917–1918," MMP.

106. MM to Albert Maverick, Sept. 18, 1918, and MM to Mrs. AM, Sept. 26, 1918, "Gen. Corr., 1912–1918," MMP.

107. In Remarque's *All Quiet on the Western Front*.

108. "Narrative of Lieutenant Maury Maverick," "Military Papers, 1917–1918," MMP.

109. Ibid.

110. *A Maverick American*, pp. 124–125.

111. Original date Sept. 6, 1918; note appended June 8, 1931, "Military Papers, 1917–1918," MMP.

112. See pp. 61–62.

113. If one may judge by his liquor bill during a four-day stay at the Hotel Bellevue, Nov. 21–24, 1918, "Misc. Notebooks and Diaries—Receipts," MMP.

114. *A Maverick American*, pp. 140–141 and record of discharge, "Military Papers, 1917–1920," MMP.

115. General Order No. 1, Jan. 1, 1940, by command of Maj. Gen. Summerall, "Mil. Papers, 1917–1920," MMP.

116. Letters to various priests in Dublin, May 4, 1919, "Gen. Corr., 1919–1920," MMP.

117. Letter to Mrs. AM, March 3, 1919, "Gen. Corr., 1919–1920," MMP.

118. The account of this trip is pieced together from hotel bills, jottings on personal cards, receipts, and copies of books mentioned in "Misc. Notebooks and Diaries—Receipts," MMP.

119. Mrs. AM to MM, March 18, 1919, "Gen. Corr., 1919–1920," MMP.

120. Mrs. AM to MM, March 29, 1919, "Gen. Corr., 1919–1920," MMP.

121. Mrs. Webb, interview.

122. *Washington Wife*, p. xix.

123. Ibid.

124. Mrs. Webb, interview.

125. Quoted in "This is Texas," *Houston Post* supplement, Jan. 29, 1961.

126. MM to MM, Jr., April 4, 1937, "Gen. Corr., 1937–1938," MMP.

127. MM, Jr., to MM, Dec. 4, 193[6], "Gen. Corr., 1936," MMP.

CHAPTER 2. THE BOOTLEG DECADE

1. *A Maverick American*, pp. 143–145 and *The Whereas*, Dec. 13, 1921, "Printed Material, Legal Documents," MMP.

2. Ibid., p. 145.

3. Mrs. Webb, interview.

4. *A Maverick American*, p. 146.

5. Ibid.

6. See black, looseleaf notebook in "Misc. Notebooks and Diaries, 1924–1953," MMP.

7. Inside front cover of MM's copy of James Q. Dealey, *Sociology, Its Development and Applications*, The University of Texas Library.

8. "Grand Jury Notebook," MMP.
9. Ibid.
10. See p. 11.
11. *A Maverick American*, pp. 235-236.
12. Ibid., pp. 236-237.
13. See "Washington Day Speech," "Speeches: 1920; 1930-1932," and "Gen. Corr., 1932-1935," MMP.
14. "Funny Stuff," campaign speech, Aug. 20, 1934, "Speeches: 1934-1935," MMP.
15. "Literary Productions, 1930-1939," MMP.
16. See p. 239.
17. *A Maverick American*, p. 231.
18. Nov. 6, 1914, and Nov. 7, 1914.
19. This item appears to have been a speech by MM. The only identifying data on the set of yellow, typed sheets is a penciled note in MM's handwriting, "Sometime in 1920's," "Speeches, 1920; 1930-1932," MMP.
20. *Daily Texan*, Feb. 27, 1923.
21. *Austin American*, May 8, 1923.
22. Ibid., May 13, 1923.
23. *Daily Texan*, May 25, 1923.
24. Ibid., May 26, 1922.
25. Ibid., Nov. 7, 1922.
26. Ibid., Dec. 16, 17, 1924.
27. Ibid., Feb. 8, 1922, and Jan. 12, 1923.
28. Ibid., Aug. 2, 4, 8, 1921.
29. Brooks, "Maury Maverick," pp. 157-158.
30. Letter from the Office of the President, The University of Chicago, Dec. 29, 1938; the signature is indecipherable, "Gen. Corr., 1937-1938," MMP.
31. "A Fiery Texan," *New York Sun*, June 26, 1937.
32. In Horace J. Bridges, ed., *Erasmus: In Praise of Folly*. Other works were J. A. Froude, *Life and Letters of Erasmus*; John A. Faulkner, *Erasmus: His Life and Character*; J. Huizinga (trans. by F. Hopman), *Erasmus*; Ephraim Emerton, *Desiderius Erasmus*, and Erasmus, *The Praise of Folly*. All of these works are in The University of Texas Library.
33. Smith, *Erasmus*, p. 441, MM's copy in University of Texas Library.
34. Walter P. Webb, introducing MM at a meeting of the Texas Historical Association, April 28, 1950, copy in "Misc. Materials—not by Maverick," MMP.
35. Interview with Prof. Arnold Ben Wacker, July 1, 1958.
36. Mrs. Webb, interview.
37. MM to H. L. Mencken, Feb. 10, 1928 and reply, Feb. 14, 1928, "Gen. Corr., 1926-1931," MMP. MM and Mencken became acquainted when MM sent the Baltimore writer materials for his *The American Language*; see note dated Aug. 15, 1924, "Gen. Corr., 1923-1924," MMP. The two men eventually met at the Democratic National Convention in Houston in 1928.
38. "Lt. Harrick" manuscript in three fragments in "Literary Productions: to 1930," MMP.

The Bootleg Decade 317

39. MM's copy in The University of Texas Library.

40. *Express,* Nov. 16, 1924. The articles were sometimes not identified, but examples were Percy A. Hutchinson, "Anatole France, Stylist and Satirist," *Literary Digest International Book Review,* Nov. 1924, pp. 851–852; John Macy, "Master Anatole," *Nation,* Nov. 25, 1924, p. 487; Robert Littell, "Anatole France," *New Republic,* Nov. 5, 1924, p. 250.

41. "Anatole France, the Internationalist," November 24, 1924, publication not identified, copy inserted in MM's copy of *The Latin Genius.*

42. See *A Maverick American,* pp. 303–304, for a particularly good example.

43. The judgments expressed or implied in the foregoing paragraph are based upon a careful examination of the books in MM's library, a similar examination of all of his correspondence, and many conversations with Mrs. Webb and MM, Jr.

44. Some of the works that Maverick marked with the dates on which he read them, but in which he made no notations, were Niccolo Machiavelli, *The Prince;* The *Meditations of Marcus Aurelius,* intro. by W. H. D. Rouse; P. J. Proudhon, *Proudhon's Solution of the Social Problem,* intro. by Henry Cohen; Charles Cotton, trans., *The Essays of Michel de Montaigne,* 3 vols.; John Ruskin, *Ruskin's Views of Social Justice;* H. I. Woolf, ed. and trans., *Voltaire's Philosophical Dictionary;* Oscar Levy, ed., *The Complete Works of Friedrich Nietzsche.* (Inside the front cover of the latter volume Maverick jotted a note to himself to reread a criticism of Schopenhauer, but he did not identify the piece); and the works concerning Erasmus noted above. There were, of course, many works in Maverick's library not marked in any fashion; virtually all the significant philosophers were represented.

45. Albert J. Nock, *Jefferson,* p. 117.

46. Jefferson to John Adams, April 11, 1823, "Memorial Edition," XV, 429.

47. Quoted in "A Gentleman With a Duster" (pseudonym of an English novelist, Harold Begbie), *Painted Windows: Studies in Religious Personality,* p. 82. MM then read L. P. Jacks' *Religious Perplexities.*

48. George Bernard Shaw, "Preface on the Prospects of Christianity," *Androcles and the Lion,* p. xxxvii.

49. Ibid., p. ci.

50. Upton Sinclair, ed., *The Cry for Justice,* pp. 210–211.

51. Ibid., in the order mentioned, pp. 233, 466, 466, 129, 630, 788, 453, 756.

52. Ralph Waldo Emerson, *Essays,* p. 56–57.

53. Ibid., p. 63. Among other works which Maverick indicated he was reading in this precongressional period were: Helen M. and R. S. Lynd, *Middletown;* Ernest J. Hopkins, *Our Lawless Police,* a study of police brutality and other violations of procedural rights; James Harvey Robinson, *The Humanizing of Knowledge;* W. E. Woodward, *George Washington: The Image and the Man;* A. V. Dalrymple, *Liberty Dethroned,* an indictment of the Ku Klux Klan; *Memoirs of Benvenuto Cellini,* ed. Ernest Rhys; *The Social and Economic Views of Mr. Justice Brandeis,* ed. Alfred Lief; A. Edward Newton, *The Amenities of Book Collecting;* Edward Creasy, *The Fifteen Decisive Battles of the World;* James Truslow Adams, *The Epic of America* (Maury wrote in criticism inside

the front cover, "The only vision of the American Businessman has been the lining of his pockets"); Norman Thomas, *Is Conscience a Crime*; Stefan Zweig, *Joseph Fouche: The Portrait of a Politician*; and Charles A. Beard, *America Faces the Future*. Maverick was also reading Sigmund Freud and Havelock Ellis at this time, but he did not specify which works, and the books were not in his library. Letter to H. L. Mencken, Feb. 10, 1928 and letter to Dhan Gopal Mukerji, March 22, 1928, "Gen. Corr., 1926–1931," MMP.

54. See inside front cover of Tagore's *The Gardner*; MM's copy in The University of Texas Library.

55. "Literary Productions: to 1930," MMP.

56. Fragment of "Harrick" manuscript, p. 5, MMP.

57. Ibid., p. 4.

58. For which he earned the comment: "He has a way of discovering factors which have escaped men of less realistic perspective and less penetrating vision," in Edward M. Sait's review of Holcombe's *The Middle Class in American Politics* in *The American Political Science Review* 35 (Feb. 1941): 145.

59. Undated speech (about 1928), "Speeches: 1920: 1930–1932," MMP.

60. Ibid.

61. MM to Dr. Harvey Cushing, Harvard Medical School, July 27, 1929, "Gen. Corr., 1926–1931," MMP.

62. Daniel J. Boorstin, *The Genius of American Politics*, p. 1; for the New Deal, see pp. 20 and 178.

63. Letter to the writer, July 7, 1958; Schlesinger once assisted MM with the preparation of speeches and reports in the War Production Board days of World War II.

64. Boorstin, *Genius of American Politics*, pp. 20 and 26.

65. MM to the late Dhan Gopal Mukerji, March 22, 1928, "Gen. Corr., 1926–1931," MMP. Mukerji was the author of *My Brother's Face, A Son of India Answers*, and a number of other books.

66. The paper was edited by Donovan Weldon; in order to appreciate the title, one must know that "Bexar" is rendered as "bare" in the local San Antonio pronunciation of the Spanish word.

67. Green Peyton, *San Antonio: City in the Sun*, p. 177.

68. *The Bexar Facts*, January 24, 1930.

69. Ibid., July 25, 1930; see also in the same issue a note on an Associated Press Dispatch of July 16 that referred to poll-tax conditions in Hidalgo County as "worse than Bexar county."

70. E. B. Chambers, brother of Mayor C. M. Chambers, was indicted for conspiring with leaders of a bootleg ring while he was an assistant district attorney in Bexar County; *The Bexar Facts*, December 13, 1929.

71. Ibid., February 12, 1930.

72. Ibid., May 23, 1930.

73. Ibid., April 25, 1930.

74. Ibid., December 20, 1929.

75. Ibid., December 27, 1929.

76. This issue is actually dated "January 3, *1929*," but it is certainly a misprint.
77. *The Bexar Facts*, January 17, 1930.
78. Ibid., January 24, 1930.
79. *Light*, Feb. 21, 1930. See also an advertisement in *The Bexar Facts*, Feb. 28, 1930.
80. Ibid., February 21, 1930.
81. "Scrapbook, 1928–1931," MMP.
82. Ibid., March 1–7, 1930. See also the *Light*, February 28, March 1 and March 8. In the March 7 issue of *Facts*, the editor printed the text of a telegram to William Randolph Hearst in which he praised the *Light* for "objective" coverage of the event that other papers had "attempted to cover up."
83. *The Bexar Facts*, April 11, 1930.
84. Ibid., May 5 and May 16.
85. Ibid., June 27, 1930.
86. Ibid., May 16, 1930.
87. Ibid., May 23, 1930. Members of the nominating committee were Guy S. McFarland, William Aubrey, R. J. Boyle, Marshall Hicks, F. C. Davis, Joe S. Sheldon, Henry Hirschberg, D. S. Davenport, G. J. Lucchese, Walter W. McAllister, and M. L. Roark.
88. Ibid., June 6, 1930.
89. Letter to Ernest Brown, San Antonio banker, June 14, 1930, "Gen. Corr., 1926–1931," MMP.
90. Ibid.
91. Ibid., July 25, 1930.
92. Ibid., August 1, 1930.
93. *Light*, December 10, 1930.
94. Chabot, *The Mavericks*, pp. 7–8; Peyton, *San Antonio*, p. 185.
95. *Evening News*, May 9, 1931.
96. Memorandum, May 16, 1931, "Gen. Corr., 1926–1931," MMP.
97. *A Maverick American*, p. 150.
98. See correspondence in Nov., 1932 in "Gen. Corr., 1932–1935," MMP.
99. Copy of statement from Governor Ross Sterling in "Diga Colony and Relief," MMP.
100. See complete records in "Diga Colony and Relief," MMP.
101. Letter to MM, Nov. 26, 1932, "Diga Colony and Relief," MMP.
102. "Diga and Relief," MMP.
103. Maverick explained that the name "Diga" was an anagram of the letters from "Agricultural and Industrial Democracy," which was in turn inspired by the League for Industrial Democracy. There was also the notion that the people might "dig" themselves out of their predicament. *A Maverick American*, p. 169.
104. MM to Robert Kelso, Reconstruction Finance Corporation, c/o Governor Ross Sterling, Dec. 12, 1932, "Diga and Relief," MMP.
105. Just how many cars he obtained is not certain. The Colony inventory

shows only twenty-three; one contemporary account said twenty-seven; and Maverick said there were "forty or more." *A Maverick American*, p. 167.
106. Ibid.
107. Interview with Dr. Montgomery, professor emeritus of economics, The University of Texas, Aug. 21, 1966.
108. "Diga and Relief," MMP.
109. *A Maverick American*, p. 167.
110. "Diga and Relief," MMP.
111. Quoted in the *Express*, Dec. 11, 1932.
112. Jan. 29, 1933.
113. Feb. 7, 1933.
114. *Semi-Weekly Farm News*, Dallas, March 24, 1933.
115. See the first in a series of reports, "Unemployment and Community Action," *Survey* 68 (Nov. 15, 1932): 612.
116. See first of a series in *Monthly Labor Review* 36 (March 1933): 449.
117. *A Maverick American*, p. 170.
118. Ibid., p. 172.
119. Ibid., p. 173.
120. Ibid., pp. 172–176.
121. Ibid., pp. 150–166; MM to Sterling, Dec. 15, 1932, "Diga and Relief," MMP; *Houston Chronicle* account of the trip, Dec. 31, 1932.
122. "Woodlawn Lake Speech," 1934, "Speeches: 1934–1935," MMP.
123. Oswald Garrison Villard, "Pillar of Government, Maury Maverick," *Forum* 95 (June 1936): 354.
124. Peyton, *San Antonio*, p. 173.
125. Interview with Malcolm Bardwell, San Antonio; he was long associated with MM as his assistant in the tax collector's office, Congress and the Smaller War Plants Corporation in World War II.
126. Letter to Lewis Terrell, Seattle, March 17, 1930, "Gen. Corr., 1926–1931," MMP.
127. Speech at Ford Hall Forum, Boston, April 25, 1937, "Speeches: 1936–1938," MMP.
128. *A Maverick American*, p. 84.
129. MM to Forrest Bailey, ACLU, Jan. 22, 1931, "Subject Corr., ACLU," MMP.
130. Malcolm Bardwell, interview.
131. MM to Forrest Bailey, March 5, 1931, "Subj. Corr., ACLU," MMP.
132. MM to Bailey, March 5, 1931, "Subj. Corr., ACLU," MMP.
133. Bailey to MM, March 9, 1931, "Subj. Corr., ACLU," MMP.
134. MM to William McGraw, March 31, 1931, "Gen. Corr., 1926–1931," MMP.
135. MM to Sen. J. W. Hornsby, April 10, 1931, and Bailey, same date, "Subj. Corr., ACLU," MMP.
136. Letter to Hornsby, April 10, 1931, MMP.
137. See correspondence with Bailey, Oct. 1928, "Subj. Corr., ACLU," MMP; with Arthur Garfield Hays, March 1951; with Bruce Bliven and Thomas Sanc-

ton of *New Republic*, Sept. 1953 and June 1945; with MM, Jr., Nov. 8, 1943 in "Gen. Corr." of appropriate years, MMP.

138. Letter to MM, Jr., April 30, 1945, "Gen. Corr., Jan.–Dec. 1945," MMP.
139. MM, Jr., interview.
140. *Express*, June 9, 1954.
141. Mrs. Webb, interview.
142. *A Maverick American*, p. 147.
143. MM to Mrs. AM, Jan. 17, 1935, "Gen. Corr., 1932–1935," MMP.
144. "Private Notes of Albert Maverick," 287 and 301, "Maury-Slayden-Maverick Family Papers, Albert Maverick: Notes & Memoranda," MMP.
145. Quin in the *Express*, Aug. 18, 1934, and Davis in the *Light*, July 21, 1934.
146. Copy in "Scrapbook-1934," MMP.
147. *Dallas News*, Aug. 27, 1934.
148. The course of MM's critical operation and recovery is discussed in Albert Maverick's "Notes," MMP; *A Maverick American*, p. 148; *San Antonio Evening News*, Dec. 26, 1934; and MM to Mrs. AM, Jan. 17, 1935, "Gen. Corr., 1932–1935," MMP.
149. *A Maverick American*, p. 148.

CHAPTER 3. MAURY AND HIS MAVERICKS

1. Mrs. Webb, interview.
2. Mrs. Webb, interview. A set of the weight charts is in "Misc. Notes & Memoranda, 1917–1954," MMP.
3. A news feature on the House barbershop expressed the view that MM had the "most unruly hair on the Hill." *Washington Times*, Feb. 4, 1936.
4. J. August Wolf, "Sketches from Life," *St. Louis Post-Dispatch Magazine*, July 16, 1935; copy in "Cong. Scrapbook No. 1," MMP.
5. *A Maverick American*, p. 11.
6. *Richmond Times Dispatch*, July 28, 1936, editorial; Heywood Broun in the *Washington News*, July 9, 1937; Franklyn Waltman, *Philadelphia Record*, Aug. 2, 1938; *New York Herald Tribune*, May 29, 1941, editorial; *New York Sun*, June 26, 1937, book review.
7. *Dallas News*, July 28, 1937, editorial; see also notes from a close friend, the late Walter Karig, with accompanying penned cartoon in MMP.
8. Brooks, "Maury Maverick," p. 151; John Janney, "Texas Firebrand," *American Magazine* 130 (Sept. 1940): 23, 70.
9. Cecil B. Dickson, in the *Seattle Post Intelligencer*, March 21, 1937.
10. Brooks, "Maury Maverick," p. 151.
11. Letter to the writer from Jerry Voorhis, friend and MM's colleague in the House of Representatives, July 1, 1958; letter to the writer from Jonathan Daniels, editor of the *News and Observer* (Raleigh), June 18, 1958.
12. Harry S. Truman, interview, Sept. 5, 1958.
13. Edward Bergin, ed., *Burke's Speeches at Bristol*, pp. 142–143. Professor Brooks said that Maverick *probably* was not familiar with Burke's view, but this

does not seem likely in view of the Texas congressman's vast reading; see Brooks, "Maury Maverick," pp. 163-164.

14. Radio speech over station KTSA, San Antonio, July 24, 1934, MMP.
15. Draft in Maverick Papers; speech in *Congressional Record*, 74th Cong., 1st sess. (March 6, 1935): 3040-3042.
16. *Congressional Record*, 75th Cong., 2nd sess. (May 12, 1938): 6807.
17. *Philadelphia Record*, July 26, 1938.
18. "Fortune Faces," Fortune 32 (Oct., 1945): 274.
19. See the hilarious discussion of some of his admitted demagoguery in *A Maverick American*, pp. 182-187.
20. Ibid.
21. Villard, "Pillar of Government," p. 354.
22. "Maverick's Advice to New Congressmen," *New Republic* 120 (Jan. 17, 1949): 20.
23. High, "The Neo-New Dealers," p. 10.
24. Editorial in *News and Courier* (Charleston, S.C.), Aug. 11, 1936.
25. On the other hand, he once offered his colleagues an eight-page disquisition comparing the British and American legislative processes to accompany his argument for permitting American cabinet officers to appear on the floor of Congress; *Congressional Record*, 75th Cong., 2nd sess. (Dec. 10, 1937): 1292-1300.
26. *Congressional Record*, 74th Cong., 2nd sess. (Feb. 21, 1936): 2608-2609.
27. *Congressional Record*, 75th Cong., 1st sess. (March 3, 1937): 575. Other reviews in ibid., Jan. 12, 1937, Appendix, p. 60; Feb. 17, 1937, Appendix, pp. 245-247; June 1, 1937, Appendix, pp. 1587-1588 and 1589 (two reviews).
28. The original draft of the review and the correspondence is in a file in MMP.
29. *Baltimore Evening Sun*, Oct. 2, 1937. Max Lerner found that Lippmann had "bungled" the "dissection of collectivism," and that he had clothed "incredibly naive statements with a magisterial solemnity"; in "Lippmann Agonistes," *Nation* 145 (Nov. 27, 1937): 589. Lewis Browne said that *The Good Society* contained "contradictions so massive as to be intellectually discreditable" to a man of Lippmann's attainments; in "Mr. Lippmann's Heresy Hunt," *New Republic* 80 (Sept. 29, 1937): 219. Norman Cousins found nothing new in the book and opined that Lippmann's strong points were no more than a matter of grace, skill and facility for persuasion. "*The Good Society*," said Cousins, "should cement the ties to all the author's present friends;" *Current History* 47 (Nov. 1937): 14-16.
30. Herbert Little, *Washington News*, June 26, 1937; review of *A Maverick American*.
31. MM, Jr., interview.
32. Walter P. Webb. See note on Rep. Henry B. Gonzales in Willie Morris, *North Toward Home*, p. 222.
33. "Jefferson in Bowers," *New Republic* 88 (Oct. 21, 1936): 317.
34. Undated copy in "Cong. Scrapbook No. 1," MMP.

35. Letter to MM, no date, from A. B. Smith and reply, Dec. 27, 1937, "Gen. Corr., 1937–1938," MMP.
36. *New York Times*, March 22, 1935, 4: 6.
37. Memorandum, Sept. 17, 1951, "Gen. Corr., June–Sept., 1951," MMP.
38. Obituary in *Proceedings of the Philosophical Society of Texas* 19 (Dec. 4, 1954): 18–20.
39. "Business Hand from the Rio Grande," March 1944, p. 36.
40. Introduction by Charles A. Henderson, the Atwater Kent Foundation, to MM's article, "Maverick's Advice to New Congressmen," *New Republic* 120 (Jan. 17, 1949): 20.
41. Letter to the writer, June 16, 1958; Mrs. Roosevelt was associated with Maverick in his work with prison industries on the War Production Board of World War II.
42. Interview, Sept. 5, 1958.
43. "Speech at CIO—Galveston," "Speeches: 1936–1938," MMP.
44. Mrs. Webb, interview.
45. MM to Joe E. Brown, Oct. 17, 1945, "Gen. Corr., Jan.–Dec., 1945," MMP.
46. Interview, July 1, 1958; MM, Jr., with equal candor, has said approximately the same thing.
47. *Congressional Record*, 74th Cong., 2nd sess. (Feb. 6, 1936): 1663.
48. Sigrid Arne, "Washington Off the Record," *Allentown* (Penn.) *Call*, July 28, 1935.
49. Sometime in 1936, "Gen. Corr., 1936," MMP.
50. Karig to MM, July 2, 1936, "Gen. Corr., 1936," MMP.
51. Lionel V. Patenaude, "The New Deal and Texas," Ph.D. dissertation, University of Texas, 1953, p. 93. This study indicates an exhaustive examination of sources dealing with the influence of Texans on the New Deal and the operations of the New Deal in Texas.
52. *New York Times Index*, 1935, pp. 216 and 1680.
53. "Congressional Scrapbook No. 1," MMP.
54. Schlesinger, *The Coming of the New Deal*, p. 554.
55. Mrs. Webb, interview.
56. March 10, 1935; see also *New York World-Telegram*, March 10, 1935.
57. Letter to the writer, June 2, 1958, from Aubrey W. Williams, editor of the *Southern Farmer* and formerly executive director of the National Youth Administration and Deputy Administrator of the Works Progress Administration in the New Deal.
58. *Washington Herald*, March 10 and 16, 1935.
59. *Washington Star*, March 13, 1935.
60. *Congressional Record*, 74th Cong., 1st sess. (March 14, 1935): 3629–3631.
61. *New York Times*, March 15, 1935, 1.
62. *Washington Times*, March 15, 1935.
63. *Congressional Record*, 74th Cong., 1st sess. (March 14, 1935): 3659–3661. MM's hometown paper, the *San Antonio Express*, reported in its news columns that the group was "figuratively yanked onto the House floor for what was in-

tended as a public spanking," under the headline "Maverick Flirts with House Pinks, Struts across Floor while Replying to Attack on Newly Formed Group."

64. *Congressional Record,* 74th Cong., 1st sess. (March 15, 1935): 3729–3731.
65. *New York Times,* March 17, 1935, 33.
66. Ibid. See also *Washington Post,* March 10, 1935.
67. *Congressional Record,* 74th Cong., 1st sess. (March 14, 1935): 3629.
68. *New York Times,* March 20, 1935, 4: 2.
69. *New York Times,* April 14, 1935, IV, 10: 6.
70. *Congressional Record,* 74th Cong., 1st sess. (March 22, 1935): 4310–4311.
71. *New York Times,* Jan. 25, 1936, 1: 8 and Jan. 28, 1936, 1: 8.
72. Ruth Finney in *New York World-Telegram,* April 12, 1935; see also the *San Antonio Light,* April 7, 1935.
73. "War and Peace," Nov. 28, 1933, "Speeches: 1933," MMP.
74. "Merchants of Death," July 3, 1934, "Speeches: 1934–1935," MMP.
75. *American Neutrality Policy,* Hearings before the Committee on Foreign Affairs, House of Representatives, 74th Cong., 1st sess. (June 18 and July 30): 1935, 105.
76. *Washington Herald,* Jan. 11, 1935.
77. See *New Republic* 83 (June 19, 1935): 156–157, and MM's comments in *Congressional Record,* 74th Cong., 1st sess. (April 3, 1935): 4953.
78. Ibid., Feb. 12, 1935, p. 1887.
79. Ibid., April 3, 1935, p. 4953.
80. Ibid., April 4, 1935, pp. 5050–5051, 5057.
81. Ibid., April 5, 1935, p. 5155.
82. Ibid., April 6, 1935, p. 5181.
83. *Newsweek* 5 (April 20, 1935): 11; emphasis supplied. See also Ruth Finney, *Washington News,* April 15, 1935.
84. MM's bound copy of his remarks and speeches from *Congressional Record,* 74th Cong., 1st sess., 2347, in The University of Texas Library.
85. Ibid.
86. Robert A. Divine, *The Illusion of Neutrality,* p. 91. Except where otherwise noted, most of this account is taken from Professor Divine's excellent, searching study of neutrality legislation in the 1930's.
87. Ibid., pp. 95–96.
88. *Boston Herald,* August 24, 1935.
89. Oswald Garrison Villard, "Pillar of Government, Maury Maverick," *Forum* 95 (June 1936): 354.
90. *Congressional Record,* 74th Cong., 1st sess. (June 24, 1935): 9983.
91. Ibid., Aug. 21, 1935, p. 13999.
92. *New Republic* 83 (June 19, 1935): 156–157.
93. *New York Times,* May 22, 1935, 9: 1; see also the *News-Week in Business* 28 (June 1, 1935), no pagination, clipping in MMP.
94. *New York Herald-Tribune,* May 25, 1935; also *New York Times,* 1: 4, same date.
95. Benton J. Stong, *Birmingham* (Alabama) *Post,* June 20, 1935. Similar

views were expressed in *New York Times*, May 25, 1935, 1: 4 and the *San Antonio Light*, June 5, 1935.
96. *Congressional Record*, 74th Cong., 1st sess. (July 8, 1935): 10774–10776.
97. Ibid., July 9, 1935, Maverick at pp. 10872–10876; other TVA speeches were in ibid., June 24, 1935, pp. 9980–9985 and June 27, 1935, pp. 10347–10348.
98. *Washington News*, July 10 and 11, 1935. See also *Washington Star*, July 10, 1935. For Roosevelt's objections, see *Washington Post*, June 25, 1935.
99. *Congressional Record*, 74th Cong., 1st sess. (July 11, 1935): 11040 and 11038.
100. Ibid., July 17, 1935.
101. Ibid., pp. 13994–14010.
102. Ibid., p. 13967.
103. *Austin* (Texas) *American*, September 5, 1935. The Guffey coal bill was a controversial piece of New Deal legislation that essentially provided for price stabilization and fair-trade practices in the coal industry.
104. *Washington Daily News*, July 2, 1935.
105. Ibid., Aug. 7, 1935.
106. *New York Herald Tribune*, June 26, 1935.
107. *Washington Times*, July 16, 1935; see also Schlesinger, *Politics of Upheaval*, pp. 316–317.
108. Lilienthal to MM, April 12, 1935, "Gen. Corr., 1932–1935," MMP. The address is printed in MM's extension of remarks in *Congressional Record*, 74th Cong., 1st sess. (April 11, 1935): 5464.
109. FF to MM, June 22, 1935, signed "The Cat," which MM explains in a marginal note as being the result of his having given Frankfurter the sobriquet of "Felix the Cat," during one of their conversations, "Gen. Corr., 1932–1935," MMP.
110. *Washington Times*, July 16, 1935.
111. Schlesinger, *Politics of Upheaval*, pp. 316–317.
112. Ibid., pp. 323–324.
113. Letter to the writer, June 12, 1958.
114. See p. 13.
115. Letter to Charles W. Ervin, Bronxville, N.Y., April 19, 1951, "Gen. Corr., Jan.–May, 1951," MMP.
116. *A Maverick American*, pp. 118–119.
117. See Jean Gould, ed., *Homegrown Liberal: The Autobiography of Charles W. Ervin*.
118. *Book Review Digest*, 1955, p. 284.
119. Mrs. Webb, interview.
120. Letter to Jean Gould, Amalgamated Clothing Workers of America, Feb. 24, 1953, "Gen. Corr., Jan.–Feb., 1953," MMP.
121. MM to Ervin, April 6, 1951, "Gen. Corr., Jan.–May, 1951," MMP.
122. Ervin to MM, April 10, 1951, "Gen. Corr., Jan.–May, 1951," MMP.
123. "The Old Oaken Bigots," speech on radio station KTSA, San Antonio, Aug. 10, 1934, "Speeches: 1934–1935," MMP.

124. *Congressional Record*, 74th Cong., 1st sess. (March 6, 1935): 3040.
125. John P. Roche, "We've Never Had More Freedom," *New Republic* 134 (Jan. 23, 1956): 15. See also Walter Berns, *Freedom, Virtue and the First Amendment*, p. 23.
126. Senate Bill No. 2253, 74th Cong., 1st sess.
127. *Congressional Record*, 74th Cong., 1st sess. (June 24, 1935): 9972.
128. Ibid.
129. *Congressional Record*, 74th Cong., 1st sess. (March 6, 1935): 3041–3042.
130. See correspondence in "Subj. Corr., ACLU," MMP.
131. MM to Swanson, March 29, 1935, "Subj. Corr., ACLU," MMP.
132. Swanson to MM, April 15, 1935, "Subj. Corr., ACLU," MMP.
133. *To Punish for Exerting Mutinous Influence upon the Army and Navy*, H. Rept. 1603, 74th Cong., 1st sess., p. 1.
134. Ibid., "Minority Views," pp. 13–27.
135. *Congressional Record*, 74th Cong., 1st. sess. (July 17, 1935): 11318.
136. Ibid., from the *Newark Evening News*, July 15, 1935.
137. Ibid., July 22, 1935, p. 11608.
138. A comparable story by Jay C. Haydeon appeared in the *Detroit News*, July 16, 1935.
139. "The Dangers of the Military Disaffection Bill," Aug. 1, 1935, "Speeches: 1934–1935," MMP.
140. Letter to MM from Gilbert B. Stinger, Press Relations Director of the National Council for Prevention of War, July 23, 1935, "Subj. Corr., ACLU," MMP.
141. *Congressional Record*, 74th Cong., 1st sess. (Aug. 31, 1935): 12969–12972. MM's collection of clippings demonstrates that he did not exaggerate.
142. "Insulting the Army and Navy," *Baltimore Evening Sun*, undated clipping in "Cong. Scrapbook No. 1," MMP; Maverick's remarks were also quoted with approval by Arthur Krock, *New York Times*, July 24, 1935, 16: 5.
143. H.R. 6247, 74th Cong., 1st sess. (March 5, 1935).
144. See MM's remarks in *Crime to Promote Overthrow of Government*, hearing before subcommittee no. 2 of the Committee on the Judiciary, House of Rep., 74th Cong., 1st sess. (May 22, 1935): 109–120.
145. *Congressional Record*, 74th Cong., 1st sess. (Aug. 19, 1935): 13731.
146. Ibid., Aug. 22, 1935, p. 14204.
147. *Crime to Promote Overthrow of Government*, Hearing before Subcommittee No. 2 of the Committee on the Judiciary on H.R. 4313 and H.R. 6427, 74th Cong., 1st sess., (1935).
148. *Congressional Record*, 74th Cong., 1st sess. (Feb. 20, 1935): 2323–2324.
149. Ibid., Aug. 13, 1935, p. 12969: "Calendar Wednesday" refers to the fact that regular rules of the House call for an opportunity for committee chairmen to call up bills for consideration on Wednesday, but the practice is to pass over Calendar Wednesday and rely upon special rules from the Rules Committee to take up measures.
150. Ibid., June 3, 1935, p. 8601.

151. See passage of H.R. 6670 in ibid., August 5, 1935, pp. 12509–12510; MM's copy in The University of Texas Library.
152. Ibid., June 14, 1935, pp. 9315–9317.
153. *San Antonio Express*, June 1, 1935.
154. *Congressional Record*, 74th Cong., 1st sess. (June 21, 1935): 9886–9888; emphasis supplied.
155. *Nashville Tennessean*, Sept. 1, 1935.
156. *San Antonio Evening News*, September 25, 1935.
157. *San Antonio Light*, October 18 and 19, 1935.
158. *Denver Rocky Mountain News*, November 10, 1935.
159. *Albuquerque Journal*, November 13, 1935.
160. *El Paso Herald*, November 15, 1935.
161. *St. Louis Globe Democrat*, November 26, 1935.
162. "Liberty and the American Liberty League," December 11, 1935, speech to Galveston Open Forum, "Speeches: 1934–1935," MMP.
163. *Houston Press*, December 12, 1935.
164. *San Antonio Light*, December 20, 1935.
165. *New York Herald Tribune*, December 24, 1936.

CHAPTER 4. TWO COWBOYS ARE BETTER THAN ONE

1. William E. Leuchtenburg, *Franklin D. Roosevelt and the New Deal*, p. 170.
2. *New York Times*, Jan. 3, 1936, 2: 5.
3. FDR to MM, Jan. 6, 1936, "Gen. Corr., 1936," MMP.
4. *New York Times*, Jan. 23, 1936, 24: 5.
5. MM to Robert S. Allen, July 10, 1936, "Gen. Corr., 1936," MMP.
6. *Washington Post*, Dec. 31, 1935.
7. *Atlanta Constitution*, Dec. 29, 1935, clipping in "Cong. Scrapbook No. 1," MMP.
8. For comparisons of the two approaches, see *New York Times*, Jan. 4, 1935, 1: 6, and *New York Herald Tribune*, Jan. 5, 1935; *Congressional Record*, 74th Cong., 2nd sess. (Jan. 6, 1936): 87–89 and Divine, *Illusion of Neutrality*, pp. 136–139.
9. Ibid., p. 145.
10. Ibid., pp. 155–157 and *Congressional Record*, 74th Cong., 2nd sess. (Feb. 17, 1936): 2241–2242.
11. Divine, *Illusion of Neutrality*, p. 160.
12. *Express*, Feb. 12, 1936.
13. "The Menace of False Patriotism: Some Reflections on 'Liberty' and on War," *Common Sense*, Jan. 1936, pp. 16–17.
14. Speech to Virginia Press Assoc., Richmond, Jan. 17, 1936, *Congressional Record*, 74th Cong., 2nd sess. (Jan. 20, 1936): 709–711.
15. Town Hall Club, New York, April 20, 1936, "Speeches: 1936–1938," MMP.
16. Quoted in the *Chicago Tribune*, Jan. 2, 1936.

17. "The Gag Threatens!" *Forum* 95 (May, 1936): 295.
18. *Congressional Record*, 74th Cong., 2nd sess. (Jan. 20, 1936): 710; ibid. (Feb. 7, 1936): 1663-1664.
19. Ibid., Jan. 31, 1936, p. 1306.
20. Ibid., Feb. 7, 1936, p. 1663.
21. "The Gag Threatens!" p. 295; emphasis supplied.
22. *Crime to Promote Overthrow of Government*, 74th Cong., 1st sess. (1935): 112-113.
23. Typed draft of "The Gag Threatens!" not in the article as published, "Literary Productions, 1930-1939," MMP.
24. *Congressional Record*, 74th Cong., 2nd sess. (March 4, 1936): 3283.
25. Ibid., pp. 3280-3281; see also *Crime to Promote Overthrow of Government*, 74th Cong., 1st sess. (1935): 113.
26. *Congressional Record*, 74th Cong., 2nd sess. (March 4, 1936): 3269, 3280.
27. *Washington Herald*, Feb. 15, 1936.
28. *Congressional Record*, 74th Cong., 2nd sess. (March 4, 1936): 3279.
29. Ibid., March 10, 1936, pp. 3543-3544.
30. MM's copy in The University of Texas Library, p. 2416.
31. *Congressional Record*, 74th Cong., 2nd sess. (March 4, 1936): 3277.
32. Ibid., March 5, 1936, p. 3354.
33. *Washington Post*, Feb. 1, 1936.
34. Cyrus L. Baldridge, *Americanism—What Is It?* Newspapers in New York and New England commended the Legion committee for the twelve-hundred-word booklet, designed as a prize for school children, that simply elaborated the thesis that "The true American spirit—Americanism—is expressed in a determined and magnificent human struggle to achieve democracy, justice and liberty." See *Congressional Record*, 74th Cong., 2nd sess. (April 28, 1936): 6295 for newspaper accounts and editorials. The entire text of the slim volume was reprinted on pp. 6294-6295.
35. Copy of letter from H. L. Gailaux, director of the National Americanism Commission of the American Legion, to Joseph V. McCabe, commander of the New York County American Legion organization, undated, but sent to MM by McCabe April 28, 1936, "Subj. Corr., ACLU," MMP.
36. See MM's extensive correspondence, identified by penned or penciled notes on each item as "Red Reader" material, "Subj. Corr.," MMP. Speech in *Congressional Record*, 74th Cong., 2nd sess. (April 28, 1936): 6293.
37. McCabe to MM, May 8, 1936, "Subj. Corr., ACLU," MMP.
38. *Congressional Record*, 74th Cong., 2nd sess. (April 28, 1936): 6296
39. 109 U.S. 3 (1883).
40. Mencken to MM, April 13, 1935 and MM to Mencken, April 20, 1935, "Gen. Corr., 1932-1935," MMP.
41. April 23, 1935, "Gen. Corr., 1932-1935," MMP.
42. Mencken to MM, Dec. 7, 1936, "Gen. Corr., 1936," MMP.
43. MM to Mencken, Dec. 10, 1936, "Gen. Corr., 1936," MMP.
44. From copy of draft in Mencken to MM, Dec. 18, 1936, "Subj. Corr., ACLU," MMP.

45. Correspondence between MM and Roger Baldwin, Dec. 1936–May 1937, "Subj. Corr., ACLU," MMP.
46. H.R. 2889, 75th Cong., 1st sess. (Jan. 13, 1937).
47. MM to John F. Finerty, Dec. 11, 1936 and to Mencken, May 23, 1938, "Subj. Corr., ACLU," MMP.
48. Mencken to MM, May 13, 1938, and MM to Mencken, May 23, 1938, "Subj. Corr., ACLU," MMP.
49. *Congressional Record*, 74th Cong., 2nd sess. (Jan. 30, 1936): 1282; ibid. (Jan. 31, 1936): 1300–1303.
50. Ibid., 74th Cong., 1st sess. (July 23, 1935): 11698.
51. Ibid., 2nd sess. (March 19, 1936): 4068–4070.
52. Ibid. (March 27, 1936): 4539.
53. Ibid. (April 15, 1936): 5520–5525.
54. FDR to MM, April 29, 1936, "Age of Roosevelt Scrapbook," MMP.
55. Ickes to MM, April 21, 1936, "Gen. Corr., 1936," MMP.
56. Richmond, May 4, 1936, in *Congressional Record*, 74th Cong., 2nd sess. (May 15, 1936): 7370–7372.
57. Ibid., 74th Cong., 1st sess. (Feb. 20, 1935): 2349.
58. Ibid., 74th Cong., 2nd sess. (April 19, 1936): 5268–5269.
59. For a history and an appraisal of the agency's work, see Charles E. Merriam, "The National Resources Planning Board: A Chapter in American Planning Experience," *American Political Science Review* 38 (December 1944): 1075–1088.
60. *Washington News*, March 17, 1936.
61. *Congressional Record*, 74th Cong., 2nd sess. (Feb. 21, 1936): 2552.
62. Ibid., April 9, 1936, p. 5287.
63. *Washington Star*, Jan. 7, 1936.
64. *Light*, March 15, 1936.
65. *A Maverick American*, p. 182.
66. *St. Louis Post-Dispatch*, March 15, 1936.
67. Letter and attached note, June 9, 1936, "Subj. Corr., Campaign 1936," MMP.
68. Koppleman to MM, June 20 and Aug. 1, 1936, "Subj. Corr., Campaign 1936," MMP.
69. *Congressional Record*, 74th Cong., 2nd sess. (June 19, 1936): 10064.
70. *Light*, March 16 and 23, 1936.
71. *San Antonio Evening News*, June 12, 1936. Maverick's irreverent wit was contagious. Mrs. Maverick wrote in "Cong. Scrapbook No. 3," MMP, opposite the Alamo pictures, "Maury—so modest and unobtrusive," and where FDR was caught with his fingers on the bridge of his nose, she jotted, "Someone suggested the title of this picture should be 'It Smells.' "
72. FDR to MM, July 10, 1936. MM apparently used this note in one of his campaign speeches, because it was originally attached to a copy of a speech he made over station KTSA, San Antonio, July 11, 1936. See "Subj. Corr., Campaign 1936" and "Speeches: 1936–1938," MMP.
73. *Light*, June 14, 1936.

74. MM to Corcoran, June 18, 1936, "Gen. Corr., 1936," MMP.
75. Pearson to MM, July 8, 1936, "Subj. Corr., Campaign 1936," MMP.
76. "Cong. Scrapbook No. 3," MMP.
77. Corcoran to MM, July 14, 1936, "Subj. Corr., Campaign 1936," MMP.
78. Ickes to MM, June 29, 1936, "Gen. Corr., 1936," MMP.
79. MM to Ickes, June 30, 1936, "Gen. Corr., 1936," MMP.
80. Ickes to MM, July 7, 1936, "Subj. Corr., Campaign 1936," MMP.
81. See pp. 138–140.
82. *Light*, July 9, 1936.
83. *Light*, July 11, 1936.
84. *A Maverick American*, pp. 184–185.
85. Campaign speech, KTSA, July 11, 1936, "Speeches: 1936–1938," MMP.
86. MM to Walter Karig, Aug. 1, 1936, "Gen. Corr., 1936," MMP.
87. *Light*, July 11, 1936.
88. *San Antonio News*, July, 1936.
89. *Washington News*, July 16, 1936.
90. *Washington News*, July 20, 1936.
91. *San Antonio News*, July 28, 1936.
92. FDR to MM, Aug. 5, 1936, "Age of Roosevelt Scrapbook," MMP. It appears that Tullis was attempting to get another job and Maverick was determined to block it.
93. *Baltimore Evening Sun*, July 29, 1936; *Des Moines Register*, Aug. 1; *Newport (Va.) News Press*, Aug. 3; *Richmond Times-Dispatch*, July 28; *Pittsburgh Press*, Aug. 2 and *Houston Chronicle*, July 31.
94. *Evening Sun*, July 29, 1936; the editorial was probably written by MM's friend, H. L. Mencken. Much the same view was expressed in an editorial in Virginius Dabney's *Richmond Times-Dispatch*, July 28, 1936.
95. "It Seems to Me," *Daily News*, July 30, 1936.
96. Farley to MM, Aug. 13, 1936, "Gen. Corr., 1936," MMP.
97. See, for example, his criticisms of the leadership in the Democratic Party in *Congressional Record*, 74th Cong., 2nd sess. (May 7, 1936): 6854–6856.
98. Undated note from Frank to MM, "Gen. Corr., 1937–1938," (probably misfiled), MMP.
99. *Dallas News*, Sept. 12, 1936.
100. See account in *New York Herald Tribune*, May 5, 1935.
101. See *Daily Texan*, resumé, "Maverick Champions Texan's Civil Liberties," Aug. 6, 1936.
102. *Texan*, June 21, 1936; June 25, July 9, 1936. See also *Light*, Aug. 4, 1936.
103. *Texan*, Aug. 6, 1936 and *New York Times*, Aug. 5, 1936, 17: 7.
104. *Texan*, Aug. 6, 1936.
105. *Texan*, Aug. 9, 13, 1936, and Nov. 10, 1936.
106. *Texan*, Dec. 10, 11, 15, 1936; Feb. 27, 1937; March 7 and June 2, 1937.
107. *San Antonio News*, Oct. 16, 1936; *Express* and *Light*, Oct. 17.
108. *Light* and *Express*, Oct. 17, 1936.
109. *Houston Post*, editorial, Oct. 20, 1936.

Ever Insurgent Let Me Be 331

110. *Houston Press,* Oct. 27, 1936.
111. *Light,* Oct. 29, 1936.
112. Ibid.
113. Ibid., Oct. 30, 1936.
114. Ibid.
115. Ibid.
116. Ibid., Nov. 5, 1936.
117. FF to MM, Nov. 21, 1936, "Gen. Corr., 1936," MMP.
118. *Albuquerque Tribune,* Dec. 2, 1936.
119. *New York Times,* Oct. 29, 1936, 20: 6; *Austin American,* Oct. 28, 29 and Nov. 1, 2, 1936.
120. "I. Congress," *New Republic* 89 (Nov. 25, 1936): 99–101.

CHAPTER 5. EVER INSURGENT LET ME BE

1. Villard, "Pillar of Government, Maury Maverick: A Texas Norther in Congress," *Forum* 95 (June 1936): 354.
2. Hamilton Basso, "Maury Maverick: A Portrait," *New Republic* 90 (April 21, 1937): 315.
3. *Congressional Record,* 75th Cong., 1st sess., Appendix (Feb. 3, 1937): 410.
4. *United States* v. *Butler,* 297 U.S. 1 (1936).
5. *Congressional Record,* 75th Cong., 1st sess. (Feb. 19, 1936): 2392.
6. Ibid., March 4, 1936, pp. 3247–3250. He said much the same in a speech to a student group, "Veterans of Future Wars," at Princeton University, April 17, 1936, copy in "Speeches: 1936–1938," MMP.
7. Interview with MM in *Albuquerque Tribune,* Dec. 2, 1936.
8. *Light,* Jan. 10, 1937.
9. Copy of NBC speech, "Is the General Welfare Constitutional," Jan. 28, 1937, "Speeches: 1936–1938," MMP.
10. Schlesinger, *Politics of Upheaval,* pp. 490–496.
11. MM, *In Blood and Ink,* p. 130.
12. *Washington Star,* Feb. 6, 1937.
13. James McGregor Burns, *Roosevelt: The Lion and the Fox,* p. 294.
14. Ibid., also *San Antonio News,* Feb. 8, 1937, and *New York Times,* Feb. 14, 1937.
15. Undated clipping, *Brooklyn* (N.Y.) *Citizen* in "Cong. Scrapbook No. 3," MMP.
16. *San Antonio News,* Feb. 10, 1937.
17. Quoted in the *Light,* Feb. 22, 1937.
18. Copy of report of "Should the President's Proposals Regarding the Supreme Court be Adopted," America's Town Meeting of the Air, series 2, no. 13, copy in "Speeches: 1936–1938," MMP.
19. *Washington News,* Feb. 19, 1937.
20. *Congressional Record,* 75th Cong., 1st sess. (May 13, 1937): 4508.
21. Speech to Fort Worth Open Forum, Oct. 25, 1937, ibid., Appendix (Nov. 18, 1937): 121–126.

22. Untitled draft of an article, Sept. 20, 1937, for the *National Lawyers Guild Journal*, "Literary Productions: 1930-1939," MMP. See also *A Maverick American*, pp. 310-312.
23. *In Blood and Ink*, pp. 131-132.
24. MM to critic, John I. Palmer, Sagnache, Col., Jan. 18, 1937, "Gen. Corr., 1937-1938," MMP.
25. *A Maverick American*, p. 296; emphasis in the original.
26. Ibid., pp. 297-298.
27. Alpheus T. Mason and William H. Beaney, *The Supreme Court in a Free Society*, pp. 318-319.
28. Speech at Ford Hall Forum, Boston, April 25, 1937, "Speeches: 1936-1938," MMP. See similar views in *A Maverick American*, p. 301 and *In Blood and Ink*, p. 154.
29. Speech at Ford Hall Forum.
30. See pp. 110-112.
31. The complete history of the measure is given in *Congressional Record*, 74th Cong., 2nd sess. (May 4, 1936): 6628-6630, 6639.
32. William A. Slade to MM, Nov. 11, 1935, "Gen. Corr., 1932-1935," MMP.
33. "Subj. Corr., ACLU," MMP.
34. *New York Herald Tribune*, Dec. 1, 1935.
35. See p. 88.
36. *Congressional Record*, 74th Cong., 2nd sess. (Jan. 20, 1936): 711.
37. Ibid., May 4, 1936, pp. 6639-6640.
38. *Washington Times*, April 17, 1936.
39. MM to *Baltimore Sun*, Dec. 10, 1936, "Gen. Corr., 1936," MMP.
40. *Congressional Record*, 75th Cong., 1st sess. (Feb. 8, 1937): 1000-1002.
41. Ibid., (May 4, 1937): 4986-4988.
42. *New York Enquirer*, Jan. 17, 1937.
43. *Boston Chronicle*, Jan. 9, 1937.
44. Undated clipping in "Cong. Scrapbook No. 3," MMP.
45. *Congressional Record*, 75th Cong., 1st sess. (April 15, 1937): 3536-3537.
46. Speech by MM to students at Brandeis University, Nov. 13, 1952, "Speeches: 1952-1954," MMP.
47. *Richmond Times-Dispatch*, April 19, 1937.
48. Speech to International House Students, New York City, Feb., 1938, "Speeches: 1936-1938," MMP.
49. See pp. 111-112.
50. *A Maverick American*, p. 18.
51. *Congressional Record*, 75th Cong., 1st sess. (April 8, 1937): 3284-3286.
52. Ibid., March 17, 1937, pp. 2370-2372.
53. Ibid., May 27, 1937, pp. 5064-5065.
54. Ibid., p. 5079.
55. *Dallas News*, Editorial, Nov. 30, 1937.
56. 16 (May 15, 1937) 12.
57. *A Maverick American*, p. 12.
58. *Time* 29 (May 31, 1937) 83.

59. *Washington Daily News*, July 9, 1937.
60. *Washington Times*, June 26, 1937.
61. *Washington News*, June 26, 1937.
62. Unidentified clipping, "Scrapbook, 'Maverick American,' " MMP.
63. David Warren Ryder, "American Notes," *New English Weekly*, March 12, 1938, p. 85.
64. *Washington Star*, June 26, 1937.
65. Copy in "Scrapbook, 'Maverick American,' " MMP.
66. "Scrapbook, 'Maverick American,' " MMP, which contains all pertinent materials relating to the publication of *A Maverick American*.
67. FDR to MM, June 28, 1937, "Gen. Corr., 1937–1938," MMP.
68. *Congressional Record*, 75th Cong., 1st sess. (June 21, 1937): 6107–6108.
69. *Austin American*, July 28, 1937; *Washington Star*, April 30 and May 4, 1937; *Washington Herald*, May 3, 1937; and *Abilene News Reporter*, especially good article by L. T. Easley, Aug. 4, 1937.
70. *Congressional Record*, 75th Cong., 1st sess., Appendix (May 28, 1937): 1478.
71. Ibid., July 1, 1937, p. 3010; also Aug. 11, 1937, p. 2044.
72. Ibid., Dec. 13, 1937, p. 1407.
73. Quoted in the *Light*, May 16, 1937.
74. *Congressional Record*, 75th Cong., 1st sess. (Feb. 2, 1937).
75. Ibid., June 17, 1937, p. 1517.
76. Interview with MM reported in *The Rattler*, student newspaper, Saint Mary's University, San Antonio, Sept. 30, 1937.
77. *Congressional Record*, 75th Cong., 1st sess. (June 22, 1937): 6163.
78. Ibid., July 2, 1937, pp. 6766–6777. See also *Washington Post*, July 3, 1937.
79. *Express*, July 3, 1937; clipping in "Cong. Scrapbook No. 4," MMP.
80. *Emporia* (Kansas) *Gazette*, July 3, 1937.
81. *New York Times*, July 5, 1937.
82. Quoted in the *Philadelphia Record*, Feb. 24, 1937.
83. *Time* 32 (Aug. 1, 1938): 13.
84. *Congressional Record*, 75th Cong., 2nd sess. (Dec. 13, 1937): 1411.
85. Ibid., Dec. 17, 1937, p. 1812.
86. Ibid., 75th Cong., 1st sess., Appendix (July 9, 1937): 2009.
87. *Baltimore Sun*, editorial, Aug. 26, 1937.
88. Speech to National Lawyers Guild (of which Maverick was a member) in *Congressional Record*, 75th Cong., 1st sess., Appendix (June 29, 1937): 1648.
89. *Dallas News*, editorial, January 16, 1937.
90. *Literary Digest* 123 (March 27, 1937): 8.
91. Rodney Dutcher in the *Chilicothe* (Ohio) *News-Advertiser*, Feb. 18, 1937.
92. Villard, "Pillar of Government," *Forum* 95 (June 1936): 354.
93. "Honesty," in the *Light*, November 19, 1937.
94. *Congressional Record*, 75th Cong., 1st sess. (Feb. 18, 1937): 1376.
95. Ibid., April 30, 1937, p. 4057.
96. Ibid., May 14, 1937, p. 4617.
97. *London Times-Mirror*, Leesburg, Virginia, April 22, 1937.

98. *Gloucester* (Virginia) *Gazette*, April 22, 1937.
99. *New York Times*, April 26, 1937, 21: 2; *Literary Digest*, May 8 and 9, 1937, and many others in "Cong. Scrapbook No. 4," MMP.
100. Quoted in the *Washington Star*, April 29, 1937.
101. *Saturday Evening Post* 209 (May 22, 1937) 10.
102. Clipping of Lippmann column, identified only by the notation, "early May, 1937," "Cong. Scrapbook No. 4," MMP.
103. *Congressional Record*, 75th Cong., 1st sess., Appendix (April 6, 1937): 725.
104. Ibid., May 14, 1937, p. 4616.
105. *Peoria Journal Transcript*, June 6, 1937. See many clippings in "Cong. Scrapbook No. 4," MMP.
106. *Congressional Record*, 75th Cong., 1st sess. (July 23, 1937): 7542.
107. Ibid. (June 2, 1937): 5244.
108. "Cong. Scrapbook No. 4," MMP.
109. Ibid., June 21, 1937, p. 6104.
110. *Washington Herald*, June 22, 1937.
111. "Washington Merry-Go-Round," *Washington Herald*, June 23, 1937; see also *Philadelphia Record*, June 17, 1937, for Stephen Early's statement concerning charges of aloofness of FDR.
112. *Light*, June 23, 1937.
113. *New York Herald Tribune*, June 24, 1937.
114. *Philadelphia Record*, June 24, 1937.
115. *Washington Daily News*, June 25, 1937.
116. Ibid.
117. *Washington Post*, June 26, 1937.
118. News story on the Jefferson Island meeting, written by MM for the United Press, *Washington Daily News*, June 26, 1937.
119. *Washington Post*, June 26, 1937.
120. MM's story, *Washington Daily News*, June 26, 1937.
121. Radford Mobley, "The Man of the Week," *Progressive*, June 26, 1937.
122. *Washington Daily News*, Nov. 20, 1937.
123. *Washington Star*, June 26, 1937.
124. *Time* 30 (Aug. 30, 1937) 14. See similar report in *Saturday Evening Post* 209 (Oct. 9, 1937): 24.
125. NBC Red Network, July 31, 1937, reprinted in *Congressional Record*, 75th Cong., 1st sess., Appendix (Aug. 9, 1937): 2095.
126. Ibid., August 19, 1937, pp. 9408–9409.
127. *Philadelphia Record*, Aug. 28, 1937.
128. *Congressional Record*, 75th Cong., 2nd sess. (November 18, 1937): 148.
129. Ibid., Dec. 10, 1937, pp. 1292–1300.
130. See clippings in "Cong. Scrapbook No. 5." MMP.
131. NBC network, Nov. 16, 1937, copy in "Cong. Scrapbook No. 5," MMP.
132. *Congressional Record*, 75th Cong., 2nd sess. (Dec. 18, 1937): 1897–1898.
133. *Sioux City Journal*, editorial, March 20, 1937.

Sultan of the Young Turks

134. *Sioux City Tribune*, March 17, 1937.
135. *Tribune*, May 14, 1937.
136. *New York Times*, April 24, 1937, 6.
137. *Congressional Record*, 75th Cong., 1st sess. (Jan. 6, 1937).
138. Ibid., Jan. 26, 1937, p. 454.
139. Editorial in the *Progressive*, Jan. 16, 1937; clipping in "Cong. Scrapbook No. 5," MMP.
140. See clippings in "Cong. Scrapbook No. 4," MMP.
141. See *Congressional Record*, 75th Cong., 1st sess., Appendix (June 1, 1937): 1583.
142. *New York Times*, Nov. 27, 1937, 15: 8.
143. Undated clipping from the *Jacksonville* (Fla.) *Times*, "Cong. Scrapbook No. 3," MMP.
144. Quoted in *Philadelphia Record*, Dec. 28, 1937.
145. Frederick L. Collins, "Who Will the Six New Justices Be?" *Liberty*, April 24, 1937, p. 7; clipping in "Cong. Scrapbook No. 4," MMP.
146. Thomas L. Stokes, *Washington News*, July 31, 1937.
147. *San Antonio News*, Sept. 18, 1937.

CHAPTER 6. SULTAN OF THE YOUNG TURKS

1. *Washington Daily News*, Jan. 3, 1938.
2. "Candid Faces on Capitol Hill," Rotogravure Section, *New York Times*, Jan. 2, 1938, copy in "Cong. Scrapbook No. 5," MMP.
3. *San Antonio Express*, Feb. 6, 1938.
4. Postcard, MM, Jr., to MM, May 16, 1938, "Gen. Corr., 1937–1938," MMP.
5. *Minneapolis Journal*, Jan. 9, 1938.
6. *Hartford* (Conn.) *Times*, undated clipping (sometime in April, 1937) in "Cong. Scrapbook No. 4," MMP.
7. *Congressional Record*, 75th Cong., 3rd sess. (Jan. 28, 1938): 1244–1245.
8. Ibid., Jan. 28, 1938, pp. 1244–1246.
9. Ibid., Feb. 14, 1938, p. 1890.
10. *New York Times*, Feb. 16, 1938, 4: 6.
11. Town Meeting of the Air Report, "Should Congress Adopt the President's Armament Proposals?" 3 (Feb. 12, 1938), copy in "Speeches: 1936–1938," MMP.
12. *Congressional Record*, 75th Cong., 3rd sess. (Feb. 24, 1938): 2392.
13. Ibid., p. 2395.
14. *Washington Post*, Jan. 28, 1938.
15. See accounts of the meeting in *Philadelphia Record*, Feb. 9, 1938; *Baltimore Morning Sun*, Feb. 9 and Pearson and Allen's "Washington Merry-Go-Round," *Washington Herald*, Feb. 12, 1938.
16. *New York Times*, Feb. 26, 1938, 17: 1, and *San Antonio News*, Feb. 23, 1938.
17. *New York Times*, March 13, 1938, 37: 3.

18. *Congressional Record*, 75th Cong., 3rd sess. (March 14, 1938): 3330–3333.
19. "The Capitol Parade," otherwise unidentified clipping in "Cong. Scrapbook No. 5," MMP.
20. *Congressional Record*, 75th Cong., 3rd sess. (March 25, 1938): 4151.
21. Ibid., April 12, 1938, pp. 5334–5335.
22. CBS, March 13, 1938, printed in *Congressional Record*, 75th Cong., 3rd sess., Appendix (March 14, 1938): 1012. See also MM's "War Built to Order," *Collier's* 102 (July 2, 1938): 12.
23. *Congressional Record*, 75th Cong., 3rd sess., Appendix, April 21, 1938, p. 5663.
24. *San Antonio Light*, April 22, 1938.
25. *Waterbury* (Conn.) *Democrat*, May 26, 1938.
26. *Congressional Record*, 75th Cong., 3rd sess. (May 7, 1938): 6411.
27. Ibid., May 31, 1938, pp. 7756–7757 and June 2, 1938, p. 8015.
28. Ibid., Appendix, June 8, 1938, p. 2459.
29. Ibid., Jan. 12, 1938, pp. 387–388.
30. Ibid., pp. 549–551.
31. Quoted in Schlesinger, *Politics of Upheaval*, p. 375.
32. *Congressional Record*, 75th Cong., 3rd sess. (Feb. 7, 1938): 1565.
33. Ibid., March 3, 1938, p. 2760.
34. Ibid., March 30, 1938, p. 4394; *New York Times*, March 28, 1938, 2: 5.
35. See account in George B. Tindall, *Emergence of the New South*, pp. 447–453.
36. MM jotted this note in the margin of his copy of Frederick Lewis Allen's *The Big Change* at p. 159, The University of Texas Library.
37. Divine, *Illusion of Neutrality*, p. 220.
38. *Congressional Record*, 75th Cong., 3rd sess. (April 2, 1938): 4649.
39. Berle to MM, April 4, 1938, "Gen. Corr., 1937–1938," MMP.
40. MM to Berle, April 11, 1938, "Gen. Corr., 1937–1938," MMP.
41. See his statement in *Congressional Record*, 75th Cong., 3rd sess. (May 11, 1938): 6652.
42. Ibid., March 18, 1938, p. 3863.
43. James T. Patterson, *Congressional Conservatism and the New Deal*, p. 244.
44. *Congressional Record*, 75th Cong., 3rd sess. (May 23, 1938): 7291–7292.
45. Ibid., Appendix, NBC speech, Jan. 10, 1938, in *Record* (Jan. 11, 1938): 137–138.
46. Ibid., Jan. 24, 1938, p. 348; see also *Philadelphia Inquirer* and *New York Times*, Jan. 23, 1938. For Berle's concept, see his *Power without Property*.
47. *Congressional Record*, 75th Cong., 3rd sess. (May 26, 1938): 7574–7576.
48. Unidentified clipping, Dec. 10, 1937, in "Cong. Scrapbook No. 5," MMP.
49. *Congressional Record*, 75th Cong., 3rd sess. (May 11, 1938): 6703.
50. *San Antonio Express*, Feb. 20, 1938.
51. *Light*, Feb. 25, 1938.
52. *Light*, March 13, 1938.
53. Elizabeth Dilling, *The Roosevelt Red Record and Its Background*, p. 156.

54. MM's copy in The University of Texas Library.
55. *San Antonio Evening News*, March 16, 1938.
56. Ed Kilman in the *Houston Post*, March 17, 1938.
57. *Light*, March 30, 1938.
58. *Express*, June 28, 1938.
59. Ibid.
60. Harlan Miller in *Washington Post*, April 21, 1938.
61. Fred Williams, "The New Southerner," *New South*, Nov. 1937, p. 9, published at Chattanooga, Tenn., by the Communist party.
62. Mike Gold, *Daily Worker*, editorial, March 22, 1938.
63. See p. 167.
64. *Light*, April 3, 1938.
65. Owen P. White, "Machine Made," *Collier's* 100 (Sept. 18, 1937): 32.
66. *Light*, April 4, 1938.
67. *Light*, April 5, 1938.
68. White, "Machine Made," and special feature in *Light*, May 28, 1937.
69. *San Antonio News*, June 28, 1938.
70. *Express*, July 1, 1938.
71. *Light*, July 4, 1938.
72. *Light*, July 12, 1938.
73. *Light*, July 9, 1938.
74. *San Antonio News*, July 11, 1938.
75. *Light*, July 12, 1938.
76. MM to Corcoran and McIntyre, June 25, 1938, "Gen. Corr., 1937-1938," MMP.
77. Sumners to MM and Connally to MM, June 28, 1938, "Gen. Corr., 1937-1938," MMP.
78. "Texas Topics," *Austin Statesman*, April 27, 1938.
79. *San Antonio News*, July 27, 1938.
80. *Light*, July 26, 1938.
81. *San Antonio News*, July 26, 1938.
82. *Fort Worth Star-Telegram*, July 26, 1938.
83. *Light*, July 25, 1938.
84. *Light*, Aug. 9, 1938.
85. *New York Post*, July 27, 1938.
86. "Tis of Thee," *Saint Louis Star-Times*, Aug. 8, 1938.
87. "Cong. Scrapbook No. 6," MMP.
88. "Washington Merry-Go-Round," *Philadelphia Record*, Aug. 1, 1938.
89. "Merry-Go-Round," *Record*, Dec. 1, 1938.
90. *Light*, July 28, 1938. *Saint Louis Star-Times*, July 26, 1938.
91. *Washington Tribune*, July 30, 1938; similar appraisal by Marshall McNeil in *Fort Worth Press*, Aug. 5, 1938.
92. Quoted in the *Washington Herald*, July 25, 1938.
93. MM to Patterson, Aug. 10, 1938 and Patterson to MM, Aug. 15, 1938, "Gen. Corr., 1937-1938," MMP.
94. *Baltimore Sun*, July 26, 1938.

95. George Rothwell Brown, special to *Light* from Washington, July 30, 1938.
96. *Philadelphia Record*, July 28, 1938.
97. *New York Times*, July 26, 1938.
98. Quoted by Paul Y. Anderson in *Saint Louis Star-Times*, July 27, 1938.
99. *Portland Oregonian*, July 26, 1938.
100. *San Francisco News*, July 28, 1938 and *Cincinnati Post*, Aug. 2, 1938.
101. *Saint Louis Star-Times*, July 26, 1938.
102. *Philadelphia Record*, July 26, 1938.
103. *Emporia Gazette*, July 29, 1938.
104. *Dallas News*, editorial, July 28, 1938.
105. See collection in "Cong. Scrapbook No. 7," MMP.
106. Harlan Miller, "Over the Coffee," *Washington Post*, Jan. 3, 1938.
107. Amlie to MM, July 26, 1938, "Gen. Corr., 1937–1938," MMP.
108. Thomas R. Amlie, *Progressive*, Nov. 1938. In addition to MM and Amlie, five other key members of the original Mavericks did not return to Congress in 1939, including Paul J. Kvale (F-L, Minn.), who had presided at their first meeting in 1935. Others were Charles G. Binderup (D.-Nebr.), Charles R. Eckert (D.-Penn.), George J. Schneider (Prog.-Wisc.), and Byron N. Scott (D.-Calif.).
109. *Light*, Aug. 21, 22, 28, 1938.
110. 1932 campaign speech, "Speeches: 1930–1932," MMP.
111. See correspondence with John P. Davis, secretary of the National Negro Congress, "Gen. Corr., Jan.–Sept., 1940," MMP.
112. See p. 224.
113. See pp. 223–225.
114. *Light*, Aug. 30, 1938 and *San Antonio News*, Aug. 31, 1938.
115. *Light*, Dec. 15, 1938.
116. Herbert Agar, note to MM attached to galley proof of "Time and Tide," which appeared in the *Chicago Daily Times*, July 28, 1938, "Cong. Scrapbook No. 7," MMP.
117. G. R. Brown, *Light*, July 30, 1938.
118. *El Mundo*, San Juan, Puerto Rico, quoted in *Macon* (Ga.) *Telegraph*, Sept. 20, 1938.
119. *Light*, Oct. 12, 1938.
120. *Light*, Oct. 25, 1938.
121. See itinerary for Nov. 18, 1938 to Jan. 19, 1939 in "Scrapbook, Mayor—1940," MMP.
122. Quoted in *American Guardian*, Dec. 16, 1938, copy in MMP.
123. Black to MM, from Denver, Colorado, July 26, 1938, emphasis in original, "Gen. Corr., 1937–1938," MMP.

CHAPTER 7. A TEXAS LA GUARDIA

1. *San Antonio Light*, Dec. 9, 1938 and *San Antonio News*, Dec. 10, 1938.
2. *Light*, Dec. 16, 1938.
3. *San Antonio Express*, Dec. 16, 1938.
4. *Light*, Dec. 31, 1938; Jan. 10, 1939; Jan. 1, 1939; Dec. 30, 1938; Jan. 2,

A Texas La Guardia 339

1939; Feb. 9, 1939; Dec. 21, 1938; Jan. 10, 1939; Jan. 26, 1939; Feb. 3, 1939 and Feb. 12, 1939.

5. *Express*, Feb. 12, 1939.
6. *Express*, Feb. 12, 1939.
7. *Light*, Feb. 23, 1939; *San Antonio News*, same date.
8. La Guardia to MM, March 1, 1939 and MM to La Guardia, March 4, 1939, "Gen. Corr., 1939," MMP.
9. *San Antonio News*, Feb. 21, 1939.
10. Political advertisement, *San Antonio News*, Feb. 16, 1939.
11. "Unbranded Bullfrog," *Time* 33 (May 22, 1939): 22.
12. *Light*, May 9, 1939.
13. *Time* 33 (May 22, 1939): 22.
14. *Express*, May 10, 1939.
15. *New York Times*, May 11, 1939, 6: 4.
16. Bob Humphreys to MM from the Press Gallery, U.S. House of Rep., May 26, 1939, "Gen. Corr., 1939," MMP.
17. *Express*, May 12, 1939.
18. *Boston Herald*, June 4, 1939.
19. Telegram, May 10, 1939, in "Age of Roosevelt Scrapbook," MMP.
20. Arnold to MM, Dec. 11, 1939, "Gen. Corr., 1939," MMP.
21. Daniels to MM, May 11, 1939, "Gen. Corr., 1939," MMP.
22. Black to MM, May 26, 1939; Cushing to MM, May 11, 1939; "Gen. Corr., 1939," MMP.
23. *Austin Statesman*, May 11, 1939; for other newspaper comment, see "Mayor—1940 Scrapbook," MMP.
24. "San Antonio's Mayor Maverick," June 4, 1939.
25. *Light*, May 13, 1939.
26. *Time* 33 (May 22, 1939): 22.
27. *Sacramento Bee*, May 20, 1939.
28. *Houston Press*, June 7, 1939.
29. La Guardia to MM., May 26, 1939, "Gen. Corr., 1939," MMP.
30. *New York Post*, July 26, 1939.
31. *Time* 38 (Oct. 20, 1941): 67.
32. See treatment of parallels in the two careers in *New York Times*, May 11, 1939, p. 24.
33. *New York Daily News*, July 27, 1939.
34. *Houston Post*, March 30, 1941.
35. Morris, *North Toward Home*, 294n.
36. Quoted in the *Los Angeles Times*, Jan. 21, 1940.
37. John Janney, "Texas Firebrand," *American Magazine*, Sept. 1940, p. 22.
38. See complete recapitulation of the Maverick administration in *Light*, June 1, 1940; see also "Fortune Faces," *Fortune*, Oct., 1945, p. 274.
39. See comments in *Kansas City Times*, Dec. 11, 1939; *Madison* (Wisc.) *Times*, Dec. 17, 1939; and *Saint Louis Star-Times*, March 11, 1940.
40. *Time* 34 (Dec. 18, 1939): 17.
41. *Express*, Dec. 9, 1939 and *New York Herald Tribune*, same date. For

other accounts of the trial and acquittal, see *New York Times*, Dec. 3 to Dec. 9 and *Newsweek* 14 (Dec. 11, 1939): 20.

42. Ickes to MM, Dec. 19, 1939; Arnold to MM, Dec. 11, 1939; Thomas to MM, Dec. 11, 1939; Daniels to MM, Dec. 18, 1939; "Gen. Corr., 1939," MMP.

43. Anderson, "Maury Maverick in San Antonio," *New Republic* 102 (March 25, 1940): 398.

44. Anderson to MM, Jan. 2, 1936; MM to Anderson, Feb. 27, 1936; Anderson to MM, dated only "Sunday"; MM to Anderson, March 9, 1936; Anderson to MM, March 4, 1936; "Gen. Corr., 1936," MMP.

45. Anderson, "Maury Maverick," p. 399.

46. Mrs. Webb, interview.

47. *An Honest Preface*, pp. 120–121.

48. Anderson, "Maury Maverick," p. 399.

49. For MM's pride in La Villita, see *Express*, June 8, 1954 and his "La Villita" file in MMP.

50. *San Antonio News*, Aug. 3, 1939.

51. Most of this account is taken from "Reconstructing the Mexican 'Little Village' of San Antonio," by MM in a special "Pan-American Good Will Edition" of *Hoy*, the Mexican magazine, Nov. 30, 1940, p. 18.

52. *Chicago News*, Feb. 1, 1941.

53. *Dallas News*, June 30, 1940.

54. *Express*, Nov. 16, 1940.

55. *New York Times*, May 12, 1940, X, 7: 4.

56. For descriptions of an excellent guide to the many historical and cultural attractions of San Antonio, see Charles Ramsdell, *San Antonio: A Historical and Pictorial Guide*.

57. Anderson to MM, Jan. 6, 1940, in *Letters of Sherwood Anderson*, pp. 456–457.

58. May 13, 1939.

59. *New York Times*, May 14, 1939, IV, 6: 6.

60. *Philadelphia Record*, Aug. 2, 1938.

61. "Maury Maverick's Election," *New Republic* 99 (May 24, 1939): 72.

62. Mrs. Webb, interview.

63. Tindall, *The Emergence of the New South*, p. 692.

64. See p. 181.

65. *Dallas News*, May 20, 1939.

66. *Washington Sunday Star*, May 21, 1939.

67. *New York Times*, July 26, 1939, 20: 3; Aug. 2, 1939, 4: 1; and Sept. 20, 1939, 16: 3.

68. Jay Franklin, "We, the People," *Washington Evening Star*, April 25, 1940.

69. *Newsweek* 15 (May 13, 1940): 31.

70. Berle to MM, May 16, 1940, "Gen. Corr., Jan.–Sept., 1940," MMP.

71. This account was reconstructed from *New York Times*, April 16, 1940, 19: 1; April 27, 1940, 6: 7; May 1, 1940, 20: 3; May 5, 1940, 4: 6 and IV, 7: 3;

He Stirreth Up the People

May 6, 1940, 1: 3, 4; May 8, 1940, 20: 2; and *Dallas News*, May 27, 28, 29 and 30, 1940. Also Mrs. Webb, interview.

72. Clipping from the *Roanoke Times*, Dec. 16, 1939, in "Mayor—1940 Scrapbook," MMP.
73. "Subject Corr., Constitution Book," MMP.
74. *Miami Herald*, Sept. 10, 1939.
75. *New York Times Book Review*, Aug. 6, 1932, 2.
76. *Richmond Times-Dispatch*, July 16, 1939.
77. *Durham Herald*, June 18, 1939.
78. *Louisville Courier-Journal*, June 16, 1939.
79. "Gen. Corr., 1939," MMP.
80. *Guardian*, Aug. 28, 1939, "Gen. Corr., 1939," MMP.
81. Letter to MM, Jan. 5, 1948, "Gen. Corr., 1948," MMP.
82. *Nation*, July 22, 1939, 106.
83. *Cleveland Plaindealer*, July 16, 1939.
84. See this writer's "The Political Philosophy of Maury Maverick Sr. with Respect to Civil Liberties," University Microfilms, 1961, pp. 104–109.
85. *In Blood and Ink*, also at p. 143.
86. Max Lerner, *America as a Civilization*, p. 730.
87. FDR to MM, Aug. 1, 1939, "Age of Roosevelt Scrapbook," MMP.
88. Louis L. Snyder, ed., *Fifty Major Documents of the Twentieth Century*, pp. 89–90.
89. Ibid., p. 92.
90. FDR, *Nothing to Fear*, p. 396.
91. Ibid.; for MM, see *In Blood and Ink*, pp. 143–144, 170.
92. Merle Curti, *The Growth of American Thought*, pp. 783–784.
93. See Henry Wallace, *New Frontiers* and *Whose Constitution*, pp. 100–104.
94. Copy of untitled speech, sometime in 1932, "Speeches, 1930–1932," MMP. For a more elaborate examination of the development of the concept of economic freedom and Maverick's role in it, see my "Philosophy of Maury Maverick," ch. VI.
95. Mencken to MM, July 18, 1939, "Gen. Corr., 1939," MMP.

CHAPTER 8. HE STIRRETH UP THE PEOPLE

1. "Speech to San Antonio Library Board," Aug. 16, 1939, "Speeches: 1939," MMP.
2. Proclamation of Good Friday, March 22, 1940, "Proclamations as Mayor," MMP.
3. Undated note, "Gen. Corr., 1939," MMP.
4. Quoted in the *San Antonio Express*, Aug. 7, 1939.
5. "Proclamations as Mayor," MMP.
6. Aug. 17, 1939, "Gen. Corr., 1939," MMP.
7. *Express*, Aug. 24, 1939.
8. *Express*, Aug. 26, 1939.

9. Mrs. Webb, interview.
10. A full account of the riot is to be found in *New York Times*, Sept. 3, 1939, IV, 10: 1.
11. *San Antonio Light*, Aug. 26, 1939.
12. *Express*, Aug. 27, 1939.
13. "Speeches: 1939," MMP.
14. Letter to Howard Le Baron, Fort Worth, Aug. 30, 1939, "Gen. Corr., 1939," MMP.
15. MM to Biddle, Sept. 16, 1939, "Gen. Corr., 1939," MMP.
16. "Gen. Corr., 1939," MMP.
17. Aug. 22, 1939; for other representative comments see the *Springfield* (Mass.) *Republican*, Aug. 27, 1939; *Hartford Courant*, Aug. 29, 1939; *Cleveland Plaindealer*, Aug. 31, 1939 and *Miami News*, Aug. 19, 1939.
18. Allen to MM, Oct. 3, 1939 and Oct. 18, 1939; MM to Ernst, Nov. 8, 1939; "Gen. Corr., 1939," MMP.
19. *Hague* v. *C.I.O.*, 307 U.S. 496 (1939).
20. 310 U.S. 586 (1940).
21. Press release, June 4, 1940, "Misc. Notes & Memoranda, 1917–1954," MMP.
22. Draft of press release, headed "Jehovah's Witnesses," "Misc. Notes & Memoranda, 1917–1954," MMP.
23. Ibid.
24. Commentary on the *Gobitis* case in Alfred H. Kelly and Winifred A. Harbison, *The American Constitution*, p. 810.
25. Copy of telegram to Emile Gauvreau, editor of the *Philadelphia Sunday Inquirer*, April 26, 1938, "Gen. Corr., 1937–1938," MMP.
26. *Schenck* v. *United States*, 249 U.S. 47 (1919). See also *Frohwerk* v. *United States*, 249 U.S. 204 (1919) and *Debs* v. *United States*, 249 U.S. 211 (1919).
27. *Crime to Promote Overthrow of Government*, p. 111.
28. Konefsky, *The Legacy of Holmes and Brandeis*, p. 221.
29. *West Virginia Board of Ed.* v. *Barnette*, 319 U.S. 624 (1943).
30. *Hirabayashi* v. *United States*, 320 U.S. 81 (1943).
31. *Korematsu* v. *United States*, 323 U.S. 214 (1944).
32. 323 U.S. 284 (1944).
33. H. F. Blackburn, "Epilogue," in J. B. Bury, *A History of Freedom of Thought*, p. 203.
34. See his *Southern Legacy*.
35. MM to Forrest Bailey, ACLU, May 14, 1929, "Subj. Corr., ACLU," MMP.
36. "Feudin' American Citizens," *Social Work Today* 5 (Nov. 1937): 5.
37. *A Maverick American*, p. 272.
38. "Let's Join the United States," *Virginia Quarterly Review* 15 (winter 1939): 74.
39. Ibid.
40. *A Maverick American*, pp. 213, 222.

He Stirreth Up the People 343

41. "Proclamations as Mayor," MMP.
42. Press release of speech to Southern Conference on Human Welfare, April 16, 1940, "Speeches: April–Dec., 1940," MMP.
43. See full text in *Atlanta Constitution*, Jan. 12, 1940.
44. Unsigned letter to MM, Jan. 13, 1940, "Gen. Corr., Jan.–Sept. 1940," MMP.
45. *New York Times*, Feb. 14, 1940, 13: 5. Other whites cited were Eleanor Roosevelt, Fiorella La Guardia, Harold Ickes, and Benny Goodman. See also comment in Francis Butler Simkins, *A History of the South*, p. 530.
46. *Congressional Digest* 20 (Dec. 1941): 307.
47. See statement on the choice of MM as witness in *New York Times*, March 17, 1940, IV, 7: 7.
48. *Congressional Digest* 20: 309.
49. Ibid.; see also MM's "Let's Join the United States," *Nation* 150 (May 11, 1940): 592. Though the title is identical, this article is not the same as the one in the *Virginia Quarterly*.
50. See speech to Descendants of the American Revolution Press Club, Washington, March 5, 1940, "Speeches: Jan.–April, 1940," MMP.
51. "Let's Join the United States," *Nation* 150: 593.
52. "Poll Taxes Are Bad," speech over NBC network, March 4, 1940, "Speeches: Jan.–April, 1940," MMP.
53. Key, *Southern Politics*, pp. 598, 618.
54. See "Let's Join the United States," *Nation* 150: 592 and *Congressional Digest* 20: 309.
55. See *Smith v. Allwright*, 321 U.S. 649 (1944).
56. Davis to MM, March 11, 1940, "Gen. Corr., Jan.–Sept., 1940," MMP.
57. White to MM, Jan. 3, 1940, "Gen. Corr., Jan.–Sept., 1940," MMP.
58. "Let's Join the United States," *Nation* 150: 592.
59. White to MM, June 6, 1940, "Gen. Corr., Jan.–Sept., 1940," MMP.
60. *A Maverick American*, p. 17.
61. White to MM, Jan. 23, 1940, "Gen. Corr., Jan.–Sept., 1940," MMP.
62. Chattanooga, April 16, 1940, "Speeches: April–Dec., 1940," MMP.
63. Campaign card in "Miscellaneous: Political Posters," MMP.
64. *Express*, April 30, 1941.
65. *Express*, *Light*, and *News*, April 30, 1941.
66. Copy in Scrapbook "Mayor Maury Maverick," MMP.
67. "Don Politico," *Light*, May 1, 1941.
68. "Don Politico," *Light*, May 4, 1941.
69. *Express*, May 9, 1941.
70. *Light*, May 10, 1941.
71. *Light*, May 17, 1941, and *Time* 37 (May 26, 1941): 8.
72. *Light*, May 19, 1941.
73. Quoted in the *Light*, May 23, 1941.
74. *Light*, May 23, 1941.
75. *San Antonio News*, May 28, 1941.
76. *News*, May 28, 1941.

77. Interview with an aide, Prof. Ben Wacker and letter to MM from businessman-supporter Paul Anderson, July 15, 1939, and other letters in "Gen. Corr., 1939," MMP.
78. June 12, 1939, "Gen. Corr., 1939," MMP.
79. Penciled note by aide to MM, Sept. 5, 1939, "Gen. Corr., 1939," MMP.
80. *Louisville Courier-Journal*, editorial, June 10, 1941.
81. *State Observer*, June 2, 1941, a penned note on the copy in the scrapbook, "Mayor Maury Maverick," MMP, says that Paul Bolton, veteran Austin newsman, wrote the article.
82. *Business Week*, June 7, 1941, p. 18.
83. May 29, 1947, II, 2; for further comment see *New York Herald Tribune*, May 29, 1941, and *Light*, June 1, 1941.
84. "The Giant World of Texas," *Harper's* 192 (June 1946): 489.
85. *Light*, June 1, 1941.
86. *Light*, June 26, 1941.
87. *Light*, June 1, 1941.
88. *Express*, June 21, 1941.
89. FDR to MM, Jr., June 4, 1941, copy in "Gen. Corr., Jan.–Dec., 1941," MMP.

CHAPTER 9. AN ISOLATIONIST'S CHANGE OF HEART

1. "Pillar of Government, Maury Maverick," *Forum* 95 (June 1936): 354.
2. Letter of Oct. 22, 1940 from Sen. Morris Shepard, "Gen. Corr., Jan.–Dec., 1941," MMP and note of Sept. 24, 1940, from Eleanor Roosevelt, "Gen. Corr., Jan.–Sept., 1940," MMP.
3. Speech to Young Democrats Jackson Day banquet, Jan. 8, 1940, "Speeches: Jan.–April, 1940," MMP.
4. See extensive correspondence with Adlai E. Stevenson and others reflecting the importance attached to Maverick in "Subj. Corr., Comm. to Defend America by Aiding the Allies" file, MMP.
5. Sept. 18, 1940, "Speeches: April–Dec., 1940," MMP.
6. "Tentative Draft," "Speeches: April–Dec., 1940," MMP.
7. Speech over radio station KTSA, San Antonio, Nov. 6, 1940, "Speeches: April–Dec., 1940," MMP.
8. Quoted in *Saint Louis Globe-Democrat*, Nov. 22, 1940.
9. See p. 165.
10. "What Should Be U.S. Policy Toward Japan?" *American Forum of the Air* 3 (Aug. 10, 1941).
11. *Baltimore Sun*, Nov. 9, 1941.
12. FF to MM, Oct. 30, 1941, "Gen. Corr., 1941," MMP.
13. MM to FF, Oct. 31, 1941, "Gen. Corr., 1941," MMP.
14. *New York Herald Tribune*, May 29, 1941.
15. *The Secret Diary of Harold L. Ickes*, vol. III, *The Lowering Clouds, 1939–1941*, p. 205.
16. HH to MM, Sept. 13, 1941, "Gen. Corr., 1941," MMP.

An Isolationist's Change of Heart 345

17. *New York Times*, Oct. 26, 1941, IV, 2: 1.
18. Will P. Kennedy, "Capital Sidelights," *Washington Star*, Oct. 26, 1941.
19. *Light*, Oct. 23, 1941.
20. *New York Times*, Jan. 14, 1942, 1: 1.
21. Bruce Catton, *The War Lords of Washington*, p. 126. Chapter 11 is devoted entirely to MM's efforts in this matter.
22. Ibid., p. 128.
23. Ibid., p. 132.
24. Ibid., pp. 132–138. MM carried on a voluminous correspondence on this matter; see "Gen. Corr., Jan.–June, 1942," and "Gen. Corr., July–Dec. 1942," MMP.
25. Cartoons in *Washington Star*, Dec. 21, 1942, and Jan. 17, 1943; *Detroit Free Press*, Feb. 15, 1943; *Seattle Star*, April 20, 1943; *Seattle Post-Intelligencer*, April 15, 1943; *Chicago Sun*, Feb. 13, 1943; *Christian Science Monitor*, Feb. 12, 1943.
26. *Salt Lake City Tribune*, April 18, 1943.
27. *San Francisco Examiner*, June 18, 1943.
28. *Washington Post*, Jan. 18, 1944.
29. See account of visit to Maryland Penitentiary in *Baltimore Sun*, Feb. 20, 1943.
30. Tom Sancton to MM, postcard, Nov. 1, 1943, "Gen. Corr., April–Dec., 1943," MMP.
31. MM, "American Prisons Go to War," *New Republic* 109 (Nov. 22, 1943): 712; MM told essentially the same thing to the Pennsylvania Prison Society, Philadelphia, Jan. 20, 1944; "Speeches: 1942–1944," MMP.
32. See clippings in "Scrapbook, Smaller War Plants, 1942–1943," MMP.
33. *Business Week*, Dec. 25, 1943, p. 8.
34. Quoted in *Current Biography*, March 1944, p. 456.
35. Quoted by Pearson and Allen, *Louisville Courier-Journal*, Jan. 20, 1944.
36. *Business Week*, Jan. 22, 1944, p. 22.
37. *PM*, Jan. 14, 1944.
38. See "Congratulatory Letters" in "Gen. Corr., 1944," MMP.
39. "Fortune Faces," *Fortune* 32 (Oct. 1945): 274. See also *New York Times*, Jan. 15, 1946, 33: 1; H. Corey, "Business Hand from the Rio Grande," *Nation's Business* 32 (March 1944): 36; and many clippings in "Smaller War Plants" scrapbook, MMP.
40. Memo in *Program and Progress Reports*, SWPC, no. 113 (May 1, 1944): 57.
41. "The Case against Gobbledygook," *New York Times Magazine*, May 21, 1944, p. 11 and "The Curse of Gobbledygook," *Reader's Digest* 45 (Aug. 1944): 109.
42. *Washington Post*, March 30, 1944.
43. Benton to MM, May 24, 1944, "Gen. Corr., 1944," MMP.
44. See, for example, *Public Administration Review* 4 (spring 1944): 151; Albert Lepawsky, *Public Administration*, p. 619; Rudolf Flesch, "More About Gobbledegook," *Public Administration Review* 5 (summer 1945): 240; and Her-

bert A. Simon, et al., *Public Administration*, p. 231, in which the word is consistently misspelled as "gobbledegook," as in the preceding article by Flesch.

45. John O'Hayre, *Gobbledygook Has Gotta Go*.

46. FDR to MM, June 5, 1944, "Age of Roosevelt Scrapbook," MMP.

47. "Gen. Corr., 1944," especially piece by MM for *Washington Post*, Sept. 24, 1944 and letter to MM, Jr., Aug. 28, 1944, MMP.

48. MM, "Symbol of Freedom," *New York Herald Tribune Magazine*, Nov. 4, 1945. See also *New York Times*, July 21, 1945, 5: 4.

49. Catton, *War Lords of Washington*, chs. 20 and 21.

50. Ibid., pp. 252–254, 279, 290–291. See also *Problems of American Small Business*, Hearings before a Subcommittee of the House Special Committee to Study and Survey Problems of Small Business Enterprises, 78th Cong., 2nd sess., parts 35, 46, 55; *Mobilization and Demobilization Problems*, Hearings before the Committee on Military Affairs of the U.S. Senate, 78th Cong., 2nd sess., part 15; "Fortune Faces," *Fortune* 32 (Oct. 1945): 274 and *New York Times*, March–Nov., 1944. See also MM's "Small Business Must Get the Breaks," *Saturday Evening Post* 217 (Sept. 16, 1944): 14.

51. Allen Drury, *A Senate Journal*, pp. 165, 247.

52. Quoted by Charles G. Ross, *Washington Sunday Star*, April 16, 1944.

53. Speech to Committee on Post-War Planning of the National Lawyers Guild, Washington, Dec. 15, 1944, "Speeches: 1942–1944," MMP.

54. *Chicago Tribune*, April 21, 1944; *Wall Street Journal*, May 4, 1944; *This Week*, Aug. 13, 1944; *Dallas News*, Aug. 13, 1944, editorial cartoon depicts "Good Old Uncle Maury" holding child (small business) up to get some of the "apples" off the tree.

55. Catton, *War Lords of Washington*, p. 302.

56. MM to Lauchlin Currie, Sept. 6, 1944, "Subj. Corr., Trips Abroad—England, 1944," MMP.

57. Currie to MM, Sept. 9, 1944 and Krug endorsement on letter from MM, Sept. 6, 1944, "Subj. Corr., Trips Abroad—England, 1944," MMP.

58. Copy of letter, MM to Hull, Sept. 12, 1944, and note to Berle, Sept. 13, 1944, with penned note by Berle, "quite OK," "Subj. Corr., Trips Abroad—England, 1944," MMP.

59. Undated copy of memo in "Subj. Corr., Trips Abroad—England, 1944," MMP.

60. "Day-by-day account of trip to England by Maury Maverick and A. B. Wacker," Oct. 27, 1944, "Subj. Corr., Trips Abroad—England, 1944," MMP.

61. "Subject Corr., Trips Abroad—England, 1944," files, MMP.

62. Annette Ebsen, BBC, to MM, Feb. 6, 1945; MM to Isa Benzie, March 1, 1945; MM to Halifax, Feb. 23 and May 1, 1945; Halifax to MM, April 20, 1945, "Gen. Corr., 1945," MMP and "Speeches: 1945–1946," MMP.

63. MS, "Odyssey of a V.I.P.," "Literary Productions," MMP.

64. Ibid., p. 57.

65. Ibid., pp. 68–73.

66. Notebook No. 2, "Notebooks on a Trip to France," MMP.

67. MS, "Odyssey of a V.I.P.," p. 107.
68. Ibid., pp. 176–177.
69. Ibid., pp. 196–208.
70. Ibid., pp. 217–220.
71. Ibid., pp. 222–225.
72. "Report on France: A Descriptive and Factual Statement," Smaller War Plants Corporation, April 2, 1945, mimeographed, "Printed Materials and Press Releases, Smaller War Plants Corporation," MMP.
73. *Washington Post, New York Times* 17: 4, and *Philadelphia Inquirer*, Jan. 13, 1945.
74. *Chicago Tribune*, Feb. 24, 1945.
75. *San Francisco News*, May 11, 1945.
76. Nelson to MM, May 15, 1945, "Gen. Corr., 1945," MMP.
77. Arthur Sylvester in the *Newark News*, Aug. 1, 1945.
78. *Washington Star*, Sept. 23, 1945.
79. HST to MM, Nov. 1, 1945, "Age of Roosevelt Scrapbook," MMP.
80. Two memos from MM to A. B. Wacker, June 29, 1945, "Subj. Corr., Orient," MMP.
81. See correspondence in "Subj. Corr., Orient," MMP; also *New York Times*, Dec. 28, 1945, 21: 2.

CHAPTER 10. ASIA—"OUR BIGGEST PROBLEM"

1. Pacific Notebook No. 1, p. 41; "Notebooks & Diaries, Trips Abroad 1944–1945," MMP. All subsequent references to "Notebooks" in this chapter refer to this file.
2. Pacific Notebook No. 2, p. 7.
3. Ibid., p. 23.
4. "Maury Maverick—Notes, Thoughts on Japan—Bought in Tokyo, Nov. 22, 1945."
5. Pacific Notebook No. 4, pp. 39–41.
6. Pacific Notebook No. 3.
7. Pacific Notebook No. 4, pp. 6–9.
8. Ibid., pp. 51–55.
9. Ibid., pp. 55–58.
10. Ibid., p. 60.
11. Ibid., pp. 62–67.
12. Ibid., pp. 78–79.
13. Tang Tsou, *America's Failure in China*, 388. This book is one of the most definitive accounts of our China policy problems at the time of MM's trip.
14. Pacific Notebook No. 4, pp. 88–90.
15. Pacific Notebook No. 5, pp. 7–12.
16. Ibid., pp. 13–15.
17. Ibid., p. 18.
18. Ibid., pp. 21–31.

19. Ibid., pp. 32–42.
20. Ibid., pp. 51–54.
21. Ibid., p. 62.
22. Ibid., p. 87.
23. Ibid., p. 104.
24. Ibid., p. 105.
25. Ibid., pp. 86–89.
26. Pacific Notebook No. 6, pp. 1–38.
27. Pacific Notebook No. 7, pp. 36–76.
28. Ibid., pp. 69–82.
29. Pacific Notebook No. 8, pp. 5–22.
30. Pacific Notebook No. 9, pp. 12–13.
31. Ibid., p. 20.
32. Ibid., pp. 22ff.

CHAPTER 11. LIKE RIPPLES ON A POND

1. HST to MM, Jan. 26, 1946, "Age of Roosevelt Scrapbook," MMP.
2. HST, Sept. 5, 1958, interview.
3. Robert S. Allen, ed., *Our Fair City*, ch. 17, p. 370.
4. Bowles to MM, Sept. 5, 1946, "Gen. Corr., 1946–1947," MMP.
5. MM to MM, Jr., Feb. 7, 1946, "Gen. Corr., 1946–1947," MMP.
6. "Maury's Back," *Time* 49 (Feb. 24, 1947), 28–29, and statement of Mrs. Webb.
7. Mrs. Webb, interview.
8. "Don Politico," *Light*, March 9, 1947.
9. "Maury's Back," *Time* 49: 28–29.
10. *Light*, April 2, 1947.
11. *Express*, March 29, 1947.
12. *Light*, April 22, 1947.
13. "Don Politico," *Light*, March 16, 1947, and Mrs. Webb, interview.
14. *Express*, May 17, 1947.
15. Ibid.
16. *Light*, May 25, 1947.
17. *Express*, May 28, 1947.
18. *Dallas News*, May 29, 1947.
19. See "Gen. Corr., June–Sept., 1951, and Oct.–Dec., 1951," MMP. See also accounts in *Express*, Sept. 14, 1951; *Dallas News*, Sept. 16, 1951; *Dallas Times-Herald*, Sept. 14, 1951; *Fort Worth Press*, Sept. 17, 1951, and *Beaumont Enterprise*, Sept. 20, 1951.
20. O. Douglas Weeks, *Texas Presidential Politics in 1952*, pp. 36–38, 41–42, 79–81; C. Dwight Dorough, *Mr. Sam*, pp. 440–441 and *New York Times*, July 19, 1952, 7: 1; July 20, 20: 4, 5; July 21, 13: 1, 20: 4, 6; July 22, 11: 7; July 23, 1: 8, 12: 3 and 15: 3; July 24, 13: 2; July 25, 7: 2; Aug. 12, 12: 2; Oct. 19, 1: 5. The argument of the Maverick delegation is presented in *Before the Credentials Committee of The Democratic National Committee, at Chicago, July, 1952—In*

the Matter of the Texas Delegations, a printed brief with annotations by MM in "Printed Material, Legal Documents," MMP.

21. Peyton, *San Antonio*, pp. 191, 193.

22. The Far East collection was sold to the University of Houston where it was made a part of the regular holdings of the library—Mrs. Webb, interview.

23. *Congressional Record*, 74th Cong., 1st sess. (Aug. 19, 1935): 13732-13736; cf. Crane Brinton's analysis of the "Rightist" and "Popular" revolutions in *The Anatomy of Revolution*, p. 22, and D. W. Brogan, *The Price of Revolution*, pp. 76, 79-80.

24. MM's copy of Harold J. Laski's *Where Do We Go From Here*, The University of Texas Library.

25. Speech to the Executives Club of Chicago, April 6, 1945, "Speeches, 1945-1946," MMP.

26. George F. Kennan, *American Diplomacy: 1900-1950*.

27. Speech to the Junior Foreign Trade Association of Southern California, Los Angeles, Dec. 4, 1946, "Speeches: 1945-1946," MMP.

28. Article rejected by *Nation*, Aug. 30, 1941, "Literary Productions: 1940-1949," MMP.

29. See "Gen. Corr., 1949," MMP.

30. HST to MM, "Gen. Corr., 1949," MMP.

31. See letter of MM to John E. Peurifoy, Assistant Sec. of State, Jan. 25, 1950, "Gen. Corr., Jan.-Sept., 1950," MMP.

32. MM to Drew Pearson, July 7, 1950, "Gen. Corr., Jan.-Sept., 1950," MMP.

33. Fairbank to MM, July 28, 1950, "Gen. Corr., Jan.-Sept., 1950," MMP. See also letter of Edward Weeks, editor of the *Atlantic Monthly*, Dec. 13, 1950, "Gen. Corr., Oct.-Dec., 1950," MMP.

34. See correspondence with Robert and Roland Wong, in "Gen. Corr., 1950-1953," MMP.

35. "Memorial and Memorandum," June 12, 1950, "Misc. Notes and Memoranda, 1917-1954," MMP. Cf. Robert P. Casey, *Religion in Russia*, p. 152, which MM read in "early 1950."

36. Speech entitled "Early and Official Laws of Texas," April 28, 1950, "Speeches: 1948-1951," MMP.

37. Draft of an article, "Let's Let China Join the World," April 26, 1951, rejected by *New Republic*, May 10, 1951, "Literary Productions: 1950-1954," MMP.

38. Speech to the Organized Voters League, Witte Museum, San Antonio, Oct. 22, 1950; the speech is partly written and partly in rough notes, "Speeches: 1948-1951," MMP.

39. MM's "Notes, 3/10/52" written on the back leaf of his copy of *The Holy Quran*, vol. II, text, translation, and commentary by A. Yusef Ali; now in The University of Texas Library. MM filled this work with almost as many commentaries as had been provided by the editor. His notes were written in preparation for an article on Eastern symbolism in the Great Seal of the United States for the internationally distributed Egyptian magazine, *Egypt*. See "The Great

Seal of the United States," *Egypt* (spring 1952): 6, in which MM discusses briefly some of the notions set forth here. See also his notes in Phillip K. Hitti, *History of the Arabs*, p. 121, in The University of Texas Library.

40. MM's copy of Thomas Jefferson Randolph, ed., *Memoir, Correspondence and Miscellanies, from the Papers of Thomas Jefferson*, IV, 173; MM wrote his note beneath Jefferson's remarks to James Maury: "We believe no more in Buonaparte's fighting for the liberties of the seas, than in Great Britain's fighting for the liberties of mankind." Inside the front cover MM indicated that he was rereading this work in Dec. 1952; copy in The University of Texas Library.

41. Joseph Gavorse, ed., *The Complete Writings of Thucydides*, p. 13.

42. *Quran*, I, 505.

43. *The Present State of Russia*, the author given simply as "An Eminent Person," (London, 1671).

44. *Quran*, II, 747.

45. Ibid., I, 177.

46. See also correspondence with Bruce, "Gen. Corr., Mar.–July, 1953," MMP.

47. Bruce, *The Golden Door*, pp. 210–212.

48. Ibid., pp. 226–228. See also MM's discussion of the case in a letter to the editor of *Nation* 176 (Feb. 7, 1953): 135.

49. Bruce, *The Golden Door*, p. 219 and *Les Misérables*, trans. Charles E. Wilbour, pp. 174–175.

50. *Express*, May 22, 1967.

51. Letter to HST, June 19, 1952 and Memorandum, June 13, 1952, "Gen. Corr., Jan.–June, 1952," MMP.

52. July 3, 1952, "Gen. Corr., July–Oct., 1952," MMP.

53. LBJ to MM, May 25, 1954, "Gen. Corr., Mar.–June, 1954," MMP.

54. See Edward Corsi, "Let's Talk About Immigration," *Reporter* 12 (June 2, 1955): 22.

55. 327 U.S. 1 (1946).

56. MM to Dies, Aug. 18, 1939, "Subj. Corr., ACLU," MMP.

57. MM to Dies, Nov. 13, 1940, "Subj. Corr., ACLU," MMP.

58. Rough draft of an article, "Books and Congressmen," *New York Times Book Review*, March 13, 1949, p. 5; the statement quoted not appearing in the printed article, "Misc. Notes & Memoranda, 1917–1954," MMP.

59. "Maverick's Advice to New Congressmen," *New Republic* 120 (Jan. 17, 1949): 21–22.

60. MM to Sokolsky, May 11, 1951, "Gen. Corr., Jan.–May 1951," MMP.

61. MM's copy of Edmund Holmes, *The Holy Heretics*, p. 53, The University of Texas Library.

62. "American Activities Committee Bulletin," 1 (Jan.–Feb. 1954): 1, copy in "Gen. Corr., Jan–Feb., 1954," and "Mimeo. Materials, 1953–1954," MMP.

63. MM to Mrs. Elizabeth T. Taylor, San Francisco, July 17, 1953, "Gen. Corr., Mar.–July, 1953," MMP.

64. "American Activities Bulletin," 2, "Mimeo. Materials, 1953–1954," MMP.

65. An excellent summary of the book-stamping controversy and the incep-

Like Ripples on a Pond 351

tion of the American Activities Committee may be found in the *New York Times*, June 7, 1953, 61: 1.

66. Copy of "Charter" in "Gen. Corr., Mar.–July, 1953," and "Legal Documents, 1950–1954," MMP.

67. Copy of bylaws in "Legal Documents, 1950–1954," MMP.

68. See *Times* account, June 7, 1953, p. 61, and letters to MM asking advice on establishment of similar organizations, in "Gen. Corr., Mar.–July, 1953," and "Aug.–Dec., 1953," MMP.

69. Letter to the writer from Mrs. Freeman Lee, 127 Canterbury Hill, San Antonio, Nov. 18, 1959.

70. MM to Daugherty, March 5, 1954, "Gen. Corr., Mar.–June, 1954," MMP.

71. Mrs. Webb, interview.

72. Speech to Town Hall Meeting, Houston, Feb. 25, 1954, "Speeches: 1952–1954," MMP.

73. "The enumeration in the Constitution of certain rights shall not be construed to deny or disparage others retained by the people."

74. Jackson, *The Supreme Court in the American System of Government*, pp. 74–75.

75. Letter to the writer from Patterson, Sept. 25, 1959; Patterson was the unnamed "lawyer friend" mentioned by Jackson.

76. See Patterson's view in *Ninth Amendment*, p. 70.

77. See James D. Carroll, "The Forgotten Amendment," *Nation* 201 (Sept. 6, 1965): 121.

78. Notes on an "Advance Program Information" sheet for the radio program, "Town Hall," ABC, June 30, 1953, which featured the question, "Is the Fifth Amendment Being Abused?" Copy in "Gen. Corr., Mar.–July, 1953," MMP.

79. Speech, "How to Read a Newspaper," not otherwise identified. Mrs. Webb said the talk was given to a San Antonio group sometime in the spring of 1954; "Speeches: 1952–1954," MMP.

80. Speech to Junior Chamber of Commerce, San Antonio, sometime in March, 1954, "Speeches: 1952–1954," MMP.

81. Speech to Town Hall Meeting, Houston, Feb. 25, 1954, "Speeches: 1952–1954," MMP.

82. *Crime to Promote Overthrow of Government*, p. 119.

83. Speech to the National Blue Key Organization, San Antonio, Dec. 29, 1950, "Speeches: 1948–1951," MMP.

84. See, for example, draft of speech to a CIO meeting in Feb., 1953, "Speeches: 1952–1954," MMP.

85. MM to Strubinger, Dec. 12, 1953, "Gen. Corr., Aug.–Dec., 1953," MMP.

86. MM to Chiles, April 9, 1953, "Gen. Corr., Mar.–July, 1953," MMP.

87. MM to Hoover, April 9, 1953, "Gen. Corr., Mar.–July, 1953," and "Memorandum" to Hoover, Oct. 16, 1953, "Gen. Corr., Aug.–Dec., 1953," MMP.

88. Minot F. Jelke, III, was being tried in 1953 for the alleged offense of "compulsory prostitution," and the press was excluded from a part of the proceedings. See *New York Times*, Feb. 10, 1953, 1: 1 and Nov. 16, 1953, 26: 3.

89. MM to American Civil Liberties Union, March 7, 1953, "Gen. Corr., Mar.–July, 1953," MMP.
90. MM to Straight, March 31, 1954, "Gen. Corr., Mar.–June, 1954," MMP.
91. MM to LBJ, April 2, 1954, "Gen. Corr., Mar.–June, 1954," MMP.
92. MM to LBJ, April 19, 1954, "Gen. Corr., Mar.–June, 1954," MMP.
93. See p. 253.
94. MM to MacArthur, June 30, 1948, and MacArthur to MM, July 10, 1948, "Gen. Corr., 1948," MMP.
95. Jackson to MM, Nov. 10, 1949, and MM to Jackson, Sept. 9, 1950, "Gen. Corr., 1949," and "Gen. Corr., Jan.–Sept., 1950," MMP.
96. He wrote to MM, Jr., from Okinawa, Nov. 21, 1945: "I am convinced . . . that all these yellow races are going to be surging around from now on. Their intelligence seems high. All of them talk of education and know that it is the ultimate road to freedom. . . ." "Gen. Corr., 1945," MMP.
97. Letter to Derk Bodde, Dec. 29, 1953, "Gen. Corr., Aug.–Dec., 1953," MMP.
98. B. L. Simpson, *Conflict of Colour*.
99. MM to Carey McWilliams, *Nation*, May 8, 1951, "Gen. Corr., Jan.–May, 1951," MMP.
100. Quoted by MM in speech to Americans for Democratic Action, Dallas, Feb. 3, 1953, "Speeches: 1952–1954," MMP.
101. Rough notes from which MM spoke to students at Brandeis University, Nov. 13, 1952, "Speeches: 1952–1954," MMP.
102. Speech to convention of National Association of Claimants' Compensation Attorneys, Shamrock Hotel, Houston, Aug. 28, 1952, "Speeches: 1952–1954," MMP.
103. "San Antonio—More Fire Fighters than Fire," *New Republic* 128 (June 29, 1953): 12.
104. Letter to Herbert Gambrell, Dallas, July 18, 1953, "Gen. Corr., Mar.–July, 1953," MMP.
105. Letters to Thurgood Marshall and Adam Clayton Powell, Jr., Feb. 11, 1954, "Gen. Corr., Jan.–Feb., 1954," MMP.
106. MM to Marshall, March 15, 1954, "Gen. Corr., Mar.–June, 1954," MMP.
107. Fragmentary notes for a speech to the Young Democrats Club of San Antonio, May 9, 1954, "Speeches: 1952–1954," MMP.

CHAPTER 12. I AM THAT GADFLY

1. C. B. Marshall to MM, April 22, 1952, "Gen. Corr., Jan.–June, 1952," MMP.
2. McAlister to MM, April 9, 1952, "Gen. Corr., Jan.–June, 1952," MMP.
3. *The Role of Politics in Social Change*, MM's copy in The University of Texas Library.
4. Salter, *The American Politician*, pp. 150–174.
5. MM's copy in The University of Texas Library.

6. Schlesinger to MM, March 16, 1943, "Gen. Corr., Jan.–Mar., 1943," MMP.
7. Boyd to MM, March 29, 1947, "Gen. Corr., 1946–1947," MMP.
8. Ford to MM, June 15, 1951, "Gen. Corr., June–Sept., 1951," MMP.
9. Nixon to MM, Dec. 18, 1952, "Gen. Corr., Nov.–Dec. 1952," MMP.
10. Boller to MM, March 27, 1954, "Gen. Corr., Mar.–June, 1954," MMP.
11. Crosskey to MM, Feb. 24, 1954, "Gen. Corr., Jan.–Feb., 1954," MMP. Crosskey referred here to his *Politics and the Constitution in the History of the United States.*
12. Sachar to MM, Aug. 11, 1952, "Gen. Corr., July–Oct., 1952," MMP.
13. Sachar to MM, Nov. 17, 1952, "Gen. Corr., Nov.–Dec., 1952," MMP.
14. Letter to the writer, June 24, 1958.
15. "Toynbee in Texas," *Dallas News*, June 7, 1952.
16. Letter to MM from Otto Schumann, Oberbayern, Germany, Aug. 20, 1950, "Gen. Corr., Jan.–Sept., 1950," MMP.
17. Letter to MM from Franz Krezdorn, Munich, Germany, Sept. 25, 1950, "Gen. Corr., Jan.–Sept., 1950," MMP.
18. Nehru to MM, Jan. 20, 1954, "Gen. Corr., Jan.–Feb., 1954," MMP.
19. MM's copy in The University of Texas Library.
20. Letter to the writer, June 29, 1958.
21. Browne to MM, Feb. 4, 1940, "Gen. Corr., Jan.–Sept., 1940," MMP.
22. Evjue to MM, Nov. 28, 1952, "Gen. Corr., Nov.–Dec., 1952," MMP.
23. A copy of the commemorative booklet (dated "Christmas, 1951") which describes the miniature silver books is in the "Famous Autographs" file, MMP.
24. *Texas Observer* (Austin), Sept. 12, 1958.
25. "The Great Seal of the United States," *Egypt* (spring 1952): 6. See also Treasury Department Press Release No. 5–59, Aug. 15, 1935.
26. Brooks, "Maury Maverick," p. 171.
27. *San Antonio Express and News*, May 21, 1967.
28. *Express*, June 10, 1954.
29. *Manchester Guardian*, June 9, 1954.
30. *A Maverick American*, p. 145.
31. Mrs. Webb, interview.
32. MM to Clayton Hildebrand, Mass, Michigan, Jan. 20, 1953, "Gen. Corr., Jan.–Feb., 1953," MMP.
33. Rep. George M. Rhodes (D.-Pa.), in *Congressional Record*, 83rd Cong., 2nd sess., Appendix (June 16, 1954): 4453.
34. *Express*, June 9, 1954.
35. See "We've Never Had More Freedom." *New Republic* 134 (Jan. 23, 1956): 15.
36. Letter to the writer, June 12, 1958.
37. Letter to the writer, July 1, 1958.
38. For a more extensive treatment of the genesis of the new position of the Court, see my "Political Philosophy of Maury Maverick," pp. 127–134, 279–280.
39. *Apology* in *The World's Greatest Thinkers, Man and Man*, Saxe Commins and Robert N. Linscott, eds., p. 200.
40. Patenaude, "The New Deal and Texas," p. 101.

41. Willie Morris, *North Toward Home*, p. 294.
42. Letter to the writer, June 12, 1958.
43. *Proceedings of the Philosophical Society of Texas* 19 (Dec. 4, 1954): 18–20.
44. Letter to the writer, June 26, 1958.
45. Letter to the writer, June 26, 1958.
46. Letter to the writer, July 28, 1958.
47. Harry S. Ashmore, *An Epitaph for Dixie*, p. 144.

BIBLIOGRAPHY

Unpublished Material

Maury Maverick Papers

From the time of his earliest political activities to his death, Maverick seems to have kept every scrap of paper containing any pertinent information on his career. An examination of the papers of Franklin D. Roosevelt revealed that there was no significant correspondence that Maverick did not have, and several items in Maverick's files are apparently not in the FDR papers.

The Maury Maverick Papers are held in The University of Texas Archives, Austin, and are cataloged in the following major categories with box numbers:

I. General Correspondence, 1912–1959—A 28/1–26
II. Subject Correspondence—27–37
III. Speeches, 1920, 1930–1954—38–50, and Proclamations (as Mayor)—51
IV. Literary Productions—51–53
V. School Papers—53
VI. Military Papers—54
VII. Notebooks and Diaries—55–57
VIII. Newspapers and Clippings, 1919–1954—58–62
IX. Photographs—63–66
X. Cartoons and Drawings—65
XI. Cuts—66
XII. Scrapbooks, 1912–1951—67–71, 88–116
XIII. Printed Material—72–79
XIV. Miscellany—80–83, 117–122
XV. Maury-Slayden-Maverick Family Papers—84–87

I have been advised by the University archivist, Dr. Chester V. Kielman, that in the not too distant future the box numbers will be changed. Consequently my references are to the *titles* of the various files and sections thereof, which will not be changed with the numbers.

Bibliography

Letters to the Author

Agar, Herbert. Author of various works on southern liberalism. August 24, 1958.
Allen, Robert S. Syndicated columnist. June 16, 1958.
Ashmore, Harry S. Editor of the *Arkansas Gazette*. June 19, 1958.
Baldwin, Roger N. Former director of the American Civil Liberties Union. June 12 and June 22, 1958.
Benton, William. Former United States Senator and publisher of the *Encyclopaedia Britannica*. July 28, 1958.
Bowles, Chester. United States Representative from Connecticut. June 26, 1958.
Black, Hugo L. Associate Justice of the United States Supreme Court. July 1, 1958.
Cohen, Benjamin V. New Deal adviser and administrator. June 26, 1958.
Cooke, Alistair. *Manchester Guardian* columnist. June 13, 1958.
Dabney, Virginius. Editor of the *Richmond Times-Dispatch*. June 18, 1958.
Daniels, Jonathan. Editor of the *News and Observer*, Raleigh, North Carolina. June 18, 1958.
Dobie, J. Frank. Late English professor at The University of Texas, Austin, and leading author of works on folklore of the Southwest. June 29, 1958.
Douglas, William O. Associate Justice of the United States Supreme Court. June 12, 1958.
Fischer, John. Editor of *Harper's* magazine, June 19, 1958.
Green, A. Leon. Distinguished professor of law at The University of Texas, Austin. June 16, 1958.
Haney, Lewis H. Professor emeritus of economics at New York University. June 16, 1958.
Hays, Brooks. Former congressman from Arkansas. June 12, 1958.
Henderson, Leon. New Deal economist, adviser and administrator. August 22, 1958.
Hutchins, Robert M. President of the Fund for the Republic. June 26, 1958.
Johnson, Lyndon B. June 12, 1958.
Lee, Mrs. Freeman. San Antonio artist and one of the organizers of the "American Activities Committee." November 18, 1959.
Lerner, Max. Philosopher, teacher, and columnist. June 24, 1958.
Mumford, Lewis. Author of various works dealing with American philosophy and ideologies. June 10, 1958.

Neuberger, Richard L. The late United States Senator from Oregon. June 10, 1958.
Patterson, Bennett B. Houston, Texas, attorney and author of *The Forgotten Ninth Amendment*. September 25, 1959.
Pearson, Leon. National Broadcasting Company commentator. August 19, 1958.
Roosevelt, Eleanor. June 16, 1958.
Roosevelt, Franklin D., Jr. June 20, 1958.
Schlesinger, Arthur M., Jr. Historian. July 7, 1958.
Straight, Michael. Former editor of the *New Republic*. June 19, 1958.
Thomas, Norman. Socialist party leader and author. June 16, 1958.
Truman, Harry S. July 21 and October 29, 1958.
Voorhis, Jerry. Former New Deal congressman and now executive director of the Cooperative League of the U.S.A. July 1, 1958.
Williams, Aubrey W. Former New Deal administrator and editor of the *Southern Farmer*. June 2, 1958.
Young, Stark. Poet, novelist and critic. August 3, 1958.

Interviews

Bardwell, Malcolm. Former Maverick aide. San Antonio, June 15, 1958.
Giles, Palmer. Rancher and boyhood friend of Maverick. Comfort, Texas, March, 1969.
Green, A. Leon. Distinguished professor of law at The University of Texas, Austin. June 20, 1958.
Maverick, Maury, Jr. Dozens of conversations from 1957 to August 1959.
Truman, Harry S. Independence, Missouri, September 5, 1958.
Wacker, Arnold Ben. Former Maverick aide. San Antonio, July 1, 1958.
Webb, Walter Prescott. The late distinguished professor of history at The University of Texas, Austin; a number of discussions from 1957 to 1959.
Webb, Mrs. Walter Prescott (formerly Mrs. Maury Maverick). San Antonio and Austin. Discussions on a near-weekly basis from 1957 to December 1959 and intermittently to date.

PUBLISHED MATERIAL

Books and Articles by Maverick

"American Prisons Go to War." *New Republic* 109 (November 22, 1943): 712–714.

"The Case Against Gobbledygook." *New York Times Magazine*, May 21, 1944, p. 11.
"The Curse of Gobbledygook." *Reader's Digest* 45 (August 1944): 109–110.
(With H. Jerry Voorhis) "Don't Sell out Prosperity." *Nation* 144 (May 15, 1937): 557–558.
"Feudin' American Citizens." *Social Work Today* 5 (November 1937): 5–7.
"The Gag Threatens!" *Forum* 95 (May 1936): 295–300.
"The Great Seal of the United States." *Egypt*, spring 1952, pp. 6–9.
"How the Immigration Service Treats Political Refugees." *Nation* 176 (February 7, 1953): 135.
In Blood and Ink. New York: Modern Age Books, 1939.
"Jefferson in Bowers." *New Republic* 88 (October 21, 1936): 317.
"Let's Join the United States." *Virginia Quarterly Review* 15 (winter 1939): 64–77.
"Let Us Defend Ourselves." *Vital Speeches* 7 (October 15, 1940): 5–8.
(With Robert F. G. Harris.) "Los Angeles—Rainbow's End." In Robert S. Allen, ed., *Our Fair City*. New York: Vanguard Press, 1947.
A Maverick American. New York: Covici-Friede, 1937.
"Maverick's Advice to New Congressmen." *New Republic* 120 (January 17, 1949): 21–22.
"The Next Four Years." *New Republic* 89 (November 25, 1936): 99–101.
"Not Now, Maybe Later." *Nation* 142 (March 11, 1936): 305–306.
"Opportunities for Veterans." *New York Times Magazine*, September 30, 1945, p. 12.
"Resolved: That the Power of the Federal Government Should Be Increased." *Vital Speeches* 7 (January 1, 1941): 169–170.
"San Antonio—More Fire Fighters than Fire." *New Republic* 128 (June 29, 1953): 12–13.
"Should Congress Enact a Federal Sedition Law?" *Congressional Digest* 14 (October 1935): 237.
"Should Congress Vote the President Power to Enlarge the Supreme Court?" *Congressional Digest* 16 (March 1937): 85–86.
"Small Business Must Get the Breaks." *Saturday Evening Post* 217 (September 16, 1944): 14.
"The South Is Rising." *Nation* 142 (June 17, 1936): 770–772.
"T.V.A. Faces the Future." *New Republic* 89 (November 18, 1936): 64–66.
"War Built to Order." *Collier's* 102 (July 2, 1938): 12–13.

Government Documents

Annals of Congress. Vol. I. Washington: Gales and Seaton, 1834.

Smaller War Plants Corporation. *Program and Progress Report.* Eleventh Bimonthly Report of the Smaller War Plants Corporation. Washington: Government Printing Office, May 1, 1944.

U.S. Congress. *Congressional Record.* 74th Congress, 1st session through 75th Congress, 2nd session. Washington: Government Printing Office, 1935–1938.

——. *Congressional Record.* 83rd Congress, 2nd session. Washington: Government Printing Office, 1954.

U.S. Congress, House of Representatives. Committee on Military Affairs. *To Make Better Provision for the Government of the Military and Naval Forces of the United States by the Suppression of Attempts to Incite the Members Thereof to Disobedience.* Hearings before the Committee and Subcommittee No. 10 on H.R. 5845. 74th Congress, 1st session. Washington: Government Printing Office, 1935.

——. Committee on Military Affairs. *To Punish for Exerting Mutinous Influence upon Army and Navy.* House Report No. 1603, to accompany S. 2253. 74th Congress, 1st session. Washington: Government Printing Office, 1935.

——. Committee on the Judiciary. *Crime to Promote Overthrow of Government.* Hearing before Subcommittee No. 2 of the Committee on the Judiciary on H.R. 4313 and H.R. 6427. 74th Congress, 1st session. Washington: Government Printing Office, 1935.

——. House Special Committee to Study and Survey Problems of Small Business Enterprises. *Problems of American Small Business.* Hearings before a Subcommittee. Parts 35, 46, and 55. 78th Congress, 2nd session. Washington: Government Printing Office, 1944.

U.S. Congress, Senate. Committee on Military Affairs. *Mobilization and Demobilization Problems.* Part 15. 78th Congress, 2nd session. Washington: Government Printing Office, 1944.

Other Books and Articles

"Agency to Watch: New Chief Demands Real Aid for Small Business." *Business Week,* April 8, 1944, p. 42.

Anderson, Sherwood. *Letters of Sherwood Anderson.* Edited by Howard Mumford Jones. Boston: Little, Brown and Co., 1953.

Arnold, Thurman W. *The Future of Democratic Capitalism.* Philadelphia: University of Pennsylvania Press, 1950.

Ashmore, Harry S. *An Epitaph for Dixie.* New York: W. W. Norton, 1958.

Baldridge, Cyrus L. *Americanism—What Is It?* New York: Farrar and Rinehart and Co., 1936.
Basso, Hamilton. "Maury Maverick: A Portrait." *New Republic* 90 (April 21, 1937): 315–317.
Bay, Christian. *The Structure of Freedom.* Stanford: Stanford University Press, 1958.
Beard, Charles A. *An Economic Interpretation of the Constitution.* New York: Macmillan Co., 1913.
Becker, Carl. *The Declaration of Independence.* New York: A. A. Knopf, 1942.
Boorstin, Daniel J. *The Genius of American Politics.* Chicago: University of Chicago Press, 1953.
Brann, W. C. *The Complete Works of Brann, the Iconoclast.* Edited by J. D. Shaw. 12 vols. New York: Brann Publishers, 1919.
Brinton, Crane. *The Anatomy of Revolution.* New York: Norton, 1938.
Brogan, D. W. *The Price of Revolution.* New York: Harper, 1951.
Brooks, Robert C. "One of the Four Hundred and Thirty-five: Maury Maverick, of Texas." In J. T. Salter, ed., *The American Politician.* Chapel Hill: University of North Carolina Press, 1938.
Bulletin of the University of Texas. Austin, 1916.
Burke, Edmund. *Speeches at Bristol.* Edited by Edward Bergin. New York: American Book Co., 1916.
Burns, James M. *Roosevelt: The Lion and the Fox.* New York: Harcourt, Brace and Co., 1956.
Carver, Charles. *Brann and the Iconoclast.* Austin: University of Texas Press, 1957.
Catton, Bruce. *The War Lords of Washington.* New York: Harcourt, Brace and Co., 1948.
Chabot, F. C. *The Mavericks* (pamphlet). San Antonio: Privately printed, 1934.
Coker, Francis W. *Recent Political Thought.* New York: D. Appleton-Century Co., 1934.
Cole, G. D. H. *A History of Socialist Thought.* 3 vols. New York: Macmillan Co., 1957.
Commager, Henry Steele. "The Pragmatic Necessity of Freedom." In *Civil Liberties under Attack.* Edited by Clair Wilcox. Philadelphia: University of Pennsylvania Press, 1951.
Commons, John R. *Legal Foundations of Capitalism.* New York: Macmillan Co., 1932.
Congressional Quarterly Almanac. Vol. X. Washington: Congressional Quarterly News Features, 1954.

Bibliography

Cooke, M. L. "Maury Maverick and the TVA." *New Republic* 94 (March 9, 1938): 133–134.
Corey, Herbert. "Business Hand from the Rio Grande." *Nation's Business*, March 1944, p. 36.
Corsi, Edward. "Let's Talk about Immigration." *Reporter* 12 (June 2, 1955): 22–26.
Corwin, Edward S. *A Constitution of Powers in a Secular State.* Charlottesville, Virginia: Michie Company, 1951.
Cronon, E. David. "A Southern Progressive Looks at the New Deal." *Journal of Southern History* 24 (May 1958): 151–176.
Crosskey, William W. *Politics and the Constitution in the History of the United States.* 2 vols. Chicago: University of Chicago Press, 1953.
Cupples, George. *Eulogy on the Life and Character of Hon. Samuel A. Maverick.* San Antonio: Privately printed, 1870.
Curti, Merle. *The Growth of American Thought.* 2nd edition. New York: Harper and Brothers, 1951.
Cushman, Robert E. "Ten Years of the Supreme Court: 1937–1947." *American Political Science Review* 42 (February 1948): 32–67.
Davis, Jerome. *Capitalism and Its Cultures.* New York: Farrar and Rinehart, 1935.
Dilling, Elizabeth. *The Roosevelt Red Record and Its Background.* Chicago: Privately printed, 1936.
Divine, Robert A. *The Illusion of Neutrality.* Chicago: University of Chicago Press, 1962.
Dorfman, Joseph. "The Economic Philosophy of Thomas Paine." *Political Science Quarterly* 53 (September 1938): 372–386.
Dorough, C. Dwight. *Mr. Sam.* New York: Random House, 1962.
Drury, Allen. *A Senate Journal.* New York: McGraw Hill, 1963.
Dumbauld, Edward. *The Bill of Rights and What It Means Today.* Norman: University of Oklahoma Press, 1957.
Easton, David. *The Political System.* New York: A. A. Knopf, 1953.
Ebenstein, William. *Great Political Thinkers.* Chapter 18. 2nd edition. New York: Rinehart and Co., 1956.
———. *Modern Political Thought.* Chapter I. New York: Rinehart and Co., 1954.
———. *Political Thought in Perspective.* New York: McGraw-Hill, 1957.
Egbert, Donald D. and Stow Persons. *Socialism and American Life.* Vol. I. Princeton: Princeton University Press, 1952.
Ely, Richard T. *Studies in the Evolution of Industrial Society.* New York: Macmillan Co., 1918.

Emerson, Thomas I. and Haber, David. *Political and Civil Rights in the United States.* Buffalo: Dennis and Co., 1952.
Ervin, Charles W. *Homegrown Liberal: The Autobiography of Charles W. Ervin.* Edited by Jean Gould. New York: Dodd, Mead and Co., 1954.
———. *The Story of the Constitution of the United States.* New York: Privately printed, 1946.
Fellman, David. *The Defendant's Rights.* New York: Rinehart and Co., 1958.
Flesch, Rudolph. "More About Gobbledegook." *Public Administration Review* 5 (summer 1945): 240.
"Fortune Faces." *Fortune* 32 (October 1945): 274.
George, W. L. *Anatole France.* New York: Henry Holt and Co., 1958.
Gilman, Wilbur E. "Milton's Rhetoric: Studies in His Defense of Liberty." In *The University of Missouri Studies.* Vol. XIV. Columbia: University of Missouri, 1939.
Granneberg, Audrey. "Maury Maverick's San Antonio." *Survey Graphic* 28 (July 1939): 420–426.
Green, Rena Maverick, ed. *Samuel Maverick, Texan: 1803–1870.* San Antonio: Privately printed, 1952.
Grierson, Herbert J. C. *Milton and Wordsworth; Poets and Prophets: A Study of Their Reactions to Political Events.* New York: Macmillan Co., 1937.
Hallowell, John H. *Main Currents in Modern Political Thought.* New York: Henry Holt and Co., 1950.
Harding, Arthur L., ed. *Natural Law and Natural Rights.* Dallas: Southern Methodist University Press, 1955.
———. *Origins of the Natural Law Traditions.* Dallas: Southern Methodist University Press, 1954.
Henderson, Herbert C. "Unbranded Maverick." *Today,* November 21, 1936 [A specially bound copy without a volume number or pagination in Maury Maverick's library, now in The University of Texas Library].
Hessler, William. *Our Ineffective State.* New York: Henry Holt and Co., 1937.
High, Stanley. "The Neo-New Dealers." *Saturday Evening Post* 209 (May 22, 1937): 10–11.
Holbrook, Stewart H. *Lost Men of American History.* New York: Macmillan Co., 1948.
Holcombe, Arthur N. *The Middle Class in American Politics.* Cambridge: Harvard University Press, 1940.

Bibliography

Hugo, Victor. *Les Misérables.* Translated by Charles E. Wilbour. E. P. Dutton and Co., n.d.
Huson, Hobart. Letter to editor. *Southwestern Historical Quarterly* 68 (January 1964): 435.
Hutchinson, F. E. *Milton and the English Mind.* New York: Macmillan Co., 1948.
Ickes, Harold L. *Secret Diary,* vol. 3, *The Lowering Clouds.* New York: Simon and Schuster, 1954.
Irish, Marian D. "Recent Political Thought in the South." *American Political Science Review* 46 (March 1952): 121–141.
Jackson, Robert H. *The Supreme Court in the American System of Government.* Cambridge: Harvard University Press, 1955.
Janney, John. "Texas Fire Brand." *American Magazine* 130 (September 1940): 22–23.
Jefferson, Thomas. *The Writings of Thomas Jefferson.* Vol. III. Edited by Paul L. Ford. New York: G. P. Putnam's Sons, 1899.
Jensen, Merrill. *The New Nation.* New York: A. A. Knopf, 1950.
Jones, Howard Mumford. *The Pursuit of Happiness.* Cambridge: Harvard University Press, 1953.
Kallen, Horace M. *The Liberal Spirit.* New York: New School for Social Research and Cornell University Press, 1948.
Kelly, Alfred H. and Winifred A. Harbison. *The American Constitution.* New York: W. W. Norton and Co., 1948.
———. *Foundations of Freedom in the American Constitution.* New York: Harper and Brothers, 1958.
Kenealy, William J. "Civil Liberties: The Philosophy of American Democracy." *Vital Speeches* 22 (January 15, 1956): 220–221.
Kennan, George F. *American Diplomacy: 1900–1950.* Chicago: University of Chicago Press, 1951.
Key, V. O., Jr. *Southern Politics in State and Nation.* New York: A. A. Knopf, 1949.
Konefsky, Samuel J. *The Legacy of Holmes and Brandeis: A Study in the Influence of Ideas.* New York: Macmillan Co., 1956.
Lambert, G. "Maverick Defies the Mob." *Nation* 149 (September 16, 1939): 287–288.
"Leisure Could Mean a Better Civilization." *Life* 47 (December 28, 1959): 62–63.
Lepawsky, Albert. *Public Administration.* New York: A. A. Knopf, 1949.
Lerner, Max. *America as a Civilization.* New York: Simon and Schuster, 1957.

———. *The Mind and Faith of Justice Holmes.* New York: Random House, 1954.
Leuchtenburg, William E. *Franklin D. Roosevelt and the New Deal: 1932–1940.* New York: Harper and Row, 1963.
Lippmann, Walter. *An Inquiry into the Principles of the Good Society.* New York: Atlantic Monthly Press, 1937.
Locke, John. *John Locke on Politics and Education.* Edited by Howard R. Penniman. New York: D. Van Nostrand Co., 1947.
MacIver, Robert M., ed. *Great Expressions of Human Rights.* New York: Harper and Brothers, 1950.
Maclay, William. *Journal of William Maclay.* Edited by Charles A. Beard. New York: A. and C. Boni, 1927.
Mason, Alpheus T. and Beaney, William M. *The Supreme Court in a Free Society.* Englewood Cliffs, New Jersey: Prentice-Hall, 1959.
——— and Leach, Richard H. *In Quest of Freedom.* Englewood Cliffs, New Jersey: Prentice-Hall, 1959.
"Maury's Back." *Time* 49 (February 24, 1947): 28.
Maverick, Albert. *A Maverick Abroad.* Edited by James S. Maverick. San Antonio: Principia Press of Trinity University, 1965.
Maverick, Mary A. *Memoirs.* San Antonio: Alamo Printing Co., 1921.
"Maverick." *Scholastic* 27 (January 25, 1936): 315–317.
"Maverick Bounces Back." *New Republic* 99 (May 10, 1939): 5–6.
"Maverick Out." *Time* 37 (June 9, 1941): 22.
Meiklejohn, Alexander. *Free Speech and Its Relations to Self-Government.* New York: Harper and Brothers, 1948.
Monthly Labor Review 33 (March 1933).
Morris, Willie. *North Toward Home.* Boston: Houghton Mifflin Co., 1967.
Munz, C. C. "Gunning for Maverick." *Nation* 149 (December 16, 1939): 673–674.
———. "Odds on Maverick." *Nation* 152 (May 10, 1941): 557–558.
Murray, Henry A. "A Mythology for Grownups." *Saturday Review* 43 (January 23, 1960): 10–12.
Myers, Henry Alonzo. *Are Men Equal: An Inquiry into the Meaning of Democracy.* Ithaca: Cornell University Press, 1955.
Niemeyer, Vic. "Frustrated Invasion." *Southwestern Historical Quarterly* 67 (October 1963): 213.
O'Hayre, John. *Gobbledygook Has Gotta Go.* Washington: Government Printing Office, 1967.
Oppenheim, Felix E. "Interpersonal Freedom and Freedom of Action." *American Political Science Review* 49 (June 1955).

Paine, Thomas. *Agrarian Justice in Thomas Paine.* Edited by Harry H. Clark. New York: American Book Co., 1944.

———. *Dissertation on the First Principles of Government in Thomas Paine, Common Sense and Other Political Writings.* Edited by Nelson F. Adkins. New York: Liberal Arts Press, 1953.

———. *Rights of Man.* Edited by M. D. Conway. New York: G. P. Putnam's Sons, 1894.

Parrington, Vernon D. *Main Currents in American Thought.* Vols. I and III. New York: Harcourt, Brace and Company, 1930.

Patenaude, Lionel V. "The New Deal and Texas." Ph.D. dissertation. Department of History, The University of Texas, 1953.

Patterson, Bennett B. *The Forgotten Ninth Amendment.* Indianapolis, Bobbs Merrill Co., 1955.

Patterson, James T. *Congressional Conservatism and the New Deal.* Lexington: University of Kentucky Press, 1967.

Peyton, Green. *San Antonio: City in the Sun.* New York: McGraw-Hill, 1946.

Plato. *Apology.* In *The World's Greatest Thinkers, Man and Man: The Social Philosophers.* Edited by Saxe Commins and Robert N. Linscott. New York: Random House, 1947.

Pritchett, C. Hermann. *The American Constitution.* New York: McGraw-Hill, 1959.

———. *The Political Offender and the Warren Court.* Boston: Boston University Press, 1958.

Ramsdell, Charles. *San Antonio: A Historical and Pictorial Guide.* Austin: University of Texas Press, 1959.

Remarque, Erich Maria. *All Quiet on the Western Front.* Boston: Little, Brown and Co., 1929.

Roche, John P. "We've Never Had More Freedom," *New Republic* 134 (January 23, 1956): 12; ibid. (January 30, 1956): 13; ibid. (February 6, 1956): 13.

Rodell, Fred. *Nine Men.* New York: Random House, 1955.

Roosevelt, Franklin D. *Nothing to Fear.* Boston: Houghton Mifflin Co., 1946.

———. *Public Papers and Addresses of Franklin D. Roosevelt.* Vol. I. Edited by Samuel I. Roseman. New York: Random House, 1938.

Rousseau, Jean Jacques. *The Social Contract.* Introduction and translation by G. D. H. Cole. New York: E. P. Dutton and Co., 1913.

Rutland, Robert A. *The Birth of the Bill of Rights.* Chapel Hill: University of North Carolina Press, 1955.

Schapiro, Salwyn. *Liberalism: Its Meaning and History.* New York: D. Van Nostrand Co., 1958.
Schlesinger, Arthur M., Jr. *The Age of Roosevelt,* Vol. III, *The Politics of Upheaval.* Boston: Houghton Mifflin Co., 1960.
Shields, Currin V. "The American Tradition of Empirical Collectivism." *American Political Science Review* 46 (March 1952): 104–120.
Simkins, Francis B. *The South: Old and New.* New York: A. A. Knopf, 1947.
Simon, Herbert A., et al. *Public Administration.* New York: A. A. Knopf, 1964.
Simpson, B. L. *Conflict of Colour.* New York: Macmillan Co., 1910.
Slayden, Ellen M. *Washington Wife.* Edited by W. P. Webb. New York: Harper and Row, 1963.
Snyder, Louis L., ed. *Fifty Major Documents of the Twentieth Century.* New York: D. Van Nostrand Co., 1955.
The State Records of North Carolina. Vols. XXI and XXV. Edited by Walter Clark. Goldsboro: Trustees of the Public Libraries of North Carolina, 1903.
Stilwell, Hart. "Maury the Maverick." *Nation* 179 (July 17, 1954): 53.
Strauss, Leo. *Natural Right and History.* Chicago: University of Chicago Press, 1953.
Sullivan, James. "The Antecedents of the Declaration of Independence." In *Annual Report of the American Historical Association for the Year 1902.* Vol. I. Washington: Government Printing Office, 1903.
Tawney, R. H. *Equality.* London: George Allen and Unwin, 1931.
Thomason, J. W., Jr. "Maverick on Parade." *American Mercury* 42 (September 1937): 111–116.
Thompson, Waddy. *Recollections of Mexico.* New York: John Wiley and Sons, 1847.
Tindall, George B. *The Emergence of the New South: 1913–1945.* Baton Rouge: Louisiana State University Press, 1967.
Tsou, Tang. *America's Failure in China: 1941–50.* Chicago: University of Chicago Press, 1963.
"Unbranded Bullfrog." *Time* 33 (May 22, 1939): 22.
"Unemployment and Community Action." *Survey* 68 (November 15, 1932): 612–615; ibid. (December 15, 1932): 694–697.
Villard, Oswald Garrison. "Pillar of Government, Maury Maverick." *Forum* 95 (June 1936): 354–358.
———. "Issues and Men." *Nation* 143 (August 22, 1936): 212.
———. "Issues and Men." *Nation* 147 (July 23, 1938): 89.

Bibliography

"Voices Out of the Past." *Time* 58 (October 1, 1951): 19.
Voltaire, F. M. A. de. *Candide*. New York: Book League, 1940.
Von Eckhardt, Ursula M. *The Pursuit of Happiness in the Democratic Creed*. New York: Frederick A. Praeger, 1959.
Wallace, Henry A. *New Frontiers*. New York: Reynal and Hitchcock, 1934.
———. *Whose Constitution: An Inquiry into the General Welfare*. New York: Reynal and Hitchcock, 1936.
Warner, Rex. *John Milton*. New York: Chanticleer Press, 1950.
Wayland, John W. *The Pathfinder of the Seas: The Life of Matthew Fontaine Maury*. Richmond: Garrett, Garrett and Massie, 1930.
Webb, Walter P. *An Honest Preface*. Boston: Houghton Mifflin Co., 1959.
———. "Obituary." *Proceedings of the Philosophical Society of Texas* 19 (December 4, 1954): 18–20.
Weeks, O. Douglas. *Texas Presidential Politics in 1952*. Austin: Institute of Public Affairs, The University of Texas, 1953.

Newspapers

The Bexar Facts, San Antonio, November 1929 to August 1930.
The Blunderbuss, April 1, 1915. [A clandestinely published newspaper, issued by University of Texas students on April Fools' Day].
Dallas Morning News, 1934–1954.
Daily Texan, The University of Texas, 1913–1915, 1921–1927, 1935–1937.
Manchester Guardian, June 9, 1954.
New York Times, 1934–1954.
San Antonio Express, 1934–1954.
(Newspaper notes without page numbers are from Maverick's collection of clippings).

Books Annotated by Maverick or Inscribed to Him

IN THE UNIVERSITY OF TEXAS LIBRARY

Agar, Herbert, et al. *The City of Man: A Declaration on World Democracy*. New York: Viking Press, 1940.
Allen, Frederick Lewis. *The Big Change*. New York: Harper and Brothers, 1952.
Beard, Charles A. *America Faces the Future*. Boston: Houghton Mifflin Co., 1952.
Begbie, Harold. *Painted Windows: Studies in Religious Personality*. New York: G. P. Putnam's Sons, 1922.

Brann, William C. *Brann, the Iconoclast.* Edited by J. D. Shaw. 2 vols. Waco, Texas: Knight Printing Co., 1903.

Bruce, J. Campbell. *The Golden Door: The Irony of Our Immigration Policy.* New York: Random House, 1954.

Carr, E. H. *Studies in Revolution.* London: Macmillan and Co., 1950.

Carter, Hodding. *Where Main Street Meets the River.* New York: Rinehart and Co., 1953.

Casey, Robert P. *Religion in Russia.* New York: Harper and Brothers, 1946.

Clarke, James Freeman. *Ten Great Religions.* Boston: Houghton Mifflin Co., 1882.

Cobb, Thomas R. R. *An Inquiry into the Law of Negro Slavery in the United States.* Philadelphia: T. and J. W. Johnson and Co., 1858.

Coulter, E. Merton. *William G. Brownlow.* Chapel Hill: University of North Carolina Press, 1932.

Cousins, Norman. *Modern Man Is Obsolete.* New York: Viking Press, 1945.

Dabney, Virginius. *Liberalism in the South.* Chapel Hill: University of North Carolina Press, 1932.

Dealey, James Q. *Sociology: Its Development and Applications.* New York: D. Appleton and Co., 1920.

Dean, Vera Micheles. *Foreign Policy Without Fear.* New York: McGraw-Hill Book Co., 1953.

―――. *The United States and Russia.* Cambridge: Harvard University Press, 1947.

Demosthenes. *The Public Orations of Demosthenes.* Vol. I. Translated by Arthur Wallace Pickard-Cambridge. Oxford: Clarendon Press, 1912.

Emerson, Ralph Waldo. *Essays.* New York: John B. Alden, 1886.

Erasmus, Desiderius. *The Praise of Folly.* New York: Peter Eckler Publishing Co., 1922.

―――. *Erasmus: In Praise of Folly.* Edited by Horace J. Bridges. Chicago: Covici, 1925.

Faulkner, John A. *Erasmus: The Scholar.* New York: Methodist Book Co., 1907.

Ford, Ford Madox. *The March of Literature.* New York: Dial Press, 1938.

Friedel, Frank. *Franklin D. Roosevelt.* Boston: Little, Brown and Co., 1952.

Froude, J. A. *Life and Letters of Erasmus.* New York: Charles Scribner's Sons, 1894.

Bibliography

Hamilton, Alexander, et al. *The Federalist.* Edited by Edward M. Earle. Washington: National Home Library Foundation, 1937.

Hays, Arthur Garfield. *Let Freedom Ring.* New York: Boni and Liveright, 1928.

Hessler, William. *Our Ineffective State.* New York: Henry Holt and Co., 1937.

Hitti, Philip K. *History of the Arabs.* 5th ed. New York: Macmillan Co., 1951.

Hoffer, Eric. *The True Believer.* New York: Harper and Brothers, 1951.

Holmes, Edmund. *The Holy Heretics.* London: Watts and Company, 1948.

Holmes, O. W. *Representative Opinions of Mr. Justice Holmes.* Edited by Alfred Lief. New York: Vanguard Press, 1931.

Huson, Hobart. *The Religious, Moral and Ethical Teachings of Pythagorus Reconstructed and Edited.* Refugio, Texas: Privately printed, 1947.

Humphreys, Christmas. *Buddhism.* Harmondsworth, England: Penguin Books, 1951.

Hunter, Robert. *Poverty.* New York: Macmillan Co., 1904.

Ibáñez, Vicente Blasco. *The Four Horsemen of the Apocalypse.* Translated by Charlotte B. Jordan. New York: E. P. Dutton and Co., 1919.

Jefferson, Thomas. *Memoir, Correspondence and Miscellanies, from the Papers of Thomas Jefferson.* Vol. IV. Edited by Thomas Jefferson Randolph. Charlottesville, Virginia: F. Carr and Co., 1829.

——. *The Writings of Thomas Jefferson.* Memorial Edition. Edited by Andrew A. Lipscomb. 20 vols. Washington: Thomas Jefferson Memorial Association of the United States, 1903.

Jennings, W. Ivor. *Cabinet Government.* New York: Macmillan Co., 1936.

Laski, Harold J. *Where Do We Go from Here?* New York: Viking Press, 1940.

Lawson, James F. *The General Welfare Clause.* Washington: Privately printed, 1934.

Lengyel, Emil. *World Without End.* New York: John Day Co., 1953.

McWilliams, Carey. *Witch Hunt.* Boston: Little, Brown and Co., 1950.

Merriam, Charles E. *The Role of Politics in Social Change.* New York: New York University Press, 1936.

Miller, John C. *Sam Adams: Pioneer in Propaganda.* Boston: Little, Brown and Co., 1936.

Mitrany, David. *The Progress of International Government.* London: George Allen and Unwin, 1934.

Morris, Clarence. *How Lawyers Think*. Cambridge: Harvard University Press, 1938.
Mowrer, Edgar Ansel. *The Nightmare of American Foreign Policy*. New York: A. A. Knopf, 1948.
Mumford, Lewis. *Faith for Living*. New York: Harcourt, Brace and Co., 1940.
Nock, Albert J. *Jefferson*. New York: Harcourt, Brace and Co., 1926.
The Present State of Russia. (The author is given only as "An Eminent Person") London: John Winter, 1671.
Raper, Arthur. *The Tragedy of Lynching*. Chapel Hill: University of North Carolina Press, 1933.
Rhys, Ernest, ed. *The Growth of Political Liberty*. New York: E. P. Dutton and Co., 1921.
Ruskin, John. *Ruskin's Views of Social Justice*. Edited by James Fuchs. New York: Vanguard Press, 1926.
Sandburg, Carl. *Abraham Lincoln: The Prairie Years*. New York: Blue Ribbon Books, 1931.
Sayles, John. *The Constitutions of the State of Texas*. Saint Louis: Vernon Law Book Company, 1893.
Schroeder, Theodore, ed. *Free Press Anthology*. New York: Free Speech League, 1909.
Shaw, George Bernard. *Androcles and the Lion*. New York: Brentano's, 1916.
Sinclair, Upton, ed. *The Cry for Justice*. Chicago: Regan Publishing Corp., 1915.
Smith, Preserved. *Erasmus*. New York: Harper and Brothers, 1923.
Tagore, Rabindranath. *The Gardner*. New York: Macmillan Co., 1923.
Thomas, Norman. *Is Conscience a Crime?* New York: Vanguard Press, 1927.
Thucydides. *The Complete Writings of Thucydides*. Edited by Joseph Gavorse. New York: Modern Library, 1934.
Trunk, Joseph V. *A Thomistic Interpretation of the Civic Right*. Dayton: University of Dayton, 1937.
Werner, Max. *Battle for the World*. Translated by Heinz and Ruth Norden. New York: Modern Age Books, 1941.
Yusefali, A., ed. *The Holy Quran*. 2 vols. 3rd ed. New York: Hafner Publishing Co., 1938.

INDEX

Acheson, Dean: 278
"ADA": MM's proposal for, 267–268
Adamusia, Zygmunt (Polish refugee): 282
administrative reorganization bill (1937): 172
Advisory Board on National Parks, Historic Sites, Buildings and Monuments: 94
Agar, Herbert: 209
agriculture legislation: MM supports Agricultural Adjustment Act (AAA), 97; MM supports and praises Resettlement Administration, 113; MM on soil conservation and rural electrification, 115–116; MM argues that first AAA was constitutional, 132, 137; MM praised for support of farm tenants legislation, 158; Gillette-Maverick bill, 160–161; second AAA, 161
Alamo, Battle of: 95
Allen, Robert S.: 117, 181, 182, 217, 247
Allred, Gov. James V.: 125, 185
Alsop, Joseph: 168
Amarillo Daily News: 18
A Maverick American: 143–144
American Activities Committee: 286–287
American Bankers Association: 249
American Bar Association: 150, 215
American Civil Liberties Union (ACLU): MM's reason for joining, 57; criticized by MM, 59; address to, on free speech, 103; aids MM in draft of civil rights law, 111; MM urges intervention of, in Jelke case, 291; mentioned, 44
American Legion, Americanism Commission: 109
American Liberty League: denounced by MM, 96–97, 103, 104
American Youth Act: 162
Amlie, Rep. Thomas R.: 153, 184–185
Anderson, Paul Y. (journalist): 116
Anderson, Sherwood: on social obligations of writers, 197; characterization of MM as mayor, 197; on Mexican-Americans, 199; proposes drama on San Antonio heritage, 201–202
anti-lynching law: MM supports, 140
anti–poll-tax bill (Geyer bill): 223–224
Appeal to Reason (socialist periodical): 11
Argonne offensive: 24
Arneson River Theatre (San Antonio): 201
Arnold, Thurman: on MM's election as mayor, 192–193; aids MM on *In Blood and Ink*, 208
Ashmore, Harry S.: 309
Ashworth, Ray (San Antonio police chief): hired by MM, 196; injured in auditorium riot, 216
Asia policy: 278
Astor, Viscountess: 244
Aubrey, William (San Antonio attorney): 47
auditorium riot. SEE riot at auditorium
Australia: 266–267

Avila Camacho, President Manuel: 200

"Babies Ball": 52
Bailey, Forrest (ACLU official): 59
Baker, Paul (theater director): 202
Baldwin, Roger: on MM as champion of civil liberties, 87–88, 138; mentioned, 59
Ballard, Frederick A. (ACLU lawyer): 91
Bankhead, Rep. William B.: 75
Bardwell, Malcolm (aide to MM): 273
Barton, James (director of *Drama of the Alamo*): 202
Baruch, Bernard: 80
Battle of the Bulge: 246
Beard, Charles A.: helps MM on review of *Good Society*, 70; opposes military disaffection bill, 91; supports MM on rigid neutrality measure, 100; aids MM on *In Blood and Ink*, 208; mentioned, 162
Beaverbrook, Lord: 245
Bedichek, Roy: 12
Bellinger, Charles (San Antonio Negro leader): linked with "machine," 178; attacked by MM, 185; mentioned, 227
Bellinger, Valmo (son of Charles): denounced by MM, 227; and attempted recall of MM, 228–229
Benedict, H. Y. (University of Texas dean and president): victim of probe of religious views, 36–37; on censorship of *Daily Texan*, 124
Benson, Elmer: 123
Benton, Sen. William: lauds MM's gobbledygook article, 240; on MM as leader, 309
Berger, Rep. Victor: 15
Berle, A. A., Jr.: praises MM's speech on reorganization bill, 172; on nature of large corporate enterprises, 174; and FDR's third-term intentions, 205; approves MM's trip to England for SWPC, 243
Bertetti, Lawrence (Bexar County Democratic chairman): 304
Bevan, Aneurin: 300
Bexar Facts, The: 47–51

Biddle, George: directs art activities at La Villita, 200; MM comments to, on auditorium riot, 217
"Bill of Rights" for prisoners: 238
Black, Hugo L.: attends National Conference of Progressives, 123; joins MM to support Supreme Court reform, 135; on MM's defeat for Congress, 186–187; congratulates MM on victory in mayor's race, 193; H. L. Mencken on, 211; on Japanese relocation cases, 220; on influence of MM, 307
Blanton, Rep. Tom: MM clashes with, 107–108; supports "red rider" legislation, 139
Bliven, Bruce: 129
Blunderbuss: 17
Board of Trade (British): 243
Boileau, Rep. Gerald J.: 78
Boller, Prof. Paul F., Jr.: 299
Bone, Sen. Homer T.: 117
Boorstin, Daniel J.: 46
Borden, Gail: 70
Bowles, Chester: 272
Boyd, Julian P.: 299
Boyle, R. J.: 128
Bradley, Gen. Omar N.: 258
Brandeis, Louis D.: 242
Brandeis University: 295, 299–300
Brann, William Cowper: 12
Brewster, Rep. R. Owen: 87
Brogan, William F. (Citizens League associate and campaign manager for MM): 118
Brookings Institution Conference (San Antonio, 1952): 297–298
Brooks, Mrs. Emma Tenyuca (San Antonio Communist party leader): 214–215
Brooks, Raymond (Austin columnist): 37, 180, 193
Brooks, Robert C.: on MM's self-education, 19; on MM as scholar, 39; importance of MM, 298; on MM's failure to seek relaxation, 304; mentioned, 16
Broun, Heywood: applauds MM's 1936 primary victory, 123; reviews *A Maverick American*, 143, 144; advises "Mavericks" on Jefferson Is-

Index

land meeting, 156; on Garner's opposition to MM, 203
Browder, Earl: denounces MM, 167, 177
Brown, John: 295
Browne, Lewis: 302
Brownell, Herbert: 289
Bruce, J. Campbell: 282
Bryan, William Jennings: 14
Buchanan, Rep. James P.: 125
Bulwinkle, Rep. Alfred L.: 145
Bureau of Government Requirements: 236
bureaucrats: defense of, 112–114
Burke, Edmund: 66
Burkean view of role of representative by MM: 66, 120–121
Bush, Vannevar: 237
Byrd, Sen. Harry F.: on MM, 63; MM on, 152
Byrns, Speaker Joseph W.: 75

Cadmus, W. M. (San Antonio union official): 53
California: MM's sojourn in, 272
Calendar Wednesday: 94
Callaghan, Mayor Alfred (San Antonio): 274
campaigning: MM's attitude toward, 121
campaign train incident (1938): 181–182
"Campus Buzzards": 17
Candide: influence of, on MM, 40–41
Cantor, Eddie: 217–218
Cardozo, Benjamin: encounter with Carl Sandburg, 99
Carter, Amon G.: 206
Carter, Hodding: 221
Cassidy, Col. James E. (lobbyist): 84
Catton, Bruce: 237, 243
Central Relief Committee (San Antonio): 52
Central Veterans Committee (San Antonio): 52
"Ceremony of Kava": 268
Chaffee, Zechariah, Jr.: 91
Chamber of Commerce, San Antonio: 95–96
Chamber of Commerce, U.S.: 96
Chambers, Mayor C. M. (San Antonio): 48

Chase, Stuart: 70
Chiang Kai Shek: comment on, 256; MM interviews, 263–264
Chiang Kai Shek, Madame: 260
Childs, Marquis: 116
Chiles, M. P. (San Antonio FBI agent): 290
China policy, U.S.: MM critical of, 256–265, 278; "Memorial and Memorandum" on, 278–280
Chinese, Nationalist: MM's impression of, 256
Chow Kan P'en, Mrs. (Chinese communist): 262
Chun-Mai Carsun Chang (delegate to San Francisco UN conference): 249
Citizens League of San Antonio: organized, 49–50; supports MM for Congress, 62; endorses MM in second race for Congress, 118; disintegration of, 177
civil liberties: championed by MM, 57–58, 60; MM as leader of, in Congress, 87–94; MM's early views on, 89; and censorship of *Daily Texan*, 124–126; of speakers in San Antonio and Houston, 127; MM warns of threat to, 130; and loyalty oaths, 138; and House Committee on Un-American Activities, 175; MM's proclamation on, 214; and Communists' use of San Antonio auditorium, 214–215; and MM's position on freedom of assembly, 218–219; and government investigations, 285–289; and denials of procedural rights to immigrants, 282–284; and interpretation of Ninth Amendment, 288; and Fifth Amendment guarantee against self-incrimination, 289; and theory of "freedom of information," 290–292; and federal loyalty program, 292; and war-crimes trials, 292–294; MM called "great leader" in, 309
civil rights legislation: encouraged by H. L. Mencken, 110–111; MM drops support for, 112; MM supports, in 1950's, 294–296. SEE ALSO Negroes
civil service: extension of, 173

Clapper, Raymond: 156
Clark, Sen. Bennett C.: 82
Clark, Edward: as Texas secretary of state, 185; as leader in FDR third-term movement in Texas, 205
Clark, Grenville: 215
Clayton, W. L. ("Will"): 97
Clemens, Ernest W. (Republican opponent of MM, 1936): 128
Cochran, J. C. (San Antonio school superintendent): 127
Coffer, John D. (Texas "Loyalist" leader): 276
Cohen, Benjamin: 308
Cohn, Morris E. (Los Angeles law partner of MM): 272
Committee to Defend America by Aiding the Allies: 233, 234, 235
communism: MM's analysis of, 280–281; and Diga Colony experiment, 55; charges of, against MM, 61, 119–120, 176–177, 207, 226
Communist Manifesto: 280
Communist party: MM grants use of San Antonio Municipal Auditorium to, 214
communists: MM's attitude toward, 58–60, 105; interviewed by MM in China, 261–262
Conflict of Colour: influence of, on MM, 294
Congressional Medal of Honor for arts and sciences: proposed by MM, 161
Congress, reform of: MM advocates, 94, 155; and attack on Rules Committee, 158–159
Connally, Sen. Tom: MM on, 156; Kilday and Connally on, 179–180; mentioned, 225
Conrad, Joseph: 68
conservation: MM on, 115
conservatives: and New Deal, 164, 183
Cooke, Alistair: 304
Cooke, Morris L.: 129
Corcoran, Thomas: attends strategy meeting on "death sentence," 87; helps MM with political enemy, 118–119; MM seeks support of, 179
Corey, Herbert: 73
Costigan, Sen. Edward F.: 123

Covici, Pascal (publisher): on MM's contribution to Erasmus book, 40; publishes *A Maverick American*, 142–143
Cox, Rep. Eugene: attacked by MM, 147; has MM labeled "buffoon," 148
Crosskey, William W.: 299
Currie, Lauchlin: 243
Curti, Merle: 210
Cushing, Dr. Harvey: 193

Dabney, Virginius: on MM's support of anti-lynching law, 140–141; on MM's stand on Communists' use of auditorium, 217
Daily Texan (University of Texas student newspaper): censorship of, by regents, 124–126
Daily Worker: criticizes MM, 177
Dallas News: supports MM's attack on denials of civil liberties in Dallas, 142; supports MM on Communists' use of San Antonio auditorium, 217; praises MM as mayor, 274
Dalton, Hugh (president of British Board of Trade): 244
Daniels, Josephus: congratulates MM on victory in mayor's race, 193; on MM's acquittal in poll-tax trial, 196–197
Davis, Frank C. (one-time Citizens League leader): 48, 62
Davis, John P. (Secretary of National Negro Congress): 224
"death sentence": in public utilities holding company bill, 86–87
Debs, Eugene V.: 11, 177
Delano, Frederic: 151
demagoguery: MM's view of, 67; example of, 120
Demagogues Club of Congress: 156
Democratic conventions: Texas (1940), 206–208; National (1940), 232; Texas (1952), 275; National (1952), 275–276
Demosthenes: 235
Dern, George H.: 106
Dickson, Fagan (head of San Antonio "Better Government"): 227
Dickson, Charles M.: 190–191

Index

Dickstein, Rep. Samuel: 141–142
Dies, Rep. Martin: comment on, by Roger Baldwin, 88; inducts FDR into Demagogues Club, 156; as member of House Rules Committee, 158; and House Committee on Un-American Activities, 175; as chairman of Committee, 285; temporary rapprochement of MM with, 285
Diga Colony: 53–56
Dilling, Elizabeth: 176
Dirksen, Rep. Everett M.: 81
Divine, Robert A.: on MM as leader on neutrality legislation, 82; analysis of failure of "Mavericks" in opposition to compromise neutrality measure, 102
Dobbs, Terrell Louise. SEE Webb, Mrs. Walter P.
Dobie, J. Frank: on meeting of MM and Carl Sandburg, 301; mentioned, 99
Donovan, Weldon (*Bexar Facts* editor): 48
Dos Passos, John: 116
Douglas, William O.: on Japanese relocation cases, 220; on influence of MM, 307
Drama of the Alamo: 94, 202
Drossaerts, Archbishop Arthur (San Antonio): 214
Drought, H. P. (Texas WPA administrator): 134
Drury, Allan: 241–242
Dubinsky, David: 226
Dutcher, Rodney (journalist): 121–122
Dworaczyk, Father Julias, 282

Early, Stephen: 74, 181
Economic Club of New York: 151
economic liberty: MM's concept of, 209–211
Edgerton, John E. (textile manufacturer): 145
Eisenhower, Dwight D.: 246, 275, 276
Elliott, Dr. William Y.: 245
Emerson, Ralph Waldo: 43
Endo, Ex parte (1944): 220
Erasmus: 40
Ernst, Morris: 218, 291
Ervin, Charles W. (labor leader and socialist): influence of, on MM, 88–89; mentioned, 162
Estournelles de Constant, d': 21
Evjue, William T. (editor and publisher): 302

Fairbank, John K.: accompanies MM on visit with Chinese communists, 261; praises MM's research on China policy, 278–279
Farley, James A.: fails to use MM as speaker for national ticket, 123; MM on, 186
Ferguson Island: 266
Ferguson, Gov. James E.: 205
Fertig, Col. Wendell W. (leader of Philippine guerrillas): 266
Fiesta Noche del Rio: 201
Fiesta San Jacinto: 201
Fiji Islands: 268
Finney, Ruth (journalist): 122
Fish, Rep. Hamilton: 235
Fishbein, Morris: 245
"Flag of Liberation": 241
Ford, Guy Stanton: 299
foreign aid: MM urges for postwar Europe, 247; need for U.S. supervision of, 259
Forrestal, James: 250
France, Anatole: 41, 74
Frank, Jerome: on third party movement, 123; at anti-Supreme Court bloc meeting, 133
Frankfurter, Felix: praise for MM on holding company bill speech, 87; congratulates MM on election victory (1936), 129; discusses role of U.S. in world affairs, 235
Frantz, Joe B.: 300
freedom of assembly: 214, 218–219
freedom of expression: defense of, 90; "safety valve" theory of, 104; theory of limits of, 105–106
freedom of information: 290–292
freedom of press: and military disaffection bill, 92; and Kramer anti-sedition bill, 93; MM fights suppression of, 109; and censorship of *Daily Texan*, 124–126
freedom from want: 210
Frisch, Rabbi Ephraim: 127
Fuller, Rep. Claude A.: 77–78

Fusion Ticket: 191
Futrell, Harry: 57

Gaitskell, H. T. M. (British price administrator): 244
Gandhi, Mohandus K.: 46–47
Garner, John Nance: MM's relationship with, 203; MM opposes for presidency, 204; mentioned, 128, 162
German soldiers: MM on, 23, 24
Germany, E. B. (steel executive): 206
Geyer anti–poll-tax bill: 223
Gifford, Rep. Charles L.: 164–165, 166
Gilchrist, Rep. Fred C.: 79
Giles, Palmer (rancher and boyhood friend of MM): 8, 10
Gillette, Sen. Guy: 160–161
Gillette-Maverick bill: 160–161
Gitlow, Benjamin: 58
Glass, Sen. Carter: 156
gobbledygook: MM's memorandum and article on, 239–240; mentioned, 34, 305
Great Seal of the United States: 303
Green, Dr. A. Leon: 19
Green, William: and minimum-wage law demands, 149–150; boasts of contributing to MM's defeat, 180–181; mentioned, 147
Groce, Walter (San Antonio lawyer): 50
Grotius, Hugo: 88
Guffey coal bill: 85–86
Gunther, John: 229

Hague, Mayor Frank (Jersey City): MM denounces, 175; MM says FDR should take stand against Hague and other corrupt bosses, 186
Hague v. CIO (1939): 218
Halifax, Lord: 244
Halpenny, Marie S. (San Antonio writer): 286
Han-fu Chang (Chinese Communist editor): 261
Harris, Edward A. (journalist): 249
Harris, Robert E. G.: 272
Hegel, G. W. F.: 69
HemisFair: 201
Henderson, Herbert C. (Austin writer): 208

Henderson, Leon: assists MM with *A Maverick American*, 143; assists MM with tax speech, 173; aids MM on *In Blood and Ink*, 208; in Office of Production Management, 236; joins MM in WW II discussion with Lord Beaverbrook, 245
heroism: MM discusses, 24
High, Stanley: 153
Hill, Edwin C.: 151
Hillman, Sidney: 123
Hitler, Adolf: 233–234
Hodge, Ed (editor of *Daily Texan*): 124–126
Hodge, Gen. John R.: 256
Holcombe, Arthur N.: 45
Holcombe, Oscar F. (mayor of Houston): 207
Homma, Gen.: tried for war crimes, 266
Hoover, J. Edgar: 290–291
Hopkins, Harry: attends meetings of "Mavericks," 77; defended by MM, 113; meets with "Mavericks" before Jefferson Island meeting, 156; on federal appointment for MM, 236
"hors d'oeuvres reform committee": 152
House Judiciary Reform Group: 135
Houston Open Forum: 127
Howland, Charles P.: 298
Huey, K. A. (San Antonio restaurant owner): 283
Huey, Maury Maverick: 283
Huey, Maury Maverick, Jr.: 283
Hugman, Robert H. (San Antonio architect): 201
Hull, Cordell: confers with MM on neutrality legislation, 82; approves MM's WW II trip to England, 243
Hunter, Robert: 11
Huntress, Frank (publisher of *San Antonio Evening News* and *Express*): 48
Hurley, Gen. Patrick J.: 263
Huson, Hobart: 15
Hutchins, Robert Maynard: 125, 309

Ibsen, Henrik: influence of, on MM, 44
Ickes, Harold: defended by MM, 113;

Index

as butt of humorous letter to FDR, 114; on MM in primary, 119; congratulates MM on acquittal in poll-tax trial, 196; challenges Garner-for-president group, 206; doubts MM's administrative abilities, 236; mentioned, 118
Iconoclast (radical paper): influence of, on MM, 12
immigration laws and policies: 282–284
In Blood and Ink: 208–210
Institutum Divi Thomae: 236
International Ladies Garment Workers Union: 196
investigations: MM's views on, 285–289
isolationism: 233–234

Jacks, Dr. L. P.: 42–43
Jackson, Justice Robert H.: on Ninth Amendment, 288; asks MM's alternative to war-crimes trials, 293
Jackson, Dr. Dudley (San Antonio surgeon): 144
Japan: threat of, before WW II, 234–235; proposals for reform of, 254–255
Jefferson Island Rod and Gun Club: 155
Jefferson Island meeting: 155–157
Jefferson, Pat: 56
Jefferson, Thomas: influence of, on MM, 13, 42, 88; mentioned, 243, 281
Jehovah's Witnesses: 218–219
Jelke case: 291
Johnson, Carl Wright: 196
Johnson, Gen. Hugh S.: 70, 80
Johnson, Lyndon B.: election of, to Congress, 135; supports Court reform, 135; and minimum-wage bill, 173; active in FDR third-term movement, 205; seeks compromise in FDR-Garner fight, 206; on administration of immigration laws, 284; complaint to, by MM on federal loyalty program, 292; on MM's importance, 308; mentioned, 179, 231
Johnson, Gen. Robert W.: 239

Johnson, Wylie (San Antonio city manager): 286
Jones, Jesse: advice of, to MM, 76; on MM as president, 308; mentioned, 162
Joyce, James: influence of, on MM, 41

Karig, Walter: 74–75, 92
Keller, Rep. Kent E.: 78
Kelly, Mayor Edward: 238
Kelso, Robert (field director for RFC): 55
Kennan, George F.: 278
Kennedy, Rep. Ambrose J.: 139
Kenny, Robert (Los Angeles law partner of MM): 272
Key, V. O., Jr.: 224
Kilday, James E. (brother of Paul J.): 176
Kilday, Owen (brother of Paul J.): 176, 189, 226, 227
Kilday, Rep. Paul J.: opposes MM in 1938 primary, 176; says MM supports John L. Lewis for president, 179; defeats MM, 180; MM comments on, 181, 227; speaks for Quin in 1941 mayor's race, 227
King, Sen. William H.: 135, 165
Kleberg, Rep. Richard M.: 61
Knutson, Rep. Harold: 171
Koppleman, Rep. Herman P.: 117
Korean War: MM predicts, 255, 278; MM on germ-warfare charges in, 291
Klutz, Jerry (columnist): 240
Kramer bill (anti-sedition measure): MM opposes, 93, 103; dropped, 107
Kramer, Rep. Charles: 93, 107
Kriesler, Fritz: 30
Krug, J. A.: 243
Ku Klux Klan: MM attacks, 30; in MM's first campaign for Congress, 62
Kvale, Rep. Paul J.: leader of "Mavericks," 77; commended by H. L. Mencken, 92

labor, organized: MM's sympathies toward, 67, 68, 146; and sit-down strikes, 147–148; MM critical of,

149–150; in 1938 campaign, 179–181
Lattimore, Owen: 291
La Follette, Gov. Phillip: 123
La Follette, Sen. Robert M.: 15
La Guardia, Fiorello H.: attends National Conference of Progressives, 123; MM seeks advice of, 191; congratulates and encourages MM, 194; and parallels to MM's career, 194–195; falling out of, with MM, 195; mentioned, 157
Latin American policy: MM's proposals for, 162
La Villita: origin and historical background of, 199; development and success of, 200–201
Lee, Robert E.: 138
Lemke, Rep. William: 79
Lerner, Max: on MM's concept of liberalism, 210; on MM's visit to Brandeis University, 299–300
Lewis, John L: attends National Conference of Progressives, 123; at anti–Supreme Court bloc meeting with MM, 133; on John Nance Garner, 205; mentioned, 129, 177
Lewis, Rep. David J.: 133
Lilienthal, David E.: 86, 171
Lincoln, Abraham: 46
Lippmann, Walter: 70, 153
Little, Herbert (book reviewer): 143
Llewellyn, Prof. Karl N.: 91
Locke, Edwin A. (aide to HST): 249
Los Angeles: MM on, 272
Lovett, Prof. Robert M.: 127
"Loyalists" (faction of Texas Democrats): 275–276
loyalty program: 292
Lubin, Isador (New Deal administrator): 76
Ludlow amendment: 171
Lyttleton, Oliver (British minister of production): 244, 245

Maas, Rep. Melvin J.: 79
McAlister, Prof. Sam B.: 298
McAllister, Mayor Walter M. (San Antonio): 49
McCarran-Walter immigration law: 284
MacArthur, Gen. Douglas: on war-crimes trials, 253, 293; mentioned, 241, 277, 300
McCabe, Joseph V.: 109
McCarthy, Sen. Joseph R.: MM's view of, 287; State Department fear of, 297; mentioned, 285, 300
McCarthyism: MM on nature of and causes, 287; fought by MM, 308
McCormack, Rep. John W.: 90
McCrory, Judge W. W. (Texas district judge, San Antonio): 188, 189
McFarlane, Rep. W. D.: 179
McGown, Floyd (aide to MM): 207
"machine" (San Antonio-Bexar County political ring): 1929–1930 attack on, 47–48; *San Antonio Evening News* and *Express* associated with, 48; attacked by Rep. Harry M. Wurzbach, 51; defeated by Citizens League, 51; supports Paul Kilday against MM, 176; charged with election irregularities, 189–190; and Negro vote, 178, 185, 228–229
McIntyre, Marvin: 179, 181
Mackey, Argyle R. (immigration official): 282
McNinch, Frank R. (ch. of Federal Power Commission): 133
McNutt, Paul V.: 245
McSwain, Rep. John J.: 80, 85
Madero, President Francisco I.: 15
Main Avenue High School (San Antonio): 15
Malik, Charles: 281
Mann, Thomas: 301
Manus Island: 266
Mao Tse-tung: 261
Marcantonio, Rep. Vito: "decorated" by MM, 72; comment on, by Roger Baldwin, 88; opposes military disaffection bill, 91; prevented from "aiding" MM in mayor's race, 192; MM denies making speech for, 273
Marshall, Gen. George C.: 253, 258
Marshall, Thurgood: 295
Martin, Homer (United Auto Workers president): 149
Marxism: SEE communism
Masterson, Bert (United Press editor and writer): 209

Index

Mauermann, Mayor Gus B. (San Antonio): 273-274
Maury, Rev. James: 6
Maury, Matthew Fontaine: 6
"maverick": origin of term, 4
"Maverick, The," (streetcar house): 305
Maverick, Albert (father of MM): youth of, 5; trip abroad of, and marriage of, 6; relationship of, with MM, 6-7, 9, 10; and education of MM, 13; economic views and interests of, 14; and 1930 annexation suit, 49; on MM's war wounds, 61; swears in MM as mayor, 193; death of, 272
Maverick, Dr. George (brother of MM): 40
Maverick, Jane (mother of MM): characteristics of, 7; relationship of, with MM, 10-11; on MM's love letters, 26
Maverick, Maury:
—as administrator: Bexar County tax collector, 51-53; attacks Depression problems in San Antonio, 52-57; reform program of, for San Antonio, 195-196; and restoration of La Villita, 199-200; achievements of, 229-230; WW II service of, 236-239; chairman of Smaller War Plants Corporation, 239-250; 251-269; gobbledygook memorandum of, 239-240; fights for small business reconversion, 241-243
—as champion of civil rights and civil liberties: attacks Ku Klux Klan, 30; charges University of Texas regents with inquisitorial tactics, 36; early views of, 89; fights military disaffection bill, 90-92, 103; fights Kramer anti-sedition measure, 93, 103; fights American Legion suppression of booklet on Americanism, 109; promotes general civil rights measure, 110-112; attacks University of Texas regents for censorship of *Daily Texan*, 125-126; defends speakers in San Antonio and Houston, 127; fights "red rider" loyalty oath for teachers, 138-140; opposes establishment of House Committee on Un-American Activities, 175; attacks abuses in U.S. immigration administration, 282-284; temporary rapprochement of, with Martin Dies, 285; attacks McCarthyism and inquisitions, 285-288; blasts federal loyalty program, 292. SEE ALSO civil liberties
—as congressman: leads "Mavericks," 76-77, 153-154; leads fight for extension of TVA powers, 83; influence of, in passage of holding company bill, 86-87; gains legislation for preservation of historic sites, 94; leadership of, recognized by FDR, 99; pushes rigid neutrality law in 1936, 100-102; dubbed "Congressman of the Year" by Pearson and Allen, 117; secures passage of cancer research measure, 144-145; champions minimum-wage law, 145-146; tries to push flagging New Deal, 155-160, 172; proposes "American Youth Act," 162; helps to defeat Ludlow amendment, 171; urges congressional reforms, 94, 155, 159
—, education of: early reading and study, 11, 13; at Virginia Military Institute, 16; at University of Texas, 16-19; influenced by grand jury duty, 31-32; as self-taught scholar, 32-35, 39-44; and overemphasis on athletics at University of Texas, 37-38; at St. Mary's University, 161; and self-education in late career, 277-281
—, nominations and elections of: as tax collector, 51; and first race for Congress, 61-62; and second race for Congress, 116-122; and defeat of, in third race for Congress, 175-187; and first race for mayor of San Antonio, 190-192; and 1940 anti-Garner movement, 203-208; and second race for mayor, 225-228; and third race for mayor (1947), 272-274; and contest for congressman-at-large, 274; as leader of Texas "Loyalists" (1952), 275-276
— and Negroes: need for aid to mi-

norities, 60; support of anti-lynching law, 140–141; general views, 221–225; and end to poll tax, 223–224; and desegregation, 294–296. SEE ALSO civil rights; "machine"

—, personal characteristics of: general, 64–74; as youthful agitator, 15; war wounds and suffering, 28, 61–62; as "weight watcher," 63–64; as humorist, 71–73; as "Texas La Guardia," 194–195; and appraisal of past career and future, 268–270; and types of hobbies, 302–303

—and religion: liberal views of parents, 14; Jehovah's Witnesses, 218–219; extremes of, 254; and Chinese communism, 279

—and Supreme Court: early attack on, 94; and "court packing" bill, 134–135

—, theories of: on Depression, 45–46; on communal experiments (Diga Colony) and reasons for failure, 55–56; and "War on Poverty" concept, 95; on limits of free expression, 105–106; and concept of economic liberty, 209–211; on prison reform, 238; and concept of "freedom of information," 290; on revolution, 42, 253, 277, 280, 294

—and trips abroad: to British Isles for legal research (1919), 25; to Britain, as chairman of SWPC, 244–245; second WW II trip to Britain and European battle fronts, 245–248; mission to Asia as SWPC chairman, 251–270

—and war: efforts to enter armed forces (1916), 21; enlists at outbreak of U.S. involvement in WW I, 22; wounded in Argonne offensive, 23–24; decorated for gallantry in action, 25; on tragedy and absurdity of war, 24–25, 80, 81, 280; clashes with FDR on naval expansion, pushes development of air defenses, 164–167; reversal of antiwar views, 232–235

—, writings of: attempted war novel, 45; as poet, 44–45; as book reviewer, 70; *A Maverick American*, 142–143; *In Blood and Ink*, 208–210; and chapter on Los Angeles, 272

Maverick, Mrs. Maury. SEE Webb, Mrs. Walter P.

Maverick, Maury, Jr.: on MM's war wounds and suffering, 28; sees famous father in film, 163; receives FDR letter on father's defeat for mayor, 231; follows MM's footsteps, 283; suggests name of "American Activities Committee," 286; victory of, in civil rights case, 295; at University of Texas, 302; campaigns for Texas Legislature, 304

Maverick, Sam (of Boston): 58

Maverick, Samuel (of Pendleton): 4

Maverick, Samuel A. (MM's grandfather): 4, 5, 138, 193

Maverick, Terrelita: 28, 194

"Maverickos": 273

"Mavericks": origin and organization of, 76; attacks on, by House leaders, 77–78; aims, program, and leaders of, 78; defeat Vinson bonus bill, pass Patman bonus bill, 79; fight for neutrality legislation, 82–83, 102; attack lagging New Deal, 153–154; prepare for FDR's Jefferson Island meeting, 156; success of, on farm tenancy bill and appropriations for NLRB, 158; urge more New Deal legislation, 167. SEE ALSO Maury Maverick as congressman

May, Rep. Andrew J.: 83–84

Mayfield, Sen. Earle B.: 47

Mencken, H .L.: comments on MM's attempted war novel, 41; lauds MM's fight on military disaffection bill, 92; offers draft of general civil rights bill to MM, 110–111; opposes MM's concept of economic liberty, 211; on Hugo Black, 211

Menefee, R. S.: 122

Merriam, Charles E.: 298

Mexican-Americans: MM defends and assists in WW I training, 22–23; MM defends in House speech, 107; MM's aid to, as mayor, 199; and plight of low-paid pecan shellers, 199

military disaffection bill (Tydings-McCormack bill): provisions of, 90;

Index

MM condemns and organizes fight against, 90–92; renewed attack on, 103–104; dropped, 106
Miller, Monsignor Cletus A.: 236
Miller, Mayor Tom (Austin): as FDR third-term leader, 205; fight of, with MM, 207
Minersville School District v. *Gobitis* (1940): 218
minimum-wage law: MM champions, 145–146; signs petition to bring to House floor, 173
Minute Women: 286
Mitrany, David: 298
Montgomery, Dr. Robert H.: on inquisition by University of Texas regents, 36; gives economics lectures to Diga colonists, 54; target of "red hunt" by Texas Legislature, 129
More, Sir Thomas: 40
Morgan, Arthur E.: 84, 129, 171
Morgan, Harcourt A.: 170–171
Morris, Grover C. (worker for Fusion Ticket): 191
Morris, Willie: 308
Morrison, Ralph W. (Federal Reserve Board member): 122
Morrow, Wright: 275–276
Murphy, Justice Frank: 284
Murrow, Edward R.: 276

Nami, Herman G. (San Antonio American Legion leader): 127
Nathan, Robert: 237
National Association for Advancement of Colored People (NAACP): 224–225, 295
National Cancer Research Institute: 145
National Conference of Progressives: 123
National Labor Relations Board (NLRB): 158
National Lawyers Guild: 150
National Parks Trust Fund Board: 94
National Resources Board: 115
National Youth Administration (NYA): 199–200
natural rights: 23, 88
Nazis: 234
Nearing, Scott: 17

Neff, Pat M.: 37
Negroes: MM opposed to social equality for, 112; MM urges equal economic treatment of, 160; general views of MM on, 221–225; MM opposed to segregation of, 294
Nehru, Dr. S. S. (president of International Union of Lawyers Associations): 301
Nelson, Donald M.: and MM's proposal for Office of Technical Development, 237; picks MM to head SWPC, 239; reconversion plans and departure of, from government, 241; praises MM for SWPC work, 248
Neuberger, Richard L.: 143
neutrality legislation: MM introduces bill on, 81–83; and Nye-Clark-Maverick bill, 100–101; MM opposes compromise measure on, 102
New Britain: 266
New Deal: MM anticipates, 45–46; MM's contribution to ideology of, 210–211
New Guinea, 266
New Zealand: 267–268
New York County American Legion: 109
Ninth Amendment: 288
Nixon, Prof. H. Clarence: 116, 299
Norris, Sen. George: MM's view of, 28; at National Conference of Progressives, 123; at anti–Supreme Court bloc meeting, 133; mentioned, 163
Nye-Clark-Maverick bill. SEE neutrality legislation
Nye Committee: 82
Nye, Sen. Gerald P.: 82, 100

Office of Production Research and Development: 238
Office of War Information (OWI): 259
Okinawa: 252
Olmstead, Allan S. (ACLU lawyer): 91

pacifism: 42, 80, 232
Paine, Thomas: influence of, on MM, 13, 88; MM's work likened to, 209

Parran, Dr. Thomas (surgeon general of the U.S.): 178
Parten, Maj. J. R. (Texas "Loyalist" leader): 275
Passamaquoddy Dam: 87
Patman bonus bill: 79
Patman, Rep. Wright: 79
patriotism: follies of, 41; MM demonstrates, 232, 240–241; MM's views on, 281–282
patronage: MM's impatience with, 173, 228
Patterson, Bennett B. (author of *The Forgotten Ninth Amendment*): 288
Patterson, Eleanor: 182
Patterson, J. J. ("Jack"): 191
Patton, Gen. George S.: 246–247
Pearl Harbor attack: 235
Pearson, Capt. Conrad A. (aide to MM): 265
Pearson, Drew: praises MM as "Congressman of the Year," 117; on campaign train incident, 181–182; on clash of MM and Eddie Cantor, 217; on incident of Patton slapping soldier, 246–247
Pearson, Leon: 143
Pei Tsu Yi (Bank of China): 260
Penton, Brian (Australian author): 267
Perkins, Frances: 147
Pershing, Gen. John J.: 10, 21–22
Philippine Islands: 266
Point Four program: 271
poll tax: frauds in Bexar County (1930), 50; and MM's trial, 196; and MM's testimony for Geyer anti–poll-tax bill, 223
Powell, Thomas Reed: 129, 162
President's Committee on Administrative Management: 172
prison reform: 238
"Progressive Democrats": 129
P. S. Ho (Bank of China): 263
public utilities holding company bill (Wheeler-Rayburn bill): 86–87
Public Works Administration (PWA): 113
Pufendorf, Samuel von: 88

Quin, Mayor C. K. (San Antonio): opposes MM in first race for Congress, 61; supports MM in 1936 general election, 128; supports Paul Kilday against MM (1938), 176; indicted for election irregularities and indictments quashed, 188–190; responds to charges of election irregularities, 190; flays city commissioners and loses organization, 191; defeated by MM, 192; defeats MM (1941), 227–228; mentioned, 162

Rabelais, François: influence of, on MM, 40–41; mentioned, 59
radicalism of MM: 68
Rankin, Rep. Jeannette: 80
Rankin, Rep. John E.: 86, 87, 142
Rayburn, Sam: 122, 162, 173, 206
Rector, George: 153
"red rider" (loyalty oath measure): MM opposes, 138–140
Resettlement Administration: 113
revolution: 42, 253, 277, 280, 294
Reyes, General Bernardo: 15
Rhee, Syngman: 255
Rich, Rep. Robert F.: MM extends time to, for attack on Democrats, 112–113; gives time to MM to answer attack by Rep. Cox, 148; chides Democrats on Jefferson Island meeting with FDR, 155
riot. SEE San Antonio Municipal Auditorium
Robbins, Lionel (British economist): 244
Roberts, Mary Carter (book reviewer): 144
Robinson, Sen. Joseph T.: 136
Roche, Prof. John P.: 90
Rodriguez, Polycarpio (Indian fighter and scout): 5
Rodriguez, Santos (caretaker of MM's home): 306
Rogers, R. R. (commander of Diga Colony): 53–54
Roosevelt, Eleanor: 73, 238
Roosevelt, Elliott: 182
Roosevelt, Franklin D.: MM anticipates election of, 46; MM's letter to, seeking appointment with Stephen Early, 74; vetoes bonus bill, 79; opposes neutrality legislation, 82–83; commissions MM to father

Index

TVA measure, 85; consults MM on "death sentence" in holding company bill, 86; State of the Union address (1936) of, 98; letter of, recognizing MM's leadership, 99; opposes Nye-Clark-Maverick bill, 101; humorous letter of, 114; visits MM in San Antonio, 118; private congratulations of, to MM on 1936 primary victory, 122; receives support of National Conference of Progressives, 123; MM predicts victory of, over Landon, 127; and Supreme Court "packing" plan, 132–134; calls Jefferson Island meeting, 155; inducted into Demagogues Club, 156; characterized by MM, 164; and naval construction program, 164–167; and naval construction program criticisms, 167; persuades MM to oppose Ludlow amendment, 171; support by, of MM in 1938, 179; wires congratulations to MM on victory in mayor's race, 192; congratulates MM on poll-tax trial acquittal, 196; MM urges renomination of, in 1940, 204; suggests MM as possible running mate, 205; commends MM on *In Blood and Ink*, 210; letter of, to MM, Jr., praising MM as mayor, 231; appoints MM as chairman of SWPC, 239; humorous note of, 241; advice to MM on Negro rights, 294–295; mentioned, 95, 193

Roosevelt, Henry L. (assistant secretary of the Navy): 91

Rubiola, Jacob (San Antonio parks commissioner): 193

Rucker, Fred (Democratic state committeeman from San Antonio): 207

Rules Committee, U.S. House of Representatives: 158–159

Rural Electrification Administration (REA): 116

Russians: MM's view of, 281

Sabbath, Rep. A. J.: 117
Sachar, A. L.: 300
Salter, Prof. J. T.: 298
Samoa: 268
San Antonio: in Texas Revolution, 4, 5; Albert Maverick as citizen of, 7; view of, from Sunshine Ranch, 8; MM promotes Carnegie Library for, 32; charges of political corruption in, 47–48; Citizens League organized in, 49; depression in, 52–57; and *Drama of the Alamo*, 94, 202; health conditions in, 95, 178; attempt to bar speakers in, 127; "machine" government in, criticized, 177–178; MM charged with "defaming," 192; MM's reform of, 195–196; MM restores color of, 198; and La Villita, 199–201; river development and other attractions of, 201–202; riot at Municipal Auditorium in, 214–217; MM's achievements for, 229–231; MM's streetcar home in, 305

San Antonio Bar Association: MM as president of, 30; opposes FDR's court reform plan, 134

San Antonio Civic League: 49

San Antonio Conservation Society: 200

San Antonio Evening News: charged with support of "machine," 48; attacks MM as tax collector, 52; reports San Antonio visit of Elizabeth Dilling, 176; on MM's congratulations to Mayor Quin, 228

San Antonio Express: charged with support of "machine," 48; on MM as "buffoon," 148–149; on machine, 176; opposes MM for mayor, 192; on auditorium riot, 215, 216

San Antonio Light: recommended to readers by *Bexar Facts* editor, 48; commended by MM, 49; on investigation of 1936 election, 121; on charges of election irregularities of Quin and "machine," 189–190; on auditorium riot, 216; report of MM's achievements as mayor, 229–230

San Antonio Municipal Auditorium: riot at, 214–217; as political issue, 273. SEE ALSO civil liberties; Communist party

San Antonio River beautification: 201

Sanchez, Johnny (political organizer for MM): 273

Sandburg, Carl: encounter of, with Benjamin Cardozo, 99; impression of MM, 301
San Jose Mission State Park: 94
Schlesinger, Arthur M.: 298
Schlesinger, Arthur M., Jr.: impression of MM's philosophy, 46; on election of "Maverick" group, 75; on working for MM, 298–299
Schneider, Rep. George J.: 78
Schomburg Collection award: 223
Sciortino, Pasquale (Italian alien): 282
Searls, Fred, Jr. (WPB member): 237
Seeligson, Lamar (MM's major opponent in 1936 primary): 116, 120
Shaw, George Bernard: 43
Sheppard, Sen. Morris: 21, 121
Shintoism: 253, 255
Shivers, Gov. Allan: 275–276
"Shivercrats" (faction of Texas Democrats): 275
Shook, John R. (Bexar County district attorney): involved in election irregularities of "machine," 188, 189; brings MM to trial on charge of buying poll-tax receipts, 196
Sinclair, Upton: 43
sit-down strikes: 147
Slayden, Ellen Maury (Mrs. James L.): as mentor to MM, 18–21; on MM's war wounds, 25; on MM as "lady killer," 26; mentioned, 39
Slayden, Rep. James L (MM's uncle): 15, 22, 25, 27
small business: MM aids Donald Nelson in reconversion plans for, 241; MM's fight for, 241–243
Smaller War Plants Corporation (SWPC): MM made chairman of, 239; criticisms of, 248; to be abolished, 249; MM reports on, 271. SEE ALSO Maverick, Maury as administrator; Maverick, Maury and trips abroad
Smith, A. Abbot (director of SWPC): 248
Smith, Preserved (Erasmus scholar): 40
socialized medicine: 245
Sokolsky, George E.: 285
Sons of the American Revolution: 140

Soule, George: 129
Southern Conference on Human Welfare: 222–223
Southern Policy Committee: 116
Soviet Union: U.S. policy toward, 256
Sperti, Dr. George S.: 236
Splawn, Dr. W. M. W.: 37
Stark, H. J. Lutcher (chairman of University of Texas Regents): 36, 37, 38, 125
Starving Artists Show: 201
states' rights: MM critical of, 129
steel strike (Memorial Day 1937): 147
Steffens, Lincoln: 195
Steinbeck, John: 143
Sterling, Gov. Ross: 52
Stevenson, Adlai E.: joins MM in organization of Committee to Defend America by Aiding the Allies, 233; lauds appointment of MM to chairman of SWPC, 239; as presidential candidate (1952), 276
Stokes, Rose Pastor: as victim of WWI sedition laws, 106
Stone, Harlan: 133
Stone, I. F.: 239
Straight, Michael: 292
Strauss, Isador (New Deal administrator): 77
streetcar house ("The Maverick"): 305
Strubinger, D. B. (U.S. Customs official): 290
Studebaker, Dr. J. W.: 125
Sumners, Rep. Hatton W.: 179
Sun Fo (president of China's Yüan): 259, 263
Sunshine Ranch: 8, 9, 305
Sun Yat Sen: 260
Supreme Court: MM's attack on (1935), 94; FDR's reform plan for, 132; MM introduces bill on, 134; MM's view of, 137–138
Swanson, Claude A.: 91

Tagore, Rabindranath: 44
Taiwan: 255–256
tax policy: 174
Tennessee Valley Authority (TVA): MM tries to extend powers of, 83–

Index

85; extension bill for, passed, 85; MM supports investigation of, 170
Tenyuca, Emma. SEE Brooks, Mrs. Emma Tenyuca
Terrell, R. W. B.: as spokesman for "Constitution League" of San Antonio, 128
"Texas Dynasty": MM named as part of, 162
Texas Gulf Sulphur Company: 125
Texas Philosophical Society: 72
Texas Senate: MM addresses, 95; upbraided by MM for opposition to FDR's court reform plan, 134
Texas State Historical Association: 280, 295
Texas State Historical Theatre: 202
The Bexar Facts (San Antonio weekly tabloid, 1929–1930): 47–51
third party movement (1936): 123–124
Thomas, Norman: 196
Thucydides: 281
Tingfu F. Tsiang (Director of Chinese National Relief): 263
T. L. Chao (China Bank of Communications): 260
T. N. Lee (China Bank of Communications): 261
Torchbearer of the Revolution (review of by MM): 34
Townsend Plan: 67, 97
Toynbee, Arnold J.: 300–301
Treaty of Portsmouth: 256
Troyanovsky, Alexander (Soviet ambassador): 177
Truman, Harry S.: on MM's irreverence, 66; on MM's compassion, 73; approves Asian mission for MM, 249; on influence of MM's ideas, 271; on efforts to reform immigration administration, 284; mentioned, 283
Tugwell, Rexford Guy: target of MM's joshing, 33; defended by MM, 113; mentioned, 129
Tullis, Richard A. (San Antonio FHA administrator): 118–119
Turner, Frederick Jackson: 46
T. V. Soong (foreign minister of China): 260
Twain, Mark: 46, 71, 143

Tydings-McCormack bill. SEE military disaffection bill
Tydings, Sen. Millard E.: 90
Tynan, Sen. Walter: 117–118, 274

Ulysses: 41
Un-American Activities, Committee on: opposed by MM and defeated, 141; established, 175; limited support by MM (1939–1940), 285; condemned again (1949), 285
Un-American Activities, Special Committee on: 90
"unconditional surrender": MM opposed, 247
United Auto Workers: MM's speech to, 146
United Nations: concept of, 235; MM's view of, 281
United Nations Relief and Rehabilitation Administration (UNRRA): 259
United States Air Academy: proposed by MM, 169
University of Texas: MM attacks inquisition at, 36; MM on overemphasis on athletics at, 37; regents of, censor *Daily Texan*, 124; "red hunt" at, 129
Untermeyer, Louis: 131

Vandenburg, Sen. Arthur H.: 81
Velde, Rep. Harold H.: 300
Villard, Oswald Garrison: 232
Vinson bonus bill: 79
Vincent, John C.: 249
von Pufendorf, Samuel: 88

Wacker, Arnold Ben (aide to MM): on MM's compassion, 74; accompanies MM to Britain, 244
Wallace, Henry: attends meeting of "Mavericks," 76; MM charges with lagging in support of farm legislation, 154, 161; on economic liberty, 211; mentioned, 129, 200, 292
war: MM's views on, 24–25, 80, 81, 232–235, 280
war-crimes trials: MM's reasons for opposing, 293
"War on Poverty": 95
war profits legislation: 80–82

War Production Board (WPB): 236
War Research Development Corporation (proposed): 237
War Veterans Relief Camp. SEE Diga Colony
Weakley, A. B. (chairman of Citizens League): 50
Webb, Walter Prescott: on MM's university high jinks, 16; and anecdote about MM and Mexican band, 198; with Toynbee in Texas, 300; on MM's contributions, 308
Webb, Mrs. Walter P. (Terrell Louise Dobbs, Mrs. Maury Maverick): meets MM, 26; life with MM, 27–28; encounter with Senator Harry Byrd, 63; comments on treatment of MM by San Antonio newspapers, 148–149; helps MM to stay on delegation to 1940 Democratic National Convention, 208; at 1952 Democratic Convention, 276; characterizes MM, 305
Wedemeyer, Gen. Albert C.: 257
welfare department: MM proposes, 173
Wells, H. G.: 198
Welles, Orson: 198
Wheeler-Rayburn public utilities holding company bill: 86–87
Wherry, Sen. Kenneth S.: 239
White, Jack (San Antonio mayor): 286
White, Owen P.: 177

white primary: 224
White, Walter (head of NAACP): 224–225
White, William Allen: says "buffoon" vote against MM unjustified, 149; deplores defeat of MM for Congress, 184; joins MM in Committee to Defend America by Aiding the Allies, 233
Williams, Talcott (journalist and critic): 18
Wilson, Charles E.: 241
Wilson, Woodrow: 20, 168
Wirtz, Alvin J.: 206
Wong Wen-Hao (Chinese minister of economic affairs): 249, 260
Wood, Frederick H.: 135
Woodring, Harry: 128, 179
Woodrum, Rep. Clifton A.: 170
Works Progress Administration (WPA): defended by MM, 113; and amendment to keep workers from demonstrating, 142; MM supports investigation of, 154
Workman, Rev. James W.: 127
Wurzbach, Rep. Harry M.: 51

Yamashita, in re (1946): 284
Yelvington, Ramsey (Texas playwright): 202
Young, Stark: 17
Youngman, W. S., Jr. (president of China Defense Supplies, Inc.): 249